— A —
FORTUNATE
LIFE

— A —
FORTUNATE
LIFE

The Autobiography of

Paddy Ashdown

Aurum

First published 2009 by Aurum Press Ltd
7 Greenland Street, London NW1 0ND
www.aurumpress.co.uk

ISBN 978 1 84513 419 8 hardback
ISBN 978 1 84513 494 5 export paperback

Book designed and typeset by Robert Updegraff
Printed and bound by MPG Books Group

Unless otherwise credited all photographs are from the author's personal collection.

CONTENTS

To my wife, Jane,
who has ridden the turbulent wave
with such gentleness and grace

The life of things passes by like a rushing,
galloping horse, changing at every turn,
at every hour

Lao Tse 369–286 BC

Acknowledgements

Memory is a most fickle and unfaithful thing. Unlike the love described in Shakespeare's famous Sonnet 116, it does 'alter when it alteration finds and bends with the remover to remove' – and does so, moreover, all the time and in the most inconvenient manner.

If I had had to write this book relying only on my own defective memory, it would have been crammed full of grievous inaccuracies and gross distortions.

I am therefore most grateful to those old colleagues and friends who have been kind enough to look through the text and correct it. They include Mike Aaronson, Max Atkinson, Mark Ashdown, Tim Ashdown, Julian Astle, Cathy Bakewell, Alan Beith, Michael Boyce, Julian Braithwaite, Nick Clegg, Tim Clement-Jones, Tim Courtenay, Sherard Cowper-Coles, Alison Downing, Sarah Frapple (who has kept my diaries over many years), certain Government authorities, Greg Jefferies, David and Dorothy Hartridge, Archy Kirkwood, David Laws, Alan Leaman, Ed Llewellyn, Roger Lowry, Bob MacLennan, Colin McColl, Tom McNally, John Murphy, Sead Numanović, Sue O'Sullivan, Nick South, Nick Speakman, David Steel, SBS Poole, Roger Taylerson, Archy Tuta, Pat Troy, Rupert van der Horst, Shirley Williams and Amela Zahiragić.

Others, even more heroic, have not only corrected my memory but have also been kind enough to read and advise on what I have written. Their amendments and suggestions have resulted in great improvements. Amongst them are: Simon Ashdown, Steph Bailey, Rosemary Billinge, Ellen Dahrendorf, Les Farris, Miranda Green, Andrew Phillips, Steve Radley, Chris Rennard, Carol Ross, Kate Theurel and David Walter.

From Chapter 12 onwards I have been able to check my memory of events by referring to the diaries I started keeping when I became Leader of the Liberal Democrats at the end of July 1988 and most of the passages reproduced as direct speech in these later chapters, for example my conversation with Tony Blair on the eve of the 1997 election, were recorded in my diary on the day in question.

I also owe a debt to some who have been most generous in providing information and material which has been invaluable to me. In this category I am especially grateful to the authorities of Bedford School, and particularly to Gina Warboys and the team of sixth-formers who were tasked by the then Headmaster, Dr Evans, with searching through the school's old records and digging up past reports and references to my time there. My thanks also go to the Royal Navy for my service records and reports, as well as to Michael Brunson, Richard Lindley, David Mitchell, Dr Peter Sercombe and those people in Rathfriland who made Jane and me so welcome (especially the Reverend Phillip Thompson), all of whom have been so generous and helpful with facts and advice.

And then there are two people who have done all of these things and more. My wife Jane, whose idea it was that I should write this book, has read, re-read, corrected and advised with great patience and wisdom. And my old friend and colleague Ian Patrick, who through his dedication to detail, good judgement and diligence has, in this enterprise as in so much else I have done, saved me from numberless errors and improved the final outcome immeasurably.

Finally, I would like to thank Michael Sissons of PFD for encouraging me to write this book and Aurum Press for publishing it – especially Piers Burnett of Aurum, who has advised me during the writing of it and, with great skill, edited what I have produced, as well as John Wheelwright, who, with extraordinary patience and a fearsome attention to detail and grammatical correctness, copy-edited it.

All of these, and no doubt more, have made this book better than it would otherwise have been. But none bear any responsibility for whatever infelicities, inaccuracies or inadequacies it may contain.

A Distillation of Days

T HE WOMAN'S FACE was stained with sweat and waxy-white and heavy with hopelessness and fear. Her flower-pattern dress hung around her, grimy and formless, but still hinting of a young body and strong limbs. A child of perhaps four clung to one hand, while with her other she pushed a pram laden with assorted cheap household items: some worn clothes, a collection of cooking pots, a coffee *djezva** and an incongruous tin of Nestlé's powdered baby milk. Behind her trudged an older woman carrying a baby which was crying pitifully and an old man bent over a stick. They made up just a small ripple in the miserable stream of dusty stragglers tramping towards the school buildings at Trnopolje under a burning sun, as our convoy, led by a Serb jeep, bumped past them. My mind flew back to that first remembered image – the one that used to haunt me and grow into exaggerated forms in the nightmares of my childhood – the brief glimpse, snatched from between the folds of my mother's skirt, of a single platform under a boiling sun, carpeted with dismembered bodies, the gore and the smell of putrefaction and that other smell that I recognised now – the odour of animal fear.

Little more than twenty-four hours before I had been sitting up until the cool, starlit hours of the early morning with the 'President' of the Bosnian Serbs, Radovan Karadžić, at his mountain headquarters high above Sarajevo, drinking *slivović †* and talking of philosophy and poetry, of the eternal tragedies of the Balkans and of his life as a psychiatrist and poet. The wonderful, brave *Guardian* journalist, Maggie O'Kane (who, with other journalists, had accompanied me on my visit to see the Serb side of the three-month-old Bosnian war), had warned me earlier that evening that Karadžić was evil and a liar. But, sitting in front of him, drinking plum brandy, I did not believe her. I accepted his assertion that he wanted a just peace if 'the Muslims'

* Bosnian coffee pot.
† Plum brandy.

1

would only compromise. I accepted his acknowledgement that the Serbs, too, had done some bad things and his promise that they would be punished. Not yet understanding very much about the Balkans and knowing nothing of Karadžić's ability (shared, I later discovered, by his backer, President Slobodan Milošević of Serbia) to lie straight into your eyes without wavering, I still believed, naively, that it must be possible to see great evil in a man's face

Of course, I knew there was another side. Two weeks earlier, in the last days of July 1992, I had, on a whim, hitched a lift on an RAF Special Forces *Hercules* and flown into besieged Sarajevo, spent three days there, met the President of the Bosnian Muslims, Alija Izetbegović, been sporadically shelled on Sarajevo airport and made statements urging the West to intervene to stop the carnage.

It was because of this that Karadžić had written to me suggesting that, having seen 'the Muslim' side, I should see the Serb side too. The letter had arrived in my London office and was read out to me over the phone as my wife Jane and I were visiting Monet's garden in Giverny at the start of our annual summer holiday in France. By this time (thanks in large measure to another outstanding *Guardian* journalist covering the Bosnian war, Ed Vulliamy), the first stories had begun to emerge about the Serb death camps at Keraterm and Omarška. Nevertheless, Karadžić's invitation, civil and quietly framed, seemed to me entirely reasonable – I *should* see both sides. I abandoned our planned holiday in France and, setting only two conditions – that I should take my Lib Dem colleague Russell Johnston with me, and that we should have free access wherever we wished to go – flew from Paris to Budapest and then drove across the Danube plain to Belgrade, from where, in the most frightening helicopter ride I have ever taken, we flew over the Bosnian battlefields to Karadžić's headquarters at Pale in the mountains of Eastern Bosnia, from where he was directing the siege of Sarajevo.

The day after my *šlivović* evening with Karadžić, Russell Johnston and I nursed our hangovers through another long car journey, this time behind Serb lines and through what looked to me like relatively peaceful countryside, to the Serb capital, Banja Luka. It was only ten years later that I discovered that the countryside here looked peaceful because Serbian irregulars who called themselves the White Eagles had just swept through, killing hundreds, raping and crucifying women naked on their own front doors, burning houses, laying waste to the land and driving out all that remained of the Muslim population. Ten years later I was to see their dolls, toys and the remnants of the clothes they wore amidst the tangle of broken bones that was all that was left of around some six hundred of them, men, women and children, at one of the biggest of the mass graves at nearby Crni Vrh.

We arrived in Banja Luka at around three in the afternoon, having been held up by an ambush on the road. The journalists accompanying us had travelled by a different route and arrived before us. They were abuzz with rumours of a new 'death' camp which had not yet been visited – Manjača. I insisted that we should go there immediately, reminding the Serb military commanders in charge of this sector of their 'President's' promise that I would be given unimpeded freedom to go wherever I wished. They refused, saying there was a curfew, and I would be shot if I went. I responded that they would have to shoot me in front of the journalists who were accompanying me, and this would not do their cause any good in the face of world opinion, which was now turning against them.

What I found when we got to Manjača that evening was not an extermination camp like Keraterm and Omarška, but a brutal prison in which were incarcerated about two thousand Bosnian Muslim men and boys of potential fighting age who had been picked up by the Serbs in local towns and villages during recent ethnic cleansing. Conditions were harsh, even inhuman; medical supplies for the wounded were either rudimentary or non-existent and, although killing was not the specific purpose of the camp, prisoners were being killed, either in random acts of brutality by the guards, or on the instructions of the authorities. That night television images of what we saw were broadcast on news bulletins around the world. Shortly afterwards the Red Cross got access to Manjača. Ten years later, when I was giving evidence at the trial of Milošević in The Hague, one of the prosecutors told me that several of the inmates I had seen in Manjača on that day had, in the course of their evidence, said that there had been many killings at the camp until one day a British MP had come and brought the television cameras with him. After that the killings stopped.

I count this as the best day's work of my life.

The following day at Trnopolje I count as the worst.

A little beyond the young mother and the remnants of her family and the dusty river of refugees on the road, we came to Trnopolje Middle School.

The scene is still as deeply etched on my mind as that massacre of my young nightmares. The smell of faeces and neglected bodies hung thick in the still hot air. Here were old men, scarcely more than skeletons; wounded, lying on fly-blown mattresses; young mothers with terror on their faces, trying to comfort desperate children; old women sitting on their haunches, staring vacantly into a chasm of misery. A few pathetic torn curtains were erected on poles here and there, for shade or privacy. Most seemed to have abandoned their dignity and submitted themselves to degradation and hopelessness amidst the little stinking piles of carelessly deposited human excrement with which they shared their living space. Amongst them – moving gently and with infinite compassion – was an ITV crew who had also just got there and whose presenter, Penny Marshall, was making a film which later won her a prestigious award.

These were the wives and children and fathers and mothers and grandparents of the emaciated men and boys we had seen the previous day, at Manjaca. One elderly woman told me the nights were the worst. That was when the gangs of marauding Serbs came in to take away the young women to be raped and then, she thought, often killed; for many just disappeared, leaving their children to be cared for by the rest as best they could.

I have never before or since felt such hopelessness or shame, and wept because of it. On my way back to Belgrade I wrote a letter to Prime Minister John Major, telling him what I had seen and begging him immediately to declare Trnopolje a safe haven, under UN protection.

But my shame that day pales into insignificance alongside the greater shame that swept over me nearly ten years later when, back in Bosnia as the International Community's High Representative, I learned that about three days after my visit (I sometimes torture myself with the thought that it may even have been because of it) the Serbs took away almost all those I had seen, herded them, old men, women and children, to the edge of a cliff on nearby Vlasić mountain and machine-gunned them all into the ravine below. I went to see their splintered bones and broken skulls and the little shards of clothes and toys amongst the weeds – all that was left of those I had seen, who had died in such misery and horror because of the shameless inactivity of my country and those who were in charge of what we are pleased to call 'Western Civilisation'.

Perhaps it is true of all of our lives that we can pick out a day, or a handful of days, which stand out in Technicolor detail from the grey procession of weeks and months and years. Some, because we are proud of them; some, because they give us pain or shame. Perhaps these are one way of distilling the pattern, range and purpose of a life.

I have, so far at least, led a most fortunate life. I was soldier at the end of the golden age of imperial soldiering; a spy at the end of the golden age of spying; a politician while politics was still a calling; and an international peace-builder backed by Western power, before Iraq and Afghanistan drained the West of both influence and morality.

I seem, in all, to have travelled a long way and had great luck. But two of my Technicolor days, the best and the worst, fall consecutively in the second week of August 1992. Together they form not just a memory but also somehow a distillation of the theme of my life; that of conflict and its human consequences when the beast of intolerance and bigotry gets loose. Looking back, this seems like a subterranean stream which has appeared, vanished and re-emerged, never completely leaving me, since my very earliest days.

CHAPTER 1

Ancestors and Early Years

THEY WERE A PRETTY RUM LOT, my ancestors.

Four themes run steadily through the nine unbroken generations that my brother Mark has managed to trace, back to the middle of the eighteenth century: the public service, India, Ireland and adventurism.

The earliest Ashdown root we know of goes back through a family of land agents in Shropshire to an innkeeper and his wife in Shifnal, and the link to the Welsh Marches remained strong right down to my father's time. The family's earlier attempts to raise themselves up to the middle class were rather erratic and largely focused on the Midlands. By the 1850s, however, they had dispersed towards London, where my paternal great-grandfather, John Ashdown, set up as an architect – and apparently a rather good one, for I remember from my youth that one of my parents' treasured possessions was the silver medal for the Inigo Jones Prize which he won. It was he who anchored the family firmly in the middle classes. He married a Charlotte Durham, who was the daughter of a Buckinghamshire land agent and had pretensions to descent from a long line with noble connections originating in Scotland. It was he who, following the middle-class practice of the time, began adding the name 'Durham' to the plainer 'Ashdown' to mark this, at best, extremely distant and probably dubious aristocratic connection. To this day, the male Ashdown line carries the name Durham as a third Christian name.

John Ashdown was one of the chief architects involved in laying out the town plan for Victorian Llandudno and later worked for South Eastern Railways. Apparently he designed all the stations from Victoria to Folkestone and may well have had a hand in No. 4 Cowley Street, then the Headquarters of South Eastern Railway and now serving the same function for the Liberal Democrats. He also, I fear, bore at least some responsibility for St Pancras Station, for I have seen his sketches of it in a book of his drawings. He lost all his fortune in the great South Eastern Railway crash of the late 1800s, which might be viewed as appropriate retribution for his part in that horrible confection of brick and Victorian fancy.

My grandfather, his son, was educated at Heidelberg at the height of the era of student duelling and often used to regale us with gory tales of sawdust sabre fights in the taverns of the city. He, too, must have done well, for he later became the companion of the young Earl of Warwick and accompanied him on a Grand Tour of Europe, before gaining a much-sought-after place in the Indian Civil Service, starting off as a District Officer in the Punjab and rising to become the Inspector General of Police for what was then known as United Provinces, now Uttar Pradesh. My grandmother died when my father was eight years old, at which time he was sent away to school in England, where he was placed under the guardianship of an uncle, the huntin', shootin' and fishin' Vicar of Snitterfield in Warwickshire (one of the other waifs from the Raj sheltered by this country parson at the time was Vivien Leigh, the star of *Gone with the Wind*, with whom my father appears to have had an early romantic connection).

My father did not see his father again until the age of nineteen, when the latter returned to England for home leave just as my father was finishing his officer training at Sandhurst. My grandfather retired to Guernsey in 1927, the same year as my father left England to join a Punjabi regiment of the Indian Army, their ships, according to family legend, literally passing on the passage.

To be honest, I am not at all sure that the Ashdowns, as a whole, were very nice people – my father excepted. They tended to have nasty tempers, a strong streak of snobbishness and, as far as the Ashdown women were concerned, a marked capacity for being catty, especially to those they considered below them in social standing.

My paternal grandmother's bloodline was at once more romantic and rather wilder than that of my grandfather. One of her great uncles declares his profession in the 1851 Covent Garden census as the entrepreneurial combination of 'boot maker and brothel keeper', presumably having discovered that attending to clients' boots whilst they were otherwise occupied was a good way to add value to a thriving business. By the time she was born, however, her branch of the family, the Cliffords, were firmly rooted in India. The Cliffords were plantation Irish and Catholic to the core. It is through them that my line runs back to Daniel O'Connell, the father of Irish nationalism, emancipator of the Catholics and generally roguish politician of the mid-nineteenth century. In 1995 the Irish government got to hear of this connection and put on a little Press event to mark it when I was visiting them in December of that year. Afterwards they sent me off to see the great man's grave in Glasnevin Cemetery outside Dublin. On the way the driver said in a thick Dublin accent, 'I gadder dat you are the descendant of the great Dan O'Connell?' I confirmed that I was. He replied 'Do you know what dey used to say about him?' I knew perfectly well that they called him 'The Liberator', but I wanted him to tell me that, so I pretended I didn't. 'Dey used to say dat you couldn't trow a stone over an orphanage wall but you'd hit one of his children!' It was the best put down I have ever endured. Clearly, being able to claim descent from O'Connell was a less exclusive distinction than I had supposed.

O'Connell's granddaughter, Anna Mary Fitzsimmons, married Richard Clifford, my great-grandfather on the maternal side and followed him to India. She wrote a Victorian monograph *On the March*, describing the life of an Indian Army officer's wife in the second half of the nineteenth century, which I still have. The Cliffords were, with exceptions, more steadily illustrious than the Ashdowns. My fifth great-grand-uncle by the Clifford line was the celebrated traveller, orientalist and Chinese expert, Sir George Staunton, who accompanied Lord McCartney as one of the first British emissaries to the Manchu (Qing) Emperors in Peking in 1793 and was the inventor (or, to be precise, discoverer) of Earl Grey tea. The Indian branch of the family was established by his great nephew William Henry, whose father served with variable distinction in an Irish Regiment, the 3rd Dragoon Guards, in Wellington's Peninsular army (he was at one time imprisoned for being absent without leave as result of a female entanglement). William Henry, his son, was born in Wexford 1800 and later went to India as an Irish soldier-adventurer with the East India Company. He first comes to notice in 1825, for being cashiered from his regiment, the Madras Cavalry, and exiled from India to Hong Kong as a result of a fight over a woman. Apparently he was provoked over breakfast by a fellow officer.

(It seems that for the military there is something especially provocative about being insulted over breakfast which does not apply to other meals. I once saw a grizzled and much respected veteran of the war-time SBS* and former Colditz prisoner tip a bowl of porridge

---

* The Special Boat Section (now Special Boat Service) of the Royal Marines.

over a startled Guards officer in his own mess. Apparently, in the Guards, it is – or was – the tradition that, if an officer wore his hat to breakfast, it was meant as a signal that he didn't want to be talked to. My SBS friend having collected his porridge plumped himself down next to a Guards officer just so attired and said a cheery 'hullo'. Receiving no response he said it again and then, with increasing menace, a third and fourth time. The recipient of this cheery greeting then said in a very drawly upper-crust voice, 'Don't y'know, old man, that in the Guards the tradition is that, if we don't want to be spoken to at breakfast we wear a hat.' To which my friend replied, with a growl, 'In the Royal Marines the tradition is that if we are rude at breakfast we get to wear a plate of porridge,' and tipped the lot over his head.)

Anyway, the authorities in India in the early nineteenth century seem to have taken the view that William Henry's offence was mitigated by the fact that the provocation took place over breakfast and duly reinstated him, after a helpful intervention from his illustrious relative 'Chinese' Staunton. In 1832 he made the sea journey back to India with someone else's wife (who he eventually married) and founded the Clifford dynasty in India, which lasted until the British left nearly a century and a half later.

Being Irish and therefore dedicated to the proposition that a good story should not be spoiled by too much concern for the truth, the Cliffords have handed down many legends which would be fun to believe, but for which I can find no evidence. For instance, one of my female ancestors supposedly left Peshawar in the autumn 1841 to join her husband in Kabul and was one of the very few to avoid the wholesale slaughter of the British which we know as the 'Massacre in the Snows' and which, in January 1842, brought the First Afghan War to a disastrous end. The story (for which, I repeat, I can find not a shred of evidence) gets even more romantic: she was said to have crossed the Himalayas back into India in the company of a doctor whom she eventually ran off with (the early Cliffords seem to have had rather a tendency to untidy private lives).

Solidity, however, was a definite feature of my mothers' ancestors, the Hudsons. The Hudsons were as steady, Protestant and Northern Irish as the Cliffords were wild, Catholic and from the South. They came to Ulster with the Cromwellian plantation from, we think, Northumbria.

The first Hudson we know of was Robert, who lived in the little County Down market town of Rathfriland, under the shadow of the Mourne Mountains. He, like my Ashdown ancestor from Pimlico (and at about the same time), was a boot- and shoemaker by trade – though we may be certain that, as a good Northern Ireland Presbyterian, he did not combine this with a brothel-keeping sideline. Succeeding Hudsons were variously musical reed-makers, grocers, and auctioneers and valuers. My grandfather, Robert Hudson, whose sisters were missionaries in China and India, must have done rather well for himself, for the three Rathfriland houses in which he lived reveal a steady progression up the middle-class ladder. He combined his profession as Rathfriland's auctioneer and valuer with that of newsagent, bookshop-owner, cycle agent and occasional dancing master, while still finding time to play in the local hockey team, train the church choir, serve on the local School Management Committee, conduct the choral society, be married twice and sire, in all, twelve children. His second wife, my maternal grand-mother, was a Hollingsworth. They came over to Ireland, probably also from Northumberland, in the 1660s, were fiercely Protestant and served as clergy with the army of William of Orange.

My grandfather was largely self-educated, a great believer in the Victorian virtue of self-improvement, and deeply engaged in the affairs of his local community. It is his strong Northern Irish genes that sweep all before them and march largely unchecked through all his grandchildren and my children, right down to my grandson, all of us carrying his indelible mark of a robust frame, a tendency to run to weight, a broad forehead, deep-set eyes and a marked cleft in the chin. He was said to have an extraordinary feel for glass, which he valued for Christies, and to have been an expert in fine furniture, apparently able to assess the age, date and value of a friend's dining table simply by running his hands along its underside during dinner. He must have been quite progressive, because he went to Paris in 1898 and returned with the first car in Ireland, an Orient Express. It was described in a book of the time as 'petrol-driven, single-cylinder, leather belt, Brampton chains, 36-inch black wheels and costing £210 [sic]'. On my office wall, I have a picture of him sitting in it, outside his stable in Rathfriland in the last year of the nineteenth century. He was fasci-nated by automobiles and all that went with them, and predicted, in the face of some derision, that they would completely reshape the way society worked. His capacity to predict the future was not, however, flawless. He was once approached by a Belfast friend called John Boyd Dunlop, who told him of his new invention, the pneumatic tyre, and asked him if he would like to join with him in a manufacturing enterprise to produce them. My grandfather took one look at his friend's new contraption, declared it would never work and declined.

He is described in a book of Rathfriland reminiscences of the time as being widely read with a well stocked library and as someone who, being 'forceful of personality, . . . influenced most of the cultural and social side of life in the district'. His funeral oration adds that, though a weak church-goer, he was a strong Mason. His portrait, in the full regalia of his Lodge (looking, to be honest, rather like a Sicilian bandit), still hangs in the Masonic Hall in Rathfriland. He was also involved in local politics, being at one stage a member of the Irish Liberal party (a fact I did not discover until I was a Liberal MP). Although a Mason, he hated the Orange Lodge. My mother used to tell me that, during the 'troubles' of 1917–1920, when the Protestant Black and Tans rampaged through the countryside and she could see Catholic farms burning from her bedroom window, he took considerable risks to give shelter to Catholic families in his home. But he was a good Ulsterman and was amongst the quarter of a million men and women who signed the Ulster Covenant of September 1912 against Home Rule.

He died before I was born, and I am very sorry never to have met him.

◆

My mother, Lois, was the eighth child of Robert Hudson. She was striking rather than classically beautiful, had extraordinary grace (despite heavy bones), a strong face and a beautiful voice, because of which she was known by her father as Merle (thrush) and was at one time selected to be trained as an opera singer. One of my earliest childhood memories is of her singing around the house, especially Irish folk songs. Her favourite, which she sang with an almost unbearable poignancy, was 'Down by the Sally Gardens', which my daughter still sings to her children before sleep every night. But instead of training for the opera, my mother trained as a nurse at Belfast Royal Infirmary. I do not know why she went to India, but I think it was because she joined the Queen Alexandra's Royal Army Nursing Corps (QARANCs), which provided nursing services to the armed forces, and was posted there. She met my father and married him on 3 November 1938 in Rawalpindi. The wedding was, to be frank, something of a surprise to the rest of my family.

My father had already been engaged no less than seven times, leading my grandfather, according to family legend, to bet a substantial sum with a friend that this engagement would go the way of all his previous ones. I think some of my rather snobby Ashdown aunts also took the view that my mother's family was somewhat inferior, judging by their behaviour to her even to the end of her life, a fact which my mother, strong woman that she was, affected to either ignore or disdain.

My father was not a big man. He had a light, sinewy frame, a demeanour which gave off a constant sense of physical alertness and eyes from which a twinkle was never far away. His most powerful weapon was his charm, which I have seen bowl people over, especially women. He had, to put it euphemistically, a very active social life in India before he met my mother.

She told two stories on the subject of my father's conquests before her, which, if not apocryphal, were probably somewhat exaggerated. The first was that, when they first started seeing each other seriously, my father suggested that she should go down to the local bazaar and visit a particular leather shop, where he had left the skin of a python that he had recently shot. She should, he said, ask the leather wallah* if he would make her up some shoes and a matching bag from it. She duly visited the shop and made her request. The leather wallah smiled knowingly and advised her, 'Memsahib, this would not be possible.' He then showed her all that remained of the skin. 'A small purse, perhaps Memsahib, but the demand to date has been quite great!' My Mother kept the tiny piece of skin, which she would later produce whenever she told the story, eventually giving it to my sister-in-law.

The second story concerns their wedding night, which was spent in a friend's hill station bungalow where my father had stayed often before. On the following morning the *ayah*† came in with a tray on which was a teapot and one cup. This she put down by my father's side of the bed announcing, 'Tea, Sahib.' She then went round to my mother's side of the bed, lifted the mosquito net, pulled back the bed clothes, slapped her on the bottom and declared, 'Time for you to go home now, missy!'

Not long after they were married, the war came. My father, as a young Captain in the Royal Indian Army Service Corps, commanded a small unit of pack mules. His troops, apparently to a man, volunteered to leave India and join the British Expeditionary Force in

* Leather artisan.
† Maidservant.

France. They embarked for Europe on 10 December 1939 and were the first troops from India to go into action with the BEF. He was posted just south of Lille, where his unit was used primarily for ammunition supply near the front line. When the retreat to Dunkirk began he received orders to head for the coast. He turned his mules loose and marched his men to the sea, narrowly avoiding capture on several occasions. At one stage of the journey a staff officer told him that the order had gone out for British officers of Indian regiments to leave their men and make their way to the coast individually. My father refused and managed to get his men, without loss, onto the last ship to leave the Dunkirk mole and back to England. He was subsequently threatened with a court martial for disobeying an order, but the charge was wisely dropped, and the officer who gave the order was reprimanded instead.

My father used to joke that he was involved in both the great British retreats in the war (Dunkirk and the retreat through Burma to Imphal) and had a son after each of them. I was Dunkirk and my first brother, Richard, was Imphal. On the day of his return from Dunkirk he met my mother (who had followed him from India) in a Folkestone hotel, and nine months later I was born, the eldest of seven children, on 27 February 1941.

By this time they were back in India and in Delhi, where my father was serving in Army Headquarters. According to my Mother, the day before I was born, she accompanied my father on a snipe shoot over a local *geel** and was bitten by a rabid dog. She was rushed to hospital and given the standard treatment for rabies, a large injection direct into the stomach through the stomach wall. Whether this had any direct bearing on my birth in the Willingdon Nursing Home in New Delhi at 4.30 p.m. the following day, history does not relate.

———◆———

Three months later, on 8 June, I was christened – at Christ Church in the hill station of Simla by the Reverend E. Claydon – with three names: Jeremy, John (after my father), Durham (the Victorian family name adopted by my upwardly mobile great-grandfather). My father came down to breakfast the day after my christening to be greeted by a puzzled and angry delegation of Indian soldiers from his regiment,

* Bog or marsh.

who protested loudly about the fact that he had called me Jeremy. 'Sahib,' they complained, 'We are at war with the Jerries so it is very improper for you to call your first son after the enemy!'

Shortly afterwards my father was posted with his regiment to Burma, arriving just in time to begin the long retreat back to the borders of India. The fighting was bitter and the conditions terrible. My mother, distraught with worry, tried to get as close to the Indian/Burmese border as she could, so as to be nearby when he got out. To start with, I accompanied her, which meant staying down in the plains during the hot season, rather than going up into the hills as most Anglo-Indian families did. Somehow, around the age of two, I contracted serious tonsillitis and had to have my tonsils removed urgently. Apparently the nearest hospital was an Indian one, and at that stage in the war there was a severe shortage of anaesthetics, because they were desperately needed at the front. Indian hospitals, in consequence, were very short of supplies, and the one I was sent to had run out by the time I got there. So my tonsils were removed without the benefit of anaesthesia. I recall only something to do with masks and the salty taste of blood and, not so much pain, as terrible discomfort. My mother said that for the rest of my younger years I used to scream whenever I saw a nurse in uniform.

My father had a brief leave after escaping from Burma, as a result of which, in due time, I acquired a brother, Richard, of whom I have only a very dim memory of a frail, small child with wispy fair hair. For Richard did not live long. He contracted some kind of unidentified tropical fever and died at around eleven months, the first of no less than three children that my parents lost in their infancy or early adult years. I do not know how they bore these losses with such fortitude. But I do know that they affected them greatly, especially in their latter years, when both of them became attached to spiritualism which seemed to provide some kind of antidote to their grief. My mother's last words on her deathbed were that she could 'see all her little ones, gathered around her'. I remain perplexed as to why two entirely rational beings could believe in such things. But I do not begrudge it to them. For I know that I could not have coped at all if what happened to them as parents had happened to me. For, even as a brother, my siblings' deaths have marked me, too. I often feel that my luck in life has been bought at the cost of my parents' terrible trials and losses, and, even to this day, I dissolve into panic whenever one of my children or grandchildren falls ill.

Around the time of my brother Richard's death, my mother moved back up to the Punjab. She spent much of her time in war work and, later, in nursing my father, who had returned from the victorious campaign in Burma terribly debilitated by illness and exhaustion. As a consequence much of my early upbringing fell to our Indian household, which consisted of an *ayah*, Aisha, a *sais* (or groom) called Hamid, a gardener whose name I have forgotten, and a father and son, Nur Mohamed and Eid Mohamed, who guarded the house and looked after our needs in my father's absence. I loved them all dearly, and by the age of four understood the rhythms and symbols of Islamic life and spoke Hindi better than I did English. I am sure that my later apparent facility with languages comes from this early bilingual period of my life.

My father delighted in keeping strange and unusual pets, many of which he would bring back from his shooting expeditions in the jungle. We had snakes and (but not together) a tame mongoose, a small pigmy deer and a scaly anteater with a long trunk; at mealtimes the latter used to wander in and circumnavigate the room, hoovering up ants and termites from the skirting boards of our wooden bungalow with all the efficiency of a four-legged Dyson vacuum cleaner (and making a very similar sucking noise). But my favourite was a monkey who went by the very original name of: Monkey. He was a little older than me, but about the same size. We were inseparable companions. But what made our friendship even warmer was that we shared not only our lives, but also our chastisements. He would be beaten for some misdemeanour one day; me the next. This was the true cement of our fellow-feeling. Until one day Monkey was especially severely beaten for some sin and, in retribution (as I remember it), walked calmly over to a coffee table on which stood a blue Wedgwood bowl with nymphs dancing round it. This bowl was the last of my parents' breakable wedding presents to have survived their many moves around India, and I knew it was my mother's most valued possession because it was given pride of place whenever there was a dinner party, or drinks, or a bridge evening. And Monkey knew it, too. But it did not stop him. For he scooped the bowl up and ran out of the door and down our long front drive, with my mother and the gardener in hot pursuit. At the bottom of our drive, near the gate, there was a tall mango tree. Monkey, still grasping the bowl in one hand, scrambled up this at high speed. Once at the top he held out the bowl in one hand . . . and dropped it! And then, just at the very last moment, as the bowl passed his foot, the foot shot out and caught it. Monkey continued to do this for half an hour (or so it seemed), with my mother and the gardener dashing backwards and forwards to position themselves beneath the bowl each time it threatened to fall, while trying vainly to entice him down between times. Finally, Monkey descended the tree, laid the bowl at the foot of the trunk and sauntered off, in carefree manner, back to the house. I swear that if monkeys could whistle he would have done so. He never got beaten again – which was bad news for me. And I have, ever since, felt myself somehow deficient for lack of prehensile toes.

In May 1945 my second brother, Tim, was born. And a year later, when the war in the Far East ended and it became clear to my parents that the days of the British in India were drawing to a close, it was decided that my mother should take my brother and me back to Northern Ireland, where she would set up home and wait for my father to return after the British hand-over in India was concluded. At the time we were living at Simla, in the foothills of the Himalayas, so our journey to Bombay took us down the length of the Punjab and into India proper. Although the full-scale partition riots and ethnic massacres which accompanied the end of British rule did not really begin until a year later, in August 1946, there were, even at this time, a number of communal riots and mass killings. It must have been the aftermath of one of these – glimpsed from the folds of my mother's skirts on our last journey across India to Bombay and the boat home – that formed the indelible childhood memory described in the Prologue. Whether the bodies I saw were those of Muslims killed by Hindus or the other way round, I do not know. Nor can I, with confidence, describe the detail of what I saw that day, for I fear this has become too distorted and exaggerated by childhood terrors and nightmares to be reliable. But smell is a more accurate hook for memory. A quarter of a century later the whole scene came flooding back in Technicolor when I next smelt that sickly sweet odour of putrefaction, this time from the long-dead bodies of our enemies on a riverbank after one of our actions in the Borneo war.

Bombay in 1946 gave me my first ever sight of the sea, and I was immediately captivated by it, making a solemn promise, along with a shipboard friend of the same age, that we would both go into the Royal Navy, which later (if you count the Royal Marines as part of the Navy) we both did.

Our first home in Northern Ireland was in a collection of coastguard cottages which stood sentinel over the mouth of Belfast Lough, called Lisnarynn. My memories of this time are of sea-lashed bluffs, vertiginous scrambles down to wild rocks and pools of indescribable romance and treasure, the blaze of whin (gorse) blossom in the spring and hedgerows festooned with wild fuchsia in the summer. And of an old anti-aircraft gun position at the back of our house, littered with faeces and old French letters (not that I recognised them as such at the time), where, to my mother's despair, I loved to re-enact the wartime defence of Belfast against German bombers. My father meanwhile, now promoted to Colonel, stayed behind in India to help manage the British handover, returning home in 1947.

It was on his return that we moved from our isolated coastguard cottages to the nearby seaside town of Donaghadee, directly facing Portpatrick in Scotland across Beaufort's Dyke and the North Channel. We lived on the first floor of a gloomy old late Victorian house within a hundred yards of the seashore, and there my third brother, Robert, named after my mother's father, was born.

I remember three of our Donaghadee neighbours, especially. The first was an old retired couple downstairs, who would always give me sweets and had a Victorian print called 'The Last Survivor' hanging on their wall; it depicted Dr Brydon, the only survivor of the Massacre in the Snows of 1842 (which my ancestor is supposed to have escaped by the skin of her teeth), approaching a Khyber hill fort on an exhausted horse. The second was an eccentric neighbour with an unpronounceable Greek name but, according to local gossip, an impeccably English aristocratic pedigree. He was given to practising yoga by standing on his head every morning in front of the huge picture window of his bungalow, stark naked and with all his appurtenances dangling in reverse. Our Northern Irish 'daily', a good Catholic girl called Bridie, who always referred to the male organ as 'the article' (and to the female genitalia as 'the underneaths' – as in 'Old Mrs So-and-so is having terrible trouble with her underneaths'), took care to be scandalised by this apparition on her arrival every morning. Best of all, however, was the fact that my bedroom window gave me a perfect view not only of 'the article' itself, but also – and much more interestingly – of unwitting passers-by taking a morning stroll along an adjacent path. This was so aligned that they did not suspect the affront to decency which lay in ambush for them until they turned the final corner, to be confronted face to face (as it were!) and at a range of only a couple of yards or so, by this tableau of body hair and inverted human biology. I used to make my mother peal with laughter by putting on a little play every day over her morning coffee, re-enacting the contortions of horror and scandal I had witnessed earlier.

Our third neighbours were the parents of my bosom pal, Willy Orr. His father, Captain 'Willy' Orr*, was to become the Ulster Unionist MP for South Down, and they lived in a house which seemed to me the very pinnacle of luxury and grandness. And Captain Orr himself, in my eyes, was just as grand as was necessary to go with it. But his son and I were scamps who got into every mischief possible for small boys living in a carefree society with a whole wild foreshore as a playground. On one occasion I was so offended by what I regarded as an unfair upbraiding from my father that I concluded that my parents didn't really want me, so I would sail away for ever. Willy and I jumped in an old potato box and set off to paddle out to sea. Fortunately, the box was so unseaworthy that it sank after only a few yards, while still within comfortable wading distance (even for seven-year-olds) of the shore and safety. Later, we conspired to tempt the school mistress of the little Donaghadee primary school we were by now both attending (whom we hated with a passion), into the stationery cupboard, after which we locked the door on her and ran away home. For this we were both severely (and very reasonably) chastised.

In the bitter winter of 1947 my parents took me 'across the water' for a trip to England. I remember being stunned at the size of London and the grime and the scale of the destruction. It seemed to me a city of bombsites connected by occasional streets of houses. I remember also the cold (this was the worst winter in living memory) and huddling round the gas fire in our room in the Army and Navy Club. And, of course, I remember Hamleys toyshop, which I thought the Aladdin's cave of my dreams when my father took me there. We also visited my father's eccentric relatives, who lived in a beautiful (but rather dog-eared and ice-cold) Elizabethan manor called Thorne House outside Yeovil. There is a photograph, taken in February of that year, of me standing in the grounds with snow up to the top of my Wellington boots. Little did I realise that this was to be the place I would in due course call home and, thirty-six years later, represent in Parliament.

* Captain Lawrence 'Willy' Orr, MP for South Down 1950–1974 (succeeded by Enoch Powell).

CHAPTER 2

A Northern Ireland Childhood

I N 1948, A YEAR OR SO after my father returned from India, we moved from Donaghadee on the coast, to the little market town of Comber, lying at the head of Strangford Lough in County Down. The town's most famous son was General Sir Robert 'Rollo' Gillespie, killed in front of a Indian fort in 1814, apparently uttering the unlikely last words, 'One more shot for the honour of Down' (County Down). He played a key part in the British conquest of India and has a statue, in the manner of a mini-Nelson's column, in the town square. The great family of the town, however, were the Andrews, one of whom, Thomas Andrews, was both the chief designer and a victim of the 'unsinkable' Titanic (built at the Belfast shipyard of Harland and Wolfe).

The town was also famous as the home of Comber Whiskey, produced in an old distillery (now sadly closed) which I passed on my way to our family home on the south-eastern outskirts of the town. The warm, steamy smell of mashing and distilling whiskey is one of the most evocative smells of my early youth.*

My father and a business partner bought an old nineteenth-century flax mill in the centre of the town† and turned it into a pig farm with over a thousand head of pigs. My father sank all his army savings into the business, which was called The Comber Produce Company. For his partner, a Northern Irish businessman, this was a speculative investment. But for my father, who ran the business, it was a full-time job. To start with, they prospered, but then they were hit very hard in the mid-fifties, when UK markets were opened to continental produce, and Danish bacon flooded the shops. By the second half of the fifties, the business was in steady decline, with my father taking more and more desperate measures to save it and my mother doing the same to ensure that the family lived within our increasingly straitened means.

---

* The Comber distillery closed down in 1956, before we left.
† It is a car park and supermarket now.

When we moved to Comber, we first took up residence in a rented nineteenth-century town house called Glenbank on the outskirts of the town. Here my siblings increased from three to six with the arrival of my sister Alisoun and, finally, the twins, Mark and Melanie. Later my parents bought one half of a 1930s house, Eusemere (previously owned by Sir James Andrews, the Lord Chief Justice of Northern Ireland), which had recently been divided in two. It was in Eusemere that I spent most of my adolescent years, and they were, despite the gathering financial clouds, very happy ones.

My parents had one of those marriages which are built on opposites. My father, to whom I was completely devoted, had three great loves in his life: shooting, fishing and strong arguments, and I was bought up with a gun in one hand, a rod in the other and a head full of disputatious opinions.

In the winter, even from the age of ten or so, I would go shooting with him, either on the bogs of Northern Ireland after snipe, or wildfowling on Strangford Lough, a vast bottle-shaped tidal inlet so named by the Vikings, whose shores lay no more than a half mile from our back garden. The best of all our shooting expeditions were those that took us to shoot duck and geese across a winter moon on the great Lough's mudflats. This was a dangerous pastime, as the tide comes in fast on Strangford, and the tangle of mudbanks and water channels can be very confusing. But we soon learned the Lough's secrets from local friends, and especially from a larger-than-life local cattle-dealer and all-purpose rogue called Billy Thompson (of whom more later).

To be honest, I was never very good with a shotgun in comparison to my brother Tim or my father, who was an outstanding shot, despite very poor eyesight. So I would often come back empty-handed. But I loved the wildness and desolation of Strangford, its bleak mudbanks crouched against the tide while racing clouds flew by on a northerly wind, and the wild calls of a skein of geese filled our ears as they wheeled and circled round us, seen only as brief black shapes across a silvery moon.

My father loved shooting. But the passion that exceeded all others was for his rod and line. I remember as a boy that, when the Farlows fishing catalogue arrived from London in early January, we would both spend hours poring over it together and deciding what flies and spinners and reels and tackle we would need for the season to come.

In spring we would load up our battered Standard Ten car (my father was completely uninterested in material possessions, especially cars – this one, I recall, had a top speed of 58 miles per hour downhill with the wind behind us, and you could see the road through a rust hole in the floor by the back seat) and on atrocious roads thread our way south through Northern Ireland's little towns for eighty miles to fish for salmon on Lough Melvin on the Fermanagh–Leitrim border. We always stayed in the same rather primitive fishing hotel, The Melvin Hotel in the little town of Garrison. There was a huge stuffed brown trout in a glass case above the bar, which they claimed had been caught in the Lough, and my boyhood dreams were all about catching one like it and of how proud my father would be.

My memories of these trips are of being bitterly cold while telling my father I wasn't; of long hours in the back of the boat trawling spinners or casting a wet fly on leaden water; of sardine sandwiches and hard-boiled eggs, which we seemed to have to wait an eternity to eat, and of bars of Highland Toffee (my father had a very sweet tooth) and ginger beer in stone bottles. We always paid a second visit to the Lough in the summer, which I loved even more. Then we would fish for a trout special to Lough Melvin – the beautiful, golden gillaroo – by 'dapping' with a daddy longlegs. 'Dapping' involves using a very light line that you allow to blow in the wind so that you can then gently lower the daddy longlegs onto the surface of the water from five or six yards away. It worked best when the fish were lying in shallow, weedy water over a sandy bank on a hot August day. The other special Lough Melvin trout is the sonaghan, also found nowhere else in the world. They do not grow big, but are tremendous fighters.

But it was the salmon we were chiefly there for, and I caught my first one, weighing ten-and-a-half pounds, at the age of eleven. Actually, I had caught one the year before, but our boatman, John Murphy, took one look at it, swore and, to my horror, threw it back. I was so furious I wanted to throw him after it, until my father explained that it was a 'kelt' or spent fish (i.e., a female which had just spawned), and so could not be taken and had to be returned.

Besides fishing, we had a second and more clandestine excitement during our twice yearly trips to Lough Melvin – smuggling. For my father, though an ex-Indian Army Colonel and to all appearances a pillar of the community, was no great respecter of any law he regarded as irksome.

The border between Northern Ireland and the Republic of Ireland runs through the middle of Lough Melvin. Our boatman, John Murphy (to whom my father used to send Christmas cards every year – even after he himself had emigrated to Australia) came from the Irish side. No trip was ever made backwards and forwards across the Lough without carrying some contraband or other. It was my job to sit on top of the cartons of whatever it was most profitable to smuggle at the time. The favourite was butter, which was much cheaper in the south than the north, but I have sat long hours on Melvin, in rough weather and smooth, on crates containing everything from cigarettes to Irish whiskey, depending on what my father and John Murphy thought at the time would return the best profit. On one occasion we went on a rather larger smuggling trip, which we undertook in a dilapidated truck. I was positioned at the rear and equipped with a large sack of tin tacks. I asked what these were for and was told that if we were chased by the police or the customs I was to throw as many handfuls as I could onto the road behind us to puncture the tyres of our pursuers.

Smuggling across the border was a regular business at the time, and many were the stories of near escapes told in the bar of The Melvin Hotel. My favourite was of a local man who was big in smuggling and well known for it to the local police and customs. On one occasion he was observed cycling backwards and forwards past the customs post many times a day, for several days. The customs knew he was smuggling something, but, however many times they stopped and searched him, they could find nothing. Some time later, at a local bar, they bearded him with their suspicions:

'You were smuggling weren't you?'

'I was.'

'But we searched your bicycle and never found anything. What were you smuggling?'

'Bicycles.'

In the spring of 2008, while researching for this book, my wife Jane and I paid a visit to Melvin and found old John Murphy, then well into his nineties, in his little house in Garrison. His gnarled old hands, still calloused and rough from a lifetime of rowing, were arthritic and bent, and his hearing was almost totally gone. But he still had a fund of stories of these times and of my father, of the smuggling and of the fish we had caught together. Sadly, he died a few months after our visit.

Among the laws my father omitted to respect was the law giving the well-to-do (as my father saw it) the ownership of fish. Or to be more precise, the ownership of pieces of water in which one could fish. He used to say, 'Fish are wild. Catching them should depend on skill, not on how rich you are. I accept that people can own a piece of water, but how can you own the fish in it, for they could have come from anywhere?' This unconvincing logic (which he never applied to anything else – pheasants, for instance) gave him, in his own eyes, all the justification he needed to poach. This he did with relish, his Ulster friends and me, whenever I was home from school.

We had two favourite poaching spots, the Hollywood Reservoir, which is in the hills above Belfast, and Lough Island Reavy, nestling under the Mourne Mountains. The fishing rights to both were owned at that time by the Belfast Anglers Association, who employed ghillies to guard their water and its fish. So we fished at night, especially during the moonless period, starting around midnight (when, we reasoned, all self-respecting ghillies would be tucked up in bed) and continuing till the dawn. Afterwards we called in for a monster breakfast at one of the workmen's cafés on the way back home – or, better still, went onto the mudflats on Strangford or the Whitewater estuary in Dundrum Bay, near Newcastle, County Down, for a feast of raw cockles, dug up and consumed on the spot.

Normally, people do not fish at night. But we used a technique which my father's cattle-dealer friend, Billy Thompson, taught him and which I have never used or heard of being used since. It depended on the fact that trout come into shallow water to feed at night and, once you had learned the technique, it proved highly successful. It involved using a fly rod with a worm as bait and casting as far out as possible with a very stiff arm (so as not to lose the worm) and then drawing the line in very slowly. You could feel the trout picking up the bait and the trick was to let him run with it a bit and then strike when you judged the worm to be fully taken. We caught some magnificent fish using this method. But we ourselves were nearly caught several times, too.

Our method for escaping ghillies was simple, effective and, again, taught us by Billy Thompson. Part One was avoidance. We would nearly always be able to hear the ghillies coming some time before they heard or saw us. Then, if we thought they hadn't actually seen us, we would simply lie down in the dark, pull our overcoats over us and make like a stone. Ten times out of ten, the ghillies, not knowing we were there, walked past unseeing, leaving us to make good our escape. But if we knew we had been spotted, then we implemented Part Two: evasion. We would start walking round the lake keeping a good distance in front of our pursuer. If he ran, we ran. If he walked, then we did, too. If he shouted (which they always did) we would keep silent. And then, when we judged him frustrated, and choosing a point at which we were briefly out of sight, we would one by one drop to the ground, pull our overcoats over us, lie still and hope he would walk past us. And that was always what happened. Then it was just a question of making good our escape and meeting at the car, which my father had always taken the precaution of parking some distance away in an unlikely spot.

My father, however, was not very fit, having lost a lung in the war and being a heavy smoker. So it always fell to me to be the last person to drop out; it was reasoned that I had the best chance of outwalking – if necessary outrunning – our pursuer. I am not quite sure how it was we were never caught – but we never were. And in the process I learned some techniques of nightcraft that were invaluable to me much later in the Royal Marines.

Fishing was our spring and summer occupation, and shooting our winter one. But argument was an all-year-round affair. My father loved his discussions fierce, noisy and over family dinner for prefer-ence. This drove my mother to distraction as she tried to intervene to make space for food, or part us as the decibels went up and the insults grew more furious. He would take us all on together, giving no quarter to any of us and accepting none for himself. When losing he could, however, be completely unscrupulous and even fall back on the tired old tactic of telling us we were too young and would know better when we were older – that was when we knew we were winning. He would often take up an opinion contrary to his own in order to get an argument going, and then become ruthless in defence of the unten-able. His opinions were surprisingly left-wing for a man of his upbringing and background. He was (though much later, of course) well ahead of me or any of my radical friends of the sixties in oppos-ing the Vietnam war. The techniques of argument I learned at our din-ner table have been invaluable all my adult life – but more valuable still was the lesson I learned from him not to be afraid to hold a minority opinion. I am sure it was my father who planted in me the latent seeds of liberalism that were to flower much later in my life.

He was impish, had a sense of humour (often bawdy) to go with it and boundless energy. He loved poetry in general, and Kipling in particular, and would read to us almost every night. He was a Catholic (the Ashdown family religion) but wore his faith very lightly (in fact hardly at all), often quoting a saying which he claimed came from the Quran (though I have never found it there): 'There is one God but many ways to him'. And he would say that if he had been born in a Muslim country he would certainly have been a Muslim. He hated all religious bigots equally, but since we were a predominantly a Unionist and Protestant community in Comber, he had a special contempt for those of the Protestant persuasion. I suffered quite a lot in early life, at school and from the lads in the area, because I came from a mixed marriage. My father's solution to the question I was frequently asked, 'Are youse a Protestant or are youse a Catholic?', was that I should reply that I was a Muslim. I tried it once, only to be met with the supplementary, 'But are youse a Catholic Muslim, or a Protestant Muslim?'

He was as uninterested in his clothes and class as he was in cars. He used to say that a gentleman was not to be distinguished by what he wore or where he came from, but by how he behaved. His favourite clothes were his most threadbare ones, and his favourite hat had fishing flies stuck all over it, in case he saw a piece of water or a fish rising which might require one of them to be put into service (when fishing he had the disconcerting habit of wearing spare flies stuck in his exceptionally bushy eyebrows – making him a rather frightening figure to the unwary). His complete lack of sartorial awareness and interest used to drive my mother mad, for she was a very trim dresser with a special passion for shoes (especially outrageous high-heeled ones, into which, even at an advanced age, she would still cram her terribly bunioned old feet). My mother used to say that you could tell what a man wanted you to think of him by his tie; but you could tell what he thought of himself by his shoes. She was unable to influence my father's dress (his ties, when he wore them, were usually regimental, splattered and severely moth-eaten), but his shoes were always sparkling.

Consistent with his dislike of bigotry, he had no side, no snobbery and a deep dislike for those who had either. But he was not an easy man to live with and could from time to time be destructively, even cruelly, self-centred, especially when things were not going his way.

My mother was a saint to put up with him, for I think he led her a merry dance. They often, especially in the early years of my adolescence, had furious rows – chiefly, as I recall, over money, which was always difficult. But they were devoted to each other and, after age had burred the sharp edges, were like a couple of lovebirds in their latter years.

My mother was in all senses his opposite, except when it came to her total dedication to us children, who always came first for both of them. She was the calm centre around whom this maelstrom of shouting and argument and adventure raged. She was the balm who mended the bloody aftermath of our fights (sometimes, but not often, physical ones). She was the bromide who would calm my father's rage when one of us did less well than he thought we should have done at school or offended in some way that he considered heinous. She was the bottomless dispenser of unconditional, tactile love to all six of her children equally. It was to her that we confided our deepest miseries and confessed our worst transgressions, which she magicked away with hugs and eternal understanding. She rarely put her foot down with my father, but, if she did, nearly always got her way in the end, for she knew the mystery, which completely eluded the rest of us, of how to handle him and turn his seemingly implacable will. She was, in short, the person who actually made the family work.

Although of true Northern Irish Protestant stock, she regarded herself as Irish, not just British, and she regarded the South – and especially its culture – as part of her heritage and genetic make up. She loved the Abbey Theatre in Dublin, the poetry of W.B. Yeats and Louis MacNeice and the writings of James Joyce and George Bernard Shaw. But her passion (not shared by my father) was music. I remember, as yesterday, the earth-shaking epiphany I experienced when she first introduced me to Beethoven's Fourth Piano Concerto (her favourite piece), and it is to her that I owe a lifetime's love of classical music, which has given me constant enjoyment and discovery, as well as much solace in time of need.

She was, however, a firmly practising Protestant and a believer. She even persuaded me eventually to go to Sunday School and, in my early teens, to get confirmed in her faith, which I did more out of love and respect for her than from any sense of conviction. Like my father, I will, if pressed, admit to being a Christian, because I find the code for living contained in Christianity best suits the way I want to live my life in the context of time and place in which I find myself. I do not find it difficult to acknowledge the presence of God. Indeed, I do so in prayer every night and regard the glorious little Parish Church of

St Mary the Virgin in Norton sub Hamdon* as the earthly anchor point of my spirituality – though, God knows, except for religious high days like Christmas, I attend its services infrequently enough, for Northern Ireland has made me like my churches better empty than full.

As for creeds, I know of none in any religious catechism which I would prefer as a compass to the little poem of Rabindranath Tagore:

> *We are all the more one, because we are many.*
> *For we have made an ample space for love in the gap where we were sundered,*
> *Our unlikeness reveals its breadth of beauty, with one common life,*
> *Like mountain peaks in the morning sun.*†

My mother had two helpers who completed our extended family. Bella Bailey, a mountain of a woman whose heart was as big as her frame, through which ran one of the most pure and marked seams of common sense I have ever known. Bella helped with the housework, while her colleague, Lottie Hoskins, only a handful of years older than me, looked after us children, to whom she dispensed love in great clotted-cream helpings. But, though she loved us children equally, she loved my mother most, regarding her, I think, as a saint whom providence had placed amongst us. I still remain regularly in touch with her by Christmas card, telephone and occasional visits.

I was a rather sickly child, suffering especially badly from whooping cough, along with all the usual childhood ailments. I have an early memory of lying in bed on a summer's evening, racked with coughing and listening to my parents in the garden below discussing my health in terms of real concern. At one stage my mother (who, having already lost one of her children, was alert to the point of paranoia about her children's illnesses – a trait I have inherited from her) was so worried about my tendency to anaemia that I was put (along with millions of others during those days of rationing in post-war Britain) on a diet of raw liver, regularly prescribed doses of Radio Malt and treatment under a sunray lamp at the local hospital.

It is one of the most terrible deprivations of my life that I saw my parents only three times a year, at best, after I went away to school in England at the age of eleven (and was inconsolably homesick), and

---

* St Mary's is referred to in Pevsner's *The Buildings of England: South and West Somerset* (1958) as 'the jewel of Somerset'.
† Sir Rabindranath Tagore (1861–1941), 'Unity in Diversity' – from his anthology *Oriental Caravan*.

was to see them for perhaps a total of only a year or so between the age of eighteen and their deaths during my fifties. But I loved them both without limit, and they gave me all that a boy and a man could need in a life of many changes and a good deal of self-imposed turbulence. If there has been a single driver during what I suppose has been a pretty driven life, it has been to do things which would have earned the approval of my father.

❧

My proper formal education began at the age of seven, when I was sent to a fee-paying 'preparatory school' called Garth House on the outskirts of the County Down seaside town of Bangor. It was a curious establishment, run by a retired army officer and Irish cricketer, Captain Wilfred Hutton, and a terrifying woman called Miss Swanton, who was of gargantuan proportions with horribly bunioned feet crammed into cut-away shoes whose squeaks entered the room a good ten yards before she did. Garth House was located in a late-nineteenth-century house that had clearly at some time been the home of a well-to-do family and was set in what to me, as a young boy, seemed sumptuously extensive grounds, including woods and a large paddock turned into a rather good sports field.

So far as I remember there were no Catholics in Garth House, which was determinedly Protestant in its teaching and outlook. It was here that I first experienced the ferocity of the religious division in Northern Ireland, for these were completely absent in my home life. I can still remember the feeling of intense disapproval from my school contemporaries when I asked our religious affairs teacher why the Protestant religion was so good and Catholicism so evil if we all believed in the same Christian God.

To be honest, I was not very good at school. I was especially bad at mathematics (which my father was especially good at) and was rather bored by the discipline of learning, which I regarded as a waste of good fishing or shooting time. (I was not, of course, at this age allowed a real gun, but I did have an air rifle, which I could use to good effect against the magpies and pigeons who raided our garden.) My school reports fell, pretty well without exception, below the academic standard which my parents (and especially my father) hoped for and expected. I still remember the dread, shame and pain I felt when my father received the end-of-term reports.

28

But I was good at sport, especially athletics, which I enjoyed enormously. (I have always been rather better at sports which require individual, rather than team effort.) I broke, and held for some time, the school high-jump record and was faster than all my contemporaries on the running track. I have only played one really good game of soccer in my life, and that was at my prep school. Soccer normally required more finesse and control than I was capable of; in this particular game though, for some reason my feet seemed to be on fire, and I could make the ball do whatever I wanted it to, to the cheers of my schoolmates and my parents, who were watching. I have, sadly, never been able to repeat the performance.

Garth House was too distant from our home in Comber for me to return home at night, so I used to board during the week and be collected at weekends by my parents. By the time I was nine, however, I was regarded as being old enough to make the journey by myself on the bus. This involved changing buses in the town of Newtownards. On one occasion I missed the connecting bus home and – aged, I suppose, ten – walked five miles or so along what was, even then, a pretty busy main road, causing my parents much worry until I turned up at last. One of my fellow bus passengers at the time was a very pretty Newtownards girl with whom I fell deeply in love – from a distance. Her name was Ottilie Patterson, and she was seven years my senior. She was to become famous as a jazz singer and the wife of one of the great British jazz masters of the sixties, Chris Barber. She would never have known of my love, of course, for it was as undeclared as it was unrequited.

In fact all my loves were unrequited at the time. But they were beginning to be there all right. We had a statuesque matron with Titian hair and breasts as sharp as missiles. I can remember, as early as ten, becoming highly disturbed by her regular monthly physical examinations, and especially by the nightly squeak of her stockings on the dormitory stair.

It had all along been planned that I should be sent to Bedford School in England at the age of eleven. This was the school my father had been to and, as an 'old boy', he had special rights to a place for his children, should he wish it. Which was just as well, because the alternative would have been for me to take the Eleven Plus examination which most of my contemporaries had to take to gain access to a grammar school. I have no doubt whatsoever (and neither had my parents or teachers) that, if I had been required to take this exam, I would have failed it. This would have consigned me to the lower tier of education and, consequently, a lifetime on the lower rungs of opportunity, from which at that time it was almost impossible to climb free.

In the event, I only had to take the Common Entrance exam for public schools – a much less rigorous test, but one which, nevertheless, I only just scraped through. At the age of eleven I was finally informed that I would be given a place at Bedford. My education after this was thus the result of only one thing – not ability on my part, but the privilege inherited from my parents and my class.

This fact was to have a profound influence on me later. But at the time I was submerged under a tidal wave of excitement and apprehension at going to school 'across the water' in England, tinged only with the dread of partings from my family which would be measured in future, not in weeks, but in months.

CHAPTER 3

Teenage Years and Bedford

W HEN I WAS SENT there in 1952, Bedford School was a rather traditional middle-ranking, boys-only public school with about a thousand pupils. It was divided into what were essentially three separate schools: the Incubator (or 'Inky') which took children from 7 to 11; the Lower School, for boys from 11 to 13, and the Upper School, which continued pupils' education through to 18. Set in the middle of the town of Bedford, the school was said to have existed as a Church school since before the Domesday Book. In 1552 Bedford's School was issued with letters patent by Edward VI as a Grammar School. But, like so many other similarly founded schools, it raised itself to the status of an independent Public School in the mid-1860s. In my time it was less a forcing ground for achievement than the educational institution of choice for Bedfordshire's yeoman farmers and its middle classes. In one respect, however, the school's reach went well beyond the county. It had a strong reputation for educating the sons of military officers and the colonial civil servants who ran the Empire. My father had been sent home from India at the age of eight, to be educated first at a Jesuit college and then at Bedford. Indeed, he went to the same boarding house that I subsequently attended.

The school in the 1950s (no doubt it is very different now) was not particularly famed for its academic prowess (though my year had a fair crop of bright students who went on to glittering careers in academia). Most of its students were at the hearty, rather than brainy, end of the spectrum. Sport was thus a very important part of school life. We had a good rugby team which in my time briefly included Budge Rogers, seven years my senior, who later won many England caps and was acknowledged as one of the best rugby players of his generation.

The River Ouse runs placidly through the middle of the town, providing perfect facilities for rowing which, ahead of cricket, was the major sport of the summer. In all these sports, as well as in athletics and boxing, we played in the usual rounds of independent-school tournaments, whose membership included most of the major public schools of England from Eton downwards.

Although primarily a market and light industrial town (which in the 1950s had become something of a magnet for post-World-War-Two Italian immigrant families), Bedford, the home of John Bunyan, had (and still has) an unusual number of educational facilities. There was Bedford High School*, the female equivalent of Bedford School, a boys' secondary modern (known as Bedford Modern, and now an independent co-educational school in its own right) and the Dame Alice Harper Girls School, a grammar school for girls. The last two were viewed with a good deal of rather unpleasant snobbish disdain by Bedford School staff and pupils (though this did not stop them regularly beating us at sports). And on top of all that, there was Bedford College, which at the time was one of the nation's foremost establishments for educating physical training teachers. All this made for quite a sizeable, if not particularly prestigious academic community, as well as a great deal of opportunity for (at the time strictly illicit) fraternisation between the boys and girls of school and college age.

In the manner of public schools at the time, 'japes' were regarded as being an essential part of school life, even if formally frowned on. These were pranks which sometimes involved personal danger, but nearly always resulted in damage of some sort or another to public (or school) property. They were at the time looked upon as 'good clean fun', provided they were carried out by the 'young gentlemen' of the town, rather than its 'yobs'. The legendary jape, carried out long before my time, but still talked of with admiration and approval while I was there, was the nocturnal painting of red footsteps down from John Bunyan's statue in the town square, into a nearby ladies lavatory and back up to the statue again. (They could, apparently, be seen for many months afterwards, despite determined attempts by the Council to erase them.) The best such prank in my time was the painting of the words 'Frying Tonight' on the gym roof, which also stayed for many months, but could not be said to be so witty. The other prank, spoken of in hushed whispers, was 'beam walking', which consisted of walking at night along the beams which held up the roof of the Great Hall, three storeys and some forty feet above the floor. One of my friends, two years my senior, became so addicted to the business of japes that

* Now Bedford High School for Girls.

he took his skills with him to Cambridge and claimed to have been one of those involved on the fringes of the famous jape of putting an Austin Seven on the roof of the University Senate House in 1958.

It was into this, to me utterly strange, environment that I was plunged in the early 1950s, just as Britain was entering the last decade of Empire, privilege and class – soon to be swept away by the 1960s. My father made the first journey from Belfast to Bedford with me. Thereafter, from the age of eleven until eighteen, I made the journey alone, waving goodbye to my parents standing on Belfast dock as the ship for Liverpool bore me away for a three-month parting from them. Next morning the ship would dock under the Liver Birds statues on Liverpool dock, and I would make my way to Lime Street Station, through the grime and bustle of Liverpool's crowded streets. From Liverpool, the train went to Crewe, where I changed and, after an hour or so's wait, caught the train to Bletchley. Here I changed once more for the train to Bedford. I can still remember the journey intimately. But most of all I can remember the fear of missing the train engendered in me then (and never since lost). I can recall perfectly the cold and misery of sitting out on the platform of a wintry and windswept Crewe station for half an hour before the train was due, in case it should come early and leave without me. To this day, I drive colleagues and companions mad with my compulsion to arrive for trains and aircraft long before it is necessary, for fear of missing the connection.

On 31 January 1953 I had to return home from Bedford to Northern Ireland for a family funeral. This was the day of the 'Great Storm'. I was twelve years old at the time and remember the crossing of the North Channel from Liverpool to Belfast as by far the roughest and most frightening voyage of my life. In the event we were probably lucky to make it, as that same day the MV *Princess Victoria*, crossing from Stranraer to Larne, sank, with the loss of 133 lives. One of my childhood memories is of seeing the frozen bodies washed up on the Donaghadee foreshore for days afterwards.

Since I was a full-time boarder, I went into the Lower School's boarding house, called Farrar's. Here my broad Northern Ireland accent and a severe bout of early homesickness immediately attracted unwelcome attention. They nicknamed me Paddy, which remained my name right through my school years. And then as no less than thirteen of my contemporaries at Bedford also joined the Royal Marines, Paddy followed me there. Thus it was that Paddy became the name by which I have been known for the rest of my life. This, I fear, caused some distress to my parents. I, however, have always felt more comfortable with Paddy than with my given name of Jeremy, not least because it was not long before my strong Northern Irish accent was driven out of me (to my regret, with hindsight) so my schoolboy nickname now remains the only personal acknowledgement I have of my Irish blood and upbringing.

Farrar's was a pretty rough-and-tumble, physical place in my time, and I soon learned to be very self-sufficient, a habit which, together with a dislike of clubbishness, has remained with me all my life. The discipline was strict, the corporal punishment frequent and the play rough. Most of my contemporaries had been together in the Inky for four years previously, so I was something of a stranger intruding into already established relationships and found my first months there, parted from my parents and in a totally alien environment, very painful. It was not long, however, before I realised that if I wanted respect, I would have to fight for it. I became rather good at fighting in the rough-and-tumbles that were encouraged in the evenings. No damage beyond an occasional bloody nose was ever done, so far as I remember, and genuine anger in fights was something of a rarity. Indeed, the one golden rule of these scrimmages was never to lose your temper (I have a fiery Irish one, which I have always had difficulty controlling). We were more like young animals testing their strength through rough-and-tumble than genuine combatants. But it was a tough school of knocks nevertheless, and I soon found that I was bullied and teased less because I could both take it and give it on the rough-house floor. All in all it did me little harm, for I was a physical boy. But I cannot say I think it was a good way to bring up all boys, and there must have been many who found it deeply unpleasant and even permanently scarring.

My prowess on the rough-house floor and on the sports field was, once again, not matched in the classroom. I found study irksome, and my early reports were not good ones – to my father's chagrin. My Form Master's General Report for the Easter Term, when I would have turned twelve (signed off by my father in his neat hand on 27 April 1953), is pretty typical and reads:

A disappointing term; I am sure he could have done better. His effort is much too variable and his concentration poor. There is no doubt he means well, but it is a case of the spirit being willing, but the flesh weak. There has also been very little attempt to improve his handwriting.

A little over a year later, in the summer of 1954, I caught double pneumonia. The school authorities were sufficiently worried about my condition to send for my mother, who came over from Ireland and helped nurse me back to health. I have hazy memories of being delirious during this period and of nightmarish dreams in and out of which swam my mother's face and interminable wheeling columns of marching ginger biscuits (which seemed to be my staple diet when I was ill, and which I have hated ever since). It was also about this time that I started to get migraines, to start with as often as once a week. They were crippling, involving first blindness and lights and then brain-splitting headaches and nausea. I used to dread them, as they were very unpleasant, and I had to remain in a darkened room for twenty-four hours until the attack passed. They diminished in frequency and severity as I grew older, but have stayed with me, albeit in less severe form, all my life. I fear I hid them from the Admiralty authorities when I joined the Royal Marines and (with the help of friends and service colleagues who would cover for me during an attack) during my subsequent service career, for they would have disqualified me from entry at the start and could have caused me to be invalided out later.

At the age of fourteen, I contrived to break both bones in my lower left leg during an escapade in the Gym that resulted in my falling some fifteen feet onto the wooden floor. They made a bit of a mess of resetting the bones, with the result that I have one leg slightly out of alignment and shorter than the other.

In the autumn of 1954, at the age of thirteen, I moved to Bedford Upper School and a new boarding house, Kirkman's, situated about a mile from the main school on the banks of the Ouse. The first thing I saw when I entered my new home was a large board showing the names of all the previous heads of the house, amongst them my father's against the year 1925.

It was at about this time that, on holiday visits back to Northern Ireland, I started to become more and more aware of the position of Catholics in the Province, who at the time were heavily discriminated against in jobs, housing and almost all aspects of social life. The great annual Twelfth of July triumphalist celebration of the victory of the Protestant William of Orange over the Catholic Stuarts at the Battle of the Boyne often took place in a huge field opposite our house in Comber. As a child, I used to look forward to this as a

great and fascinating spectacle. But now I increasingly found its cere-
monies bizarre and its atmosphere ugly. I remember very clearly, from
about the age of fourteen, having a most powerful premonition that
this could not last, and that violence was coming.

Back at Bedford, however, my first year at my senior boarding
school meant that I was required to be a fag for one of the senior
boys, or 'Monitors'. The 'fag master' who chose me was someone I
had looked up to with something close to hero worship since I first
met him, 'Ram' Seeger. I later followed him into the Royal Marines,
where he won a Military Cross in Borneo. I also followed him into
the SBS, where he was (and still is) a legend. He subsequently saw
unofficial service in Afghanistan during the war against the Soviet
occupation, where he carried out acts of outstanding courage and
endurance. He remains one of the most extraordinary men I have
ever met. His outstanding gifts of leadership, mental focus and bravery would have better served both him and his country had he lived
in a different and earlier age, or perhaps during a time of great war.
He asked me to do none of the things normally expected of fags, like
making his bed or cleaning his shoes. Instead, I had to join him doing
PT in the backyard with a pack full of bricks on my back, or running
considerable distances along the banks of the Ouse in large boots and
the heaviest clothes we could find. He taught me the techniques of
endurance and the importance of physical fitness, alongside that of
an active mind.

I greatly enjoyed my time in the Upper School. Not that my academic work was any better, at least to start with. Here is a selection of
comments from my early Upper School reports which give the flavour:

> On the whole I am not satisfied with his work and progress. . . .
> He must try to work a little quicker. . . . Excessively Irish. . . . I
> was glad to see him show such pluck in the House boxing. . . . He
> works well but easily gets muddled. . . . He has some intelligence
> and with just a little more control over himself and some restraint
> of his high spirits, he could do quite well. . . . He has enthusiasm,
> but not always understanding. . . . His work is spoiled by careless-
> ness. . . . Very weak, but need not overly despair [French]. . . . He
> is far from being an accomplished linguist [French again], but in
> his own way he makes a contribution to the class. . . . Pleasantly
> argumentative. . . . Tries hard but finds it difficult.

Sport, however, was a different story. I was in the House rugby team for my age every year and eventually in the School's First XV. I played in various positions; first hooker, then wing forward, then No. 8 and occasionally in my last years, as I became more fleet of foot, as a wing three-quarter. My rugby, however, was more brawn than skill. Here is what my team Captain wrote in the House yearbook of Christmas 1958.

> Ashdown (2nd row). An amazing player, who never seems to run out of energy, even though leading the pack. He was the mainstay of the forwards, shoving like a maniac in the tight, leaping fiendishly in the line-outs and crashing into the loose. He inspired the pack to greater heights than we thought possible and combined them as a unit around him. He is slightly devoid of rugger intelligence, owing possibly to his fantastic energy, and is not very good at passing. Dribbles well.

I boxed, too, but hated it. At one time, in the annual blood match against Eton, the tournament depended on the result of the last bout in which I was pitched against Lord Valentine Charles Thynne*, the son of the 6th Marquis of Bath. Although he was four years my senior I was much the stronger. But no matter how many blows I rained on him, he refused to go down and succeeded in landing an equivalent number on me – each of us being spurred on with roars from our respective supporters in the audience. At the end of a most bloody fight, the bout was declared a draw.

I was, however, hopeless at cricket, which I have never really seen the point of, and so during the summer took up rowing and athletics. I was not neat enough to be a good oarsman, but in athletics I found I could excel. I loved the one-on-one competitiveness and the thrill of winning. To start with I was better at field than track events, particularly the high jump and the shot put, at which I set a new school record. But later I discovered I could run fast too, and in my last year won the Victor Ludorum for the best all-round athlete in the school.

Apart from sport, I took quite an active part in the other 'extra-curricular' school activities. I was an active member of the Debating Society from the age of twelve right through to my final year, arguing at various times against corporal punishment, against too much conformity, in favour of Sunday cinemas, in favour of suppressing gambling and against the abolition of fagging (in which I said that being a

---

* He committed suicide in 1979.

fag helped leaders to understand what it was like to be led). I also rose through the ranks to become a Warrant Officer in the School Cadet Force. But my extracurricular agenda was beginning to extend somewhat wider than official activities. As I approached my mid-teens, adolescence and puberty came roaring tempestuously into my life.

After the age of fourteen, we were all required to go to dancing classes. I was, and remain, a completely hopeless ballroom dancer and have, over the years, inflicted much grievous damage on members of the opposite sex unfortunate enough to be paired with me. But this was a chance to meet and actually touch those, to me, mythical creatures – girls! I was paranoid about my curly hair at the time and used to spend hours washing it an attempt (always vain) to get the frizziness out (in those pre-race-conscious days, the nickname my detractors gave me was 'the white wog', because my hair, though mousy blonde, was so negroid in character). I had actually had my first kiss in a hay loft on the night of the Coronation at the age of eleven, when visiting the home of my father's favourite sister (whose house in Dorset became a kind of 'home from home' during half-term holidays when I could not get back to Ireland). But this had not in any way diminished the paroxysm of nervousness and confusion into which my body was plunged whenever I was required to have social contact with a member of the opposite sex. And so, despite falling deeply in love with every single one I was nominated to dance with, I was not very successful and envied the louche and easy manner of my (straight-haired) school colleagues, who always seemed to be able to make progress where my clumsy approaches had been embarrassingly rejected.

All this changed, however, when I was just a couple of months short of my fifteenth birthday.

Two academic subjects consistently caused me problems at school. French (all my French teachers agreed on one thing – I had absolutely no aptitude for languages) and mathematics. Lack of ability in French was not regarded as being too serious. But mathematics was a different matter. By 1955 my father was in severe financial difficulties. The pig farm had folded, and my parents were now trying to make their living from a small market garden set up in the grounds of our house, where they grew vegetables for sale in Belfast market. It was therefore decided that I should try for a Naval Scholarship, which would pay my school fees from the age of sixteen, so taking enough financial pressure off my parents for them to be able to send my brother Tim to

Bedford as well. To be eligible for a Naval Scholarship, I needed to pass the Civil Service exam, of which mathematics was an essential part. Everyone agreed that I would not be able to pass this unless I received special individual, extra instruction.

Private maths lessons were arranged for me with the wife of a local businessman, who had given up teaching when she got married*. I used to see her on Wednesday afternoons, the school half-day. Since I fell in love with every member of the opposite sex who came within touching distance at the time, I naturally fell hopelessly in love with her, despite what must have been at least a fifteen-year difference in our ages. And with good reason, for she was extremely pretty with a trim figure and a habit of wearing tight Jane Russell sweaters and those narrow-waisted very full skirts with flouncy petticoats which were in fashion at the time (Bill Haley and the Comets' 'Rock Around the Clock' had just burst upon us).

I spent hours preparing to go and see her and none of it, I fear, was on mathematics. I had a slight stammer at this age, which, together with wild untameable waves of blushing, became uncontrollable in her presence. In retrospect, she could not have avoided seeing my confusion. Whether she deliberately made it worse I cannot say. But that was the effect when she leaned over me to correct some hopelessly incorrect calculation, and I could smell her perfume and feel her warmth. For brief moments I even felt her breasts brushing my shoulder and on one, much mentally reconstructed occasion, she permitted one to briefly touch the back of my hand as it steadied my exercise book while she corrected a sum. The effect on a young teenager with a head full of fantasies and a bloodstream boiling with a cauldron of adolescent hormones was predictable and, one might say, elevating. I used to dread the end of our lessons when I had to try to hide this somewhat prominent fact with my textbooks as I stood up to leave.

Things came to a head on our last lesson before the school broke up for Christmas 1955. She had clearly been to a lunchtime drinks party, for she arrived in a very boisterous and jolly mood, an especially flouncy dress tightly gathered at the waist, a silk shirt with the top button carelessly undone and her bosoms more than usually visible. The effect on me, exaggerated by the fact that she was especially close

* While the events described in the following passage are accurate as far as I can remember them, I have completely altered all personal and professional details, to disguise the identity of the person involved.

in her attention to my exercise book, was entirely inevitable. After about ten minutes of this torture, she instructed me to get a book from the bookshelf. Now there was no disguising my embarrassment and nothing to hide it with. And this time she did not pretend not to notice, but to my horror asked me whether I was embarrassed by it. I stammered that I was and, in a flame of blushes, apologised! She replied that it was nothing to be embarrassed about, unbuttoned her blouse and, gently taking my hand, placed it on her breast.

Our Wednesday afternoon affair lasted, I think, about two months after I returned from Christmas holidays. It did not do anything for my deficiency in maths – but it did teach me a very great deal that was useful for a young man to know on the edge of manhood. She dealt with my inexperience and gaucheness with kindness, tenderness and patience, and for this I have been eternally grateful to her. When it ended I was distraught and did all the things ardent boys do at that age, like hanging around her house and writing her dangerous, passionate notes. But I soon got over it, and with it my shyness towards the opposite sex – and this I owe to her, too.

I met her again four years later, between leaving school and joining the Royal Marines. At the time I was filling in time by working as on odd-job man in London, and our affair flared briefly and then died again.

This early initiation into one of the key rites of passage into adulthood marks a decisive watershed in my time in Bedford. But it was not, I fear, in any way beneficial to my academic studies, as the reports on my fourteenth and fifteenth years show only too clearly.

Corporal punishment was a feature of all public schools at the time and could be administered with up to six strokes of a cane, not only by the masters, but also by our fellow pupils who were Monitors. During my next two years I was beaten several times. Mostly this was for minor misbehaviour, though I was clearly beginning to develop a somewhat rebellious streak. One record in the punishment book of a caning by my Head of House notes:

> 4 cuts [strokes of the cane]. Talking and joking in prep [the Public School equivalent of homework] after repeated warning. Generally bad attitude. I was going to give him only 3, but when he appealed to Mr Reeve [the housemaster] in an obstreperous fashion, I gave him one extra.

A mere nine days later I got caught again – this time on my way out 'over the wall' at midnight to meet some local girls at a party. All those caught with me got four strokes, but I and one other fellow miscreant were given 'six of the best'. The note in the punishment book explains why:

> Being caught down [in the garden] fully clothed to go for a swim (so they said). The extra 2 were given [to me and my friend] for arguing to justify themselves on a blatantly obvious case of wrongdoing.

Fortunately for me, all that could ever be proved against me was that I was either preparing to be absent (as in the case above), or was absent – if we had actually been discovered in any of our secret nocturnal liaisons (often in the town's taverns), we would have been expelled.

In Bedford, apart from the Monitors, there was also a second and more junior tier of pupil authority, called 'Options'. Options had certain lowly privileges and were generally regarded as students who were on the way up to become full Monitors in due course.

So, given my record, it was to my very great surprise that, close to my sixteenth birthday, I was promoted to this first rung of student authority and appointed an 'Option'. It did not last long, however, as I was, with others, shortly afterwards discovered in an illicit (but day-time) rendezvous with some girls from one of the Bedford girls schools in an old derelict barn we had discovered on a school cross-country run. I cannot quite remember how we were discovered: I think one of the girls blurted it out to a friend, and it all fell apart from there. I should point out that nowadays what went on at these illicit ren-dezvous would be regarded as entirely tame stuff; some furtive fum-bling was about as far as it got. But it caused a great scandal, nevertheless, and I, along with others, was removed from the list of 'Options' and was again lucky not to be expelled.

Altogether my sixteenth year was shaping up to be pretty disas-trous. I managed to get seven O levels (English Language, English Literature, History, Geography, General Science, Elementary Maths, Physics), but they were a real struggle, and classroom study became an increasingly irksome chore.

Then two things happened that, together, formed the second water-shed of my school years. First, it became evident to me that my father's business was now failing fast and that, unless I got a Royal Naval Scholarship, I would effectively deny my brother a chance to go to Bedford. I *had* to pass this exam.

The second was that amongst the teachers to whom I was assigned in this year were two who literally changed my life for ever. The first was a history teacher Michael Barlen, and the second, even more influential, was a man called John Eyre, who became legendary among all those he inspired (but was, I suspect, something of a thorn in the side of the School authorities).

To these two, I shall return in a moment. But first I had to win my scholarship.

In fact, I failed at my first attempt at the Civil Service Exam (mathematics again!). But it was decided that I should nevertheless go ahead and take the second stage anyway; then, if I passed that, I could return to retake maths later. The second stage was one of those initiative tests for leadership, which went on over two days and was held in HMS *President*, then (and still) moored on the banks of the Thames, just down from the House of Commons. It was my first visit alone to London, and I was completely bowled over by the place. My memory is of fog and dirt and grime and derelict bombsites covered in rosebay willow-herb and buddleia, all overlaid with an intoxicating sense that this really was the centre of the world. I was captivated by the House of Commons, which I visited twice during the two days, and by Whitehall, in which, in my mind's eye, were all the levers which, when pulled, made things happen even in the farthest corners of the world.

I must have done quite well in the initiative tests, because I received a letter from their Lordships of the Admiralty a few weeks later, saying that the Royal Marines (always, anyway, my first choice over the Navy) would overlook my deficiency in maths and accept me. My father was delighted, and I suddenly, and perhaps for the first time, experienced the glow of being able to do something to help him.

My teachers did the rest. Michael Barlen inspired in me a fascination for history which has never since left me, and my school reports suddenly begin to be sprinkled with praise for academic and intellectual things.

But it was John Eyre who really changed my life. He persuaded me to join the Poetry Society (which all rugby playing 'hearties' resolutely despised) and gave me a lifetime love of poetry, even getting me to write some for the school magazine. Eyre lit in me a fire for literature, especially Shakespeare, which has never gone out. He persuaded me to act in the school play (not at very high level – I was a wordless monk in W.H. Auden's *The Ascent of F6*, on the basis of which success I was entrusted the following year with a single spoken line – 'Sound the alarums without!' – as a soldier in *Macbeth*). He even, with the assistance of another master in my house, got me to join a group to sing in (and win!) a madrigal competition – which, to anyone who knows my totally tuneless voice and incapacity to hold a melody, was nothing short of a miracle. Richard Lindley wrote a wonderful description of John Eyre in his obituary for *The Independent* in January 2006.

> There he would sit at his schoolmaster's desk, a theatrically tattered gown draped about his gaunt shoulders, tossing back a lank mane of hair and holding forth like some actor manager, explaining to his youthful cast the drama of life in which they were about to play a part.

John Eyre was one of those really great teachers who inspired all he came into contact with. In 1996 I joined some of the other pupils whose lives he had also changed for a lunch in the Reform Club. Amongst his past pupils present were: Michael Brunson, ITN Political Editor; Sir Michael Burton, our ambassador in Prague; Quentin Skinner, Regius Professor of Modern History at Cambridge (an exact contemporary of mine and also a considerable influence on me in these years, especially on music); Richard Lindley, BBC *Panorama* reporter; Andrew McCulloch, screenwriter and actor; John Percival, independent television producer; and Robert Hewison, the cultural historian, who wrote of Eyre:

> The red tie he wore was taken as a thin ray of radical hope by boys of a more intellectual persuasion, who found themselves trapped [at Bedford] in philistinism and rigidly enforced conformity. . . .There can have been few teachers of that period who kept a copy of Joyce's *Ulysses* on the classroom shelves.

Richard Lindley, in the 2006 *Independent* obituary, quotes me as saying:

> It's often said that we can all remember a single teacher who changed our lives by giving us a love of something we didn't know we loved. John Eyre was that teacher for me. Pretty well single-handedly he converted a rough, tear-away schoolboy interested only in rugby and sport into somebody who discovered the benefits of music, poetry (especially the Metaphysicals, who are still my favourites), literature and art which have stayed with me and probably improved me ever since.

At the end of his life John Eyre came to live close to us in Shaftesbury, and Jane and I went to see him for lunch there in 2001, five years before he died. He had lost none of his old spark, or his impish and acerbic nature. He opened our last meeting with 'Ah yes, Ashdown – you were always an interesting boy. But you were one of the few to surprise me – I never thought you would get as far as you have. Still, there's no accounting for fate is there?'

Eyre and Barlen tried hard to persuade me to give up the Marines, take my A levels and go to university. But this would have involved paying back the Naval Scholarship and would have meant, in those days, that my parents would have had to pay for me at university too. So it was out of the question. And, with the benefit of hindsight, it would have been wrong for me, as well. One of the strange features of my life has been that my wisest choices have been made by fate, not me. Had it not been for my parents' financial situation, I would probably have gone to university. And it would have been a mistake. For I still had some rough edges to be knocked off, and I fear I would have wasted my university years in an excess of rough pursuits. In due course I would take my tertiary education, but much later: in my late twenties. At eighteen, the Royal Marines were exactly the right place for me, and that was where my course was now set.

By this time, I was leading an increasingly independent life. The continued decline of my father's business meant that my parents no longer had the financial resources to keep my brother Tim at Bedford, and he was withdrawn and sent instead to Campbell College in Belfast. This tightening of family belts also meant that it became increasingly difficult to find the fare for me to return home during the shorter school holidays. So it was arranged that I should spend these with relations, and especially my aunt in Dorset. In practice, I contrived to spend much of the time I was supposed to be with her in London, living with an actress, somewhat my senior, who I had met at a joint amateur dramatic production put on by Bedford and its sister girls' schools.

My last year at Bedford was an exceptionally happy one. I was promoted to be a Monitor (which meant being allowed to wear a coloured waistcoat – in my case dove grey – and carry a cane). At the end of 1958 I was appointed as the Head of my House, so following in my father's footsteps. I loved this job and the new experience of being a leader. To my great surprise I enjoyed the pastoral side of leadership most. As Head of House I was allowed to inflict corporal punishment on younger boys with a cane. It was my proudest boast that I was the first-ever Head of a House who never did. I regarded this kind of corporal punishment, even then, as barbaric and unnecessary and, when it came to one boy inflicting it on another, dangerous and completely indefensible. The House punishment book at the end of my term as Head of Kirkman's rather mournfully records, 'The use of the cane was not required this term.'

I left Bedford before taking my A levels at the end of the Easter term of 1959, with a six-week gap to fill before joining the Royal Marines in May.

Here is what John Eyre wrote of me in my last report from Bedford:

I am so glad he has finally achieved his aim in the Civil Service examination. . . . I fear this will mean that we shall be deprived of his invigorating and mature zest in and out of class. But he has achieved a great deal here and I am sure that the value of much of the work he has done this year does NOT lie in the examination labels he was incidentally seeking and that therefore the breaking off of his A level course is insignificant. I hope he will not let himself lose touch with the world of thought in the necessarily more restricted life of the Royal Navy.

He has finished here in great style; everybody likes him and I am sure he will do well, for he has a fair ability and lots of sound common sense. He leaves with our sincere good wishes.

And my report on Bedford?

I hated the parting from my parents to go to Bedford. And during the year or so of my early misery the school did little to make things easier, while my contemporaries did much to make them worse. But the hard carapace I have ever since been able to construct when necessary, along with a certain self-sufficiency, a lifetime's resistance to the attractions of 'clubbability', and a determination to choose my friends and not have them chosen for me by my profession, have helped me to live a life in which the temptations of easy or companionable choices have never weighed too heavily in my calculations. In Field Marshal 'Bill' Slim's great book *Defeat into Victory*, his account of the defeat of the Japanese in Burma, he says somewhere that, whenever he was faced with a choice between two equally weighted options, he always chose the more difficult one. This has been, for me, something of a lifetime's motto. But I knew the truth of it before Bill Slim told me, because Bedford had already taught me.

I have also no doubt that, had I not had access to a privileged education, I would have failed my Eleven Plus exam and been consigned to the lower rungs of opportunity in the Britain of that time. I was a late developer, which our national education system in those years made no allowances for. So Bedford did me a great favour, though whether it was a just one is a different question. When it came to educating my children, I did not send them into the public school system that my father, in his time, regarded as so important and (as we shall shortly see) made such sacrifices for.

Finally, Bedford gave me four attributes that were to prove invaluable to me. A sense of confidence in myself (maybe a shade too strong – but the Royal Marines soon knocked that out of me); an enquiring mind; a burning desire to go on learning; and a very good grounding in the techniques and disciplines necessary to do so. I have, in consequence, learned far more since the end of my formal education, than I ever learned during it.

All things considered, this was not a bad armoury with which to equip an eighteen-year-old setting out to do battle with the world.

CHAPTER 4

The Royal Marines and Commando Training

T HE DATE WAS 5 MAY 1959. Out of the train window I could
see the mudflats of the Exe estuary. The tide was out, and the
great river, a spangled blue ribbon shining in the May sun, threaded
its way through brown mudbanks and haphazard battalions of tufted
salt grass. Here and there stout little boats painted in primary colours
bobbed to their moorings, and some busy oystercatchers were probing
for shellfish in the ooze, like tiny nodding donkeys in an oilfield.
South, across the river, were verdant fields, small whitewashed cottages, a huddled fishing village and the red earth of the Devon countryside rising to a wooded ridge on the skyline. There is just a hint of
Dartmoor here in the shape of the land, and the light has that soft
luminescence which only seems to occur close to the sea on Britain's
south-western peninsula. It was a strange landscape to me then, but
over the next few years this vista of intermingled sea and land would
become so familiar that I could reconstruct it in my mind's eye,
almost tree by tree and field by field, for the rest of my life.

Across the carriage from me was a young man whom I had been
furtively watching, as he had been furtively watching me. I was sure that
six weeks earlier he, like me, had received the fat envelope portentously
marked 'The Lords of the Admiralty'. It contained a magnificent scroll
saying that Her Majesty Queen Elizabeth, having complete confidence
in me, her trusty and well-beloved subject, was conferring on me the
rank and status of a probationary Second Lieutenant in the Royal
Marines, a letter instructing me to catch this train to Exton on this day,
a travel warrant for my ticket and some rather intimidating instructions
as to what I should bring with me and how I should dress. I was to be
smart, wear a jacket and tie and a hat. My travelling companion opposite me was indeed wearing a hat – a very smart brown trilby. My own
hat was stuffed in my suitcase, as I hate hats. It was a most inappropriate green felt affair, with a slightly rakish Robin Hood air to it, which I
had recently purchased and would, in the coming months, try to wear

as little as possible. He was looking very smart in a new sports jacket, cavalry twill trousers and sparkling shoes. I was wearing a duffle coat and looking pretty scruffy with a jacket that had definitely seen better days (my father had lent it to me), a rather crumpled shirt I had washed myself and very down-at-heel suede shoes. He was looking every inch the young Royal Marine officer. I was feeling very inadequate.

But then, apart from a brief return home to Ireland to see my parents, the last two months since I left Bedford had been spent in London, where I had been doing odd jobs and having a whale of a time. Mostly I had been interior decorating for a friend, rather older than me, who had just bought a couple of run-down houses in Ealing. He would go on to make a million and end in jail. I had also earned a little money washing up in Joe Lyons Corner Houses, and spent it all very fast with old Bedford friends of both sexes. All that was now being left further and further behind me with every clack of the rails under our little train rattling along the bank of the Exe estuary.

Sure enough, when the train arrived in Exton, my travelling companion and I got out together. When we did our introductions later in the day, I discovered he was called Roger Munton. He would be best man at my wedding, all but get engaged to my wife's cousin, and then be tragically killed in a car crash. But for the moment we found ourselves on the narrow platform along with eight other behatted young men being shouted at by a burly man who, we would discover, was our drill instructor, the inimitable Colour Sergeant Bert Shoesmith. He was giving us orders and referring to us as 'young gentlemen', though in a voice that told us he definitely didn't mean it. He commanded us to pick up our kit and 'embus' in some nearby three-ton military trucks. Beside him, in quiet but wordless command, was an incredibly smart, rather suave officer with black, slightly oiled hair, a cane under his arm and a Sam Browne belt with brass buckles so shiny that the sun, reflecting off them, seemed to lose none of its intensity. We were to discover that this was Lt Graham Mackie, our course officer.

We were 'marched' (if such a term is applicable to a ragged group of young men without the slightest idea of *how* to march) to the waiting truck, driven up the hill and through the gates of ITCRM (Infantry Training Centre Royal Marines), which was to be our home for the next two years. Today CTCRM (Commando has replaced Infantry) consists of a shining complex of multi-storey buildings and modern facilities; then it was just a collection of old World War Two wooden huts. Here, and on nearby Woodbury Common and Dartmoor, young commandos had trained during the war, and their ghosts were everywhere, including in initials carved in the woodwork of the huts and on the trees of the little wood inside the camp that was used for rope work, 'death slides' and instruction on how to climb rope nets on the side of a ship.

We were given a short briefing and then shown to our 'cabins' (ITCRM, Lympstone was very solidly on terra firma, but, the Royal Marines being part of the Navy, everything was in naval terminology – so the room you slept in was your 'cabin', and an evening having fun off camp was known as a 'run ashore'.) Each cabin housed two of us. We were arranged alphabetically. In the next-door cabin to me was Tim Courtenay, soon to become one of my best friends; I would marry his cousin in three years' time. I shared my cabin with Richard Armstead, who married my wife's sister a few years later.

My nine fellow trainee Second Lieutenants were:

Richard Armstead (retired as a Captain, died 2001; son joined the Royal Marines);

Jim Bartlett (retired as a Captain);

Tim Courtenay (retired as a Major and subsequently made a Lieutenant Colonel);

Peter Clough (retired as a Colonel);

Angus Gordon (transferred to the Royal Navy as a pilot and retired as a Lieutenant Commander);

Andy Moreland (retired as a Major; son joined the Royal Marines);

Roger Munton (killed 1962);

Ron Wheeler (retired as a Captain, one-time Conservative County Councillor in Devon); and

Rupert van der Horst (retired as a Brigadier after 33 years service; his son followed him into the Royal Marines and, as a much loved and respected commander of the SBS, was tragically killed in a diving accident).

Together we made up Young Officer Batch No. 19, known as YO19, or simply 'The Batch' for short. We were one of two 'batches' of young officers who joined the Royal Marines (known internally as 'The Corps') in 1959; YO20 joined six months after us.

At this stage we were all strangers. But by the end of the two-and-a-half years' training that lay ahead, we would know every detail of each other. We would know which of us would need help to cover the last few miles of a thirty-mile, seven-hour march in full kit across Dartmoor; whose mental processes were not to be trusted after three nights on the march without sleep; who would get drunk first and who would be sick first, and how many pints of beer it would take. We would know whose visio-spatial sense was so bad that, whenever he was leading us, one of the others had to be always at his shoulder to check his map-reading; we could spot early signs of bad temper in each other, even before we recognised them in ourselves; we would know who could do brilliantly at everything, but somehow could not command men; whose feet smelled worst in a wet trench, and who not to sleep close to after they had been eating beans; who snored so loudly that a would-be enemy could hear him from hundreds of yards away; we would even know the pattern of each others' bowel movements after a week in a bivouac on 'compo'*. In short, we would come to know each other probably more intimately than any other living human being (including parents and partners) ever would.

Our training began in earnest the following day. We were harried from morning to night, and the pace was frenetic. Physical training and runs were intermingled with classroom work (the history of the Royal Marines, military history, the principles of tactics, the theories of warfare, world affairs and much else). There were exercises, and instructions on field- and woodcraft, including the techniques of living out in the wild. There were tests all the time, including changing clothing quickly. There were inspections of kit at unannounced times. There was weapons training – lots of weapons training – with the whole range of weapons used by the Royal Marines at the time, from light machine-guns to rocket-launchers. But, above all, there was drill . . . and drill and more drill.

We were taught first how to clean our kit, and spent long hours deep into the night trying to make rough, service-issue leather parade boots and the equally dull officers' Sam Browne belts shine with a spit-and-polish sparkle you could see your face in. I was never very good at parades, being rather ungainly in gait, and my uniform seemed to act as a magnet for gathering pieces of fluff and general scruffiness out of

---

* Service field rations.

nowhere. I have a good voice, however, and therefore found commanding a parade rather better than being under command on one. This was not always true, though. On one occasion, when I was supposed to be in charge, I recall haplessly watching my colleagues marching off to the farthest reaches of Lympstone parade ground while my mind froze, unable to remember the command to turn them round. This caused the ever-present Bert Shoesmith to bawl in my ear, 'Come along, young sir. Say something – even if it's only goodbye!'

Drill sergeants ruled our lives in those days, and they had an inexhaustible store of choice phrases. The only difference between the vocabulary they used on the Marine recruits, who trained alongside us, and on us officers was that with us the word 'Sir' was included somewhere, no matter how eviscerating the language which surrounded it. A favourite of one of our instructors – usually shouted with his tonsils about an inch from one's nose – was, 'You, sir, are enough to make bishops bag off* and barmaids eat their young.'

We Officers used to be paraded alongside the Marine recruit squad every Sunday for church parade, which took place outside the little brick World War Two army hut that served as ITCRM's church at the time. As officers, it was assumed that we would know how to behave in church. No such presumption was, however, made about the ordinary Marines alongside us; they therefore needed a briefing from a drill sergeant. A legendary story has it that one of these briefings went as follows:

> RIGHT! In a minute you will file to the right in a horderly fashion into the church and you will all sit dahn. The next thing wot will 'appen is the Padre will walk in. You will all stand up. Then you will all sit dahn again. The next thing wot will 'appen is the Padre will say 'Let us . . . '. 'Let us' is the cautionary word of command; you do not move a MUSCLE. But when 'e says 'Pray', get down on yer knees and pray like FUCK.

A similar legend tells of a Lympstone Drill Sergeant who, spotting that one of his new recruits had not taken off his beret in church, bawled at the unfortunate:

TAKE YER 'AT ORF IN THE 'OUSE OF THE LORD – C**T!

* A Royal Marines term for the sex act.

On one occasion, during an inspection of kit, I was found to have squirrelled away more than the regulation three bits of lavatory paper we were allowed to carry in our kit. The Drill Instructor was clear:

> Only three bits of shit 'ouse paper, young sir. That's all your arse'ole needs! One up, one down and one to polish!

Shortly after we joined, one of my colleagues made the mistake of attempting to try and grow a moustache. After three weeks the wretched thing was barely visible, but Shoesmith spotted it and, pointing at the moth-eaten growth with his drill sergeant's cane from three yards away, bawled, so that the whole parade could hear:

> And what do you think this is, young sir? Yer eyebrows come down for a drink?

We also played a lot of sport, especially rugby. It was at Lympstone that I played alongside another of the great rugby players of my generation, Richard Sharp, the famous fly-half who was capped for England fourteen times and captained his country in their triumphant Five Nations victory in 1963. He was three years my senior and had joined up as an ordinary Marine in one of the last National Service intakes before conscription was abolished. He was also an exceedingly decent and modest man. The story goes that his rugby playing talents were spotted by an alert officer who put him in the Unit third team, where, of course, he excelled. Then, in the Unit second team, he excelled again. Finally, he was selected for the Unit first team. When told of this exceptional honour and given the date of the match, he said, as politely as possible, that he could not attend because of a previous engagement. His Troop Officer ordered him to cancel the engagement, which Marine Sharp, again respectfully, declined to do. 'Why not, Marine Sharp?' came the disbelieving and angry response. 'Do you not realise what a great honour it is to be chosen to play for the Unit? What on earth are you doing that can be more important than that?' 'Playing for the Barbarians at Twickenham, Sir. Sorry, Sir,' was Sharp's reply.

We spent much of our time out in the field on exercises, living rough. One exercise involved clandestinely moving across Woodbury Common at night to establish a new defensive position and digging in. This meant digging fire trenches, which were then camouflaged before first light. In these we spent the next three days, rain and shine, under simulated attack. Digging a five-foot-deep trench in the flinty soil of this outcrop of Dartmoor at night was one of the most labor-ious and miserable things I can remember from this period. By dawn the following day none of us had got deep enough to provide proper shelter, so the trenches had to be completed the following night, with horribly blistered hands. On the first morning our position was 'probed' by our simulated enemy who sent in small groups to try to identify our positions. We each took turns at being in charge, which meant, among other things, giving the order to fire when under attack. The standard fire order goes: 'Number four section, enemy to your front, four hundred yards – rapid – FIRE!' As luck would have it, my colleague in charge at the time (he turned out to be a most gifted soldier and commander) had a pronounced stammer. His fire order became a classic, long remembered and retold afterwards. He ordered us to 'stand to' in our trenches and then, when the enemy was clearly visible in the dawn light and within range, he gave his fire order: 'Number f-f-f-four section, enemy to your f-f-front, f-f-four hundred yards – F-F-F-FUCK it they've gone!'

On another exercise we were camped under makeshift winter bivouacs of sod walls for warmth with our groundsheets serving as a rudimentary roof, doing weapon training at Willsworthy Camp on Dartmoor. We rather enjoyed this camp because, although the buildings were Second World War, they were warm and mostly dry. The camp also had one of those latrine systems which consists of a series of cubicles (ten I seem to remember), each positioned over a trough with water flowing in at one end and carrying the detritus down the trough to a drain leading to a septic tank at the other. The flow in the trench was about that of a lazy trout stream, which nicely facilitated a practice we called Drake's Fireships. To play this you had to be upstream of your colleagues as they went about their morning business. You then gathered a large, loose ball of service-issue lavatory paper, set it alight and launched it towards an unsuspecting downstream defecator, much as the great Admiral launched his fireships against the Spanish Armada at anchor off Gravelines. If you got it right, and all ten downstream traps were occupied, the squeals of pain and rage issuing *seriatim* from each one gave a sort of rippling xylo-phone effect that was most satisfactory. Naturally, there was always early-morning competition for the most upstream traps.

On this occasion, however, there was none of that. Although we were quite close to the camp, we were banned from its facilities and had to make do with what we could construct or dig on Dartmoor's unforgiving hillsides. No sooner had we built our pathetic little sod bivouacs, than the skies opened and it poured . . . and poured . . . and poured. We spent three miserable days living and sleeping in a sea of mud, and then the exercise was abandoned – not because of our discomfort but because we were needed to join the rest of ITCRM, which had turned out to the last man to help Devon farmers and families, saving lives, property and stock in one of the worst floods in the county's history.

In one exercise, towards the end of this phase of our training, we were dropped on Exmoor and had to make an approach march over two nights, lying up in woods during the day, to a point just short of RAF Chivenor near Barnstaple on the north Devon coast, on which we were tasked to mount a night-time commando attack. On the third night we carried out our reconnaissance and on the following night our assault, which aimed to plant dummy bombs on their aircraft. The assault did not succeed, as the RAF Regiment guarding the airfield had been warned in advance. We were forced to pull back and then had to make our way through 'enemy-held' north Devon, using escape and evasion techniques, to a safe pick-up point in 'friendly' territory on the other side of Exmoor. We split into pairs, the better to evade the enemy. I was with my friend Tim Courtenay and it was my job to lead us across Exmoor in the dark. I made the fatal mistake of disbelieving my compass and attempted instead to find our direction by reading the land and trying to compare what I could see with what I thought I should see from the map. The night was very dark, and we got caught in some bogs (which, uniquely on Exmoor and Dartmoor, seem to occur more often on the tops of hills than on the low ground at the bottom of them). By three in the morning it was very clear that I had hopelessly lost us, so we elected to spend the rest of the night in a shallow sheep scrape and find our bearings when the dawn came. Light found us in the upper reaches of the very beautiful Doone Valley, miles from where we should have been. By now the rendezvous time for our transport back had passed. We decided that our only course was to make our way back to Lympstone, some sixty miles to our south-east, on our own. Thanks to hitches on trains, the help of a farmer on a tractor and the driver of a small delivery lorry, we made it back by nightfall, to find that there was a full-scale search on for us. My low marks for map-reading were compensated for by the high marks we received for initiative and self-reliance.

By now, however, my friendship with Tim Courtenay had another and deeper strand.

ITCRM held its annual Christmas ball on 12 December 1959, some seven months after we had joined. At this time I was 'between' girl-friends and so invited my cousin Freda, who lived close by in south Devon. Tim was in the same position. We arranged for both cousins to be put up in the nearby local, the Railway Inn (now rechristened with the rather more consumer-friendly name of 'The Puffing Billy'). The ball started, if I recall, at 7.30 p.m., so it must have been about this time that, in full Royal Marines mess kit (but nursing a huge black eye from a boxing bout the day before), I went down in a friend's car to pick up my cousin. I asked the publican, who by this time knew us all well, which room my cousin was in. But he confused the cousins and directed me to the wrong room. After a peremptory knock I opened the door to find, not my cousin, but a very pretty girl in the last stages of getting ready for the Ball. I could see she was pretty, even though her hair was in curlers. I stammered my apologies and beat a flustered retreat. It was only later at the ball (when she looked even more radiant and beautiful), that I discovered that she was Tim's cousin, Jane Courtenay. I will not say I fell in love with her that night, for we only danced together twice (a foxtrot and a waltz my wife tells me – but how could she tell, given how bad my dancing was?). But I did fall in love with her next day when, along with other colleagues and their girl friends and partners, we met for lunch in the Clarence Hotel in Exeter's Cathedral Square. I was bored with the lunch, and so was she, so we went off to look round the Cathedral together and, wandering round, found that we shared a love of architecture and classical music. Jane, it turned out, was an art student studying at Bristol and was as engaging, unpompous and fresh in her views as she was beautiful.

We started to write regularly and see each other whenever we could. I couldn't afford a car at the time, and so I relied on Tim Courtenay to drive me up to see her at her home in Burnham-on-Sea in his open-topped MG. I have very fond memories of these drives up the Exe Valley, full of anticipation at seeing Jane again. These were days when roads were less crowded, and we could stop off at a pub for a couple of pints and a sandwich without worrying about alcohol limits. And it always seemed to be summer, and the sun always seemed to be shining.

It was just at this time, as I was finding a new dimension to my life, that I lost the most important anchor on which I had relied for all of my eighteen years. Straight after the ball at which I had met Jane, I returned home to Ireland for Christmas with my parents. A day or so after I arrived home, my father took my mother, my brother Tim and me off to the Grosvenor Hotel in Belfast. This was, by family tradition, the place we always went when there was something really important to celebrate. But this was not a celebration. My father, with tears in his eyes, told us that he had failed us – his business would have to fold. He had decided, with my mother, that the only sensible course for them now was to pay off their debts and emigrate with the whole family – except me, since I was now established – to Australia, where the Government had initiated a scheme that offered British families passage and assistance in setting up in the new country for £10 (the so-called 'ten-pound Pom' scheme). They would leave in the spring. My father explained that his only lifetime ambition left was to give his children a proper start in life, and in class-conscious Britain that meant paid-for private education. It was now clear that that he would not have the money even to do this, so he would take the family to a country where it didn't matter. They had considered Canada, but the Australian scheme was all they could afford. I was heartbroken, almost as much by the sight of my beloved father with tears running down his broken face as at the prospect of being permanently parted from them all.

***

We had a pretty miserable last Christmas in a rented house in Donaghadee, where we had started in Northern Ireland, and then I returned to Lympstone at the end of the Christmas holidays. I saw them once more, a few weeks before they left from Tilbury Docks on the SS *Strathaird* on 6 June 1960. They had gone down to spend their last few days in Britain with my Dorset aunt, and I got time off to go and say farewell to them. After I had said goodbye to my brothers and sisters, my parents decided to accompany me as far as Axminster on the first leg of my bus journey back to Lympstone. It was not a wise decision. Most of the journey was spent in dumb misery, broken only by my father trying, in a choking voice, to give me advice on how I should live the rest of my life. It was on this journey that I first told them about Jane. And then, there in the town square of Axminster, I said goodbye to them both. It was dusk, raining and very cold for early summer. I remember seeing their faces out of the rain-streaked back window of the bus as it pulled out of the square, carrying me back to my life in England, as they headed off to refound their family on the other side of the world. I was to see my mother again for only three (albeit extended) occasions, and my father for four, before they died.

Many 'ten-pound Poms' found it too difficult in Australia and quickly returned to Britain. But not my parents. After a very tough beginning in a transit camp, my father took up a 'temporary' teaching post in the Victorian town of Castlemaine (they chose the town because it had the same name as a town in southern Ireland). He became, in time, a much-loved and respected teacher at the local high school. On a recent visit there to see my sister I was frequently stopped in the street by his grown-up pupils, telling me how much he had changed their lives, as two of my teachers had changed mine. My mother, also much-loved, worked as a nurse in the local hospital. Australia and Castlemaine were very kind to my parents and my brothers and sisters. Of the five of my siblings who went there with my parents, one has died, one was killed in a road accident, one, Mark, has returned to England and is a solicitor in Bristol. But the remaining two, my brother Tim and my sister Alisoun, are proud Australians and have established families firmly planted in that country's welcoming soil.

Now, however, I was on my own – apart from Jane that is. But our relationship was still in its early stages.

The next phase of our training took my colleagues and I to the Royal Naval College at Dartmouth to learn navigation and seamanship. This culminated in a three-month training voyage with the Dartmouth training squadron, consisting of three frigates, HMSs *Venus*, *Vigilant* and *Urchin*. We visited Gibraltar, Tenerife and the Cape Verde Islands before making a very rough Atlantic crossing to the West Indies, where we spent six weeks cruising the islands and calling at the major ports. We learned the routines of shipboard life, watch-keeping, gunnery, engineering, damage-control, first aid, and how to fight the ship on active service. We also had a very good time, climbing Teide (the mountain on Tenerife), visiting the strip joints in La Linea, close to Gibraltar (grubby, sweaty and sordid and enough to put me off such things for life), drinking too much rum in Barbados, and then learning the technique of negotiating the gangway on our return, under the alert eye of the Officer of the Watch, without letting it show too much.

———◆———

During these three months Jane and I kept up a regular and passionate correspondence as our relationship deepened. I spent that summer holiday with her and her family and then, in late August, sailed to Norway to take part in a joint-services expedition based in the town of Glomfjord, well north of the Arctic Circle and sheltering under the largest glacier in Europe. The town was also famous for being one of the targets of the daring SOE raids (immortalised in the film *The Heroes of Telemark*) on Norwegian power stations during the war, in order to prevent the German production of heavy water, a key ingredient for the development of a nuclear weapon.*

———◆———

Our task, however, was far less dangerous. We were to map some of the high mountains above the fjord and, in the process, learn about cartography. We lived at the time almost totally on dried rations, which share one quality of almost all service field rations, only more so: they look very much the same when they come out as they did when they went in. This is especially true of dried apple rings, which formed a major part of our diet and which, I observed, could pass through the entire intestinal tract of healthy young men without any detectable change to either their composition or their shape.

I know this because in Glomfjord I helped to construct the finest latrine upon which I have ever sat. It happened like this.

One of my fellow expeditioneers was a young Royal Engineer officer who had just finished his demolition course. He was given the job of building the camp latrine, and I was apprenticed as his assistant. After an extensive reconnaissance we finally settled on a small ravine, perhaps thirty feet wide and twenty deep, which formed a cleft in the mountain not too far from our base camp. Along the side of the ravine was a small stand of fir trees. My Royal Engineer friend selected two

---

* One of my Royal Marine colleagues who was on this expedition with me, Rupert van der Horst, would later marry the niece of one of the leaders of this raid by No 2 Army Commando, known as Operation Musketoon. Along with others on the raid, he was captured and transported to Sachsenhausen concentration camp, where he was subsequently shot.

stout ones growing close together and, using expertly placed plastic explosive, dropped them neatly across the ravine. A little work with levers was all that was then required to manoeuvre them so that they lay parallel to each other and about six feet apart. We secured them firmly to each bank with rope and spikes driven into the ground and then used them as the basis for a most impressive structure which had a narrow walkway giving access to a most magnificent eight-holer. We were miles from anywhere and some two thousand feet above the fjord, so there was no need for screens to hide us from prying eyes. I have known few more congenial experiences in my life than sitting every morning, in the company of my fellows, over a twenty-foot-deep latrine, with the mountains around us, looking down on the returning trawlers of the local fishing fleet dotting the fjord below and listening to the distinctive 'pot, pot, pot' sound of their big, single-cylinder diesel engines wafting up to us from the calm waters below.

My first act when I got back from our Norwegian adventure was to go and see Jane, who had now got a job in London. I turned up unannounced at her bedsit on the fourth floor of 13 Philbeach Gardens, Earls Court. I had fixed nowhere to sleep that night and hoped to be able to stay with her. But I reckoned without her dragon of a landlady, Miss Griffith-Jones, who instructed me in tones not to be disobeyed that 'All visitors are to be out by eleven o'clock'. So, after a scratch meal of baked beans from her fridge (all she had at the time), I left to take pot luck on the streets of London. I called in at a nearby mobile tea and buttie stand, where I met a very pleasant man of around 60, who asked if I had anywhere to stay? I said I didn't and he offered to give me a bed for the night. We walked back to his flat nearby where we sat and talked over glasses of whisky. I found him engaging, interesting and utterly charming. He introduced himself as very well-known contributor to a popular tabloid newspaper. After about two hours conversation and several more whiskies he told me that he was homosexual, was I? I said I wasn't, and the conversation then continued as though the subject had never been raised, until the early hours of the morning. I remember him as one of the most urbane, interesting and civilised people I have ever met.*

---

* The Wolfenden report had been published two years before, so homosexuality was no longer a criminal offence. But it was still socially unacceptable and could cause embarrassment, especially to the well known. The person referred to here is now dead. But he did not, to my knowledge, reveal his sexuality during his lifetime, so I have not revealed his identity here.

Next on our training agenda was the much feared Commando course, which we began in late September 1960. Newly joined Royal Marines wear the Corps's distinctive blue beret with a red patch on the front, on which is mounted the Globe and Laurel which is our insignia. The green beret of the Commandos has to be earned on a six-week course designed to test the limits of physical endurance. The centrepiece of the course is a series of forced, or 'speed', marches which must be accomplished at a pace of a mile in ten minutes, carrying full kit and rifle. These speed marches escalate from the 'five-miler' to the final march in full kit across thirty miles of open Dartmoor, which we Officers had to complete in seven hours and the Marines in eight. In addition there were exercises to test mental endurance when tired, negotiating an assault course while carrying a 'wounded' comrade over obstacles, and high rope and net work in the upper branches of a local wood. It was very tough going, but we all got through it and received our much-coveted green berets on 28 October 1960.

This brought us to the next phase of our training, in which we were posted as junior Troop officers to an active service Commando for a year. To my delight I was posted that autumn, along with my two colleagues Tim Courtenay and Rupert van der Horst, to 42 Commando Royal Marines, then serving in Singapore.

Before the start of our posting, we were given a month's leave, which I spent in part with Jane's family and in part, accompanied by Jane, with my Dorset aunt, who was now, after my father's departure, the senior member of the Ashdown family in Britain. My aunt, though at first sight soft, feminine and feline, was in reality something of a tartar, with a very strong will and decidedly settled views. She could be very intimidating when roused or displeased. But she immediately took to Jane (whom she called 'little Jane', despite being at least three inches the shorter of the two). It was during this visit, on a hilltop overlooking her house in Upwey, on a fine spring morning in May, that I proposed to Jane. I was nineteen at the time, and Jane, who is a few months older than me, was just a month short of twenty. We agreed to get married as soon as my training was over in eighteen months. At this time the services strongly discouraged officers from getting married before they were twenty-five. So we would have to ask their Lordships of the Admiralty for permission to marry, and even then would receive none of the allowances, accommodation or travel support given to married couples until I was twenty-five. Since neither of us had any money at all, life was going to be very tough for us – but, of course, we thought little of that in the excitement and joy of the moment. I think that my aunt was a little shocked, though, when we came back that day and told her the news.

But we had strong support from my parents in Australia (even though they had never met Jane) and from Jane's parents – and from one other invaluable source. One of the senior officers at ITCRM at the time was a remarkable man who was admired, respected and loved by all of us as a most just person and an outstanding soldier. He had had a glittering war record in the Commandos. He had also taken to Jane and, I think, realised that, because of my upbringing and the recent loss of my parents, I had seen more of life than most nineteen-year-olds. He supported us and it was, I am sure, because of him that we did eventually (but a year later) get permission from the Admiralty to marry. Some years later he resigned from the Royal Marines over an issue related to homosexuality in the armed forces – a tragedy for him and a terrible loss to all he commanded. Many years later, when, as an MP, I was amongst the first to campaign to have the law changed to allow homosexuals to serve in the armed services, I was doing something which I not only knew to be right but which also enabled me to repay a small debt to this outstanding man.

A month later on 15 November 1960, Jane and I said rather tearful goodbyes in the Bunch of Grapes pub on the Kings Road, Chelsea, and I left to take up my new posting in Singapore.

***

A Royal Marines Commando unit consisted in those days of around six hundred men who were divided into five rifle troops, each com-manded by a Major or a Captain and consisting of five sections and a support section armed with mortars and heavy machine-guns. Each section was commanded by a Sergeant. Each troop also had two junior subalterns (Lieutenants) whose job was to assist the Troop Commander and to command any sub-units formed from the Troop when operational circumstances required. I was assigned to be one of the junior subalterns in 'X' Troop of 42 Commando.

My colleagues and I considered ourselves most fortunate to be posted to 42 Commando, not just because it meant going to Singapore, but also because the Commando was, at the time, testing out new techniques for using helicopters for amphibious assaults from a specially converted aircraft carrier, HMS *Bulwark*. We also had a specially dedicated Royal Navy helicopter unit, 848 Squadron, assigned to us. At the time the Senior Pilot of 848 Squadron was the legendary Lieutenant Commander 'Digby' Lickfold, an outstanding flyer who lived life as fast as he flew his aircraft. His pilots, following his lead, had a spirit of élan that would not have disgraced a Battle of Britain fighter squadron and an equivalent disregard for the rules if they interfered with getting the job done. They referred to all Marines as 'grunts', but the badinage between us was very much a two-way affair, and we loved them for their willingness to take risks, especially when it meant getting us out of trouble.

At that stage we were using Westland *Whirlwind*s, which were so inadequately powered for the job that the joke was that they could carry one Royal Marine, or his hat, but not both – in reality, in tropical conditions, they could lift up to four fully kitted Marines at a time. They also ran on the highly inflammable Avgas (high-octane petrol, rather than the kerosene that later became the standard aircraft fuel) and in the event of accident were lethal firebombs.

When we arrived in Singapore the Commando was away testing helicopters in Hong Kong. The Major in charge of the element of the Commando that had stayed behind in Singapore (under whose command we fell until the Unit returned) decided on our second day in Singapore, that we should fill in our time by doing a parachute jump. When one of us hopefully pointed out that we were not trained he replied, 'I don't give a fuck if you are trained or not. If any of you don't make it, when the Commando comes back I shall just tell the Colonel that you never joined!' (What we did not know at the time was that what was planned was a jump into the sea, so we would not need training in parachute landings.) My two colleagues, Tim Courtenay and Rupert van der Horst, seemed keen, so I felt I ought to be as well. To be honest, parachuting scared me to death then and has scared me to death ever since. (Although I later qualified for my parachute wings and did more than sixty jumps with the SBS, I never managed to bring myself to believe that it is a rational thing to throw yourself out of an aircraft travelling at 120 mph a thousand feet above the ground, on the basis that the pack on your back really contains a parachute and not just a collection of old socks someone has absent-mindedly left there by mistake.) In the event we all got down without mishap.

HMS *Bulwark* left on her next cruise with the Commando embarked in the early months of 1961. This time we were to test out our newly acquired helicopter techniques in East Africa. We were to sail to Mombasa, where the Commando would disembark and move to a nearby game reserve, which we would use as a training ground for helicopter assault.

On the journey across the Indian Ocean, I was appointed the Commando's 'Mess Deck Officer', whose duties were to ensure that our Marines were properly accommodated and looked after on board. One of my heroes at the time was Nelson, who had been loved and respected by sailors throughout the Royal Navy not just for his ability as a commander but for his dedication to the welfare of ordinary sailors at a time when conditions on board were extremely harsh. He introduced a set of standards for sailors' accommodation that included a minimum space, measured in cubic feet, to be provided for each man below decks. I discovered that the space allowed to each man on *Bulwark*, with a full Commando embarked, was actually below the limit set by Nelson in 1802 (albeit in *Bulwark* the space was air-conditioned). I enjoyed the job enormously, made myself something of a thorn in the side of the ship's authorities and once again discovered, somewhat to my surprise, that I really enjoyed getting involved in pastoral issues to do with welfare and well-being.

One of my duties as Mess Deck Officer was to give references as to character for Marines who had to appear at 'Commander's Table', where shipboard discipline for relatively minor misdemeanours was dispensed. On one occasion I had to appear in this role for a Marine in my troop who had come aboard ship late at night very much the worse for wear and had been sick over the Duty Petty Officer, which was not a good thing to do. However, when he appeared before the Commander for punishment, none of the witnesses could be found, so no evidence was submitted beyond a bald statement of the facts on the charge sheet. I was then required to give my character evidence, which I did, saying that he was a Marine of good standing, etc., etc. After this the Commander passed judgement, in the best traditions of naval discipline at the time. 'Marine X, you will have twenty-eight day's stoppage of pay. And if there had been a shred of evidence against you, I would have put you inside!'

While the publicly stated purpose of our visit to Kenya, then still a British colony, was to train, there was a deeper purpose too. The Congo conflict was just erupting at this time, and numerous atrocities were being committed, including against the white settlers. This had sent shock-waves through Africa, and there was a fear that the instability would spread to Kenya. We were there to provide for the contingency that extra forces would be needed to maintain order in the Colony. So the Commando had a warm welcome when we arrived, not least from wives and daughters who had been sent to Kenya for safety by their menfolk in the Congo. Some members of the Commando took their responsibilities to protect these unfortunate unaccompanied females further than, I suspect, husbands and fathers had intended when they sent them to 'safety' under the protection of British forces amongst the palm-fringed beaches of the Mombasa coastline.

Our next stop was in Aden, to try out our helicopters in desert conditions. Sand in the engines was the biggest hazard here, on some occasions causing complete engine seizure. I was in one aircraft flying above the Aden desert at maybe three thousand feet, when, instead of the deafening clatter of the rotors above my head, there was suddenly an eerie and disconcerting silence. Fortunately, helicopter rotors in such circumstances behave like sycamore seeds and slow the descent of the aircraft, a process called autorotation. Provided the pilot times the final manoeuvre for landing (called 'flaring') and there is a flat place to land, such a descent can be managed without major mishap. We were lucky and made it down without damage or injury, but it was nerve-wracking, nevertheless. One pilot during this time so mistimed his final 'flare' before landing that the rotors came down and chopped off the helicopter's tail – causing some discomfort, but no injury to his passengers.

While we were in Aden, some of us hitched a lift up the desert to an isolated forward fort called Dhala, to spend a few days with the Marines of our sister unit 45 Commando, who were fighting the insurgents in the Radfan mountains of northern Aden, where we experienced for the first time what it is like to be shot at in anger. Although there were some quite sharp engagements during these operations in the Radfan, our experiences were of nothing more than sporadic firing at our base from a good distance away. There is a very distinct 'crack and thump' when a live bullet is fired at you – the 'crack' being the noise of the bullet breaking the sound barrier as it leaves the muzzle of the weapon, and the thump, which comes a few milliseconds later (depending on the range), the sound of its impact. We had been taught about this in training, but now for the first time we experienced it in practice.

This being the first time we had been ashore for some time, our nights off tended to be pretty boisterous affairs. I was with some Marines from my Troop in the local servicemen's club one night when a fight developed with soldiers from an army regiment based in the Colony. The RAF police were called, and I tried to escape by retreating into the Gents and hiding in one of the cubicles. Here I was found by one of my Marines, who arrived in full RAF police uniform, complete with RAF guard dog. He explained that the policeman had tried to arrest him, but he had dealt with the situation (I didn't ask how) and 'borrowed' his uniform and the dog. He then escorted me past the RAF police cordon as his 'prisoner', complete with dog, which we let go when we were well clear.

After Aden, *Bulwark* returned to Singapore, where we continued developing our helicopter techniques, this time in the jungle. But we hadn't been in port for long before we were off once again for a second Indian Ocean tour. Our first call was at Karachi for a courtesy and refuelling visit. On our second day in port, I was in a bar with some friends when the Royal Marines Police came in and ordered us back on board the ship as quickly as possible. The Commando was scrambled back to *Bulwark*, which cast off in haste from Karachi dockside and thundered off at full power towards the Persian Gulf. All the unit officers were then called to a briefing. The Iraqi dictator of the time, General Abdul Qassim, we were informed, had amassed what were estimated to be 30,000 troops, including tanks, on his southern border and was preparing to invade Kuwait, which had just received its independence from the UK. Other British units were being mobilised to defend Kuwait, but they could not get there for days. We were the closest and would be first on the scene. Our objective was to take and hold the port and airport, until reinforcements arrived.

Poor old *Bulwark*! She was known colloquially as 'The rusty B', and we used to joke that her plates were so rotten that the only thing that held her together were the layers of paint covering up the rust. She didn't need a torpedo to sink her – a can of paint remover would have been quite enough! She was, moreover, a dignified old lady and not used to rushing places any longer, let alone gallivanting off up the Gulf at a sustained and rivet-popping thirty-odd knots.

As she surged through the sparkling waters of the Persian Gulf, we prepared, as we thought, for action against a hugely numerically superior force. There was much checking of kit and weapons, much studying of maps and old aerial photographs, much briefing and rebriefing for D-day and, amongst us younger officers at least, much nervousness. Our preparations varied between the meticulous and the bizarre.

My commander's pre-D-day (known as D –1) preparations for what we all thought would be a heavily opposed landing the following day, fell clearly into the latter category. He was a much respected and admired, but slightly eccentric soldier. He called us young officers together and, as I remember it, briefed us as follows: 'Now, when we have completed our assault and driven the enemy out, our next task will be to win these Arab johnnies' hearts and minds. And I have decided that we shall do this by putting on a show of Scottish country dancing!' And so, wearing army blankets for kilts, we paraded on the bucketing deck of HMS *Bulwark* in 45° centigrade, with action in prospect the following day, and were instructed in the intricacies of the eightsome reel – which remains, to this day, the only ballroom manoeuvre that I feel confident of being able to execute pretty well flawlessly.

Fortunately for us, when our helicopter-borne assault landed in the Kuwaiti port of Mina Al Ahmedi, in the middle of a sandstorm, the Iraqis were nowhere to be seen. The intelligence about the situation in Kuwait, however, was confusing. Some said the Iraqis were still on the Kuwaiti border, others that their forward elements had reached the strategic Mutlah Ridge above Kuwait city (thirty years later, during the first Gulf War, this was the site of the 'Highway of Death' – the infamous 'turkey shoot' in which a retreating Iraqi armoured column was decimated by US airpower in terrible scenes of carnage).

The Commanding Officer called me in and gave me instructions that I was to lead a night patrol clandestinely up on to the Mutlah Ridge, seek out a suitable helicopter landing site and mark it out with fluorescent panels, so that the Commando could mount a dawn heli-copter-borne assault the following morning.

I assembled a small hand-picked group of my Marines and briefed them. We then blackened ourselves up for night operations and set off bravely. We carried out what I thought was a skilful and silent infiltra-tion onto the ridge, found our site and laid out our panels, expecting at any time to bump into a much larger Iraqi force. And, so far as I could tell, we completed our task without detection.

But what would happen when dawn broke and the Iraqis saw us? There was very little cover and we stood out extremely prominently, gathered as we were around our brightly coloured fluorescent panels, which I was sure would make just as good aiming points for enemy tanks as they would landing-site markers for friendly helicopters. I started to dread profoundly the coming of the dawn and what it would bring. So I am not sure whether it was relief at not being a tank target or embarrassment at our failure of fieldcraft which predominated the following morning, when, as dawn broke, we discovered we were surrounded, not by Iraqi tanks but by curious Bedou and their goats, who had watched and tracked our every clandestine move!

The following four weeks were spent under the scorching July sun peering from flimsy holes dug in the desert sand into the swirling dust, out of which, at any moment, we expected the mighty weight of several Iraqi tank divisions to emerge. In the end however, the 'thin red line' held, and the Iraqis stayed away long enough for the lumbering British machine to deliver enough forces to Kuwait to provide an effective defence, leaving our puny, lightly equipped 600-strong Commando to go home to Singapore.

The rest of our training tour was quieter, but by no means boring. We went up to the jungles of northern Malaya, to learn the silent arts of jungle warfare; how to live off the jungle; how to see it as a friend and, above all, how to navigate its trackless wastes. It was on one of these jungle map-reading lessons that one of us asked our instructor, QMSI McKay, a giant of an Australian from 1 Royal Australian Regiment, if he had ever been lost in the jungle? 'Naw,' he drawled, 'never lorst, but I was once temporarily misplaced for about fourteen days!'

We did not, however, overlook the opportunity to have a good time, when we could. On one occasion, after I had been with some friends to see *Ben Hur*, I was standing up in the bucket seat of a friend's MG imitating the great chariot driver, as he raced a colleague in a Riley far too fast down a local jungle road. My friend misjudged a bend, ran out of road and into a very deep drainage ditch (they were known as monsoon ditches), which sheered his front axle off and catapulted me over the bonnet and clean through the flimsy walls of a nearby shed, cutting my nose rather severely (I was extremely fortunate not to suffer worse). After the accident had been cleared up we returned to camp, where someone said that I ought to see the unit Doctor, a naval Lieutenant Commander eponymously surnamed Mends, and known by all as 'Doc Mends'. Though much loved by the Marines, Doc Mends operated on the basis that Marines were indestructible and therefore didn't need mending. So, he reasoned, if they claimed to be ill or damaged in some way they were obviously malingering. On one occasion I had sent one of my Marines to see Doc Mends because he complained he couldn't sleep. Somewhat to the Marine's surprise, given Mends' well-known aversion to offering treatment to the sick, the Doctor agreed that not being able to sleep was indeed serious, and something had to be done. He then pulled out a prescription pad on which he scribbled something and, putting it in an envelope, instructed the Marine to take it to the Quartermaster immediately. This struck my Marine as a little odd but, being an obedient fellow, he did as he was ordered. The envelope was duly handed over to the Quartermaster, who opened it and read the Doctor's prescription, which instructed 'This Marine is to return his bedding at once.'

Despite Doc Mends' reputation, on this occasion my friends decided that he should be called. He was woken and given the brief details of what had happened and who it had happened to. His reply was, 'Silly young fool – tell him to come and see me in the morning,' after which he turned over and went back to sleep. My colleagues concluded that the best medicine now was to take me and my bleeding nose to the Sergeant's Mess bar, where we stayed until five in the morning. When I went to see the Doctor the following day he decided on stitches, but did not feel it necessary to give me a local anaesthetic while they were inserted. The combination of the natural sensitivity of the nose area and the fact that by then the skin round the wound had hardened, compounded by an imperial hangover, made this an extremely painful procedure. The scar on my nose marking Doc Mends' handiwork has stayed with me all my life, as has the suspicion that this was a clear breach of his Hippocratic oath and intended less to heal me than to pay me back for being the cause of his rudely interrupted slumbers.

Our tour finally over, we returned to UK and the last phase of our training. This involved spending time with each of the Royal Marines' specialist wings: heavy weapons, cliff assault, mountain warfare, assault engineers, landing craft, the SBS, etc.

It was during this period that, together with one of my fellow officers, I bought my first car, called 'Baby May', for the princely sum of £10 off a colleague who was going abroad. At the time I could not even drive. But I still thought it a worthwhile investment, since my co-owner agreed to drive for me whenever I wanted. This was not only convenient, it was also necessary. For driving Baby May was strictly speaking a two-person affair. These, of course, were the days before the Road Test, and so there was effectively no restriction on what kind of vehicle could be put on the public highway. Even so, Baby May attracted some attention. Her chassis and engine were those of an old Austin Seven, upon which a makeshift body had been assembled from plywood panels by someone with only the most rudimentary grasp of carpentry. She had her original glass windscreen, but the rest of her windows were made of Perspex of a rather flimsy sort, the whole being tastefully set off in lively colour scheme of luminescent yellow and a particularly bright pillar-box red. She had two other unique features (as if all the above was not unique enough).

The first was that her radiator block was cracked and leaked water at the rate of about two cupfuls an hour. This deficiency was easily remedied, though, because – as her previous owner pointed out to us at the point of sale – when removed, the external radiator filler cap revealed a circular aperture just large enough to snugly take the mouth of a Gordon's Gin bottle. We could thus drive the car with a full gin bottle of water stuck into the radiator aperture and fully visible to the driver. When the gin bottle was empty, it required only a brief halt for the co-driver to leap out, exchange the empty bottle for one of the full ones from the stack we always carried in the boot, and then we could resume our journey. We reckoned that Baby May could do some twenty miles on a gallon of petrol and some thirty on a gin bottle full of water.

Her second distinguishing feature was that her electrics had been reconstructed from wiring and crocodile clips bought at Woolworths. And this, in the end, was her undoing. Before the end of our training we sold Baby May on to a fellow officer under training. One summer's day, while he was driving her on Exmouth sea front, weaving his way between the holidaymakers – most of whom clearly believed this was some kind of comic turn the local Council had put on for their amusement – Baby May's dashboard suddenly burst into flames. To the holidaymakers, this was all part of the entertainment. But my colleague knew it was not funny at all, because Baby May's petrol tank operated on gravity feed and was situated between the now burning dashboard and the engine. He retreated to a safe distance, from which he bravely tried to encourage the amused spectators not to get too close – but this only seemed to confirm to them that this was indeed all a joke. Fortunately, we could never afford to fill Baby May's tank and always ran her near empty, so, even though her Perspex and hardwood body burnt with a merry blaze, no harm was done – apart from a black smudge on the kerbstone which was all that was eventually left of poor Baby May. The black mark at the site of her demise was still just visible more than thirty years later, when in 1998 I visited Exmouth on an election campaign tour as Leader of the Liberal Democrats.

At the end of our course we had to decide which specialisation we wanted to pursue when training was over. I had by now already firmly decided that I wanted to go into the SBS. But they only took applicants after they had done a full tour in an operational Commando. So I applied instead to specialise in heavy weapons (mortars, machine-guns and anti-tank weapons), since I knew there was a shortage of specialists in this branch and a qualification here would therefore give me the best chance of being sent to an operational Commando and as far away from the dreaded parade ground and ceremonial duties as possible.

On Friday 1 September 1961, two-and-a-half years after we had all first met on the platform of Exton Station, we finally passed out as fully qualified Acting Lieutenants, Royal Marines. I was awarded the Sword of Honour for the two Royal Marines officer batches who had joined in 1959. It was decided that the 1959 Sword of Honour would be the sword which originally belonged to a young officer, Neville Spurling, who had been killed in an ambush in Cyprus. It was awarded to me at our passing out parade in Lympstone by his father, who could not hold the tears back in his eyes as he handed it to me.

I was, of course, very proud to receive it, though the citation engraved on the blade seemed a trifle understated, given what we had been through in the last two-and-a-half years. It reads:

Presented by the Lords Commissioners of the Admiralty to Lieutenant J.J.D. Ashdown, Royal Marines for meritorious results in examinations.

CHAPTER 5

Active Service: Borneo

O N 10 FEBRUARY 1962, five months after my training finished, Jane and I got married in her home town of Burnham-on-Sea in Somerset. I was twenty, and she was twenty-one, and we had precisely fifteen pounds between us. We couldn't afford a honeymoon, so straight after our wedding we caught the train down to Exmouth and moved into a one-bedroom summer holiday flat, empty for the winter, which we had rented as our first home while I was on temporary posting to Lympstone awaiting my next orders. That night we blew our last pounds on a slap-up dinner at a local entertainment centre.

Our new home was ill-equipped and cold and very basic. But we didn't mind, being newly married. And, for the first time amongst many to come, Jane turned some very unpromising accommodation into a home where we were both extremely happy.

In due course my next assignment came through. I was to go to the Army's Heavy Weapons Training School in Netheravon, Wiltshire, where I would be taught how to use the Vickers Medium Machine-gun, the new 81mm mortar, which had just come into service, and the *Wombat* recoilless anti-tank gun. Afterwards I was to rejoin my old unit, 42 Commando, Royal Marines, in Singapore on 22 June 1962, to take command of a Commando Troop.

Since we were married under age, Jane did not qualify for any assistance in getting out to Singapore, and we were entitled neither to marriage allowance nor accommodation for her while she was there. So we had to say another miserable goodbye on the rain-swept streets of London, this time, potentially, for two-and-a-half years. Jane's last words when we parted were a promise that, one way or another, she would get out to join me.

I missed her terribly during my first months in Singapore and this was made worse by the fact that I found myself underoccupied and bored. So I decided I should do something useful and learn Malay, encouraged by the fact that, according to a friend, there was one word in Malay which meant 'Let's take off our clothes and tell dirty stories'. If such a word really exists I never found it, but in the process I managed to learn my first foreign language and loved the thrill of being able to communicate using my new-found skill. To be honest, Malay is not difficult.* The tenses hardly decline, and plural nouns are achieved by the simple expedient of saying the word twice (thus, 'orang' is 'man', 'orang orang' is 'men', etc.). So, despite the comments about inadequate linguistic ability which had been such a recurrent theme in my school reports, it didn't take me long to become quite proficient.

True to her promise, Jane managed to borrow some money from her grandmother and got a cheap passage to Singapore on the SS *Chusan*, one of the last P&O liners carrying regular passengers to the Far East. She left Britain in September 1962 and crossed the Indian Ocean in the midst of the Cuban missile crisis, blissfully unaware of the fact that the world was standing on the very brink of nuclear catastrophe.

Our first few nights together were spent in a local guest house, but eventually she managed to find a tiny flat on the edge of the Malay quarter in the centre of Singapore. From our bedroom window we could look straight down the throat of the muezzin on top of the minaret of the local mosque as he called the faithful to prayer (and frequently us from our sleep), morning, noon and night. Jane also got herself a job to help make ends meet, and we got a small puppy from the animal refuge and called her Tigger.

At the time neither of us could drive, and anyway we could not have afforded a car, so we bought a rather underpowered, second-hand, red-and-white Vespa scooter on which we travelled everywhere, except to those events where the poshness of Jane's frock made it necessary to stretch our finances to the limit and take a taxi.

And so it was that, comfortably, if impecuniously, settled, we were looking forward to our first Christmas together.

---

* Although simple, Malay is, as far as the grammar and morphosyntax is concerned, comparatively straightforward *vis-à-vis* English, the sociolinguistics of the language – particularly in address forms and ways of referring to oneself and others – is substantially more complex.

But fate had other ideas.

On 8 December 1962 we joined a host of our friends at a beach party under the forbidding shadow of Singapore's notorious Changi prison, the scene of so much brutality during the Japanese occupation of the island during the Second World War. But our minds were not on the horrors of the past. We were celebrating a christening. The air was soft, the sea was warm, the moon was full, the drink was plentiful, the music was loud, the sand was comforting between my toes, and we were having a great time.

So I hardly noticed the Land Rover clattering to a halt, lights blazing, at the edge of the party – though I should have done, for the officer who jumped out was a friend who I knew was Duty Officer and therefore should have been back in camp, not here. I did take notice, however, when he shouted for silence, for there was a tone of urgency, and something else I didn't quite recognise, in his voice.

'We have just had word from London that rebels have mounted a coup and taken over Brunei, overturning the Sultan and taking a number of British hostages. You are to return to camp immediately, report to your Company Headquarters, draw kit, weapons, grenades and live ammunition. We fly at dawn.'

As a party-stopper it was difficult to beat.

As soon as we arrived back in camp, we changed into jungle-green uniform, drew our equipment, weapons and ammunition, and then checked that the Marines were all present and properly kitted. Finally we went up to the Officer's Mess, a colonnaded building of the colonial era on a hill, and said goodbye to our wives and girlfriends just as the eastern sky reddened and dawn broke, piled high with angry cumulus clouds.

It was barely more than full daylight when the *Hastings* aircraft into which we were all bundled took off, and we began a very bumpy flight across the South China Sea heading for the Island of Labuan in the Bay of Brunei, the staging post for our assault to retake Brunei city. The *Hastings*, an ageing, piston-engined transport, was noisy and bumpy and not at all to be recommended for anyone with a queasy stomach and a most decided hangover. I found myself sitting next to a cadaverous gentleman in a dark grey suit who looked, to put it mildly, out of place amongst sweating Marines with their rifles between their knees, nursing hangovers and a strong sense of apprehension about the battle ahead. My companion resolutely refused to tell me who he was or what he was doing here amidst the first wave of assault troops, dressed, as I commented to him, for a funeral rather than a battle.

I was closer to the truth than I realised, for when we arrived in Labuan we were met by the coffins of four Ghurkhas, killed the night before, whose bodies were returning to Singapore on the aircraft we had flown out in. My lugubrious, dark-suited companion immediately sprang to life, taking charge of the coffins and finally revealing himself as a member of the Commonwealth War Graves Commission who had come out especially to ensure that the dead – and, one could not help reflecting, those of us who were now quick but would soon be dead – were properly looked after! Some quite level-headed soldiers become highly superstitious before battle, and this ghoulish presence amongst us was taken by many as a bad omen. Even for the completely unsuperstitious, like me, it was not exactly a morale-booster!

That night we moved into Brunei city. The Ghurkhas had already taken the city back from the rebels, but there were one or two remaining pockets of resistance that we had to deal with before consolidating our hold on the city and preparing to move forward to take the other two rebel strongholds the following morning.

Two assaults were planned. One was an amphibious assault on the main rebel-held positions in the river port of Limbang, using two flat 'Z' lighters requisitioned from the local port for the purpose. The second attack, to which I was assigned, was to be a dawn airborne assault on the administrative centre of Lawas, where there were reported to be a number of British hostages, including the local District Officer and his family. This was to be conducted in some army *Twin Pioneer* aircraft which had just arrived on Brunei airfield ready for the operation.

Our companions designated for the Limbang assault left that night for the long, slow sea and river journey to their target, which they, too, were to attack at dawn. As for us, shortly before sunrise we filed down in silence to board our little aircraft for the thirty-minute journey to Lawas. Intelligence reported that they believed the town, airfield and surrounding area to be in rebel hands, so our best hope lay in surprise, if we were not to suffer high casualties bringing thin-skinned aircraft in to land and disembark troops on a defended airfield. The pilots brought their aircraft in very low over the palm trees which fringed the rudimentary airstrip, threw them onto the ground with a bump and we leapt out, fingers curled around triggers, ready to open up at any movement.

But, blessedly, there was none. All was silence and calm. The place was deserted.

My task was to secure the nearby town, while others made their way to the District Officer's House where the hostages were reported to be held. Running in battle formation up a low knoll on which the house stood they were surprised to be met, not with the expected storm of fire, but apparently by a florid-faced District Officer nursing a gin and tonic (it was no later than 6.30 a.m.). He hailed them heartily and bade them welcome, immediately followed by a motley collection of other people of European origin who emerged from the house, gabbling away in high spirits at our arrival.

This, according to the story we were subsequently told, is what had happened. The rebels had indeed taken over the town, and a group of some hundred or so had marched, fully armed, up to the District Officer's house in very threatening mood. He emerged alone with a service-issue Webley pistol in one hand (the story does not relate whether he had a gin and tonic in the other, but I like to imagine he did), declared himself to be Her Majesty's representative in the area and, in her name, demanded that they all lay down their arms and surrender. This they duly did, despite their overwhelming numbers, and were all locked up in the local jail.

The concern then was that other local rebel bands in the area would gather, and they might not prove so amenable as their colleagues had been. So the entire white population of the area had been called in to the District Officer's house, where the women and children were given shelter and the men set about turning the house and the knoll into a little fortress. Fire positions had been built, the frame strengthened, water points established in case of fire, and ammunition gathered and distributed – as far as this was possible, given the motley collection of weapons they were able to assemble. Most impressive of all these preparations, however, was the establishment of a dense field of *panjis* (sharpened bamboo stakes) on the flanks of the hill approaching the bungalow, each lovingly tipped with strychnine by a local American doctor from the United States Peace Corps!

That evening the news started to filter through that our colleagues carrying out the assault on Limbang had had a much more difficult time. When, at dawn, their flat lighters broke out of the mangrove swamps for a direct frontal assault on the quayside of the town, they were met with murderous fire from well-prepared positions. The day had been won by the Vickers machine-gun troop, mounted in fully exposed positions, who had continued firing through a hail of enemy bullets and eventually suppressed the defenders' fire for long enough for the assault to go in and win the day. Five of our comrades had been killed and five wounded in this attack, led by Captain Jeremy Moore, who as a result was awarded a bar to the Military Cross he had already won in Malaya in 1952. He would go on to be my much-loved company commander, and, in later years, to command the land forces in the successful Falklands invasion, for which he received a KCB. Later still he acted as one of my close advisers during the first Gulf War, when I was leading the Liberal Democrats.*

Thus began what came later to be known as 'Confrontation', or *Konfrontasi* in Malay, the little (but at times quite vicious) four-year conflict between Britain and Indonesia in the jungles of Sarawak.

The next four months were spent on relentless patrolling.

Since I was the only person in the unit who could speak Malay, I was first tasked with leading a patrol deep into the upper reaches of the Limbang River. The patrol lasted, if I recall, a little over two weeks over the Christmas and New Year period and extended into areas of primeval jungle which had seen very few Europeans since SOE (Special Operations Executive) had dropped agents into the area to raise the local tribes against the Japanese during World War Two. The tribes in the area we passed through were very welcoming and the rebels completely absent, so we spent most nights in local 'long-houses'. These were single, very long, one-storey wooden buildings, raised on stilts and with a palm-frond roof (or *atap*). Many of them were adorned with shrunken human heads, some of considerable antiquity: the revered trophies of the tribe's past battles. Typically, a long-house would accommodate an entire extended family, numbering at times up to a hundred adults. About ten days into our patrol, I heard from the headman of the long-house in which we were staying that an aircraft had 'recently' crashed nearby. I asked him how long ago, and he waved his hands and said, 'Not long ago', but refused to be more precise (precise time is not a concept much valued amongst the jungle tribes of Sarawak). My immediate reaction was that this

---

* He died in 2008.

must be one of our aircraft which had crashed since we had left our base, and I asked him how far away the crash site was. About five cigarettes away. Three hours later we came to a clearing at the bottom of a steep-sided valley and there, amongst the undergrowth, creepers and saplings, found a more-or-less intact Japanese Zero, complete with roundels, machine-guns in the wings and the skeletal remains of the pilot still sitting in the cockpit where he had died twenty years before.

This patrol was to be the first of many which took us into the Sarawak jungles. These are home to a host of different tribes, the three main ones in our area being the Iban,* the Bedayuh and the Kelabit. But in the deeper jungle there are also many smaller tribes. On this first patrol we came across several of them, including the elusive and shy Penan people,† who tend to be of much smaller stature than the other tribes of Sarawak and often have lighter, yellowish-tinted skin. Their language was unintelligible to me, but our guide told me that Penan makes very wide use of prepositions indicating 'up-river' or 'down-river' to show direction. These prepositions are used, even when there is no river in the area, in which case the preposition is applied to indicate which way water *would* flow, if there was any.

Almost all our trackers came from the Ibans and the Bedayuh (I had, at this time, started to teach myself Bedayuh, another relatively easy language). They were exceptional for their skill and bravery and could tell from a broken leaf or a snapped twig how many people had passed and how long ago (always in cigarettes, the standard measurement of time amongst the tribes of Sarawak), their approximate ages, who was carrying heavy loads and who light, whether any were wounded, and even, on one occasion, the fact that there was a woman in the band.

But we relied on them for much more than tracking. They also taught us how to read the jungle and see it as a friend. We learned to recognise the edible palm at whose heart is a soft white core (about the consistency of the base of a celery plant) which made a wonderful addition to our diet, and where to find the grubs the Ibans called *ulat tinduh*. These – like a giant version of the white grubs with brown heads that you find, especially under dock plants, in Europe – we used

---

* Sometimes known as 'sea Dayaks' to differentiate them from the Bedayuh, or 'land Dayaks'.
† Extensive and uncontrolled logging has now put these remarkable people at risk, as their livelihood and living space has been progressively destroyed. In 1986 the Penan set up a blockade in the Baram River region of Sarawak in protest against the logging operations, and this drew some world attention to their plight. But they are still inadequately protected and remain seriously endangered as a people.

to fry in our mess tins until they popped and then eat the resulting slurry as a kind of thick and very nutritious white soup. Our trackers taught us, too, how to identify the jungle vine which, if you cut it at a shallow angle, gives a stream of pure and delicious water in sufficient quantity to fill a two-pint army water bottle in a couple of minutes; how to choose, cook and eat bamboo shoots; how to extract the poison from the *ipoh* tree that the natives used to use to tip their blowpipe darts; and much, much more.

We also relied on them to supplement our map-reading with local knowledge. The maps we used had been hurriedly made from aerial photographs. Frequently, large tracts of jungle and mountain were represented on them by nothing more than a blank white space containing the unhelpful legend, 'Area hidden by cloud cover'. These blank spaces we would try to navigate by dead-reckoning, much as one might at sea, estimating the speed of the patrol and its direction and trying to guess the direction of flow of the rivers and the underlying slope of the land, in order to establish our position and, crucially, when and where we would 'reappear' on the map. In these circumstances, the tracker's local knowledge was invaluable, especially when it came to the main rivers, which formed one of our key aids to direction-finding. I began to understand why the Penans made the direction of water flow such an important part of their language.

One of the consequences of all this was that map-reading, which I had learned on Dartmoor as a precise science, became instead a matter of estimation and guesswork. I know of few things more nerve-wracking than approaching the end of a two-week patrol, with a final rendezvous point on a river somewhere ahead and twenty Marines behind who are perfectly well aware of the fact that you don't actually know precisely where you are. Inevitably, the night before we were due at the rendezvous my Troop Sergeant would whisper to me, 'The lads would like to know when we will get there, Boss'. To which my answer, given with as much confidence as I could muster, would be something like, 'Some time tomorrow afternoon, I think.' I used to dread the following afternoon ticking by without sign of a river and my Marines' eyeballs boring into the back of my neck, until, in a dreadful admission of defeat, I had to announce that we would spending another night in the jungle and offer weak and unbelieved reassurances that 'we will probably get there early tomorrow morning'. On the other hand, few things I have experienced create a greater sense of relief than feeling the ground level out into a river valley just when you thought it should, noting the tell-tale signs of a river nearby appearing just when you hoped they might, and finally bursting out of the jungle onto the banks of a river just where and when you said you would, to see the boats patiently waiting to take you home.

——————◆◆——————

The structure of our jungle patrols was very precise. At the front were the 'lead scouts'. Depending on the size of the patrol, there could be one or two of these. They would see the enemy first, usually at very close range and sometimes as little as five yards away. So they needed to be armed with something quicker, lighter and less precise than a rifle. The favourite weapon for our lead scouts in Borneo was the Browning pump-action shotgun loaded with eight cartridges, each charged with Special Grade shot, consisting of three large balls of lead. They were deadly at close range. Behind the lead scout came the body of the patrol, usually with a Bren gunner* near the front and back, so that they could be easily deployed if the patrol made contact with the enemy either to the front or from the rear. The patrol commander normally travelled close to the front Bren gunner, but if the enemy were believed to be nearby he needed to be as far forward as possible, just behind the lead scouts, so as to make a quick assessment of the battle if contact was made. And finally, at the back, were the rear scouts. Their job was to cover up tracks as best they could and to be constantly alert to what was happening behind the patrol in case of an enemy attack from the rear. The patrol was as spread out as the density of the jungle allowed, with each man ideally only having one other person in sight. This was to ensure that, if you were ambushed, the minimum number of people were caught in the ambush 'killing zone' and the maximum number were outside it and able to mount a counter-attack. There was no talking, often for days on end, unless it was absolutely necessary, and then everything was done in whispers. Otherwise all communication was by a comprehensive system of hand signals, which had to be learned.

Essential equipment carried by each member of the patrol included spare ammunition, cooking utensils, a mess-tin or billy, a small solid-

* The Bren gun was the World War Two .303 light machine-gun we carried at the time.

fuel stove, rations, identity discs, a filtration bag and sterilising tablets for water (nearly all jungle diseases are water-borne, so clean water was essential), a stock of paludrine anti-malarial tablets, a poncho or groundsheet, a hammock (usually made from the silk panels cut from a parachute), a light sleeping bag (also usually of parachute silk), a machete or heavy hunting knife, ten yards of stout string (usually parachute cord), insect repellent, a dry set of clothes in a waterproof bag, a field dressing for wounds, a small one-shot syringe of morphine and a personal first-aid and survival kit for use in case of separation from the patrol. This last, which was always carried on your body and not in your pack, contained, among other things, antiseptic cream, pain-killers, emergency K rations, a button compass and (if you could get one) a silk map of the area scrounged from the survival packs the RAF issued to their pilots. In addition, each person carried ten *panjis* strapped to the outside of their pack for ready use.

We quickly found that our service-issue rations were so heavy and bulky that it was impossible to carry enough, even for a fourteen-day patrol. They were also clumsy and difficult to cook. So most of us adopted the local practise of carrying a small sack of uncooked rice and some fish paste or dried meat for flavouring, supplemented where possible by the lighter and more nutritious items from our service field ration packs (such as chocolate).

Leeches were ever-present and unwelcome companions in everything we did. They would parade, ranged in little waving bands, on the edges of leaves, hoping to fasten onto you as you passed. If you put your foot in a pool of water, they were there waiting for you. If you crossed a stream they appeared in squadrons from the banks and rocks, arching their way towards you with single-minded intent. It was not unusual to find fifteen or so blood-filled leeches on each leg after a day's patrolling and my record, after a day spent wading waist deep in jungle streams, was fifty-three dispersed in every corner of my body. It is important not to try to pull leeches out, as they have tiny barbs which keep their heads in your flesh and do not retract unless the leech wants to withdraw. Any attempt to pull them out by force separates the body from the head, which is left embedded in your flesh and very quickly turns septic in jungle conditions. The technique for removing leeches safely is to apply either a lighted cigarette-end or a dab of mosquito repellent to their tails, causing them to withdraw their heads and drop off. The common jungle leech is small, painless and harmless, once you have got used to the unpleasant sight of festoons of little bags of blood hanging all over your body. But not so the tiger leech, which lives in grassland and has jaws strong enough to puncture the hide of a buffalo and a body big enough to carry the best part of half a pint of blood. Mostly, leeches were treated as just part of the everyday routine of patrolling. There was, however, one leech story which had wide circulation and caused much concern amongst my younger Marines. It was said that one of our Commando had got a leech attached deep inside the urethra in the centre of his penis. The leech had swollen and blocked the passage, causing great discomfort and preventing him from peeing. A cigarette end in this area of the body being clearly out of the question, the only alternative was to remove the invader with liberal doses of insect repellent, causing much excruciating pain. At the time we were issued with condoms to put over the muzzles of our rifles in order to keep their barrels dry. But most of my guys preferred to use them on the organ for which they were originally intended, in order to protect their manhood against leech attack.

Jungle patrol routine was always the same. At the end of the day the patrol stopped to bivouac for the night about an hour-and-a-half before dusk. The first task was to put sentries out some hundred yards from the camp at all four points of the compass. Next the defence of the camp was organised. Each man's ten *panjis* were stuck in the ground to create an integrated field of them around the camp perimeter, and individual fire positions were allocated and strengthened as far as possible, without making noise. Interlocking arcs of fire were established for each position, and spare ammunition was stacked close by. (These fire positions would be each man's allotted place if we were attacked and also at the routine dawn or dusk 'stand to'.) After this, each individual could start preparing for the night. The first task was to make a sleeping position. This was done by choosing two stout trees within the curtilage of the camp from which your parachute hammock was suspended about three feet above the ground, with a 'stretcher' positioned a little way back from the point of attachment in order to hold the hammock open. A line was then strung between the two trees about three feet above the hammock, forming a ridge over which your waterproof poncho or groundsheet was stretched to create a light shelter capable of keeping off the rain. The corners of this were then staked out by guys attached to branches or leading to pegs stuck in the ground. Next, you took your dry clothes out of their waterproof bag and put them on (always a delicious moment), removing the days' collection of leeches in the process, and hanging out your wet ones (clothes were always wet at the end of the day in the jungle) in the vain hope that they might dry a little overnight. It would now be time to turn to the evening meal, which needed to be cooked and eaten before dark. At dusk there was a 'stand to' at which everyone manned their allocated fire positions (dusk and dawn are the favourite times for attack) until it was fully dark. Night sentries were then put out, with lines of string or wire leading back to the camp to enable the relief sentries to find their way out and relieved sentries to find their way back at the end of their stint of duty (usually two hours long) without stumbling into the *panji* fields. It gets very dark in the jungle at night, and, since no torches were allowed, all movement had to be by feel.

The camp could then settle down for the night. No noise was allowed at any time.

The following morning the sentries woke the camp half an hour before dawn, and all 'stood to' in their fire positions until it was fully light. You then changed back into your wet clothes (a horrible moment), and carefully put your dry ones back in their waterproof protection. Then you washed and shaved as best you could, breakfasted, packed, tried to cover up traces and moved off, ideally not later than nine o'clock.

During the day the patrol would usually rest for ten minutes in every hour and have an hour's break for lunch. Smoking was not allowed (the smell of cigarette smoke carries a long way), except in the evening after the sentries were out.

The popular perception is that jungle warfare involves a lot of hacking, cutting and slashing of undergrowth. This is completely wrong. Jungle warfare is very close-quarter. In most warfare you fight with your eyes. In jungle warfare you fight with your ears. So moving silently is the essence. Cutting noisily through branches, therefore, is just what you should *not* do – and by and large it is not necessary. But there are exceptions. We always dreaded being caught in a thicket of rattan creeper (the Malay word is *rotan*), from which the famous cane furniture is made. In the jungle, rattan grows in thick, impenetrable tangles of creepers whose outer surface is covered with row upon row of extremely sharp, hard spikes. The Australian troops in Malaya christened this plant 'wait-a-while' which is a very good name; it is a much-feared menace, which has to be cut through if it cannot be bypassed.

Most of our patrols were fourteen days or less. But there were also longer patrols of three weeks and more. During these, it would be necessary to take delivery of a fresh supply of food and ammunition. This was done by picking an open patch of grassland or by cutting a hole in the jungle, which allowed us to be resupplied by helicopter or parachute drop.

I returned from one such long patrol in February, to open a letter from my mother which told me that my brother Robert had been diagnosed with leukaemia. He died on St Patrick's Day a year later, aged fourteen. It was a terrible blow, not least because I had no one with whom to share the burden of my grief. But it was the effect on my parents I worried about most.

Soon afterwards I received orders to mount an extended operation in the mangrove swamps of Brunei Bay to try to find the leader of the rebels, Yassin Effendi, who was thought to be hiding there. In my Troop at the time I had two outstanding Marines, Sergeant Gillie Howe and Marine Ted Tandy, both SBS-qualified and later to become close personal friends. Over the next three months they taught me more about soldiering and how to do it than I learned in all my two-and-a-half years' officer training at ITCRM. Our patrol in the mangrove swamps was to be entirely water-borne, so I tasked these two with adapting some local dugout canoes to take forty-horsepower Johnson outboard engines on the back. These could carry five Marines and were extremely fast but, when we needed to, we could also easily and silently paddle them along the waterways of the mangrove swamp.

My first step was to set up stationary blocking positions, each manned by five Marines posted in fishing huts guarding the main intersections and exits of the waterways that criss-crossed the mangrove swamp. Then we began meticulously to comb the swamps themselves. We often did not put a foot on dry land for days on end, sleeping at night in our hammocks, slung between the mangrove branches. The mosquitoes were terrible. I remember commenting on their size to one of my Marines, after suffering particularly badly from their carnivorous attacks one night. He told me that two mosquitoes had crawled into his sleeping bag during the night and one had said to the other, 'Shall we eat him here or shall we drag him outside?' The other had replied, 'Best eat him here. If we drag him outside, the big ones will only get him!'

Despite our best efforts we did not catch Yassin Effendi,* for, as I learned then (and relearned forty years later when we were trying to catch Radovan Karadžić in the mountains of Bosnia), it is very, very difficult to catch a single wanted person moving in inaccessible country amongst a population that is willing to support them.

But not all our searches were in vain. Indeed, in the early days we had to detain quite a number of prisoners before handing them over to the Sarawak authorities. On one occasion, after returning from a short patrol, I discovered one of our Marines hitting one of these detainees who had been captured a few days earlier. I have a furious temper, and on this occasion, to my shame, lost it completely, knocking the Marine across the room. I could easily have been court-martialled for this if anything had been made of it. But it wasn't, and from then on everyone understood that mistreating prisoners was out of order. I claim no special morality in this. My act was one of irrational fury not thought-through principle. But when the story of the My Lai massacre in Vietnam broke six years later, I knew that that act of appalling brutality and horror had just been the last step in an escalation of violence that had been tolerated in William Calley's unit. I do not think that people leap from innocence to terrible violence in one bound. I think, rather, that anyone can succumb to the evil that steals up on us, little step by little step, and that what Lieutenant Calley did at My Lai could well have appeared to him to be just a small step beyond what had probably been perfectly acceptable common practice in his unit. Evil, it turns out, is not the great Beast of myth and legend. Rather, it imitates the bilharzia worm,† slipping in imperceptibly between your compromises to start its long progress towards possession. If leaders do not have the courage or alertness to stop the relatively small transgressions against accepted values, then they risk initiating a chain of escalation which can end in horrors they would never have imagined or tolerated when it all started.

——————◆——————

When our three-month tour of duty came to an end we sailed back to Singapore in HMS *Bulwark*. In my absence Jane had had a terrible time, falling ill with a bad dose of dysentery. She came down to the

---

* Yassin Effendi was subsequently wounded in the leg and captured five months later.
† Bilharzia is a tropical disease caused by a parasitic worm. The parasites enter the skin, sometimes under the nails and then migrate through the body to the blood-vessels of the lungs and liver and thence to the bowel or bladder.

quayside with the other wives to welcome the ship home, but was so emaciated that I did not at first recognise her.

Despite this, however, it was a wonderful homecoming. But not, alas, a long one; after a brief rest with our families we started retraining and preparing for our next tour in Borneo.

By now the rebellion had been snuffed out in Brunei, but it had been replaced by a wider insurgency, which was Indonesian-supported and mounted from bases the other side of the border by the *Tentera Nasional Kalimantan Utara* (North Borneo National Army), or TNKU for short. The TNKU sprang out of the *Parti Rakayat Brunei* or PRB (Brunei People's Party), which was founded in 1956 and dedicated to bringing Brunei to full independence after British rule. The original British plan was to transition Malaya, Singapore and the three British colonies in north Borneo, Sabah, Sarawak and Brunei, into the Malaysian Federation. This was opposed, not only by Indonesia, but also by the Philippines. Although there has never been any evidence that President Sukarno of Indonesia had territorial ambitions over the three north Borneo states, as the British claimed at the time, he probably did want to have governments on the island which would be amenable to the influence of Jakarta. There was some left-wing and communist influence on the TNKU, coming chiefly from the urban Chinese population of the three states, but it was primarily a nationalist movement. It wanted full independence from Britain in the early days, and did not want to be included in Malaysia after the British left. I have to say that, given the levels of corruption I witnessed during Malay rule over Brunei, I privately had some sympathy with the rebels' wish to avoid Sarawak and Brunei being swallowed up in Malaysia. In the event, the Sultan of Brunei effectively conceded to the rebels by subsequently deciding not to join the Malaysian Federation, and in this he was followed shortly afterwards by Singapore, which also remained outside.

Whatever my opinions at the time, however, my job as a soldier was to carry out the policy of Her Majesty's Government, and that was to defeat the TNKU so that Sarawak could become part of Malaysia when British colonial rule came to an end. It was clear by now that the Brunei rebellion of December was only the beginning of a much wider affair: a long war that would extend to the whole of Sarawak.

After a couple of months in Singapore we were redeployed to Borneo. This time my troop was sent to a place called Stass, four hours' walk from the nearest road head and right up on the Indonesian border with Sarawak's First Division region.* Stass was then so isolated that all our resupplies of stores, food and ammunition were air-dropped or helicopter-delivered into a small clearing that we cut in the jungle nearby.

My Troop of around thirty Marines built a little fort under a house on stilts on the edges of the *kampong* (local jungle village), which we defended against attack by armed guerrilla groups coming over the Indonesian border with barbed wire, fields of *panjis* and improvised explosive booby traps. Every night I would lay my sleeping bag down next to the sentry, who always manned one of our Bren guns, so that I could be easily woken if he saw something. We frequently had new Marines joining us from the UK, and it usually took some time for these new arrivals to get used to the night sounds of the jungle. The result was that I would often find myself leaping from a deep sleep to the roar of the Bren gun firing and a sentry swearing on his life that he had seen something at the perimeter wire, which almost invariably turned out to be a pig or some nosy nocturnal jungle animal. These events were not always so benign, however. My neighbour manning the next 'fort' down the line, across the mountain ridge that marked the eastern edge of my area, was a young and very gifted Royal Marine officer called Ricky Rolls. He had been attacked on several occasions. One early morning the sentry alerted him to the fact there were enemy on the wire. He wasn't convinced and went forward to take a look for himself, leaving his Troop Sergeant in charge. Shortly after he had gone the Troop Sergeant saw a figure in the murky light and, assuming this to be the beginning of an enemy attack, let loose a full magazine from the Bren gun. In fact the figure was Ricky, who was killed instantly.†

We operated out of Stass for three months, patrolling and seeking to dominate our designated operational area of around a hundred square miles of jungle. To assist us, I recruited and trained a band of some fifty irregulars from among the local tribesmen. At this stage we were not allowed to cross the Indonesian border. But they could, and, knowing the jungle, were highly effective at taking the fight to our enemy. They returned from their first expedition flushed with victory and proudly related to me how they accounted for four of the enemy

---

* I am told Stass is now just another dusty roadside town in Sarawak, and all the primary jungle described here has long since vanished as a result of deforestation.
† Ricky was 20 when he died. He is buried in Singapore, and remembered in the National Memorial Arboretum at Alrewas in Staffordshire.

in an ambush. To prove their success, they produced a bag out of which rolled four human heads. I remonstrated with them, saying that, while I knew taking human heads from the dead after a battle had been their tribal tradition for centuries, in the modern age it was wrong. They looked rather offended and asked me how, in that case, they were to prove their prowess? After some discussion we compromised on ears (or, to be precise, the right ear). Out there, miles from anywhere and separated from what we are pleased to call civilisation, it seemed a fair compromise at the time. But today, with blanket Press coverage I am very clear that if this had come to light publicly, readers back in Britain would not have understood, and it would have caused a great (and no doubt justifiable) scandal about desecrating the dead.

It was vital to win the battle for hearts and minds with the local jungle tribes. We soon discovered that one of the things which made us most welcome was the medicine in our first aid packs. Every patrol included someone qualified in first aid (known as a 'medic'), and the medics very soon became known to all in the villages through which we passed. Whenever we stopped in a village, they would be inundated with people asking to have ailments and wounds treated. On one occasion I found one of our medics strapping a Paludrine tablet to the forehead of a local man who had a badly cut leg. Paludrine was a prophylactic which we took orally every day to prevent getting malaria – it had to be ingested and had no effect whatsoever against anything except malaria – so I asked my medic what on earth he was doing. He said that he and the other medics were finding themselves so overwhelmed with requests from local people for medication that, after the first day, they had no medicines left for the rest of their patrol. So they had reached agreement amongst themselves that they would announce the arrival of a new wonder drug – Paludrine, which, if strapped to the forehead, would cure anything. He even claimed that a number of his 'patients', believing that this wonder drug would cure them, had actually been cured!

But Western medicine was not always best. On one patrol on a nearby mountain feature called Gunong Raya (the scene a year or so later of a furious battle in which Rambahadur Limbu, a young Ghurkha, won a VC), I was putting out *panjis* around our night bivouac when I tripped and fell on one, cutting my left bicep nearly to the bone. Our patrol medic, a great strapping Marine who was famous for his lack of delicacy in all things, was called for. He came up enthusiastically brandishing the suture kit from his first-aid pack and making ready to sew up my wound. While I was contemplating whether leaving a gaping and painful wound would not be a better option than submitting myself to his less-than-tender ministrations, our tracker intervened to ask me if I would mind leaving it to him? Almost anything seemed a better option, so I said yes. He went to a nearby ant heap, which he had spotted earlier, and picked out, one by one, about two dozen very large soldier ants which he put in a box. Then, squatting beside me, he proceeded to close my wound with one hand and place a soldier ant with its mandibles open, one on each side of the wound. This kind of soldier ant, he explained, is blind and, once it grips, will die before it lets go. One by one, the soldier ants closed their mandibles, sealing the wound almost painlessly, after which he nipped their bodies off. After about five minutes I had some thirty neat sutures of soldier ants' heads closing my wound. Ant bites contain formic acid, which disinfected the wound, and as it healed the ants' heads fell painlessly out.

About halfway through our time in Stass one of my patrols returned with some leaflets they had found nailed to trees and scattered on a jungle path they had used. These caused much amusement among the Marines, for they turned out to be crude propaganda left by our opponents from across the border in the hope of lowering our morale and encouraging us to go home. They featured some scantily clad, but very out-of-date, ladies who looked as though they had been taken from a 'What the butler saw' slot machine of the 1890s, underneath which was printed the stern instruction, 'Go hom Johnny – someone else is fuking your wife.' They became something of a collector's piece, and it was not long before every Marine had one above his bed space, alongside the latest pin ups from the centrefold of *Playboy* magazine. One of my Marines said to me one day, 'They are obviously short of good pictures of nudes, boss. Why don't we send them some of ours?' It seemed to me harmless and rather a good joke. At the time there was still a good deal of traffic between registered trading posts across the border, with rice, vegetables and tobacco the main commodities exchanged. The flow of trade was chiefly from Sarawak to Indonesia, and every traded package was wrapped in old newspaper. So I hit upon the idea of collecting all the old unwanted copies of *Playboy* and similar magazines from the lads and giving them to the trading post to use as wrapping paper for parcels going back over the border. This did a great deal for the volume of trade from the Sarawak side and soon resulted in requests from purchasers on the other side of the border not to bother with the rice – just provide the magazines! I even got a written request from the Indonesian Army Lieutenant who was my opposite number on the other side of the frontier, proposing that we should go into business together, and please would I send him any magazines directly and not give them to the locals?

I treated all this as a great joke and reported it back only for amusement value. But one day the joke took a serious turn when a helicopter flew in and, unannounced, delivered into my care a rather elderly man with a vast shock of grey-streaked, unkempt hair, a disturbing look in his eye and a habit of speaking so fast that the words tripped each other up as they poured in a torrent from his mouth. He told me, rather conspiratorially, that he was from the Psychological Warfare Unit (which I had never heard of), based in Singapore. This turned out to be an organisation left over from World War Two and staffed by people who had learned the dark arts of their trade in that conflict. A special unit had apparently been formed in the Far East with the task of undermining morale among the Sarawak rebels and the Indonesian forces who backed them.

Judging by my new visitor's enthusiasm and the stories he told me about how they had gone about their task, this was clearly jolly good fun, though whether it had any practical effect is rather more doubtful. 'Anyway,' he exclaimed, 'we are terribly excited about your splendid idea for undermining Indonesian morale, and we want to build on it.'

He went on to explain that his unit had worked out they could get the latest edition of the main Indonesian newspaper *Berita Harian* (literally 'The Daily News') via the diplomatic bag from the British Embassy in Jakarta (which was still open, despite our 'war'), reprint it in Singapore and ship it to us in Sarawak; we would then put it into the trading posts, where it would be used as wrapping, so that it passed over the border into the hands of the Indonesian troops on the other side. All this could be done, he claimed, about two days faster than the paper could be got out to front-line Indonesian troops direct from Jakarta. His plan was to reprint the Jakarta newspaper faithfully, with only a very few minor 'tweaks', and send it down this somewhat complicated pipeline for our opponents to read before they received the real thing. For instance, he explained, the Psychological Warfare Unit knew from intercepted communications that the troops across the border were suffering a severe shortage of jungle boots. Hence, in their reprinted version, they would include a large front-page advertisement announcing a massive sale of army-surplus jungle boots in Jakarta. Warming to his theme, he added that, of course, all Indonesians were highly superstitious, and the first thing they always read in their paper was the astrological predictions for their star sign. These, too, would be rewritten, advising almost all star signs that this was not a good time for taking risks – or for going out in the jungle, etc. It all seemed great fun to me, though I was sceptical about its effect. Nevertheless, I agreed to hand over my communications line to them.

I heard nothing more of it at the time. But a few years later a friend who was then in Singapore Headquarters told me that the scheme was eventually approved and had been tried out at another border post – without, as far as he could tell, any detectable impact on enemy morale. No doubt, however, a good time was had by all.

After Stass, I did two more three-month tours of duty in Rasau and Padawan, two other forward locations in the deep jungle on the Sarawak border. One day in early March, on my third tour, our chief local tracker came running into our camp in Rasau to tell me that he had found the tracks of about fifty heavily armed men coming from the Indonesian border and heading deep into Sarawak. I radioed my headquarters and said that I intended to give chase. A troop of Ghurkhas was quickly flown in, and we joined forces to form a patrol of about forty under my command. It did not take us long to find the tracks, which we followed for three days, drawing quietly closer and closer to our enemy. I loved the Ghurkhas, who formed a ready, close and mutually respectful companionship with our Marines. (The General then in charge of military operations in Sarawak, General Walter Walker,* would allow no other regiments except Royal Marines and Ghurkhas in his area of operations.) As dusk approached on the third day our trackers told us we were now very close to our enemy, who were within three hundred yards or so of our position. I discussed with the commander of the Ghurkha contingent, an outstanding officer called Lieutenant Kakraprasad, whether we

---

* Later to become notorious as a right-wing organiser of service officers and industrialists during the period when there was much speculation that Prime Minister Harold Wilson was a 'proven communist' and that there was a 'communist cell' in No. 10 Downing Street.

could risk a reconnaissance to locate exactly where the enemy were and what were their dispositions. We agreed it was too big a risk to take. If we were discovered we would have to attack immediately, and it would be too late in the day to do a proper follow-up, giving our enemy the opportunity to escape under the cover of night.

We agreed we would attack at dawn the following morning. All fires were forbidden, as was any noise or talking, and we ordered the Marines and Ghurkhas to eat cold rations and lie down where they were for the night. The following morning we were on the move as dawn broke. I was up near the front of the column, with a Ghurkha section on point ahead of me, when a shot rang out. I discovered later that one of the enemy had come down to fill his water bottle at a stream which lay across our path and stumbled into our lead scout, who had no option but to shoot him. We would now have to go into headlong attack in order to make good our surprise. I was just calling up my Marines when the Ghurkhas, who weren't waiting for anyone's orders, tore through in a furious and uncoordinated assault on the enemy. Without waiting we all joined in and there followed a mad, surging mêlée of shouting and shooting, as we all charged through the forest towards the enemy position. I immediately saw that our opposition had made no attempt to defend their position and had not followed the normal jungle practise of 'standing to' at dawn. They were instead scattered all over the place. Some were washing, some cooking, some standing chatting and smoking in groups far from their weapons, and one was squatting down behind a tree with his trousers around his ankles. This was very fortunate, because they were numerically stronger and, had they been better prepared, we would have had a much tougher job of it.

In the event, they mostly fled in disarray, with only a handful putting up a fight. One of these fighters started to engage us with a machine-gun from behind a tree, thinking he was safe. But he did not reckon with our very high velocity SLR 7.62 rifles,* or even have time to be surprised, when one of my Marines loosed a burst of fire at him and shot him clean through the tree he assumed was protecting him.

After the engagement we cut a hole in the jungle for the helicopters of 848 Squadron and shipped out the wounded and about a ton of

---

* These were heavy, clumsy rifles with a long range that was completely unnecessary in the jungle, and we all tried to beg, borrow or steal the US Armalite if we could get our hands on one. But SLRs did from time to time have their uses, as on this occasion.

captured arms and equipment, including wirelesses, written orders giving the insurgents' destination, a list of local contacts and about 300 Malay Dollars carried by each man. The following days were spent chasing small remaining groups through the jungle and laying ambushes to catch them as they tried to get back to Indonesian territory. What I remember most from this time was the sickly smell of putrefaction as we discovered the rotting bodies of those who had died of wounds or starvation on river banks and jungle paths. We heard later that less than half of those who set out managed to make it back across the border.*

In between three-month tours in Sarawak, we went back to Singapore for time with our families, some rest and retraining. On these occasions our Commanding Officer tried to give us all as much leave as possible, but there always had to be an officer on duty, even when the Commando was effectively closed down. One of our problems was that the Commando operated on a so-called 'trickle' drafting system (i.e., the Commando always stayed in Singapore but individuals arrived, did their tour and were then replaced by new arrivals when their time came to go home).

This meant that we had a constant stream of experienced people leaving and new, inexperienced people arriving to take their place. This applied, of course, not just to the Marines, but also to their wives and families, many of whom had never been out of the United Kingdom before. To them, Singapore and the Far East was a strange and frightening place. One of the things which frequently upset newly arrived wives were the small lizards or geckoes which inhabited every house and could frequently be seen running up the walls or upside down on the ceiling, chasing flies.

On one occasion when I was Duty Officer the Guard Room put through a phone call from a newly arrived wife whose husband was away and who had demanded to speak to me. She told me, in tones close to hysteria, that she had a lizard in her kitchen. I told her that this was nothing to be frightened about, they were very common and were believed by local people to bring good luck. She seemed a little mollified and we ended the conversation. She then rang back half an

* There is an account of this operation in Harold James and Denis Sheil Small, *The Undeclared War: The story of the Indonesian confrontation 1962–1966* (London: Leo Cooper, 1967), pp. 115–16.

hour later, even more distraught and frightened. I gently calmed her again, saying that these lizards were perfectly normal, ate flies and there was nothing to be frightened about. Over the next few hours she must have rung me again three times, always with the same hysteria, to which I always responded with the same mollifying words. Finally, she rang back and said that the lizard had now left the kitchen and come into her bedroom and she was taking refuge on top of the wardrobe. I got a bit exasperated at this stage and told her not to be so silly and to come down at once, adding, 'Look Mrs X, these lizards are regarded as good luck. They do you a favour by eating the flies in your house. They can't do you any harm. How can you be so frightened about something that is only three inches long?' There was a short pause and then her small voice came back to me saying, 'This one is six foot long!'

I told her to stay exactly where she was, dashed round with a small squad of Marines and shot it. What she had in her bedroom was not a gecko, but a large iguana which had wandered in from the nearby jungle and was quite capable of breaking a person's leg with a single swish of its tail. I was a bit more careful with such phone calls after that.

Life may have been physically quite tough for us. But it was no picnic for our wives either. Not knowing what your husband was doing and always having a wary eye out for the dreaded unit Land Rover turning up with some bad news generated an emotional strain that told on many wives and marriages. Apart from getting a bad dose of dysentery (as a result of which she has suffered recurrent bouts of the disease ever since), Jane coped magnificently. Together with other wives she visited the wounded in the British Military Hospital and got involved when she could in the provision of welfare and support services for newly arrived wives from the UK, while holding down a regular job (much-needed because of our financial situation). At one stage our bank balance fell to a mere 27 cents of a Malay Dollar (at the time a Malay Dollar was worth about two shillings and sixpence – or 13p in decimal money). Money has always been one of the most contentious issues in our marriage and the cause of most of our rows. I am paranoid about running out, the consequence, I think, of seeing what happened to my father when his business failed. As a result, apart from a mortgage, we have never in our whole married life had an overdraft or been in debt, though we came perilously close to it on this occasion.

With four months to go before the end of my tour, I received my next posting instructions. To my delight, I was told that, when my tour was completed I was to take some leave and then join the next SBS training course in Poole. But I still had one more operational tour to do in Sarawak.

Jane and I were finding partings increasingly painful at this time, and somehow they were made worse because I was on active service and she was in a strange country. Someone, somewhere has said that war is ninety percent mind-numbing boredom and ten percent terrifying activity. It is a good description. Soldiers, like everyone else, have a habit of filling their empty spaces with daydreams, and I was no exception. My recurring image during the long silent patrols and the even longer sleepless nights, was of her, dressed in a black dress and ready to go out in the evening, bending over our child, with the light of a bedside lamp softly shining on her face from below. We were trying hard, but vainly, to start our family at the time.

We decided that, if we had to be parted so close to the end of my tour it would be better for her to go back to the UK to be with her parents, while I did my final three months in the jungle. She managed to hitch a lift back home with the RAF just before I left.

It was on this tour in Sarawak that the Government's policy on what we could and could not do in Borneo was secretly changed. Hitherto, regular units had not been allowed to cross the Indonesian border, even in hot pursuit of the enemy, although there had been some special forces operations which had taken place 'on the other side'. It was now decided that certain units, chiefly the Ghurkhas and the commandos, could, in future, carry the fight to the enemy on their territory. This new policy was code named 'Operation Initiative'. My Troop was at Padawan, high on a very mountainous part of the Indonesian border at the time. We were suddenly replaced by another Troop from the Commando and flown back to Headquarters, where I was called in by our Commanding Officer and told that I was to lead the first regular troop incursion into Indonesian territory, a ten-day-long ambush mounted on a track, some eight miles into Indonesian territory, which was known to be used by our enemy. This operation, which he said had been cleared at Cabinet level, was to be conducted in the greatest secrecy. I was to take my full Troop, but I was not allowed to tell them what we were doing until the operation had begun. We would be launched through one of the other Troop locations close to the border and were to return through the same location after the operation was over. I was ordered, in the firmest terms, to return immediately if the element of surprise was lost, because there was little or nothing that could be done to help us if we got ourselves into trouble. Our cover story, if discovered was to say we had made a map-reading error (easy enough to do in this largely uncharted jungle) and had strayed over the border inadvertently.

We were flown at last light into the forward position which was to be our jumping off point for the operation. The following morning, I checked everyone's kit very carefully, and then we formed up in patrol order and left, heading away from the border. As soon as we were well clear of prying eyes, I stopped the patrol, gathered them round me and informed them of our real destination and task. We then swung the patrol round and headed for the border, crossing into Indonesia a little after midday and arriving just short of our ambush position as dusk began to fall. It was too late to man the ambush, so we camped up for the night about two hundred yards from our objective. Then, in the morning, I went forward with my Troop Sergeant to carry out a reconnaissance of our ambush location.

Under normal circumstances, an ambush is a fairly simple military procedure. The first task is to choose a target, or 'killing', zone. It is in this zone that you aim to engage the enemy, and it is on this area that the main weight of firepower of the ambush is concentrated. Ideally, the target zone should be centred round some kind of obstacle; a log across a jungle path, or a stream the enemy has to negotiate, or (in the case of a vehicle ambush) a sharp bend in the road. The aim is to use this obstacle to divide the enemy forces, and so diminish their capacity to regroup for a counter-attack. The ambush is then split into two groups: lookouts – posted at both ends of the ambush, some distance from the main body, to provide as much notice of the enemy's approach as possible – and the main body, whose job is to engage the enemy in the target zone. The commander will normally be positioned next to the most powerful weapon (usually a machine-gun) in the centre of the ambush. It is he, and he alone, who has responsibility for triggering the ambush at the right moment.

Where possible, an ambush should be positioned as far from the target zone as possible within the maximum effective range of the weapons involved – about seventy yards away is usually right where small arms are used. This, too, is to make counter-attack more difficult, as well as helping with concealment and reducing the chance of discovery by casual passers by. But this is where jungle ambushes pose a problem. Lack of visibility means they must be positioned very close, sometimes as little as five yards from the target zone, making it necessary for the ambushers to be exceptionally quiet and laying them open to chance discovery by passers by (and especially their dogs).

I looked in vain for a suitable obstacle around which to base our ambush. Nor could I find any small rise from which we might be able to command the target zone from a little distance. The area we were given was flat, featureless and covered in tall grass and light scrub. I therefore chose a portion of the track which ran straight for a hundred yards or so, giving us the best available field of fire.

I divided my thirty men into three groups of ten, of which two would be active in the ambush at all times while the third was rotated out to the rest area, some hundred and fifty yards to the rear for rest, feeding and relaxation. I then posted the two lookouts on either wing of the ambush and moved the main body into position, after which the ten 'resting' men were used to silently remove all twigs and obstacles from a path which ran from the centre of the ambush to our rest area, so that we could move along this as silently as possible. We then ran a length of parachute cord from each lookout position to where I lay, attaching the ends to both of my wrists. We had previously arranged a series of signals which the lookouts were to use. One tug for passers by and a series of tugs for an approaching enemy, etc. I lay in the centre of the ambush alongside the Bren gunner, with whom I had also agreed (and rehearsed) the signals for triggering the ambush. If we received a warning from the lookout that the enemy were approaching I would lay my hand lightly on his left arm signalling that he should come to the ready position. One light tap meant that he should take the first pressure on the trigger and three sharp ones were his signal to fire, unleashing the ambush and triggering the rest to open fire as well. Every day we lifted the ambush just after dusk and replaced it just before dawn the following morning. It was not easy to lie perfectly still for long hours at a time, especially in the grassland, which the sun baked to an oven and which was infested with armies of insects. The track we were ambushing was quite well used by locals, but, unhappily, of the enemy there was neither sight nor sound. We had a very limited supply of water, which we restricted to drinking, rather than using any for washing. So by the fifth day we were all smelling pretty ripe – as I could attest, lying close to the person manning the Bren gun (and no doubt he could attest, lying close to me). On the sixth day, around midday, a party of locals came down the track. Suddenly one of their dogs, which had clearly scented us, raised its hackles up and charged into the area where we were lying, followed by his master, who quickly stumbled on our hiding positions and then turned round and ran for his life. I had to presume that he would quickly report our presence and therefore had no alternative but to order that we lift the ambush immediately and move out and back to our side of the border, as quickly and as silently as we could.

Shortly after this, our tour in Sarawak came to and end, as did my two-and-a-half years in 42 Commando. Before I returned to UK in May 1964, I managed to scrounge a lift on some RAF aircraft and flew down to see my parents and my brothers and sisters in Australia. We returned to all the old pursuits of fishing, shooting and strong argument. I discovered that, in my absence, my parents had built me up in my siblings' eyes as an absent paragon of virtue and ability, probably in order to encourage them to higher things. Though perhaps natural, this was most unfair on both my siblings and me. I had to ask my parents to stop, as it did not help in rebuilding my old relations with my beloved brothers and sisters.

We had a wonderful three weeks together – but the parting was, as always, very painful.

As a result of the new Freedom of Information laws, I have been sent my service records, which include the confidential reports written about me by my commanding officers over my service career. In these, the old faults of impetuosity and lack of attention to my appearance crop up now and again. One of my superiors even complained that, having got married young and being impecunious, I did not play much part in the activities of the Officers' Mess. This was accurate, though marriage and lack of money were not the primary reasons. I always preferred to draw my friends from a wider circle than you can meet in an Officers' Mess, a club, or, later, the House of Commons.

Such reports could be highly subjective and idiosyncratic. It is said that one commanding officer of an old cavalry regiment, who owned horses, bred horses and raced horses, wrote a one-line report on a subordinate of whom he disapproved which read simply, 'I would hesitate to breed from this officer.'

My immediate commander during my time in Borneo, in contrast, was a man whose unfailing decency and generosity of spirit were often reflected in his over-flattering view of others, a fact which, to me, often said more about his qualities than the qualities of those on whom he was reporting. His final report on me at the end of this tour was characteristically generous. But the most important bit for my future was the final sentence: 'Strongly recommended for SBS training.'

And that was exactly where I went next.

CHAPTER 6

SBS

T HE DATE IS 2 November 1965. My watch, glowing softly in the darkness, tells me that the time is 0050 – ten minutes to launch.

Over the shoulder of the man on my right, I can see the needle on the large red illuminated gauge he is studying so intently. It shows sixty feet. Around me five or six figures, all bathed in a suffused red light,* are going about their tasks with quiet and focused concentration. The air is stale and faintly tainted with the unmistakable smell of diesel that mixes indelibly with our sweat and gets into the very seams of our clothes. The intense stillness is broken only by the soft, almost inaudible hum of machinery as we glide towards our launch position.

'Stand by to come to periscope depth. Keep fifty feet. Up periscope.'

The words come from the ringmaster of all this perfectly choreographed activity. He is in his mid-thirties, rakishly thin and wears a white polo-necked seaman's sweater, topped off with a battered Royal Navy cap, set at a jaunty angle. I feel the boat† tip imperceptibly upwards as we angle towards the surface and watch the periscope column slide noiselessly out of a recess in the deck beneath us. As it passes, the Captain deftly flicks down two handles attached to its sides. They look like motor-bike handlebars and contain the controls for the powerful optics on the periscope, which will by now be slipping like a thin probe out of the waves above us, leaving a thread of white wake behind it. When the rising column reaches eye height, the Captain turns it using the handles and looks into the eyepiece. I watch him as he goes through a full circle, scanning the dark horizon above and satisfying himself that there are no ships or fishing vessels in our vicinity.

'Stand by to surface. Blow main ballast.'

It is time for me to make my way forward to my SBS colleagues who are waiting alongside our canoes in the forward torpedo compartment. By the time I get there, the submarine has broken surface and the forward torpedo hatch is already open, letting in a gust of cold night air and an occasional spray of sea water. We now have four minutes to get

---

* Red light is used in these circumstances because it does not destroy the eye's night vision.
† Submarines are always known as boats, not ships.

our canoes through that hatch and onto the submarine casing, jump into them and be ready for the sea before the submarine must submerge again in order to reduce the risk of detection by radar. At 20 inches across, the hatch is only just wide enough to permit torpedo loading, so it is not easy to get four fully laden two-man canoes, together with their crews, through it in a hurry. But we have been well practised in the drill. Once safely on deck and in my canoe, I have just time to take in our new surroundings before we must be ready for the sea. Around me in the dark are my seven companions, their blackened faces, already streaked with sea foam and sweat, shining in the soft refracted red light coming from the open torpedo hatch. All are now firmly in the cockpits of their canoes, to which they have fastened the rubber-edged canoe 'skirts' that will keep out the water once we are launched. There is a blustery north-westerly wind blowing in our faces, and the sea is quite rough, with three- or four-foot waves slapping at the side of the subma- rine casing. In the distance I can see the low dark loom of the land which is our destination, like a wavy black brushstroke on a dark grey canvas. Behind it is the glow of Plymouth, lying unseen over the hill. Here and there are dotted pinpricks of light from houses and the occa- sional long searchlight beams of cars travelling along the coast road.

The sudden sigh of escaping air below us as the submarine gently vents its tanks tells me that this is no time to be admiring the view. We check that none of us is inadvertently still attached to the sinking craft (I once caught my signet ring in the submarine's guard rail at this moment and was very lucky to get away with a badly cut finger rather than being dragged down with it) and brace ourselves for the waves as the submarine sinks beneath us. In a moment it is gone, leav- ing us bobbing on the surface in darkness and in silence. We initially have to paddle hard to get clear of the backwash of the submarine's descent and then regroup to check that all are OK and no harm has been done to our fragile, canvas-covered canoes. We then turn our lit- tle crafts' heads to the shore and our chosen landing point.

Earlier, during daylight, our submarine had run along this piece of the south Cornwall coast from Rame Head, with its prominent fourteenth- century chapel (Drake, in his time, would have used this as a key land- mark, too) to Looe Island to give me the opportunity to carry out a periscope reconnaissance of our target area. From this, and a study of the map, I have chosen a little inlet which seemed uninhabited as our landing point for that night. It is now my job to find it. I have already studied the local tide tables, to estimate the tidal flow and speed at the submarine's drop-off point, and have laid off for this and how much I estimate the wind will push us off course. This has given me a course to steer, which I now set on the luminous P11, ex-Spitfire compass mounted on the skirt in front of me, and we start paddling, four dark and almost invisible shapes slipping quietly towards the land five miles ahead.

Our canoes are heavy and cumbersome, but remarkably seaworthy. Each carries two Marines, the one at the back being responsible for steering, via two foot pedals attached to a rudder at the rear. We are heavily loaded tonight. Each craft carries two Bergen rucksacks containing our kit for the three-day operation, our weapons and four dummy limpet mines.

My navigation is not perfect but it is not bad. It needs only a little paddling up and down the shore to pick out our spot.

There is a slight scraping noise on the shingle as our bows crunch on the beach, and then we are out and running up the foreshore, carrying our craft to the shelter of some nearby sea grass. Here we silently strip down our canoes into two loads and, now with around a hundred pounds on our backs, start to climb the steep hill which is the start of our journey across the narrow isthmus separating the open sea from the long arm of the Lynher River, which is tidal at this point and runs into the estuary of the Tamar and Plymouth harbour. By the time we reach Cathole, on an inlet of the Lynher, the tide is ebbing fast, and we have only enough time before dawn to reassemble our canoes and paddle a short way to a patch of deserted swamp grass and scrub in which we will lie up for the day.

The following night we catch the ebb tide, which swiftly sweeps us down to the junction of the Lynher and the Tamar. Here we lie up again during the day, only this time in a good position to observe our target for the following night, a collection of Royal Naval ships moored at buoys and lying alongside the jetties of Plymouth naval base.

The next night we complete our exercise by planting our limpet mines on what we consider the juiciest of these targets and, after hiding our canoes as best we can, head off north in pairs to find our way back to 'safe territory'.

This exercise marks the end of the training course for the Swimmer Canoeists Class Three (SC3s) who make up the operatives of the Special Boat Section,* Royal Marines.

---

* Now known as the Special Boat Service.

The SC3 course I joined began at the Amphibious Training Unit Royal Marines (ATURM) in Poole in September 1964, following three glorious months' leave after returning from Singapore in May. Jane and I had spent this with her parents in Somerset. It was one of our most relaxed times together before our children started to arrive. We walked a lot with our new dog, Pip, on the Somerset Levels, one of our favourite excursions being to take a picnic across the flatlands behind Burnham to Brent Knoll, a prominent hill rising some two hundred feet above the Levels, on the summit of which are the remains of a Roman hill fort. Having just returned from my own isolated hill forts in the jungles of Sarawak, I whiled away many summer afternoons speculating about what it must have been like to be the young Roman hill fort commander during those early, untamed days of the Roman occupation.

In August Jane and I had gone down to Poole to stay with friends and try to find a house (we were still under age, and so not entitled to service accommodation). We eventually found one: a wooden bungalow called Barnfield, in a pretty decrepit state of repair, in the middle of some beech and silver-birch woods at Broadstone, five miles or so from Poole itself. It was fine during the summer, but so damp and cold in the winter that our clothes first gathered mildew and then froze, even inside the cupboards in our bedroom. It was also very isolated for Jane – now pregnant with our first child – when I was away (which I was, a lot). We had just bought our first family car, a second-hand mini-van, registration 907 PYD. But only Jane could drive it, as I had failed my first attempt at the driving test (driving has always bored me, and Jane does nearly all the driving in our family). I knew that when the course started I would have to leave at 0530 every morning to be on parade at 0600, and it was, of course, out of the question for Jane to drive me in at that hour. So I bought a very battered Norton motorbike, once a World War Two dispatch-rider's mount, and rode it in to work throughout the following winter, dressed in a leather greatcoat, topped off with a parachute helmet borrowed from a friend.

I started my five-month SBS course on 6 September. We were ten on the course: seven Marines and three Officers (one was a fellow YO19 colleague, Rupert van der Horst). But this time there was absolutely no distinction of rank; Officers and Marines were all treated exactly the same and did everything together, including taking it in turns to be in charge of the group.

Our first task was to learn to dive, for which we were sent to HMS *Vernon* in Portsmouth, where we joined a Royal Navy diving course in mid-September. First we learned about the physiology of diving – and especially of the danger of decompression sickness, more commonly known as 'the bends'. This is caused by the fact that, when a diver descends, the pressure increase allows his blood to absorb more gas (most notably nitrogen). If he then ascends too quickly, the excess gas 'boils off' into bubbles causing great pain in the joints and, in some extreme cases, a gas embolism in the bloodstream that can block the blood flow (much like an air-pocket in a central-heating system) and cause death. Next we were taught how to get into the 'dry' suits used for diving: one-piece rubber suits with a neck seal to keep out the water. With the aid of a partner, we had to get into and out of these in three minutes. They were supposed to be dry but, no matter how much you tried to mend them, they always seemed to develop little leaks that slowly let in the freezing sea water. After that (for reasons I could never understand) we had to learn to run in them across the mudflats of Portsmouth harbour. These 'mud runs' in full diving kit and carrying swim fins (flippers) are about the most exhausting thing I have ever done. Finally, we were allowed to put on compressed-air breathing apparatus and actually go underwater. The rest of this course I remember for its boredom and its cold. We were diving through the early winter months using a diving set that gave us ninety minutes underwater. This was chiefly spent sitting at the bottom of the old torpedo-testing trench on what used to be Horsea Island in the middle of Portsmouth Harbour, beating a rusty shackle with a hammer or pointlessly sawing bits of iron.* The only relief from the cold was to save up your pee until about an hour into the dive and then pee into your suit to warm yourself up for the last half hour.

The highlight of the course was a deep dive off one of the Napoleonic forts in the middle of Portsmouth harbour, which we did in late October. The safe diving limit for compressed air is 120 feet, and this depth could only be found in the middle of the main shipping channel north of the Isle of Wight. While I was on the bottom during this dive the *Queen Mary* passed over our heads, shaking the whole sea bed, even at that depth.

---

* This trench – about 400 yards long and 30 feet deep – has long since vanished, and Horsea is no longer an island but part of Portsmouth, although the Defence Diving School is still based there.

When we returned to Poole in November we found that our diving training had actually only just begun. The compressed air sets we used at Portsmouth let off great streams of bubbles when the diver breathed out. Indeed, this was one of the key safety features of this kind of diving, since it was always possible to see the position of the diver, and whether he was OK, from the bubbles breaking on the surface.

But our task as clandestine divers was to hide our presence, not advertise it. And for this we had to learn how to use a different type of diving set, the Swimmer Canoeist Breathing Apparatus, or SCBA. The SCBA ran on pure oxygen, carried in two small bottles on the back. These fed a 'counter-lung' made of rubber, which was carried on the front. The 'counter-lung' formed a kind of bellows which went in and out with each breath, providing you with a supply of pure oxygen. The exhaled breath then passed down a rubber tube to a refillable can containing a chemical ('protosorb') that extracted the CO_2 from the exhaled breath and recycled the left-over oxygen back into the counter-lung for the next breathing cycle to begin.

The SCBA set was very light, self-contained and gave off no bubbles. But it had two big disadvantages. The first was that oxygen can become lethally toxic at greater than two atmospheres of pressure, which meant that we were limited to a depth of 30 feet, and going deeper could be fatal. The second was that, being made of rubber, the counter-lung was very susceptible to being torn on sharp edges or underwater barbed wire. This, too, could be fatal, since water in the counter-lung not only altered the driver's buoyancy, dragging him down, but also combined with the protosorb to produce a very unpleasant 'cocktail' of caustic soda, powerful enough to strip away the gums, which surged up the breathing tube and into the diver's mouth, causing him to spit out his mouth-piece and so lose his ability to breathe.

But the complexities of underwater work in the SBS were not confined to new equipment. We had to learn some completely new techniques as well. The first was diving at night, and the second was underwater ship attack. The water around Portsmouth could often be pretty murky, and at a hundred feet the available light was often very limited. But nothing prepared us for the inky blackness of diving at night, when the only visible thing is the dim, luminous glow of your compass and depth gauge. We always swam in pairs, connected by a 'buddy line' or short length of cord attached to both swimmers at the wrist. A 'buddy's' duty was to check his partner's kit and help him out if he got into trouble underwater. After much practice on many freezing nights in an old disused clay pit close to our base, we became quite proficient at swimming on a compass bearing and estimating distance underwater in the dark. By the end we could all swim a three-leg course in total darkness at a depth of twenty feet and find our target, the hull of an old barge, with some accuracy. Finally, we were let loose on a real ship, doing a three-hundred-yard underwater approach at night, to end up beneath one of Her Majesty's frigates in Portsmouth harbour. One of the things I discovered in the SBS was that my colleagues divided pretty neatly into two: those who (like me) hated the parachuting but never minded the diving, and those who hated the claustrophobia and disorientation of diving but loved parachuting. But, even for someone who is not claustrophobic, diving in inky blackness under a major ship is a bizarre and unsettling experience. You can hear a ship, and feel the vibrations of its engines and machinery, from some distance away underwater. Underneath it, however, apart from this general sound which thrums loudly in your ear, you can also hear all the other shipboard sounds, including people hammering, someone dropping a spanner and even the metal-tipped boots of the engine room staff walking around. It is very difficult not to let your mind dwell on the twenty thousand tons of ship above you and the crew going about their routine business – only the thickness of a metal plate or two away from where you are, cocooned in coldness, darkness and blindness amongst the barnacles, the seaweed and the dead man's fingers,* just beneath them. It was also difficult not to think what it would be like for them if the charges you were planting were real.

Our biggest fear on these exercises lay in the wire-mesh-covered inlets under the ship's hull, through which cooling water is sucked for the ship's engines, and which, when the engines are running, are quite powerful enough to pull off a diver's face mask. Normally, all this machinery is carefully turned off before a diving exercise begins. But this did not always happen. Much later, on a ship attack exercise in Singapore, someone restarted an engine while we were beneath the ship, and I had a very nasty moment when I got caught in the suction and was only saved by an alert 'buddy' who pulled me clear.

It was now the turn of the year, and our course was in full swing. The day always started with Physical Training (PT) at 0600, followed by a

---

* A jelly-like seaweed, which is deathly white in colour and grows from the bottom of ships in clusters that look like fingers

near-naked swim in the icy waters of our local clay pit. Then we had a full day's instruction, ending usually with some kind of night exercise.

Apart from diving, we learned how to paddle canoes at night over long distances; how to read charts and tide tables; how to do basic coastal navigation; how to work the clandestine radio sets used by SBS at the time; and how to carry out rudimentary first aid. We also learned how to use not only the standard British Army weapons of the time but also the weapons commonly used by our enemies – including the fabled Kalashnikov AK-47, which (because of its robustness, simplicity and resistance to jamming) all of us agreed was the best battlefield weapon in the world. I found myself proficient enough with most short-barrelled weapons,* with the single exception of the pistol, with which I proved absolutely useless. It soon became clear to me that if I was armed with one of these, then by far the safest place to be was the target, for this I seemed incapable of hitting even at the closest range. This applied most especially to the World War II 'Wellrod' silenced pistol then issued to SBS combat swimmers, a single-shot affair that took about fifteen seconds to reload. If ever I had to depend on one of these, I concluded it would be easier to damage a potential enemy by throwing it at him than by trying to shoot him with it. We also learned how to shoot accurately in built-up areas and confined spaces (on a specially constructed range), unarmed combat, fieldcraft and the techniques of escape, evasion and survival.

Indeed, survival was the subject of the shortest and most effective lesson I have ever attended. The instructor, one of our Sergeants and a mountain of a man, came into the lecture room in which we were all seated, walked up to the front and put both his arms on the lectern. 'Right! Today you will learn survival. It's not complicated,' he said, pulling two very ancient pieces of bread, curled up at the edges, out of one pocket of his parachute smock. He then pulled a live frog out of the other, put it between the pieces of bread and ate it. 'If you can do that,' he said, 'you will survive. If you can't you won't!' Then, lecture over, he left the room, leaving us with our eyes out on stalks and a lesson we would never forget.

At the end of a bitterly cold December we went up to the Royal Naval base at Greenock for a week practising our submarine drills, after which we did a three-day exercise that involved being dropped

---

* Pistols and sub-machine guns.

from a submarine and paddling at night up Loch Long and Loch Goil to Lochgoilhead. Here we packed up our canoes and carried them, with full kit, over a vicious hill to Loch Fyne, near Ardno, where we reassembled them for a twenty-mile paddle, followed by a reconnaissance of a target, which we raided, before making our way south over the mountains and along Loch Eck (where I used my old poaching skills to supplement our depleted food stock by tickling trout), to a pick-up point in Glen Kin, close to the Holy Loch. It was bitterly cold, and we were permitted to carry only one sleeping bag, together with its white Arctic camouflage cover, between the two of us. My 'buddy' at this time was an outstanding Marine who came from Wincanton, called Peter Meacham, with whom I became close friends. On our first day, lying up in a pine wood on the shores of Loch Long, I discussed with him how we should divide the use of our one sleeping bag. His answer was very clear: 'I am in charge today, so I will have the sleeping bag – that's the way you officers work isn't it?' It was a joke, of course, though not an entirely unfounded one. We actually ended up sharing the sleeping bag, turn and turn about, in three-hour stretches, with the warm one sleeping and the shivering one keeping sentry and trying to get as much warmth out of the flimsy cover as he could manage. Sleep was not something we got much of at any time during those three months, but it was especially lacking on this exercise.

Towards the end of our course we were taught how to resist interrogation. The heart of this skill is to recognise that all intelligence has a life. For instance, if an operator is captured during a raid, the intelligence he possesses that the enemy desperately needs to obtain quickly is the target, the number of operatives and the escape and evasion plan. If he can keep these details secret until his comrades have completed their task and had time to get away, the intelligence he has is useless to the enemy. So the first thing to have is a good cover plan with a whole series of deeper cover plans beneath it which, like the layers of an onion, get closer and closer to the truth without actually revealing it, and to delay the peeling of each successive skin for as long as possible. Each layer of the cover plan has to be a variation of the first story and convincing in its own right, so it forces the interrogator to waste time checking whether it is true or not. In this way, the prisoner can, when he feels the need to get a break from the pressure, unpeel one layer of the onion while continuing to conceal the real truth at the centre until, hopefully, the intelligence he holds becomes redundant.

This all sounds very easy in theory. But in practice it means putting up with a very great deal of discomfort. Basically, interrogation is a battle of wills between the interrogator and the prisoner. The interrogator's job is to induce in the prisoner a kind of conditional and temporary mental breakdown, so that the prisoner abandons his values and adopts those of the interrogator in their place. The job of the prisoner is to hang onto his values and keep himself anchored in reality. Disorientation is a key part of this process, and discomfort, pain and, especially, sleep deprivation, are the most powerful tools in the hands of the interrogator. At the time when I was going through interrogation training, the techniques used by NATO interrogators included 'white noise' (playing, at very constant, loud volume, the kind of noise you get on your mobile phone when there is a bad connection), severe discomfort (especially through cold and through the use of painful restraints), hooding and total sleep deprivation. These interrogation techniques were subsequently banned as a result of public outrage when it came to light that they were being used against IRA prisoners in Northern Ireland.

On our final exercise in December 1964 we had to conduct a series of exhausting night operations testing the range of skills we had learned; and then, after three days of sleeplessness, when we were on the escape phase of the exercise, one of the chain of 'agents' through whose hands we were being passed on our way to safe territory, betrayed us. I was ambushed in a sunken lane leading to a bridge over the Stour near Wimborne Minster in Dorset. I was fully laden with a 50-lb pack and a submachine-gun. Nevertheless, I managed to clear a high wall on my left and get into the Stour to escape. But it was to no avail – I was captured the following morning lying up in a wood. After the exercise was over they took me back to the point where I was ambushed and showed me the wall I had jumped over. It was vertical, without any hand holds and about six feet high. Even unencumbered with a heavy pack and a weapon it was completely impossible for me to scale it, let alone jump over it. This showed me the extraordinary things the body is capable of when fear, adrenaline and the instinct for flight take over.

Even after we were fully trained, a period of interrogation became a feature of many of our exercises. Often these involved an escape-and-evasion exercise across Dartmoor, during which, as usual, we got no sleep and at the end of which we were taken prisoner and transferred to Bovisand Fort, an old Napoleonic fortification situated on the bluffs above Plymouth, for interrogation. Apart from special-forces operatives, RAF V-bomber pilots were also subjected to these sessions. One interrogator, who I got to know quite well, told me after one exercise that one of the RAF pilots had broken down and unloaded on a startled interrogator a full list of his targets in Russia. He was swiftly removed from the course and shortly afterwards from the V-bomber force. This same interrogator, who I always seemed to get, also told me that, if the situation had been real and he had enough time, he knew exactly how he could break me – make me sit for days and days in solitary confinement with absolutely nothing to do. He told me I was the kind of person who always had to be active and pushing against something, and that idleness, rather than pain, was my Achilles heel. It is not an inaccurate judgement.

The Poole elements of our training were now over. But there were two more stages to go before I could qualify as a fully trained SBS officer.

On 3 January 1965, I joined RAF Abingdon for my parachute course. Our first task was to learn how to land properly, using the parachute roll, which we practised interminably on the floor of an aircraft hanger. Then they taught us how to exit properly from the aircraft door, projecting yourself through it with sufficient force to break through the 120-mph slipstream. We did our live parachuting onto Weston-on-the-Green, a little World War Two grass airstrip, complete with hangars and all the usual airfield paraphernalia, alongside which runs the busy, twin-carriageway A34 road.

To qualify for parachute wings you have to do eight parachute jumps, and I hated every single one of them. But not as much as the Ghurkha officer on the previous course who, we were told, was a veritable magnet for misfortune, particularly when it came to parachuting. On his first jump he had what is known as a 'blown periphery', which means that, on opening, one of the parachute rigging lines is thrown across the canopy. The effect of this is that when you look up to check your 'chute, instead of seeing the silk canopy neatly deployed in a nice round circle looking like a plate of shrimps, it has two lobes and looks like a brassiere. This is not fatal, but it does reduce the surface area of the parachute, causing you to come down a little faster and land a little harder. On his second jump, our Ghurkha had a three-lobe blown periphery, causing his parachute to look like a somewhat crumpled shamrock, giving him a real bang when he reached the ground. On his third jump he was caught by the wind and came down on the nearby A34, narrowly escaping being run over by a large articulated lorry. At this point I am sure I would have concluded fate was trying to send me a message and quietly chosen some career that did not involve jumping out of aircraft at a thousand feet with a flimsy silk contraption on my back. But, being a Ghurkha, he continued. On the fourth jump he was followed out of the door by an exceedingly large soldier from a Scottish regiment, who, being heavier than him, not only descended faster but also succeeded in doing so right onto the top of the Ghurkha's open parachute, on which he then proceeded to trample with exceptionally large army boots. Thus locked together, the two men descended all the way to the ground, with the Ghurkha shouting 'Murderer! murderer!' at his Scottish tormentor. In the fifth jump, a night jump, our hero descended perfectly, but landed on an exceedingly dark Nigerian whom he was unable to see in the inky blackness. One's sixth jump was carried out with fifty pounds of equipment initially attached to the left leg, but then released to dangle below you on the descent, so as not to get in the way of the landing. Needless to say, in our unlucky Ghurkha's case the equipment release mechanism did not work, and he was fortunate to get away with only a badly bruised leg. I cannot remember what happened on the seventh jump, but the story of the eighth, qualifying, jump became something of a parachuting legend – of the gallows-humour variety. This was a night jump, with equipment, on an especially dark night. Our hero apparently accomplished it perfectly, then picked himself up, gathered his equipment, tucked his parachute under his arm and . . . stepped off the edge of the hangar roof and broke both his legs! He got his wings, but history does not relate whether he ever jumped again. (I suspect, though, that there must be quite a few apocryphal elements to this story.)

After the parachute course we went off to the Royal Engineers for a demolition course. This I found interesting and fun after the unremitting physical exertion of the last four months. Our first task was to learn how things were built, the better to know how to blow them up. We had a small, wiry and very Cockney Royal Engineer instructor, who introduced one of his lectures on this subject thus:

Right gentlemen. Today we are going to learn about piles for piers – and I do not mean 'aemorrhoids on haristocratic harseholes.

Before we were allowed to begin actually blowing things up, we had to learn what to blow up to create the greatest effect. The principle here was to use the relatively small amount of explosive an intruder can carry to release the much larger stored kinetic energy of the machines you are trying to destroy. So, for instance, in a power station you blow the huge spinning flywheels off their bearings, and they then run loose and smash much more machinery than you could ever carry enough explosive to destroy. In a harbour, instead of sinking a ship where it lies, it is much better, if you can, to place a small charge on its rudder which is set off by an impeller; this fires the charge when the ship is well under way and leaves the uncontrolled vessel to crash into others and destroy the dockside facilities much more effectively than you would ever have had the time or explosives to do. Similarly, it is much better, if you want to blow up a railway line, to blow up the curved rails rather than the straight ones – first, because there are fewer curved rails, which makes them more difficult to replace, and, second, because a train coming off on a bend does more damage than one derailed on a straight – and so on.

Finally, when we had absorbed all this, we were let loose with live explosives. We learned about primers, detonators, fuses, firing cable and all the other paraphernalia needed to make very big bangs. And how to set pressure switches (which go off when you put your foot on them), pressure release switches (which go off when you take your foot off them), time pencils (which rely on the predictable speed at which lead will stretch and ultimately break, under a constant pull), aniseed switches (the underwater version of time pencils, using the predictable rate at which aniseed dissolves in sea water), and how to improvise booby traps and time switches based on clocks and watches. We also learned how to set charges, make incendiary bombs using soap dishes and ferrous oxide (Jane was furious at the rate that soap dishes went missing from our home at this time) and how to make a shaped charge that would fire a heavy metal object from several yards away at electricity sub-stations, piercing their metal casings and causing a collapse in the local power distribution system (the new and deadly shaped-charge-based IEDs – Improvised Explosive Devices – used against armoured vehicles by the insurgents in Iraq and Afghanistan work on the same basic principle).

We also had a very great deal of fun setting booby traps for the unwary amongst us and blowing each other up in a minor sort of way.

Our demolition course finished, we finally became fully qualified Swimmer Canoeists in the SBS and took some leave before getting our next postings. To my delight I was sent back to Poole, where I was appointed the training officer in charge of future SC3 courses like the one I had just completed. This was a challenge for such a newly qualified SBS operative, but I loved it, for I really enjoy the whole process of teaching. It is not an accident that my father ended up as a teacher and that my sister and both my children are in the teaching profession. If my life had been different, I would have been very content to be one, too.

Jane got involved in this training as well, often acting as an 'agent' through whose hands my trainees had to pass on the escape and evasion parts of their exercises. By this time she was heavily pregnant, causing some rather strange looks from the customers of isolated pubs in the Purbeck hills, where she would sit for an hour or so as a succession of young men came in and sidled up to her to receive their instructions for the next leg of their escape, hidden usually in the folds of a local paper which she pretended to be reading. On one occasion she even baked some current buns, inside which, wrapped in grease proof paper, were the instructions for the next leg. These were left with a friendly local shop owner who was instructed to hand them over on demand to all who could offer the appropriate pre-agreed pass phrase.

Over the Easter weekend of 1965 an SBS colleague and I took part in the Devizes-to-Westminster canoe race. This involves 125 miles of non-stop canoeing, with 77 locks around or over which you have to carry your canoe. (The standing joke amongst us was that history only knows of one person who had a worse Easter than those who choose to spend it on this race.) My friend and I did this, not in one of the light, modern, rigid canoes, but in a heavy canvas folding boat similar to those we used for SBS operations. Our time was a few minutes over 25 hours, and we won our class. I remember this race, and especially the last few miles down to Westminster Bridge against a flooding tide, as physically exhausting.

By now Jane's pregnancy was reaching its term. Although I was not yet 25, and therefore not entitled to service accommodation for my wife, the authorities bent the rules on the ground that, as the SBS training officer, I had to be close to the camp. In April 1965 Jane and I moved into our first service 'quarter', a newly built house just outside the camp's perimeter fence. I immediately tried to grow things in the garden, but this was hopeless, because the soil was little more than a layer of flint and heavy clay. But I did plant a rowan tree on our back lawn, which survived and is still there.

The new SC3 course I was taking through used to parade for PT at 6 o'clock every morning just outside our bedroom window, after which we would go for our run and swim accompanied by our dog, Pip, for whom it was a point of honour to be the first into the lake, the first to swim round the buoy and the first back to land every morning.

On one occasion I took my trainees to Beaulieu in Hampshire for survival training. We first taught them which wild food they could eat, how to trap and fish, how to 'borrow' vegetables from a farmer's field without leaving traces, and generally how to live off the land. Then we left them without rations for four days, to see how they got on. Each night there was an exercise involving a raid on one of the local military bases, after which they had to make their way back during the daylight hours to their base, using natural cover to avoid being seen. They got very tired and very hungry, and I recall on one occasion seeing two of them very nearly coming to blows about how to divide up a mouse between them. On another occasion I heard the most tremendous cacophony of clucking coming from one of the trainees' hides. Investigating, I found one of our Marines (who subsequently proved to be an outstanding, determined and most courageous SBS operator) busily plucking a live chicken he had no doubt 'liberated' in a night raid on a local farm. I told him that the proper (and more humane) way was to kill the bird first and pluck it afterwards. He replied, 'I know, Sir. I couldn't bring myself to kill it. On the other hand, I am so hungry I can't wait to eat it either. So I thought I would just get on with this first, so as not to waste time, and then deal with killing her later.'

One pair of trainees on this exercise, however, seemed to be coping suspiciously well. They were always well fed, but seemed to make no attempt to set traps or lay clandestine fishing lines, as we had taught them. On one bright May morning I discovered why. About midday, I was sitting on a hill with a pair of binoculars looking at some open ground which I knew the trainees would have to cross to see if I could spot any of them. My attention was suddenly attracted to an out-of-place movement close to a large group of picnickers who had installed themselves about a hundred yards away on a pleasantly sheltered grassy sward where they had spread out their food. I trained my glasses on the group just as a hairy arm snaked out of a nearby bush and helped itself to some of their sandwiches, soon followed by

A FORTUNATE LIFE

another a few moments later! I watched, fascinated at this imaginative form of survival, to see if the group noted that they were sharing their picnic with two uninvited, invisible and very hungry Marines – but they never appeared to.

In the second week of June I was away doing a reconnaissance on Ipswich harbour for a ship attack exercise when I was contacted by the SBS office in Poole to say that Jane was in labour. I rushed back to take her into Poole Hospital with her parents, who had come down from Burnham to be with her. We all celebrated prematurely and a little too well in the Mess that evening. Before going to bed, I called the hospital from a nearby phone box (we could not afford a phone) to ask for the news and was told that the baby would definitely not come until tomorrow and that I should have a good night's sleep and call in the morning. I duly telephoned again at six the next morning, 13 June 1965, to be informed that I had a daughter, who had been born at 4 a.m. I dashed to the hospital with rather a thick head, but no flowers and nowhere to buy them from. I remedied this by 'borrowing' some flowers in a dawn raid on a Poole Borough municipal flower bed on my way. Jane says these were some exceedingly moribund sweet peas – in her words, 'more pea than sweet' – all wrapped up in an old piece of newspaper. But we were both so delighted at the arrival of our new and incredibly beautiful daughter that it didn't seem to matter too much at the time.

(Here I should confess that the morning of Kate's birth was not the only time I was responsible for damaging the civic amenities of Poole, which advertised itself as the 'Town of Flowers' and took great pride in the floral displays ornamenting its public spaces. Later the same year I was being driven through the town in an army truck when we approached a particularly large roundabout which was the site of one of these horticultural extravaganzas. I told the Marine at the wheel, as one might any experienced driver, to 'drive straight over'. Unfortunately he was only recently out of training, where he had been taught to obey an officer's orders instantly, precisely and without question. He immediately put the lorry into four-wheel drive and, before I could stop him, drove 'straight over', exactly as instructed. We fled the scene, leaving two broad swathes of mangled foliage and muddied earth to mark our passage.)

I cannot pretend that I was a very modern father – indeed, I fear I am anything but a 'new man'. On one occasion Jane left me with Kate for a few hours, with firm instructions not to forget to change her nappy. She arrived back to find Kate nappiless and naked and us both asleep on the sitting room floor after an afternoon's playing together.

In August of that year we took our first-ever family holiday together. We borrowed a car-top tent from a friend and, together with six-week-old Kate and our heavily pregnant dog Pip, spent a week camping close to Abergavenny in South Wales. We slept in the tent on the mini-van roof, and the dog slept in the van below us. One morning when we were camping at Talybont Reservoir I came down early to try to catch some fish for breakfast, to discover our numbers had increased from four to nine, Pip having given birth to five puppies overnight. The rest of our holiday was more crowded but no less fun for the additions.

In January 1966, after a very happy seven months in Poole, I was posted back to Singapore again, this time in command of an operational SBS based in the Royal Navy base on the north of the island. A month later I became 25, and so Jane and Kate were at last eligible for a free passage to join me and for service accommodation when they got there. We eventually found a little planter's bungalow in a rubber plantation not far from my work.

There were at the time two operational Special Boat units in Singapore, Nos 1 and 2 SBS. I was to command the latter, in the overall charge of an SBS theatre supremo, Captain Pat Troy. Both SBSs had been very active during Confrontation, carrying out raids and reconnaissance on Indonesian targets. Most of the operations had been canoe- and submarine-based raids and reconnaissances of various islands in the Malacca Strait that were being used as jumping-off points for terrorist groups being infiltrated onto the western coast of Malaya. On one of these the SBS party missed its rendezvous with the submarine because of strong tides and was well embarked on the long swim back to Singapore across the Malacca Strait when they were eventually (and very fortunately) found by a Royal Navy ship and rescued.

But Confrontation was now spluttering to a close,* so further operations were put on hold for the time being, for fear of disrupting the

* After General Suharto replaced General Sukarno as President, Indonesian interest in pursuing the war with Malaysia declined, and combat eased. On 28 May 1966, at a conference in Bangkok, the Malaysian and Indonesian governments declared the conflict over. Violence ended in June, and a peace treaty was signed on 11 August and ratified two days later.

delicate peace process then under way. Then what we had thought would be a temporary lull turned out to be a permanent peace.

We were now asked to see what we could do to resolve a serious tactical problem that had come to light during the Confrontation operations. It was decided that it was becoming too dangerous for submarines to surface in order to launch their SBS canoe teams, and we were tasked with finding a way to launch and recover combat swimmer teams from a submerged submarine.

Much of my first year in Singapore was spent working with the 'A'-class diesel-powered submarines of the Seventh Submarine Squadron, also based in Singapore, developing a technique codenamed 'Goldfish' at Pulau Tioman, a remote island off the east coast of Malaysia.

The procedure we devised started when the submarine first left port, usually long before the date of the intended operation. A submarine patrol can last a number of weeks during which it will probably have other tasks to accomplish, apart from landing and recovering SBS teams. Meanwhile, the SBS team needs to be kept in peak fitness and fully up to date with the developing intelligence picture. It cannot afford to be cooped up on a submarine for a long time and so should, ideally, join it as close as possible to the scheduled date of the operation.

To solve this problem, we loaded all our equipment onto the submarine before it left port and then, some twenty-four or forty-eight hours before the operation, parachuted at night to a fixed rendezvous point in the ocean, perhaps two hundred miles out to sea where the submarine could safely surface to recover the team. It proved somewhat nerve-wracking to jump into an apparently empty expanse of water, trusting that the pilot of the aircraft was right when he promised this was the correct position and there really was a submarine down there somewhere, waiting for you.

Once on board the submarine, we would have time for the last-minute periscope reconnaissance and final adjustments to the plan. Half an hour before launch time, the swimmers got dressed for the operation. Invariably, their task was to go ashore at night and spend, say, two or three days on the operation before returning to a rendezvous point in the ocean at a given time for the night-time pick-up. This meant that, although the first and last parts of the operation would be in the water, the main part would be on land. So the team had to be dressed and equipped for a normal jungle patrol, with the difference that they wore swim fins (flippers), and everything that could be damaged by

With my mother, brother Richard and our *ayah*, 1944.

On my pony, probably in Agra around my fourth birthday, 1945.

With my mother, father and brother Tim. Donaghadee, 1946.

Above: My first salmon (John Murphy in the background). Lough Melvin, 1952.

Above: With Bridie. Dongahadee, c.1946.

Right: High jump, Garth House School, Bangor, c.1950.

Kirkman's, Bedford School, 1954 (I am fifth from right, middle row). *(Photo: Bedford School)*

Bedford School 1st XV, 1958 (I am fourth from left, back row). *(Photo: Bedford School)*

YO 19 1959. Left to right, back row: Angus Gordon, Richard Armstead, Roger Munton, Ron Wheeler. Middle row: me, Peter Clough, Andy Moreland, Tim Courtenay, Jim Bartlett, Rupert van der Horst. Front row: Our weapons instructors.

The Doone Valley, Exmoor. Autumn 1959.

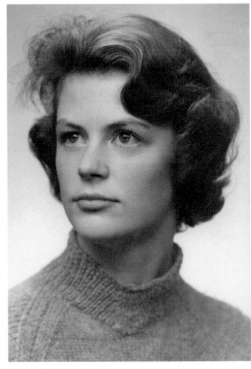

Jane, 1960.

Before my first parachute jump. Singapore, 1960. Left to right: Tim Courtenay, me, Rupert van der Horst.

Jungle training, Fort Rekum, Malaya, with Rupert van der Horst, 1961. *(Photo by Tim Courtenay)*

'Makan salamat' – a welcoming feast for my irregulars on their return home after a raid. Stass, Borneo, 1963.

Jane and Tigger, Singapore, 1963.

The helicopter landing site at Stass, Borneo, 1963.

Above: 'The Jesus Christ moment'.
HMS *Anchorite* surfacing, Pulau Tioman,
Malaysia, 1965.

Right: 'Goldfish' – riding the periscope before
re-entering the submerged submarine to return
home after an exercise. Pulau Tioman, 1966.

Driving Archie. Jahore Straights, Singapore, 1966.

Above: Ah Moy, our *amah*, Kate and Simon (with the green bucket). Hong Kong, 1968.

Above: With Kate, Jane and Tandy (between us) walking on the mountains of Hong Kong, 1968/9.

Left: Teaching Jane to fire a sub-machine gun, Stonecutters Island, Hong Kong, 1969.

Right: With my Sergeant Major (Bert Blythe), the Shankill Road, Belfast, 1970.

water (such as wireless sets, detonators, etc.) had to be very carefully sealed in plastic. The operators, complete with weapons and packs, then crammed themselves two by two into the empty escape chamber of the submerged submarine, which was fitted with rubber hoses and mouthpieces attached to the submarine's compressed-air system. The lower lid was then closed, the swimmers put the mouthpieces in their mouths, gave a signal that they were breathing off the submarine's system, and the escape chamber was flooded with water. As soon as the pressures inside the escape chamber and outside were equal, the upper lid could be opened, and the swimmers reached out to find a second compressed-air line attached to the outside of the submarine.

From this moment onwards the whole operation had to be carried out in darkness and by feel. The swimmers exchanged the mouthpieces attached to the submarine's internal breathing system for those on the external breathing lines, carefully placing the internal breathing lines back into the escape chamber and closing the lid for the next pair to follow them. They were then free to make their way up the outside of the submarine into the conning tower, using specially fitted hand lines and taking good care not to let go of them, as the submarine was still moving at two to three knots. Once in the conning tower, the leader could plug himself into an underwater communication system (called DUCS) which he could use to talk with the submarine captain. There was then usually quite a long wait as, two by two, the whole team was assembled. When all were in place the captain steered the boat to the agreed drop-off point and gave the command 'Release, release, release' to the patrol commander over the underwater communications system. The whole team then released together and popped to the surface, fully equipped with weapons, packs and everything needed for the task ahead. Now it was just a question of swimming the three to six thousand yards to the shore with the aid of swim fins. These were buried where they could be found again, and the patrol was ready to move off at daybreak and complete its mission as a normal jungle patrol.

Recovering the swimmers was done by reversing the process. Swim fins were collected from their hiding places, all the equipment not needed on the return journey was carefully buried, and the team swam out to the fixed rendezvous point for the submarine pick-up. This point was established by reference to two previously calculated bearings on prominent points (such as headlands) which could be easily seen in the dark on a moonless night (we always tried to chose the no-moon periods of the month, as these give the best cover of darkness for this kind of operation).

Having reached the pick-up point the swimmers split into two groups about a hundred yards apart with a strong piece of line (referred to as the 'snag line') running between them. The teams at each end of the lines then turned on a specially developed electronic homing device, called a 'trongle', which emitted a signal that the submarine could use to home in on the swimmers. After this it was just a question of waiting for the submarine to arrive. Its captain steered his still submerged vessel between the two signals, with his periscope up. The first sign the swimmers got that the submarine was coming was the slight 'swish' of the periscope creaming through the water. This caught the snag line between the two groups of swimmers, who pulled themselves forward to the periscope and, reaching down under water, found their breathing lines and mouthpieces attached just below the surface. They then plugged in their mouthpieces and reversed the process that they had followed to launch, stepping out in the submarine wardroom at the end of the operation.

The swimmers had to leave sufficient hours of darkness to swim back to the shore if the rendezvous was missed, get themselves hidden and prepare to try again the following night. It was always a most depressing moment when, at the end of a couple of hours treading water after a long swim out, the decision had to be made to start the long plod back to the shore again for another day in the jungle and all the uncertainties of another possible failed pick-up twenty-four hours later.

At the end of canoe-borne operations, we used to describe the moment that the submarine surfaced for the final pick up as the 'Jesus Christ' moment. But it didn't compare with the moment when, on a dark night at the end of three or four days ashore and a five-thousand yard swim to the pick up point, you suddenly heard the sound of the periscope in the dark and felt the reassuring tug of the submarine on the snag line that told you that warmth and safety were only twenty feet below you.

Where an SBS team had to be flown out to a submarine before the start of an operation, 'Goldfish' also allowed us to do this without the need for the submarine to surface where it was considered too dangerous to do so. In this case, the SBS team would sink their parachutes after the jump, stretch out their snag line, turn on their 'trongles' and wait for the hoped-for periscope to come creaming towards them, much as they might a London bus. After this it was just a question of using the 'Goldfish' re-entry process to make their way down to the still-submerged submarine. For dramatic transformations of circumstance, there cannot be many to match going from a thousand foot above a darkened sea to thirty feet below it, having experienced the fear of the jump, the elation of the descent, the nervousness of the long wait, the relief at hearing the periscope approaching, the heart-lifting sharp tug on the snag line, the satisfaction of closing the escape hatch and the sheer joy of the welcoming handshake and warm glass of Royal Navy rum at the end – all in the space of an hour or so.

While these operations were not, at this stage, being carried out against a live enemy, they were nevertheless dangerous, difficult and required the highest concentration. I have always been fascinated by the extent to which it is possible to do the seemingly impossible through a combination of teamwork, technology and a high degree of professionalism. Nevertheless, we were operating at the limits of what was sensible, even with good equipment and the most professional people it was possible to get. I developed a principle during this period which has stood me in very good stead, in politics and out, ever since – that I was never prepared to take with me into a dangerous situation anyone who was not at least as frightened as me. For the person who does not recognise fear when everyone else is gripped by it is not an asset, but a danger to success and comrades alike.

We practised and developed these techniques with our submarine colleagues until we felt we had them finely honed. The submarines, *Ambush*, *Anchorite* and *Andrew*, were our usual partners in this, and one of those with whom I worked most closely at this time was a certain Mike Boyce: then, as a young Royal Navy Lieutenant, the 'second hand' on HMS *Anchorite* responsible for launching me and my SBS colleagues in canoes or as swimmers on many a dark night off the coasts of Malaysia. Today he is Admiral Lord Michael Boyce, a former Chief of the Defence Staff and one of my colleagues in the House of Lords.

In between climbing in and out of submarines we did a lot of diving in the crystal waters off Pulau Tioman. This area is well known as a shark breeding-ground, and we nearly always saw a shark or two when we dived. They were mostly rather small, about six feet long, and no one had ever been known to be attacked by one in these waters. Nevertheless, small and benign or not, you had to be particularly insensitive not to feel your heart beat a little faster when one came to investigate, not least because, underwater, a shark – clean, sleek and swift – was so much in its element, and we – slow, lumbering and clumsy – were so much out of ours. One of my Marines developed such a hearty dislike of these regular companions to our dives that he became a cause of a good deal of gallows-humour ribbing from the rest of us. But he got his own back eventually. One day, when we were preparing to dive together, I noticed he was carrying a long sharpened stick.

'What's that for?' I asked.

'It's my shark stick, sir.'

'Don't be stupid,' I said, 'that won't keep a shark off.'

'I know sir. It's not for the shark, sir. It's to poke you and make you bleed, so I've got time to get away.'

Our real fear in these waters was not sharks, but sea snakes. These are green, yellow and duck-egg blue with darker bands, a powerful paddle tail and can run up to ten or more feet in length. They are mostly deadly poisonous, but fortunately have only very rarely been known to attack humans. They were, nevertheless, an unpleasant thing to find swimming along with you on a dark night. These seas are very phosphorescent and every paddle or swimming stroke produces clouds of green light in the water. I recall one night paddling in from a submarine launch to find that our canoes were surrounded by six or seven sea snakes, each nearly as long as our canoes, swimming along with us in great serpentine ribbons of phosphorescence.

The other threat was jelly fish, and especially the so-called 'Portuguese man-of-war', a curious creature with the ability to put up an air bladder which acts as a sail. Their sting is excruciatingly painful and can kill small children. One of our favourite expeditions in Singapore was to load our friends onto one of the Motor Fishing Vessels (MFVs) we used for diving and sail the 120 miles to Pulau Tioman for a long weekend living on the beach and swimming. The usual routine was to load all the children and families in the hold and on the deck for a night passage up the coast, on which I would do the navigation, returning three days later. On one of these trips, our boat was anchored in shallow water a little way out from the shore, while most of the families were swimming with their children. I was on the deck with one of the fathers, who suddenly spotted a flotilla of Portuguese men-of-war sailing in on the wind and heading straight for his wife and two young children. He leapt straight in between them and got himself severely stung, while his family got back to the boat.

———

We spent 1967 honing our new 'Goldfish' skills in a series of exercises that tested them to the limit. While we were satisfied that they could now be used in real operations, the shallowness of the coastal waters in this area of the world presented us with a new operational problem. In order to remain safely submerged, the submarines we were using needed a minimum of 10 fathoms (60 feet) of water. Meanwhile, the maximum distance you could reasonably ask a combat swimmer to swim, fully laden with weapons, ammunition, explosives, communications and equipment for three days was, we reckoned, 7–8,000 yards. Beyond this, exhaustion on the part of the swimmers and the effect of tides on navigation made the operation unacceptably hazardous – especially on the return journey, after several days' potentially arduous operations ashore, when accurate navigation to find the right point in the open sea for the rendezvous with the submarine was critical. However, the shallowness of the sea around the Malaysian peninsula and the Indonesian archipelago meant that the ten-fathom line was often considerably more than 8,000 yards from the shore, which limited our combat swimming teams.

We needed to find a mechanical means to deliver combat swimmer teams over longer distances. We needed, in short, a Swimmer Delivery Vehicle (SDV), which could be carried in the submarine and which swimmers could unload while the submarine was still submerged and then use for their journey ashore. This SDV would then be sunk in shallow water and camouflaged, ready to pick up on the return journey. The last such 'swimmer delivery vehicles' had been the World War Two 'Chariots' invented by the Italians* and used to attack Valetta and Alexandria harbours; they were subsequently adapted by the British, who used them mostly in the Far East. But these had long since gone out of service. So we had to start again from scratch.

* The Italians called them *maiali*, or 'pigs'.

We hit on the idea of down-rating a standard Royal Navy Mark 23 torpedo and fitting it with steering gear at the rear, a buoyancy chamber, a compass, a depth gauge and an attitude indicator. This could be unloaded by swimmers from the torpedo tube of the submerged submarine and used to infiltrate combat swimming teams over longer distances, enabling the submarines to stay further out to sea and preserving the energy of the swimmers. Our modified torpedo was given the code name 'Archie', after Archimedes, and it fell to me to try it out. It was fine on the surface, but a bitch to drive under water. No matter how you trimmed the buoyancy, the length of the torpedo in front of the driver (who was at the very back end) meant that, once the nose dipped, it was very difficult to turn the beast round before the whole contraption went deeper than thirty feet, the point beyond which the pure oxygen we were breathing could turn toxic. And, if the nose went up, it was very difficult to turn round before the whole thing, with two swimmers on its back, broke surface like a breaching whale and gave the game away. In the end, however, we became quite skilled at driving it in a moderately controlled manner, even managing some successful simulated night attacks on Royal Navy warships in the harbour of Singapore naval base – on one occasion we left a large (dummy) mine under one of Her Majesty's aircraft carriers as a calling-card.

We were rather pleased with ourselves, and even grew attached to our distinctly Heath Robinson contraption. But unfortunately (or, I suspect, fortunately – despite our enthusiasm, this was not a machine to be trusted in a real combat situation), the confrontation had by now ended, so we never had the chance to try out our new-fangled toy in anger.*

In mid-1966 Jane again became pregnant. This time she had a very difficult pregnancy, with such severe sickness that she had to be taken into hospital frequently to be put on an intravenous drip. As a result, she became skeletally thin and had to spend much of the last months of her confinement in bed, causing us all much worry. Our son Simon was, however, born without complications in the British Military Hospital in Singapore on 24 April 1967. At this time it was not usual for husbands to be present at the birth, but the wonderful Chinese midwife who delivered Simon was a woman ahead of her time and

* For further details of these Archie trials and what they led to, and of 'Goldfish' in the Far East, see John Parker, SBS: The inside story of the Special Boat Service (London: Headline, 1997).

broke the rules to permit me to stay and see him emerging into the world, for which I have always felt in her debt.

Simon was christened on HMS *Forth*, the headquarters ship of the Seventh Submarine Squadron, in June. We had a tremendous party at which Kate, aged two, was discovered drinking whatever she could find from half-filled glasses within her reach. It was only when we left the Royal Naval dockyard in high spirits on our way home that we discovered that we had left the object of the whole affair, my son Simon, back on board HMS *Forth*!

In February 1966 Denis Healey, then Secretary of State for Defence, introduced a Defence White Paper, followed by a full-scale Defence Review which concluded that all British armed forces east of Suez, with the single exception of those in Hong Kong, should be withdrawn. In October that year Mr Healey visited Singapore, and we were tasked with putting on a demonstration for him involving divers exiting a submerged submarine and some SBS frogmen parachuting into the sea alongside him. Denis Healey never forgot this incident and, unprompted, reminded me of it sixteen years later, when, after my election as an MP, we met in the corridors of the House of Commons.

Towards the end of our time in Singapore, I was given the task of taking No. 2 SBS to Hong Kong and surveying all the beaches on the mainland and larger islands of the Colony. We were told our survey was part of the contingency plans being assembled in case of a Chinese invasion and the need to evacuate British citizens in a hurry. We spent three weeks surveying all the most likely beaches for an emergency amphibious evacuation, recording their gradients, hinterland access and how load-bearing each beach was. We were told to be as unobtrusive as possible, so as not to cause alarm, so we abandoned our uniforms and military kit and appeared as holidaymakers, going about the business in a way which, we hoped, would attract as little attention as possible. In these days of sexual equality I don't suppose the sight of so many fit young men prancing about the waves together would cause much comment, but it certainly attracted an occasional odd look at the time – a fact which caused us all a good deal of amusement. At the end of our time we changed back into uniform and went up to the border with China to conduct a week's surveillance operation.

People have often asked me where, as a member of the services, I got my left-of-centre political opinions from. The answer is the SBS.

I inherited from my father a deep dislike of the class system in Britain. I hated the large part this seemed to play in the services in general and especially, at the time, in the Royal Navy – something which I saw at first hand in 1960, when I was responsible for the conditions of our Marines below decks on that first cruise to Mombasa. Since leaving school I had believed that a fairer society – in which people's ability, not their class, would determine their lives – would best be achieved under a Labour Government. I had declared myself, in consequence, a Labour supporter, something which was not always either welcome, or understood, amongst of my fellow officers. So I felt very comfortable with the culture I found when I joined the SBS, where people were valued and trusted according to their abilities and skills, not their origins. It was my good fortune during my years in the SBS to command a bunch of individuals who were, by any standards, better at the profession in which we were involved than I was. What was more, the things we did together, and our mutual reliance on each other's skills and courage in difficult moments, taught me a very great deal about the value of structures that are based not on hierarchies but on mutuality. This is not unusual. The services may have a reputation for being the Conservative Party under arms in peacetime, but the mutuality and comradeship experienced on active service nearly always remind people of the value of the things that they hold and exercise in common. It is not an accident that, after experiencing the vicissitudes of war, democracies nearly always turn left, before the selfish gene takes over again.

My horizons were beginning to widen in other areas, too.

Having largely taught myself two Far Eastern languages (Malay and Bedayuh/Dayak), I now rather fancied myself as a linguist and decided to teach myself 'Mandarin' Chinese. I started with one of those standard 'Teach Yourself' books like the one I had used to learn Malay. But I soon found out that Chinese was much, much more difficult. So I enrolled in a Chinese evening class in downtown Singapore.

Here I discovered my second problem. I was the only non-Chinese in the class; all the others were Cantonese, Fukienese and Hakka, whose native spoken tongues are mutually incomprehensible and who were trying to learn Mandarin, which Mao Tse-tung had just declared to be China's official mother tongue. This put me at a great disadvantage because, although all of China's local languages are verbally very different, they share a common written language, and this was already known to all my fellow students. So they only had one language – spoken Mandarin – to learn, whereas I had two – written Chinese and spoken Mandarin.

I made, I confess, slow progress. But in the process I became fascinated by the language, culture and history of China. By now my SBS posting was drawing to a close, so I applied to take a sabbatical from the Royal Marines and go on a full-time course to learn Chinese. Such a thing had never happened before, and certainly not in the SBS, so I was not at all confident that my application would be successful. To my delight, however, I heard in June 1967 that I was to go to Hong Kong to take a two-and-a-half-year course at the newly opened Chinese Language School in Lyemun, where I would train as a Royal Naval interpreter in Chinese.

We left Singapore as a family in August that year for home. There, after a couple of week's leave, I started to prepare for my next trip out to the Far East, this time not as a soldier, but as a student.

CHAPTER 7

Chinese

I ARRIVED IN HONG KONG on 12 September 1967, after just a month's leave back in the UK. Jane and I had decided that I should go to Hong Kong alone to start with, to begin my studies, while she, Kate and Simon would follow three months later. This enabled them to spend a bit of time with Jane's parents and recover after what had been, for her, a very tough last year in Singapore. It would also give me a chance to spend three months immersing myself totally in Chinese language and culture.

Our Chinese *alma mater* was the Joint Services Chinese Language School, situated on a rocky outcrop overlooking the Lyemun gap at the eastern end of Hong Kong island. It was through this gap that all the aircraft flew after taking off from Kai Tak airport, and all the ships entering the harbour from the east sailed. Close by was the secret Sai Wan listening station, and it was here that most of the students from the language school would eventually work.

The school had just been opened, taking over as a service-run equivalent of the London University-based School of Oriental and African Studies (SOAS), and we were to be its first students. It was run by a remarkable RAF Squadron Leader called Bob Sloss, whose looked like a somewhat eccentric academic but whose infectious passion for China, its people, culture and language, inspired us all. Our three main teachers were Mr Tang, a rather fierce northern Chinese, unremittingly demanding in what he expected of us (very much the traditional attitude to students in China; 'yong gong', or 'studious effort' was his constant exhortation to anyone he thought was slacking); Mrs Cheong, a five-foot powerhouse of dynamism and humour; and Mrs Chen, who was gentle, quiet, full of grace and loved by us all.

My eleven colleagues on the first course (including one Australian) were all serving officers, warrant officers and senior other ranks. Except for special occasions, we did not have to wear uniform and were encouraged to behave as students. After the rigours and responsibilities of SBS I loved this sense of freedom and the joy of being footloose and immersing myself in academic study. I was determined, at least until Jane and the children came out, to capitalise on this opportunity to cut myself off as much as possible from service life and Hong Kong's European community. So, instead of living in the service accommodation provided for us, I started to look for a Chinese family who would have me as a paying guest.

I soon found a very pleasant *putonghua**-speaking family called Liu. Mr Liu worked at a local factory making plastic flowers and was a rather taciturn and serious man, especially with his children. His wife, who was round, jolly and very voluble, worked as a cleaner in an office block occupied by one of Hong Kong's major insurance companies. They had two children. The eight-year-old daughter, known always by her nickname Xiao Mao (little cat), had a delightful face framed by pigtails and an irrepressible giggle she found it impossible to control. Her brother Da Zhong, her elder by two years, was serious, studious and smiled little, like his father. They treated me, I think, as a kind of curious mascot which it was their duty to protect from my own stupidity and the consequences of my clumsy Western ways.

The family, who had been quite well-to-do in previous years, had fled Shanghai during the Communist revolution and now lived on the third floor of a five-storey apartment block which was crowded cheek by jowl with factories, bars and little restaurants in a teeming quarter of the Causeway Bay district of Hong Kong. I used to eat with them morning and evening and then went off to my very small, very cramped, very hot bedroom to study. This had one window overlooking a round-the-clock, back-street ball-bearing factory, which proudly informed me – by way of a huge flashing green neon sign blasting into my window day and night – that it was 'The Far Eastern Balls Company'.

When not studying, I wandered round the Causeway Bay district, engrossed in its constant, teeming, sleepless activity. In the morning, I often stopped by the market for a bowl of noodles at a Chinese stall on my way to work. At weekends I would go for lunch with some Chinese friends to one of the little restaurants in the area for a bowl of *wuntun* soup,† or buy a steaming corn on the cob from a street barrow, or a paper bag of ten little roasted birds (rice birds, like little sparrows), which are delicious and eaten whole, head and all. When I got back in the evening, if there was no studying to do, I wandered the streets, listening to the cacophony of Chinese languages, captivated by

---

* The proper name for Mandarin Chinese.
† *Wuntun* (literally 'a thousand swallows') is a delicious soup in which float hordes of little pasta packages of meat.

all the refracted shards of culture, history and ethnicity swept into Hong Kong by war and revolution from the vastness of China, invisible but ever-present across the black water of the harbour and over the jagged rampart of the mountains to the north.

I fell in love with it all and threw myself with impatient zeal into learning the language. One of my teachers wrote of me at the time that I 'match[ed] high aptitude for the study of Chinese with considerable, not to say ferocious application'. The 'ferocious application' part, at least, was right. I am an enthusiast by nature and wanted to gulp it all down as fast as I could.

At the time, the Cultural Revolution was just beginning in China, and its effects were already being felt in Hong Kong. There were a number of strikes and riots, including some in the area where I was living. These were accompanied by a spate of political murders, especially amongst those Chinese journalists regarded as being insufficiently sympathetic to the Communist cause, or who voiced their opposition to the violence. There was also a minor, but at the time quite disturbing, spate of bombings. What I did not know then, of course, was that, though things would quieten down in Hong Kong, they would get much worse in China, and that this so-called 'Cultural Revolution' would prevent me from doing what I wanted to do most – visit China itself. At one stage the service authorities got quite worried that I was living in what they regarded as one of the major hotbeds of the disturbance and suggested I should leave my little room for more salubrious accommodation in one of the local service bases. I refused, saying that I felt quite safe. And so I did – and so I was. I never hid from my hosts or their neighbours the fact that I was in the British services, and it would have been reasonable for them to assume that I was a British spy in their midst. But I never felt threatened and was never treated with anything other than courtesy and kindness, even when I once found myself caught on the edges of a rather nasty confrontation with the massed ranks of the Hong Kong riot police. I mentioned my puzzlement at this to one of my Chinese teachers and she told me that students have a special status in China, and doubtless I was benefiting from that – though she told me not to push it too far, as 'these Communists don't know the old traditions as well as they should'.

My nastiest moment came not in the Colony but on the mountains of the New Territories, which lie between Hong Kong and the Chinese frontier, where I frequently went on expeditions with a local Chinese walking group. We would normally all meet up for these expeditions at the Star Ferry terminal on Hong Kong Island, cross on the ferry to Kowloon and then catch buses to our destination of the day. On this particular day, the group decided to visit the site of a new barrage being built at the time to close off the Plover Cove inlet, beneath the Ba Tsin (eight fairies) mountain range, in order to create a new fresh-water reservoir for the Colony. We arrived at our destination to discover that it had become the scene of a major demonstration and strike against the construction. We had just decided to go elsewhere, when over the mountain, cutting off our retreat, came an army of Chinese youths carrying red banners, chanting 'Long live Chairman Mao' and each carrying a copy of Mao's little red book. We were trapped and, as the only European, I stood out like a sore thumb – not just because of my mousy red hair (one of the Chinese words for a European foreigner is *hong tou fa* – 'the red haired one') but also because I was about half a foot taller than anyone else in the company. The Chinese friend I was with at the time told me to bend my knees and do exactly as he did. He then pulled out his Hong Kong and Shanghai Bank cheque book which, though twice as long as Mao's little red book, had a plastic cover of exactly the same hue and, holding it halfway down to reduce its apparent size, started to shout '*Mao zhu xi, wan sui!*' ('Long Live Chairman Mao!') as lustily as everyone else. I bent my knees, rummaged for my cheque book in my pack, and started chanting with the rest as the red tide swarmed through us, too intent on their chanting to notice either me or the fact that we were wishing their Chairman a long life with the most powerful icon of the capitalist Hong Kong that they were dedicated to destroying!

At this time I met two couples who became special and lifelong friends. Both were mixed marriages. Mark Tang, one of life's natural gentlemen, is a Hakka* Chinese married to a German wife, Heidi. And Bennie Wu, now sadly dead, was a Cantonese from one of Hong Kong's richest families (but who lived extremely modestly himself) and was married to Sarah, an American. Together, they taught me about the customs of the ordinary people of China, some of its history, a bit of its culture, a smattering of its folklore, but mostly (and a lot) about the glorious treasure-house of Chinese cuisine. Every Friday

---

* The Hakka Chinese are the remnants of the indigenous northern Chinese driven out by the Mongols (later known as the Manchus). The Hakka fled and took up residence as refugees in southern China – hence their other Chinese name, the *ke jia* or 'guest people'.

night we would go out to a different Chinese restaurant to taste the delicacy of the season – I used especially to love the early autumn, when we went to a nearby Causeway Bay restaurant to eat newly arrived Shanghai *da ja hai* or freshwater hairy crabs, washed down with *fa dew*, red Shanghai wine served hot, like *sake*. In spring we would visit a fishing village for seafood (the Chinese have a saying that if you eat seafood you should take a fat wallet), and in December we went to the Western District of Hong Kong to eat 'three kinds of snake' (good for heating the body, they say). Or we might seek out a little back-street restaurant at the back of Kowloon for spicy Szechuan food to ward off the winter cold (not that it ever got very cold in Hong Kong, though there were at least discernible seasons – which we had missed in Singapore). I have rather a large appetite, and this could sometimes grow to gargantuan proportions when it came to Chinese food – with the result that, around the restaurants we habitually visited, I earned the nickname *da fan tong* or 'the big rice bucket'.

My Friday evening appetite was sharpened by the fact that, in order to keep fit (always something of an obsession with me) I used to go to Hong Kong squash club every Friday at 6 p.m. and play two hours of squash against all-comers. On one occasion an older man walked into the court and asked if he could play. I said 'Of course' without taking too close a look at him, and we began a pretty furious game. He was wilier than me and, if younger, would certainly have beaten me. Something about his voice, however, triggered a spark of recognition; I turned to look at him more closely and realised that I was playing James Mason, who was in Hong Kong to make a film.

Jane came out with the children just before Christmas 1967, and this marked the end of my living as a Chinese in the Chinese quarter. We moved into a service quarter on the seventh floor of a twelve-storey block of flats called Royden Court in Repulse Bay, where we spent the next two years. There was a beach nearby for the children and boating and walking at the weekends.

Since the start of our married life we have always had a dog chosen from a local animal refuge, and Kate was soon asking when our new dog would join us. We went to the Hong Kong RSPCA and found a splendid, scruffy little half-long-haired terrier mongrel we called Tandy, because he had the same squat determination and indomitable cheerfulness as one of my ex-SBS colleagues. He quickly became the indispensable fifth member of our family, accompanying us everywhere, especially on our walks. He was a good guard dog, too – though his efforts were not always appreciated. One early morning in our second year, Jane and I were woken up at 2 a.m. by a furiously barking Tandy. I scolded him and told him to shut up, which, grumbling, he duly did. We woke up next morning to find the front door open and our money and many of our valuables gone. The thief had climbed seven storeys up the outside of the building to get in at the open window of the children's room. I suspect we would have lost more had he not been scared off by our alert and unjustly admonished little dog.

I kept up my excursions with my Chinese walking group, who, to a man and woman, fell in love with my shining blonde daughter Kate, whom I carried on my shoulders up almost every major mountain in the Colony.

Expeditions on the mountains of Hong Kong remained one of my favourite pastimes, which blew away the cobwebs of the week's study; even after Jane arrived I would occasionally take Tandy off for three days, walking by myself, staying out on the mountains overnight. My two favourite long walks were on a great saddle-backed mountain called Ma On Shan, with magnificent views of the coves and inlets of the New Territories on all sides and a shepherds' hut at the top, and on Tai Mo Shan, Hong Kong's highest peak, on whose slopes grew a single magnolia tree which was supposed to be of a genus unknown anywhere else in the world and had huge soup-plate-sized blossoms that burst out in profusion every spring.

On other occasions we would go walking as a family, catching one of the many ferries plying between the Hong Kong islands and returning at night, marvelling at the harbour sparkling with the great city's myriad constellations of lights. One of our adventures, a two-day affair, involved climbing the three-thousand-foot Ngong Ping mountain on Lantau Island, at the top of which there is a Buddhist monastery called Po Lin. We spent the night there amongst the monks, and then watched the dawn come up next morning before descending the mountain and catching the ferry home from a little harbour now buried under Hong Kong's new airport. Kate came with us on nearly all these trips. Simon, though, was too young and was looked after by our *amah*, Ah Moy, who soon became a close friend of the family as well as an indispensable source of advice, guidance and assistance.

Our other favourite pastime was boating. I crewed for a friend who raced dinghies most weekends, and we often hired a Chinese junk for family boating trips around the islands, anchoring overnight in some cove and returning the following morning.

And there were great parties, too. The sixties came late to Hong Kong but, when they did, they came with a rush. Almost overnight every woman under fifty was wearing a mini skirt, the colours of Mary Quant were everywhere on show, and the sound of the Beatles pounded out of every bar in Wanchai – at the time playing host to thousands of US servicemen, whose bleak desperation to enjoy every last second of their 'R and R' * leave spoke almost as much of the horrors to which they would soon return in Vietnam as the pictures and reports we read daily in our papers.

Curiously, none of this was spoiled, or even much affected, by the dark storm of the Cultural Revolution raging just over the Chinese border, even though dead bodies, often bearing the marks of torture, were regularly washed down the Pearl River to end up on Hong Kong's western shores. But, reading the Chinese papers every day, I was more than aware what was going on – and frightened for my family. Only thirty miles north of us huge mobs of young revolutionaries were on the rampage in a China that seemed to be dissolving into a series of fiefdoms of madness, uncontrolled by the authorities.

Hong Kong, I knew, could not be defended. It relied then (and does still) on China for the bulk of its food, and even most of its fresh water. I became at the time obsessed by the vulnerability of our little island of prosperity and gaiety amidst a sea of war, revolution and instability all round us, from Vietnam to China. Legend has it that Kowloon, across from Hong Kong island, got its name when one of the Sung Emperors sailed through the area and asked one of his court sages for the name of this magnificent harbour. The sage replied that it was called Jiu Lung (which becomes 'Kowloon' in the English corruption of the Cantonese, and means the 'nine dragons'). Chinese folklore has it that every mountain has a dragon. The Emperor counted the mountains and saw that there were only eight. So he said to his sage, 'You have it wrong – there are only eight mountains so it should be Ba Lung [eight dragons].' To which the flattering sage replied, 'No sire, for the Emperor, too is a dragon – so with you here, this is now Jiu Lung [nine dragons]. One day a thousand lights will burn here – but not for long.'

* Rest and Recuperation.

My constant fear (reflected in private, I later discovered, by the Colony's authorities) was that, one day, the Chinese mobs would simply extend the revolution over the border and swamp us in insanity, too. If they did come over the border, I reasoned, then the first days would be the worst, after which things would calm down enough to get us out. So one weekend I went up into the mountains behind our block of flats and established a hide within easy distance of one of the best beach embarkation points I had recorded for London, when in the SBS two years earlier, and stocked it with enough food for my family to sit it out for a week, if we had to. I also took Jane to the Royal Navy small-arms range on Stonecutter Island, in the middle of Hong Kong Harbour, and taught her how to fire a pistol and a submachine-gun. In the event, of course, nothing happened, and everything stayed peaceful in Hong Kong, though I learned later that it was at one time touch and go. I suspect the cache of food and equipment I carefully hid in 1968 is probably still there today.

Typhoons, or the threat of typhoons, are part of the seasonal rhythm of Hong Kong life. Normally the typhoon period begins in June and ends in September. I had already been close to one typhoon (the great Wanda, which killed over 400 people in Hong Kong) when, on our way back to Singapore in 1962, we rode out the edge of the storm on board HMS *Bulwark*. Most of the typhoons during the season missed the island, though we often had strong winds and lashing rain as they brushed past us. In the summer of 1968, however, one typhoon hit us fair and square, with the eye of the storm passing right over the island. We were all sent home and told to sit away from plate-glass windows – for, if these shattered, the flying glass could kill. Jane and I put the kids in the sheltered back bedroom, pushed the furniture against our balcony picture window and barricaded ourselves, Tandy and the whisky bottle into a sheltered corner we had constructed in our living room. I remember very clearly watching the whisky in our glasses and the water in the lavatory slopping from side to side as the block of flats swayed in the wind. But the most extraordinary feature occurred not during the storm itself but when the eye passed over us. It lasted perhaps half an hour, during which the air was almost deathly still, before the wind came howling back at us, this time from completely the opposite direction.

But the dominant feature of my two-and-a-half years in Hong Kong was, of course, study, study and more study. I spent long hours in the Chinese Language School and at home listening to taped phrases and endlessly repeating them until I had the cadences and rhythms of the language firmly locked into my head, and I sweated hour after hour learning vocabulary and script through the use of 'flash cards'. These were small pieces of white cardboard, about the size of the old cigarette cards, which carried, on one side, the English word and on the other the Chinese character and its phonetic in *putonghua*. Everywhere I went I used to carry about two hundred of them, done up in a rubber band, and in every spare moment would pull them out and go through them, only removing a card from the pile when I was able to look at the English and instantly both say and write the Chinese – and vice versa.

Chinese is not, as it is often regarded, a difficult language from a grammatical point of view. In fact the grammar is relatively simple. What makes it difficult is the fact that Chinese is monosyllabic, with the difference between one word and another being conveyed by tone. There are four tones in *putonghua* (seven in Cantonese). The first tone is a steady tone which neither rises nor falls. The second tone rises. The third dips and then rises, and the fourth falls. It is essential to get these tones right if you wish to avoid saying something completely different from what you intended. For instance the word *mai*, said in the third tone, means to buy something. But the same word in the fourth tone means to sell it.

This provides not only many traps for the unwary, but it also gives almost inexhaustible scope for punning, which the Chinese love, especially when the pun is pornographic – and most particularly when a foreigner, trying to say something polite, ends up saying instead something completely disgusting. On one occasion, at a Chinese Language School dinner, during one of those moments of silence which always seem to attend a conversational catastrophe, I attempted polite small talk with a very refined Chinese lady sitting next to me by asking her if she had ever flown in an aircraft. I got my tones wrong and asked her, instead, if she had ever sat on a flying penis. I couldn't understand why all my Chinese dinner companions collapsed in uproarious laughter. Which was hardly surprising: it was another six months before I finally got to that word in the Chinese lexicon!

The other means of distinguishing meaning is to string together a compound noun consisting of two monosyllabic words. So, for instance, an aircraft is *fei ji*, or flying machine, and a train is *huo che*, or fire car. The trap here is the order. Even if you get the tone right, reversing the order can still be catastrophic. On one occasion I did just this and found myself explaining to a full class which I had joined late, that my tardiness was due to the fact that I had left in my car, not my briefcase, but my testicles.

All this means that to learn spoken Chinese you need a good ear, a capacity to pick up cadences and a thick enough skin not to mind a disaster or two. But what you need to learn written Chinese is a prodigious memory. There is no alphabet in Chinese. Each word is represented by a pictogram which has its own meaning and value, independent of its phonetic pronunciation. Arabic numerals have this quality in European languages. Take the figure 4: the English say 'four', the French say 'quatre' and the Germans say 'vier', but the written symbol is the same in all three languages. In Chinese, this principle extends across the whole language; thus, although two people speaking the local dialects of, say, Canton and Beijing will not be able to understand each other if they speak, they can if they resort to pen and paper. It also means that the Chinese written script is one of the major unifying forces of what is, in reality, a collection of peoples as disparate as the populations of Europe. A Cantonese is as different in physique, temperament, cuisine and habits from a Manchurian as a Sicilian is from an Aberdonian Scot. But in China they can all read the same newspapers and the same literature and, above all, appreciate the same calligraphers, the greatest of whom are much revered throughout the land. Indeed one of the things which made Mao so influential in China was not just that he was a great military commander and political leader, but also a much-admired calligrapher and poet.

For poor foreigners trying to learn the language, however, the written script is not a boon, but a torture. For it means that you have to learn each pictogram, individually and one by one. Instead of 26 letters in the alphabet, there are literally countless thousands. An educated Chinese is said to know in excess of forty thousand characters. To read the Chinese equivalent of *The Times*, you need perhaps fifteen thousand, and for a tabloid newspaper around ten thousand. Our task at the end of two-and-a-half years was to be able to read a broadsheet newspaper and write essays in Chinese script – requiring a knowledge of somewhere between thirteen and fifteen thousand characters.

In late 1968 Jane and the children left Hong Kong to visit my family in Australia, flying to Singapore and then picking up a passenger-carrying freighter to Port Moresby in Papua New Guinea, where the boat broke down. It was a pretty nightmarish journey for them all, as the ship had no air-conditioning, with the result that Simon and Kate got very bad monsoon blisters. To make matters worse, the boat's guard rails were completely inadequate for young children. But Jane, resourceful as ever, managed to cash in the rest of her ticket and bought an air passage to Melbourne where she was met by my father and mother, who were meeting their daughter-in-law and grandchildren for the first time. They spent a wonderful Christmas with the family, before returning to Hong Kong in March 1969.

It was about this time that one day, completely unannounced, I got a rather mysterious call from someone introducing himself as a member of the Hong Kong Government, who asked me if I would like to join him for lunch at an out-of-the-way but rather good Chinese restaurant. Intrigued, I agreed. He spoke good Chinese, but we conversed solely in English. He said he was a member of the Foreign Office, and that they were looking for people like me who had had what he described as 'wide experience in some difficult circumstances' and could speak Chinese. Would I be interested in joining? I knew perfectly what was going on. This was not the Foreign Office proper; if this led anywhere it would end with my being asked to go abroad, not to lie for my country (as the Elizabethan Sir Henry Wotton defined the diplomat's role), but to spy for it. But I went along with the game, expressing wide-eyed surprise and, dissimulating enthusiastically, said that I had always wanted to 'work for the Foreign Office'. Although I heard nothing further from my interlocutor, merely receiving an obscure form to fill in which had 'Foreign and Commonwealth Office' at the top, this strange lunch set in motion a train of events which I neither knew of nor had hints about at the time, but which would change my life completely when I returned to UK.

By now the end of my course was fast approaching. My final exams were to be in February 1970, and I wanted to spend the last two months as I had started, living with a Chinese family and immersing myself in the language. Jane flew back with the children just after Christmas 1969, and I moved back into the habits and environment of a Chinese living in Hong Kong.

On 14 February 1970, two weeks before my twenty-ninth birthday, I took my final exams gaining a First-class Interpretership in Chinese, recognised by the Civil Service at the time as being the equivalent of a first-class degree in the language. Before I left Hong Kong, I was promoted to Captain and received my next posting. I was to return to the UK to take command of Echo (E) Company 41 Commando Royal Marines. My student days were over. It was back to soldiering again.

CHAPTER 8

Active Service: Belfast

I TOOK THE OPPORTUNITY to visit my family in Australia on my way back from Hong Kong in February 1970, spending a fortnight with them before travelling back to the UK to be reunited with Jane and the children.

We immediately started house-hunting in the Plymouth area, so that we could move the family down there as soon as I joined my new unit, which was stationed in Bickleigh, on the edge of Dartmoor between Plymouth and Tavistock.

At the time, a gratuity of a thousand pounds (a very great deal of money in those days, when the average house cost about four thousand) was given to all those who achieved a First-class Interpretership in Chinese, and we wanted to use this to buy our first house. But we could find nothing we liked and so settled for a rented cottage in Horrabridge, five miles south of Tavistock, which for the first four months of my new job we used as our home and a base for further house-hunting in the area. I took command of my new unit, Echo Company, 41 Commando Royal Marines, on 5 May 1970. To my delight I found that I had as my second-in-command an old friend, Alan Hooper, for whose soldiering skills and intelligence I had a very high regard.

Alan and I drove the Company very hard in those early days. By then the troubles in Northern Ireland had started, and I knew that it was only a matter of time before we would have to go there. So we had to move fast if we were to create an effective and cohesive unit which could cope with the pressures of the very difficult kind of soldiering we would find on the streets of Belfast. We practised the techniques of crowd control and patrolling in an urban environment, of course. But it wasn't techniques I was so interested in – anyone can acquire those. In these kinds of operations, the weight falls not on the senior officers, but on the junior commander on the spot: at the road block, or the point of interface with a hostile crowd, or in the aftermath of a bomb attack. So Alan and I spent a lot of time building up the initiative, quality and self-reliance of our junior commanders in the Company, ensuring that they had the confidence of the Marines they commanded and knew that they had our confidence, as well.

We spent a lot of time on initiative training in small groups on Dartmoor. It was on one of these in the early summer of 1976 that I was passing a flooded clay pit when I saw someone about three hundred yards away throw a package into the water. I watched for a moment and saw the package resurface and then noticed ripples circling out from it. It was alive! I reached the edge of the water just as a bedraggled and half-drowned dog emerged. I took her home to Jane and the children, who fell in love with her immediately. I said, rather pretentiously, that in view of her origins we should call her after a Chinese water nymph, but they ignored this and christened her Tina, and so she remained.

She was, I think, the best dog we ever had.

She was a half-Alsatian, half-greyhound and as fast and agile as a knife. I have seen her catch rabbits, flushed out from a hedgerow by a friend's Jack Russell terrier, in mid-field. And she would often bring me pheasants she had caught on the ground before they had time to fly. But she was, by nature, as soft as butter and adored our children. Later, when we had a cat, Boney, Tina adored her, too. Indeed, when Boney had kittens it was Tina who looked after them, carrying them in her mouth upstairs to the airing cupboard, one by one, every night, with the cat following imperiously, like an aristocratic lady supervising her nursemaid wheeling the children in the park.

I used to take her to work with me every day, where she ran with us on our morning runs and sat under my desk when I was in my office. She had, however, one distressing habit which I could never rid her of. She would sidle up to any Marine I was upbraiding for some failure or other and lick him on the hand, or even, if I was really cross, put her paws on his shoulders and lick his face in a gesture of comfort and solidarity. This, of course, did nothing to enhance the dignity and severity of my reprimand. But my Marines loved her for it.

During the summer Jane and I finally found the house of our dreams. It was a stone cottage, which, as a hunting lodge, had featured in the Domesday Book and was set in a deep valley about three-quarters of a mile from the little Devon village of Milton Combe (famous in the area for a very good pub called 'Who'd Have Thought It?'). It was called Lillipit Cottage and came with an acre of land and a lively little trout stream running through the garden. Despite the fact that it was somewhat dilapidated and needed a complete new roof, we fell in love with it at first sight and offered £6,700 for it – £200 more than the asking price. To our delight our offer was accepted, and we moved in during the summer of 1970.

Our first task was the roof, and this presented us with a real problem. It consisted of the old-style Cornish Delabole slates (smaller than modern slates) which are very much a feature of this part of Devon and, of course, unobtainable, except at an exorbitant price. But luck was on our side. We selected from the Yellow Pages a local part-time builder and part-time poacher, who came with a team of roofers and a very great deal of local knowledge. I explained the problem, and he tapped his nose and told me not to worry. 'We'm be right,' he promised – and was as good as his word. The antique slates duly appeared in sufficient quantities to complete the job. I thought it impolitic to ever ask him where they came from – though I did notice on our Dartmoor exercises that some of the abandoned barns and farmsteads in out-of-the-way places on the moor suddenly looked a bit more roofless than, I fancied, they had been before.

Jane and I then threw ourselves into redecorating, repairing and refurbishing the inside before turning our attention to the garden. Jane, who is a passionate gardener, created a really beautiful cottage flower garden, while I walled and dammed the stream, built a garage, repaired the bridge, constructed a greenhouse and a tree house for the kids and turned the front paddock into an apple orchard. Meanwhile Kate got enrolled in the local school, and we became increasingly embedded in the local community. Jane also acquired a veritable aviary of domestic fowls to go with Tina and (after Northern Ireland) Boney the cat. These included five Khaki Campbell ducks, dominated by an extremely amorous drake called Barnabas; three bantam chickens, including a cock we called Chantecleer, who was extremely elderly and moth-eaten and used to potter into our kitchen on a winter's day and, like a drunk at a bar, lean against our Aga for warmth. This feathered menagerie was further supplemented by six white doves, who went feral on us, and a succession of guinea-fowl (they call them gleenies in Devon) who, it appeared, we kept chiefly for the benefit of the local foxes, for they gratefully ate them as fast as Jane could replace them, until she finally gave up the unequal struggle.

For the first time since I had been a boy in Ireland, I felt the joy of putting down roots and having a place of permanence. It was, therefore, with mixed feelings that I received the long-anticipated orders to go to Belfast at the end of August of that year.

I found the process of going back to my home city far more painful than I had ever imagined it would be. The troubles did not come as a surprise. Even from an early age I had known that the discrimination against Catholics in Northern Ireland would be bound to lead to some reaction. But the ferocity of the violence shocked me, as did the way that it affected my old Northern Ireland friends and acquaintances. I was discovering what I would see in even sharper relief later in Bosnia: that the proximity of violence can transform even the most reasonable and civilised of people, and that the seemingly robust barrier separating civilisation from animal brutality is in fact a wispy, fragile thing which, once torn down, unleashes a bestiality that seems to empower neighbour to do indescribable things to neighbour – and which takes a very long time to put back.

Each of 42 Commando's companies was assigned an area of the city to look after. Echo Company was given the Old Park Road and Ardoyne areas in the west of Belfast and was based in an old mill building in Flax Street, just off the Crumlin Road.

This was an area I knew well as a boy. I had cousins in this part of the city and friends, too. The news reports had prepared me for the physical destruction – though I remember being deeply shocked at the Old Markets area, where, as a seventeen-year-old, I had helped my father sell his lettuces. The thing which really stunned me most, however, was the feeling that the city of my youth was being brutalised by an army of occupation – and we were that army! I knew why we were there, fully supported it and had no doubts about the need for our presence. But none of this diminished the shock that it had come to this. Or the pain of realising that, for my military colleagues, this was just another 'internal security' operation, no different from what we had done together in Aden, Malaysia and Brunei.

But for me it was different. This was my city as well as my theatre of operations. Suddenly I found the Irish jokes increasingly tiresome and the black-and-white certainties of our operational assumptions increasingly inappropriate. For the first time I was beginning to see military operations not just from the viewpoint of the soldier patrolling the street, but from that of the person living in the street as well. And I found it very uncomfortable. A friend with whom I have discussed this since has concluded that this was all because I was beginning to get tired of the profession of soldiering. But I do not think so. I felt just as dedicated to what I was doing, but much less certain that the way we were going about it was right.

We were all provided with what were called 'tribal maps' of Belfast, which showed the Catholic and Protestant estates coloured differently and the mixed areas shaded with both colours. The map showed me what, from boyhood, I already knew: that my patch was divided equally between Catholic and Protestant, with the Ardoyne being predominantly the former, the Old Park area predominantly the latter, and the Bone district fiercely divided between the two.

My day in Belfast began at 6 a.m. with a debrief of the night's patrols and receiving the reports of those on guard at fixed points on our patch. During the morning Alan Hooper and I would plan the day's patrols, trying to ensure that we always kept a stand-by unit ready for emergencies, that we treated Catholic and Protestant areas scrupulously the same, and that every part of our area had at least one visit from one of our patrols in every twenty-four-hour period. The main time for trouble came at the weekend and after darkness fell, so we would always have our operations room fully manned with one or other of us present during these times and at other moments of tension. Our day usually ended at around 2 a.m., when I would take a turn round the area in my Land Rover to make sure the 'patch' was quiet before going to bed. I do not normally need very much sleep and at the time did not find it particularly hard to maintain this routine. But when I came home at the end of our three-month tour I suddenly found myself more exhausted by lack of sleep and tension than I can ever remember being before or since.

At this time the British Army was still regarded by many in the Catholic community as saviours who had come to protect them from Protestant violence. But I could feel the mood changing. In July, shortly before we arrived, a highly unpopular curfew had been imposed on the Catholic Falls Road area, and many Catholic families had been burnt out of their homes in the largely Catholic area of the Ardoyne, where the gutted, burnt-out shells of whole terraces of houses acted as a stark reminder of the security forces' inability or unwillingness to prevent this from happening. Bloody Sunday and internment, still eighteen months away, would finally and catastrophically lose us the confidence and support of even moderate elements of Northern Ireland's Catholic community, after which it would take thirty or more years of patient politics before we would finally be able to retrieve the situation and recreate the ingredients from which peace might be built. But at this time I felt that the early confidence in us among the majority of the Catholic population of Belfast was not yet irredeemably lost. The key battle, therefore, was not for order on the streets but for hearts and minds. I started a small youth club for the deprived youth of both religious traditions in my area and took them for a two-day outing to an old fishing haunt I used to visit with my father, the beautiful lake and castle at Castlewellan. Our first trip was a great success. But the numbers then started mysteriously to decline. When I asked one of the mothers why her son had withdrawn, she told me that she had been 'instructed by the men' not to let her child go off with the British Army. In retrospect, it was probably rather naive of me to imagine that it could ever have been otherwise, but I remember being really depressed about this at the time.

Although we all knew (and our intelligence reports confirmed) that the IRA had a presence in Belfast and in the Ardoyne at the time, they appeared to me to be supported by only a relatively small minority of the Catholic population. It was the Northern Ireland Civil Rights Association (or NICRA) who were the main (and, in my private view, entirely justified) vehicle for Catholic protest. NICRA in my area was run by a remarkable old man called Frank McGlade, who lived in one of the Catholic working-class terraced houses in the Bone district, about a hundred yards from the back gate of the mill in which we were stationed. Frank was around sixty and something of a local legend among the Catholics as a man of principle and courage. He had been an Irish nationalist activist all his life, had spent a considerable amount of time in prison and was a founder member of NICRA. He was also, according to our intelligence, the commander of the local IRA unit. One day – mostly, I have to confess, on a whim – I decided I would call on him. I walked up the street to his house, unannounced, alone and without any arms (but in my uniform) and knocked on his door. My intention at the time was simply to meet him and talk about the local situation and what we could do to make it better. It was, to say the least, a naive hope and a stupid way of going about trying to realise it.

Frank McGlade's wife opened the door and, seeing my uniform, naturally believed that I had come to arrest her husband. All hell broke loose and I had to beat a hasty retreat. The next day the Catholic newspapers (including, if I recall, the *Irish Times* in Dublin) were full of stories of a British Army Captain intimidating an elderly and much respected local citizen. I have since met Frank's two daughters who remember that incident well and have even asked me to write a piece for a memorial article on their father, a man for whom I had then, and retain now, a considerable respect and admiration.

But back then it was the articles in the local papers which mattered, not my rather muddled intentions. On my next visit to Commando Headquarters, I was quietly taken to one side by the Intelligence Officer, who told me that I had now been placed on the local IRA death list. That night I jumped into my Land Rover with my two signalmen and driver to begin my usual end-of-the-day tour round the patch, to find that, with typical Marine gallows humour, they had chalked on the Land Rover door where my seat was, a big white cross and the words 'This is the bloke you want, Paddy. We're innocent. X marks the spot.'

As our tour in Belfast drew to a close, the temperature on the streets started to rise sharply. In late October 1970 the Catholic/Protestant interface at the upper end of the Shankill Road erupted, and Echo Company were called upon to deal with it.

Dante conjuring up his inferno in modern times would easily have recognised the scene which greeted me as I parked my Land Rover on the pavement and deployed one of Echo Company's Troops (about 35 strong) in full riot gear between the two sides, with orders to keep them apart at all costs.

A great pall of black smoke hung over us, and the cacophony of noise and shouting threatened to drive all rational thought out of the brain. In front of me there was a crowd of about two thousand Catholics who had marched down from Unity Flats in Brown Square, about five hundred yards away. Behind me were about the same number of Protestants coming the other way. Each was determined to get at the other. The crowd in front of me had left a trail of burning cars behind them as they marched down the street, and one enterprising group of young men had even managed to get a lorry laden with straw bales from somewhere, set it alight and rolled it down the hill at us.

Fortunately it had stopped about a hundred yards short and was now burning away merrily. Behind me they were launching all sorts of makeshift projectiles over our heads at the opposite side, and, somewhere in front, someone was firing a small calibre weapon (a pistol, I think), but from too far away to be a serious danger.

The really serious threat came, not from firearms, but from the stones, bits of pavement and, above all, lethally sharp fragments of cast-iron drain covers which both crowds now started to throw at us – having now recognised that we were the common enemy they had to dispose of before they could deal with each other. Several of my Marines had already gone down, one with a very nasty head wound, and I was getting increasingly worried that if I did not pull back, or get reinforcements fast, we would be overrun. I was on the radio asking Alan Hooper to send in our reserve Troop, prepositioned in a quiet side street just round the corner, as fast as he could, when a huge mountain of female Shankill Road Protestant fury came charging up to me, bosoms heaving dangerously and face suffused with anger. 'You fuckin' English fuckin' bastard,' she screamed above the noise,

> What are you fuckin' doing here? Why don't you fuckin' go back to fuckin' England and fuckin' leave us in fuckin' peace? Can't youse fuckin' see you're not fuckin' wanted here? And anyway why can't youse fuckin' show any fuckin' respect?

The tirade rose to a crescendo, ending explosively:

> Can't youse fuckin' see? Youse've got your fuckin' Land Rover parked outside our fuckin' church and it's a fuckin' SUNDAY!

I did not tell her I was a fellow-countryman, or that I would have dearly loved to be back in England at that particular moment, since neither fact seemed very relevant either to my fears about the situation, or to her concerns about our breach of church etiquette.

A few moments later, the reserve troop arrived. But still our numbers were insufficient to restore the situation. Eventually neighbouring units had to be called in, increasing our numbers to more than a hundred, before the riot subsided, and people went home.

In the following weeks we had a number of serious riots like this one, and it was after one of these, in the Bone area, that I came down in the morning to find a little tortoise-shell kitten sleeping on the front seat of my Land Rover. I called her Boney, after the riot of the night before, and took her home to Jane and the kids, who immediately adopted her as one of our family. She eventually became very widely travelled for a little Belfast moggie, for four years later we took her with us to Switzerland, where she used to insist on accompanying us on our boat whenever we went sailing on Lake Geneva.

The crisis came to a peak in early November, just before we went home, when there was another nasty riot on the Crumlin Road, between the Catholics in the Ardoyne and the Protestants on the other side of the road. Once again we were caught in the middle. The rioting lasted all night, and several Marines were badly injured by stones and nail bombs, which, for the first time in Northern Ireland, began to appear in the rioters' armoury. One of these seriously injured one of my Marines and blew me up against a wall, but left me otherwise unharmed. I was luckier than our much-loved and respected Colonel, Pat Griffiths, who received a near-fatal head wound from a flying rock and was lucky to survive.

Active service is very often a mixture of the terrifying and the bizarre, and Northern Ireland proved no exception. One day in late October I was summoned to the military intelligence cell in Belfast headquarters. They explained that the Government had received a request from journalists working for the Chinese *People's Daily* to visit Belfast with their cameramen. It was clear, they said, that the Chinese were intent on giving the worst possible picture of Northern Ireland (I refrained from saying that I didn't see how it was possible to give a good one). They wanted me to be part of the 'facilitation' team that looked after the Chinese delegation, without letting them know that I could speak Chinese. My job would be to hang around, listen to what they said and report back. It seemed a pretty preposterous piece of espionage to me, but I went along with it, changing into civilian clothes and skulking around trying to catch what the journalists were talking about. The itinerary requested by the Chinese took us to one of my own Company locations, where the sight of their Company Commander trying to disguise his presence while carrying out this clandestine charade caused some initial puzzlement amongst my Marines, followed by open hilarity and much leg-pulling later. As my first foray into espionage, this was hardly successful either, for, though I heard and understood almost all they said, there was precisely nothing of any interest to anyone except themselves.

Our tour in Belfast ended in mid-November, and we all returned home to a period of leave and a very welcome Christmas with our families. As usual, it was only when I got home that I realised what a burden all this had placed on Jane, who had had to look after Kate and Simon without any help from me, as well as coping with the strains of having a husband away in a battle zone. She told me that the one fixed point she and the children insisted on every night, was watching the Six-o'clock News 'to see if they could see Daddy', and the pictures of what was happening had horrified her and caused her sleepless nights, though she had, of course, kept her fears hidden from the children. Kate, aged five, was, however, more angry than horrified, and she developed the habit of accosting strange men in the supermarket and saying in a very loud voice, 'My Daddy is in Belfast. Why aren't you?'

Belfast also made me much more aware of politics. Here is an extract from an article I wrote for the *British Army Review* in 1971:

> The truth of the matter is that the Services must nowadays be regarded as as much a part of the executive organ of Government as, say, the Tax Office or the Foreign Office or the Department of Trade and Industry. Yet we are singularly ill-equipped to fulfil this role. Ask a junior commander to include 'Politics' as one of the factors he should consider in a military appreciation, and he will probably react with horror. And yet I feel certain that this is what we must learn to accept. We are, after all, primarily and fundamentally political animals. By this I mean that both the stimulus for our actions and the results of them are essentially political in nature. This has, of course, probably always been true to a degree, but our increasingly close and obvious involvement in the political scene today makes it a fact we can afford to ignore no longer . . . we must clearly understand that a greater knowledge of politics and a more easy familiarity with its ways is an essential of modern-day soldiering, and one which we ignore at our peril.*

* Captain J.J.D. Ashdown, Royal Marines, 'The Officer as a Political Animal', *British Army Review*, no. 39, December 1971.

In March the following year, I flew my Company up to Scotland to test their endurance and their ability to work in small groups. The exercise began with a night landing on a secluded beach on the Mull of Kintyre, after which we did a series of night approach marches, lying up during the day, to Campbeltown, where we carried out a raid on nearby RAF Machrihanish. We then broke up into small groups of two or three and, using escape and evasion techniques, made our way to a rendezvous point with fishing vessels on the east coast of the Kintyre peninsula. These took us across the straits to the Isle of Arran, which had to be crossed close to its highest point, Goat Fell, at night in order to make the final dawn pick up on a beach near Lochranza on the north of the island. It was a tough exercise which required both endurance and skill, and I was very proud that, with very few exceptions, all my Marines made it to the final pick-up.

When I crossed the shoulder of Goat Fell that night the sky was clear and blazing with stars, and a deep frost, sparkling under a full moon, lay over all the land below. As I crested the hill I saw the great shimmering expanse of the Firth of Clyde, pointing like a silver finger towards the loom of Glasgow's lights in the distance and edged by the dark mass of the Ayrshire coast, spangled with towns and villages spilling down to its water's edge. I am not a religious person but twice in my life I have had what I think were quasi-religious experiences, in which I felt, almost tangibly, the presence of something far beyond my comprehension and which was both sublime and omnipotent. One was in 1996, when I looked down from the top of Brunelleschi's dome to see Florence and the Arno laid out at my feet; the other was on that March night on Goat Fell on the Isle of Arran.

When I got back from this exercise, I was told that it was time for me to start preparing to go to Staff College in order to qualify for further promotion. But by now it was already clear to me that, since that mysterious lunch in Hong Kong, wheels had been turning behind the scenes, and the direction of my life was about to change again.

Shortly after I returned to UK from the Far East I had received another mysterious phone call. 'The Foreign Office' had noted my Chinese exam results. If I was interested in following up my lunchtime conversation in Hong Kong, they would like to meet again. Another lunch was duly arranged in London, this time in a most expensive and salubrious restaurant (as I later discovered, eating seems to be an important concurrent activity when it comes to both diplomacy and espionage). Again no mention was made of the true identity of my prospective employers. My lunch companion simply confined himself to outlining the procedures. There were certain exams to take, then an interview to undergo, and finally a process designed to test initiative and lateral thinking, which included a psychological profile. All this would entitle me to enter as a 'fast-stream' and 'late-entry' member of the Diplomatic Service. It would probably take a year or so to go through. Did I want to proceed? I said I did, and we agreed to launch the process but reserve final decisions for both sides until later. We then got down to a very agreeable lunch washed down, as I recall, by a fair quantity of exceptionally good wine. As a humble 'grunt' Marine, I viewed all this as rather romantic and very exciting. But I was never in any doubt about the true nature of the approach, despite my host's best efforts to disguise this with little anecdotes designed to lend verisimilitude to his claim to come from the Foreign Office.

During 1971 I completed the exams and interviews. At the end of this process, which included, without my knowing it, a rigorous check on my background, I was called into an anonymous office close to St James's Park in central London, where the real identity of my prospective employers was revealed and I was asked if I would like to join them. I affected the surprise and astonishment apparently expected of me – and immediately accepted the invitation. It was decided that I should leave the Royal Marines and start my new career in the middle of 1972.

I originally hoped that I could see out the remainder of my time in 'The Corps' as Company Commander of my beloved E Company. But events soon dictated otherwise. In June 1971 we heard that 41 Commando was to leave Bickleigh and take up temporary quarters on an old World War Two hutted camp on Dartmoor, in preparation for being posted to Malta in the autumn. Whenever a military unit goes on a foreign posting such as this, it leaves behind a 'rear party' whose job it is to look after the unit's interests at home and to assist with welfare and administrative issues that can only be resolved in the UK. Since I was about to leave anyway, I was the obvious person to command 41 Commando's rear party during their deployment in Malta.

I understood the logic of this, but I hated giving up E Company, and hated even more the drudgery of the purely administrative tasks which were now about to take up all my time. So I decided to try to learn another language and enrolled with someone who taught me German in my spare time.

With the Commando gone, the last months of 1971 were very quiet, and I thought they would remain so until I started my new life in the shadows in mid-1972. But on 29 December, after a wonderful family Christmas (my mother had come over from Australia), the phone rang in the corner of our sitting room in Lillipit. It was the MOD duty officer in London, who told me that Dom Mintoff, the Prime Minister of Malta, had just announced that he was ending more than a hundred-and-fifty years of connection with Britain and kicking all British forces off the island. The withdrawal would start immediately, with the wives and families flying back in two weeks, and the Commando following four weeks after that. There was, he explained, a severe shortage of suitable accommodation in the UK, and the only place where they could all be housed was a closed and largely derelict World War Two wooden-hutted army camp at Houndstone, outside Yeovil. I was to go there immediately, open the place up and get it ready, first for the families and then, in due course, for the Commando. I left that night in a mixture of driving rain and snow and arrived in the outskirts of Yeovil at about 11 p.m., leaving instructions for the rest of the rear party to follow the following day. When I got to the camp it was locked, and there was no one about. So I broke open the door to one of the empty wooden huts, laid out my sleeping bag and went to sleep on the floor. And that was how I spent my first night in the area which I was subsequently to represent in Parliament, both in the Commons and the Lords, and which was to become our family home for the rest of our life.

Just as I am not very religious, I am not superstitious either. So I do not believe much in premonitions. But, again, there are exceptions. The following morning was cold, the hut damp, and I was grumpy at being here rather than back at home. But through the cracked window-panes of the hut in which I had spent the night I looked out on frost-covered trees, silver meadows and a champagne December morning, and was quite suddenly hit by the unbidden and totally surprising pre-monition that this was where I was going to spend the rest of my life.

The feeling soon passed, however, as I got down to the grinding business of opening up long-deserted family quarters for the returning wives and children, doing deals with local tradesmen to provide them with the necessities of life on tick, because the families' finances had not yet been sorted out, and working with Yeovil District Council* to ensure that they were properly provided for. As with my previous experience as the Mess Deck Officer of HMS *Bulwark*, I loved it, made firm friends in the local community, learned how local councils worked and acquired a huge admiration for the skills and sense of service of most of the Council's employees.

Jane came to see me one weekend, leaving the children with her parents at nearby Burnham-on-Sea. I told her I had fallen in love with the area. When we had to leave Lillipit to go to London for my new job, would it not be a good idea to buy a little cottage here and a small flat in London? As a Somerset girl born and bred she jumped at the idea of having our roots once again in her native county, and we started looking for a house. We eventually found Vane Cottage, which sits in the middle of a terrace in Great Street in the little village of Norton Sub Hamdon, about six miles from Yeovil. It was exactly what we were looking for. We sold Lillipit with great sadness – though we were not sad about the price we got (£24,000, which meant we had quadrupled what we had paid for it in just over two years).† With the proceeds we bought Vane Cottage for £14,750 and moved into it during the summer of 1972 – it is our home still. Shortly afterwards we were also able to buy a small flat in Wimbledon, which we would use when I started my new job in September 1972.

Meanwhile, first the wives and families returned, and then the unit, and, after seeing them properly settled into the camp, I took my leave of the Royal Marines in August 1972, after thirteen years and three months of service.

---

* Now South Somerset District Council.
† On a visit to the Plymouth area in 1999, Jane and I returned to Lillipit, to discover that it had just changed hands at a price well in excess of a quarter of a million.
  I imagine that the selling price at the height of the recent housing boom would have risen to nearer a million.

CHAPTER 9

Diplomacy and Shadows

W RITING THIS CHAPTER in our lives presents me with a problem. Before I started my new job I undertook a lifetime obligation never to reveal in public either the name of the organisation for which I worked or anything beyond the barest outline of what I did. For reasons which are no doubt excellent, the authorities have asked me to stick to this undertaking and to go no further than the words used by my old friend Sir Menzies Campbell, then Leader of the Lib Dems, in an interview in the *Evening Standard* in September 2007, when he, perhaps inadvertently, admitted that I had been 'in the more shadowy side of Foreign Office activity'. And I have agreed to do that.

I started my new job with a small collection of fellow trainees, in September 1972, when Jane and I also moved into our newly purchased flat in Wimbledon. At weekends, we regularly bundled the children, the dog and the cat onto a mattress in the back of our old mini-van on a Friday night and drove down to Vane Cottage, returning on Sunday night.

Our training took place in a faceless building in south London and in an equally faceless establishment in the south of England where we learned all the skills and techniques necessary to our trade. We also learned about the past successes of the British intelligence community, such as the recruitment and running of the great British agent Oleg Penkovsky. And we learned of our failures, too: Philby, Maclean and the rest of the Cambridge five, as well as Blake. This, as I soon discovered, is a world which teeters, sometimes crazily, between high drama and danger at one end and farce and hilarity at the other.

My favourite story from these times concerns the period when I was fighting in our little conflict in Borneo (though, sadly, I have to confess it may be apocryphal, since it was vouchsafed to me one rather bibulous evening by an 'old hand' who claimed to have been there). His tale went thus. Despite the fact that Britain was, in effect, at war with Indonesia, both countries maintained diplomatic relations with each other and embassies in each other's capitals. As you might imagine, the Jakarta

Embassy was one of the biggest in the world at the time. Some way into the conflict, an expert in these things thought he spotted something in the behaviour and demeanour of the Indonesian President, General Sukarno which, he believed, could be the tell-tale signs of a fatal illness. He announced that if, somehow or another, one of the President's stools could be obtained, then not only could the illness be confirmed but a fair estimate could be made of how long he had to live. Jakarta was asked to obtain one of the articles in question, preferably in pristine condition, as a matter of the most urgent priority.

Early attempts, including the recruitment of some of the President's personal cleaning staff resulted in a series of near-misses, but, as they say, no coconut. About this time, a tunnel dug under the Berlin wall to intercept Russian communication cables on the other side was discovered and closed down by the Russians, leaving a lot of secret but now redundant tunnellers in the pay of the British Government. So the Jakarta office were instructed to obtain not only an accurate plan of the layout of the Presidential Palace, including, crucially, the drainage and sewage pipes, but also a 'safe house' as close as possible to the perimeter of the Presidential grounds. This done, a team of tunnellers were secretly flown out to Jakarta and tasked to dig a tunnel from the safe house to intercept the drain running from the President's personal loo. In this way a near pristine example of the sought-after article was finally intercepted on its journey to the outside world, carefully bagged and packed with ice to stop deterioration, and then smuggled from hand to hand, through a series of dead-letter boxes, until it finally reached the safety of the British Embassy. Here it was put into the diplomatic bag and flown with utmost urgency back to London. The story did not have the expected ending, however. When the item was examined it was discovered that the Indonesian President was in rude and robust health!

When I first joined, our headquarters was in an anonymous multi-storey tower block south of the Thames, whose existence was never supposed to be made public. Indeed, we were all instructed to approach it with discretion, taking appropriate precautions. The game was, however, rather given away by the conductors of the London buses that passed our door at regular intervals: they delighted in announcing the local bus stop with a cheery (and usually very loud) shout of, 'Lambeth Tube Station. All spies alight 'ere!'

After training, I worked for a few months in a department of the London headquarters before getting my first foreign posting – to Geneva where I was to take up the public post of a First Secretary in the United Kingdom Mission to the United Nations. Alert readers will recall that my expertise was as a Chinese-speaker, whereas in Geneva they speak French, a language in which I received the all-time record low mark of 2.5% in my school 'O' levels. In fact, however, posting me to Geneva was not quite as foolish as it might, on the face of it, have seemed. For Anglo-Chinese relations were just beginning to warm up slightly, after many years in the deep freeze following the sacking and burning of the British Embassy in Peking in 1967. One of my tasks in Geneva was to see if we could help the process of Anglo-Chinese diplomatic *rapprochement* through contact within the 'neutral' framework of the United Nations.

Nevertheless, Geneva meant learning my fifth language, French.* This led in due course to a house in France, a French son-in-law and French grandchildren – yet another way in which fortunate circumstance, rather than planning, has shaped my life.

I flew out to Geneva for a short visit to prepare for the job and find a house for the family just before Christmas 1973, taking out a lease on a very beautiful but very run-down house, Maison Kundig, on the shores of Lake Geneva. It had its own pier and boathouse in the little village of Coppet, some six miles from the city.

Before making the final move, Jane and I were told we would have to attend a 'pre-deployment course' in the training department of the Foreign Office (in full, the Foreign and Commonwealth Office, or FCO). When we got there we discovered that, rather than being an induction into the mysteries of diplomacy, this was actually devoted entirely to matters of etiquette. There were lessons in how to lay a table, how to fold napkins correctly and how to hold our knives and forks. All of which was laid out in diagrammatical form in a book they presented to us at the end of the course, in case we absent-mindedly forgot how to do things properly when far from home shores. (These things are, I imagine, no longer part of the curriculum in today's modern Foreign Office.)

* When people ask me how many languages I speak, I say I have forgotten six. The problem with languages is that if you don't use them you lose them. Whilst I still can pass the time of day and hold rudimentary conversations in all the languages I have tried to learn, I am nowadays only really comfortable in French. Though, interestingly enough, when once again immersed for any time in one of the languages I have studied, I find the old facility comes back quite quickly.

There were even lessons in how to employ and treat servants, which were given by the wife of the then head of the Foreign Office. She told us about servants in Africa (which we didn't think would have much relevance in Geneva), including one story designed, I suspect, to underline how important it was to brief your servants properly. She related how, one day when 'we' (her illustrious husband and herself) had been relatively junior and posted to some small African country, they had decided to have a gala dinner after the Queen's Birthday Party (the big event on every British Embassy calendar). To this they had invited, not only senior members of the local diplomatic corps, but also most of their host Government. Our redoubtable FCO hostess decided to splash out and serve roast suckling pig. She attended to every small detail, including supervising the cooking of the unfortunate animal, leaving only the serving to be carried out when the guests were safely at table. She firmly instructed the 'head boy' how the pig was to be served – with an apple in the mouth and sprigs of parsley coming out of the ears. When the great moment arrived the dish was duly borne in by the enthusiastic servant whose appearance was much enhanced, precisely as his mistress had instructed, by having an apple stuffed in his mouth and a sprig of parsley sticking out of each ear.

In the event, when we got to Geneva Jane initially tried to follow diplomatic practise of bringing in caterers to cook and serve the official dinners we gave. But we both found this so unpleasant that she soon decided to do the cooking herself, and we shared the job of serving it between us. We found this was more relaxing for our guests and more effective when it came to doing business.

But that was still some time ahead. At this stage we were still heavily engaged in preparing for our new life in Geneva. I was firmly informed by the Foreign Office that when I got to Geneva I would need a 'representational car'. I have never been much interested in cars, and both of us had grown rather attached to our mini-van, 907 PYD, the only car we had so far had since our marriage. Indeed Jane, who has a strong penchant for anthropomorphising almost anything, regarded 907 PYD as a fully paid up member of our extended family. It was therefore with sadness that we decided this old friend would have to be disposed of, and Jane agreed to do it, advertising for purchasers in the local paper. She quite quickly received an offer £60 from a nearby farmer who wanted to turn it into a mobile chicken shed. To my chagrin, she refused this with outrage and sold it instead for £40 to a young couple who, she said, would 'give it a good home'.

In early 1974 I took a couple of weeks' leave to help pack up our things and prepare to move house again (I remember calculating at the time that this was our twenty-first house move in twelve years of marriage). The country, meanwhile, was feverishly preparing itself for the February 1974 general election.

I had remained a Labour supporter, even in the face of the fiasco of the 1967 devaluation of the pound and the evident failures of the late 1960s Wilson Government. By this time, however, I do not think I would have called myself a socialist. My political beliefs were on the move, and I was inclined to think that the encouragement of responsible individualism and the creation of an effective meritocracy was a better route to social justice than state intervention and social engineering. But I still saw Labour – and especially its new stars, like Roy Jenkins and Shirley Williams – as the best available instrument for delivering this kind of Britain, by breaking the class structure and creating an industrial-relations system based on partnership in the workplace. I had, however become quite nervous about the power of the trades union movement, and especially about its ability to hold a government to ransom. Barbara Castle's 1969 White Paper 'In Place of Strife', which proposed a new, more constructive basis for industrial relations seemed to me, therefore, a powerful vindication of my support for Labour. I consequently felt utterly betrayed when the Labour Cabinet led by Jim Callaghan ditched this far-sighted programme in the face of union opposition. I concluded that Labour could never break its dependency on the unions and parted company with it in disgust.

I knew I could never be a Tory, of course, and thought the Liberal Party too small, too zany and too incoherent to be worth looking at. From about 1970, therefore, I turned away from politics and joined the millions in Britain whose attitude towards politicians of whatever party was basically, 'a plague on all your houses'. So, despite the fact that the 1974 election looked as though it would be an exciting one – with Labour and Tory neck-and-neck, and support for the Liberals, who had just won a stunning series of by-elections, on the rise – I felt neither excited nor engaged by the prospect of the imminent contest. My thoughts were on Geneva and what the next phase of my life would bring, and nothing else.

So the knock on my door, which came on a beautiful crisp cold day some time in the last week of January 1974, when I was digging in our back garden at Vane Cottage, was not at all welcome. I became even more grumpy, when I opened the door to discover that my caller was yet another canvasser, this time seeking my support for the local Liberals.

I am not much of a believer in Pauline conversions. With me, convictions grow slowly and take time to mature. But the actual event of my conversion to Liberalism is an exception. And the instrument of the epiphany, standing on my doorstep that sunny afternoon, took just about the most unlikely form it is possible to imagine.

I definitely remember that he wore an orange anorak, looked rather unprepossessing, and had a squeaky voice to match. But, for the rest, I suspect my memory may be playing tricks when it tells me he also had sandals and a wispy beard, since that sounds just too consistent with the then (and later) Liberal stereotype. I told him pretty roughly that I certainly would not vote Liberal, unless (which I considered highly unlikely) he could persuade me that I should. I don't quite know what happened next. But two hours later, having discussed liberalism at length in our front room, I discovered that this was what I had really always been. That Liberalism was an old coat that had been hanging in my cupboard, overlooked all these years, just waiting to be taken down and put on.

This is not to say that my visitor that day (whom I have diligently tried to find since, but without success) turned me into a Liberal activist. He had merely turned me into a Liberal voter. This was no more than the first small step on a long journey that, over the next two years, would include many other events which would slowly but inexorably change the course of my life again.

I cast my first vote for the Liberals by proxy from Geneva, in the February general election of 1974.

Just before the election we set off on our new adventure with Kate, Simon, our dog Tina and our cat Boney in a brand new and very posh British racing green Rover.

The first part did not go well. We planned to have dinner with a friend, Michael Aaronson,* who had been posted to the British Embassy in Paris. The plan was then to load ourselves and our car onto the car-transporter train which, in those days, ran between Paris and Saint-Gervais-les-Bains at the foot of Mont Blanc. From here we would drive the thirty kilometres or so to Geneva. What I did not count on, however, was Paris during the rush hour.

* Now Sir Michael Aaronson, and past Director General of Save the Children UK.

Very soon after entering the city we got hopelessly lost. Jane has many gifts, but map-reading is not one of them – just as one of mine is not keeping an even temper in these circumstances. So the inside of our car quickly became a scene out of Bedlam, with Jane and I shouting at each other in the front, the kids adding to the noise in the back, and the dog and the cat, convinced this was all a game, joining in with gusto. Eventually, in despair, I stopped the car and asked a man on one of those little French motorised bicycles how to get to the address Mike Aaronson had given me. He said he knew it well and would lead us there. So we set off behind him, weaving our way through the rush-hour traffic. It was only when I passed the same landmark for the third time that I realised that he was just as lost as I had been. He then, in his turn, stopped a motorist, who said, yes, he knew the place well and would take us there. And so our convoy was now three. But soon we were lost again. Finally, a taxi driver was hailed, and the convoy became four. And so it was that we were finally delivered to Mike Aaronson's house. Mike then led us to the station, where we loaded our car on the transporter, after which we joined him in a nearby restaurant for a splendid dinner. This was followed by a hair-raising return to the station, crammed (children, dog, cat and all) into Mike's open-topped MG. The dog and cat travelled in our sleeper with us on the long overnight journey to the Alps. The following morning I woke early and pulled the carriage blind to one side to see the snow-covered Alps sparkling above us in the sunlight. We unloaded our car and drove down the valley into the freezing fog which, as we were later to discover, frequently covers the whole of the basin of Lake Geneva in fine, still weather. Jane was initially terribly shocked when she saw how dirty and unkempt our home was, the result of being unlived in for some time. But we made a start on cleaning the house after we had unpacked our cases, and by the time we finished for the day, the sun had broken through the fog, revealing the whole great expanse of Lake Geneva before us and the Alps sparkling in the distance.

So began what was, I think, our happiest two years as a family. Kate and Simon were six and eight, and thus able to come with us everywhere. In the winter we learned to ski, first on the Jura Mountains, near St Cergue, where my grandfather had taken his annual winter holidays, and my father had learned to ski before me. (They used to stay at the Hotel Auberson, where old M. Auberson still remembered them quite clearly, whispering to me in a conspiratorial aside that my grandfather 'kept a mistress down on the lake' at the time.) Then, as our skiing improved, we regularly joined with friends to hire chalets in some of Switzerland's great Alpine resorts (Verbier was our favourite).

We joined forces with some new-found friends, Rosemary and Roy Billinge, and bought a small yacht, which we kept moored off our own jetty. It was just big enough for Jane and I and the children, at a squeeze, to sleep in overnight for summer weekend cruises on Lake Geneva. Our other summer passion was walking in the mountains, sometimes staying the night in high mountain huts with other friends from the UK Mission, Dorothy and David Hartridge, whose children became the closest of friends with ours.

For the first time in my life, I was regularly able to be home on weekdays early enough to eat with the children. This was invariably followed by half an hour or so in which I read them stories, especially from *The Chronicles of Narnia*, which they loved.

Maison Kundig, with its terrace lapped by the waves of the lake, was marvellous for parties, of which we had many. And its lawn was just big enough for a reasonable game of badminton, provided enthusiasm was sufficiently restrained to keep the shuttlecock out of the lake, or a game of croquet, with the same proviso.

My parents came over from Australia to visit us in 1975, the last time I saw them together. And my youngest brother Mark came too, climbing Mont Blanc with me in June of that year.

This was also a satisfying time from a professional point of view, as well. I found I enjoyed both facets of my work. The shadowy side of my professional life, in which Jane was also involved, took up a good deal of time, because at this time, with the Cold War still in full swing, the UN agencies in Geneva were something of a global hotbed for such activities.

The 'day job' was pretty full too. My area of responsibility in the British Mission was to look after Britain's relations with a number of UN bodies based in Geneva, particularly UNCTAD (the UN Conference on Trade and Development), the WHO (the World Health Organisation) and WIPO (the World International Property Organisation). All of these organisations inhabited totally different worlds to the one I had lived in up to now, so I had to learn new skills and new techniques which were totally alien to me: something which I always enjoy doing.

I was not, however, a natural diplomat and found it difficult to conform convincingly to the Foreign Office's bureaucratic routines, especially when it came to the FCO protocols for writing telegrams reporting events back to London. I have never thought it a particular sin to split an infinitive, especially where you want to specially emphasise a particular point. If it was good enough for George Bernard Shaw, it ought to be good enough for me. But I soon discovered that split infinitives are cardinal sins in the FCO. We had an especially fearsome Head of Chancery,* Anne Warburton,† who could spot a split infinitive at a thousand yards and terrified us all, especially me, when it came to correct grammar in telegram-writing. I recall having to write a long draft telegram to London (on, I think, an event in the disarmament talks) and, after taking great care to expunge all trace of split infinitives, sending it to her for approval with a quietly confident heart – only to have it returned with a completely different grammatical error that she had spotted. According to legend, a draft that one of my colleagues submitted was returned with an offending paragraph circled in her characteristic red pencil and an angry scrawl in the margin: 'ANOTHER BEASTLY HANGING GERUND!' I soon decided that, all things considered, it was better to give up the struggle for grammatical correctness, concluding that suffering her lashes was, in the end, easier and less painful.†

I was also part responsible for keeping an eye on human-rights issues, and it was in this capacity that I accompanied Dr Sheila Cassidy when she gave evidence to the UN Human Rights Commission on the torture she had endured under Pinochet in Chile. This event had a profound effect on me and helped to solidify my fast-developing liberal and internationalist views.

My other job in the UK Mission was Press relations, and it was in this capacity that I was co-opted onto the negotiating team headed by

---

* A Head of Chancery in an Embassy or Mission is, essentially, the second in command after the Ambassador and looks after the political side of the work.

† On retiring from the FCO Dame Anne Warburton became an honorary fellow and fourth President of Lucy Cavendish College in Cambridge. She was asked by the government to conduct an investigation into the abuse of Muslim women during the Bosnian war, producing the 'Warburton Report' in December 1993, which, for the first time established that there had been a Serb policy of systematic rape of Bosnian Muslim women and was thus instrumental in alerting the wider international community to this war crime.

† Many years later, after I had become the Lib Dem leader, I recommended her to Prime Minister Major for appointment to the Committee on Standards in Public Life (The Nolan Committee), confident that, if she frightened those in public life as much as she frightened me, the public interest would be completely secure.

the Foreign Secretary, Jim Callaghan, for the first and second Cyprus peace conferences, held in the Palais des Nations in Geneva in July and August 1974. On 20 July that year Turkish forces had invaded Cyprus, and this was swiftly followed by the first Geneva Peace Conference between Britain, Greece and Turkey, presided over by Jim Callaghan – probably the last time a British Foreign Secretary played this kind of pivotal role in a major peace conference. The first round of talks did not succeed, and a second conference was called, this time including not just the three nations, but also representatives of the Greek and Turkish Cypriots. It was during these two events that I first met a young Tom McNally, then Callaghan's Parliamentary Private Secretary, who was later to become a key ally when I was Leader of the Lib Dems and is now, as Lord McNally, my 'boss' as Leader of the Liberal Democrats in the House of Lords. I spent long hours in the sun on the lawns of the Palais des Nations between conference sessions, discussing the world, and especially politics, with Tom and Jim Callaghan's legendary Press chief, Tom McCaffrey.*

Tom McNally recollects that, even at this time, I was declaring myself a Liberal and expressing an ambition to go into politics. I do not remember this, but my discussions with him and McCaffrey certainly played a key role in my eventual decision to take the plunge and enter the field myself.

The Cyprus talks were also the context for a diplomatic *gaffe* that provided my friends and many Geneva dinner parties with much cruel amusement at my expense.

The second round of talks drew to a head on 13 August 1974, when Jim Callaghan, briefing us before the talks started, told us that he believed that Turan Günes, the Turkish Foreign Minister, was not negotiating in good faith. At this time, as throughout the talks, Callaghan was in very close contact with his US opposite number Henry Kissinger, who was using maximum US leverage (including repositioning the US Seventh Fleet) to put pressure on the Greeks and the Turks to come to an agreement.

The Foreign Secretary, who I thought played a weak hand with great skill, kept the Turks at the table as tensions rose and rose through the small hours of the following morning. At about 3 a.m. the

---

* I now work with his son, Mark, in my role as Chairman of the body trying to reach an agreement between Catholics and Protestants on the vexed issue of parading in Northern Ireland.

phone rang in an adjacent room, and Callaghan motioned me to go and take the call. I lifted the receiver to hear a long American drawl over a very bad line, culminating in the words 'White House' and 'Can I speak to Jim please?' I asked who was calling and he said 'It's Henry'. To which I replied 'Henry who?' He said, 'Just tell him it's Henry', and for some time afterwards in Geneva diplomatic circles I was known, rather unfairly I thought, as 'Henry who?'

I cannot, at this distance remember the precise moment when Jane and I finally decided that I should leave my job and go into politics. It happened very slowly over the two-and-a-half years we were in Geneva. One contributory factor was certainly that I found it increasingly painful trying to represent my country during the political chaos of 1974, with its two elections and its three-day weeks, when the international standing of Britain, already widely regarded as 'the sick man of Europe', was at rock bottom. I increasingly came to feel that there was not much point living a life of diplomatic ease, if the country you were trying to represent was falling apart before your eyes.

But not all my home thoughts from abroad were so altruistic. I also found that, though I enjoyed my job, understood its importance and greatly respected my colleagues, I increasingly wanted to have my own ball at my own feet, rather than, as a civil servant, kicking around somebody else's.

And so it was that, in February 1975, while on three weeks home leave from Geneva, I called in (on my birthday, as it happened) to see the then Chairman of the Yeovil Liberals, Brian Andrews, and told him that I was a supporter and, if ever I could be of assistance, I would like to help. I explained that, as a civil servant, I could take no active part in politics, but I could and would be happy to offer discreet advice on foreign-policy matters if ever it was needed. 'What a pity,' he replied. 'We are due to select our new candidate tonight. If only we had known you were available!' I responded rather sharply that he had completely misunderstood. I could *not* take an active part in politics. I had no interest whatsoever in being their candidate – just in helping behind the scenes, if they wanted it. And so our conversation ended.

That May the previous Yeovil Liberal Candidate, the much respected Dr Geoffrey Taylor, came to Geneva for a World Health Organisation conference and asked to see me. We invited him to lunch and, under a glorious May sky, sitting in our garden by the lake in Maison Kundig, he explained that the candidate the Yeovil Liberals had selected in February had also been selected (without their knowledge) for the Newbury seat and had decided that, Newbury being the better prospect, he would abandon Yeovil. So they were without a candidate again. Would I be interested? I cannot recall what answer I gave him, but it must have appeared to him to be at least mildly positive, for from then on he was in almost weekly contact trying to persuade me to put my name forward.

Slowly, over the summer of 1975, Jane and I took the decision that I would resign from the Foreign Office and go into politics. Most of our friends and colleagues, understanding the realities of the situation better than me, thought I was completely mad. Our closest friends were kind, but you could see even they thought we were mad, too. There were only three exceptions to this: George Steiner, a Geneva friend who was, at the time, Professor of English Literature at Geneva University; a close colleague in the UK Mission, Colin McColl (later to become a highly successful and much respected head of MI6); and the then Danish Ambassador to Geneva. The last told us he had wanted to do the same but had left it too late. 'You have to do this before your children go away to boarding school. If you leave it later, and they are already at boarding school, then you have to be very rich to be able to pay for it.' (Boarding school fees for both British and Danish diplomats were paid by their governments.) This latter argument weighed heavily with us, especially Jane, who was dreading the parting with our children that would have been necessary if I had stayed in the Foreign Service.

I have no doubt that, with responsibility for a wife and two young children, this decision to leave a well-paid career in which I believe I had a future for the insecurities of political life – especially as a Liberal candidate in a seat which had been Tory for half a century – was naive to the point of irresponsibility. It just happens also to be the best decision I have made in my life.

At the end of 1975 I formally gave in my notice. My employers fixed the time for our departure from Geneva as July the following year, adding that they would welcome me back at any time up to my forty-third birthday (I was thirty-five at the time).

These last months of our time in Geneva were not uneventful. One of my duties in the shadows involved Jane and me paying a visit to Vienna just before Christmas 1975, travelling by night sleeper across snow-covered Switzerland and Austria. We were ostensibly there on a short holiday, which, to add verisimilitude, included a visit to the State Opera, where they were putting on a performance of Verdi's *Aida*. For us this was not an onerous addition to our schedule, for we had by this time become keen opera fans, though with a strong preference for Mozart over Verdi (and no preference at all for Wagner, after seeing *Tristan und Isolde* on a boiling hot summer's evening in Lausanne, when Jane slept through almost the whole three hours, then woke up, burst into tears over the 'Liebestod' and left after the final curtain – all in the space of twenty minutes). All opera requires from its audience a certain ability to suspend disbelief, which is no doubt why comic operas tend to work better than serious ones – and why even serious ones can swiftly descend into comedy if things go wrong. On this occasion, Aida, the Ethiopian slave girl, was played by a voluptuous American soprano of very ample proportions. Radames, her lover, however, was a diminutive Italian with a torso so emaciated he looked as if he had been starved and legs so well developed they appeared to belong to someone else. He also had the wobbliest thighs I have ever seen – and they wobbled a great deal when he was borne in, on what appeared to be a Chinese restaurant table top, through cheering crowds for the triumphal entry into Thebes. I made manful attempts to believe it all, up to the point when, in a moment of passion, he was clasped between the bosoms of Aida, which engulfed his whole body from the waist upwards and completely swallowed up his voice along with it. The former only reappeared when unclasped, while the latter re-emerged, after a short pause, as a thin squeak from above the proscenium arch. At this point we both got a fit of uncontrollable giggles and had to leave, amid sternly disapproving looks from the more serious-minded burghers of Vienna.

There were tragedies, too. Tina, our dog rescued from the clay pits of Devon was wonderfully intelligent and obedient. But she was also a great hunter and was deaf to all instructions when she put up game. And this was what eventually did for her. She adored our walks in the mountains where she would often put up chamois and other mountain deer. One day, when we were walking on the edge of some forest in the Bernese Oberland, she put up a chamois and gave chase. It was the last we ever saw of her. Chamois, when chased, have a habit of taking their pursuers into forest or thick scrub and then running straight for any nearby cliff, jinking at the last moment and leaving their pursuer to go over the edge. There was indeed a cliff nearby, and I presume that this is what must have happened to my beloved dog. I searched the whole of the cliff face, high and low, for two days, but never found her. I left my telephone number with a local huntsman, together with my walking jacket to comfort her in case she was found. But she never was. We were all completely heartbroken.

Not long afterwards, our cat Boney was returning home from some mischief or other in Coppet village when she saw Kate, whom she adored, and ran across the road to greet her. A car ran straight over her and killed her instantly in front of Kate, who wept for her for days afterwards.

So there were only four of us in the car when, after an exhausting round of farewell parties, the time came to go home in July 1976 to start yet another new adventure, this time in the world of politics.

CHAPTER 10

The Winning of Yeovil

T HERE IS AN OLD Somerset saying: 'If November ice will bear a
duck, the rest of the winter will be slush and muck.' As 1976 neared
its end it brought just such a November. The evening of 16 November
was thick with fog and white with frost as Kate, Simon, Jane and I left
Vane Cottage, with instructions to be in the Liberal Hall in Crewkerne
by 7.30. We were going to the event for which I had resigned from the
Foreign Office, returned home from Geneva and was now unemployed:
the meeting of the Yeovil Constituency Liberal Party, called for the formal
adoption of a new Prospective Parliamentary Candidate (PPC).

We had been informed there were to be two candidates for them to
choose from: Dr Maureen Castle, a psychologist from Devon, and
myself. But at the very last moment the Doctor had withdrawn, giving
the dense fog as her excuse. Common sense would have been a more
compelling reason – for neither the Liberals nor the Yeovil Constituency
could be considered enticing prospects for those with political ambitions.

Like every other politician, I have many times been accused of 'only
being in politics for what I could get out of it'. I like to point out to my
accusers that, on that night, when I formally entered politics for the
Liberal cause in Yeovil, the Tories had held the seat with overwhelming
majorities for 63 years. Moreover, the local Liberals consistently came
third in elections at every level; the Party nationally was at less than
10% in the polls; Liberal candidates were most famous for losing their
deposits and regularly came behind those of both Britain's fascist
Parties, the National Front and the National Party. And my Party leader,
Jeremy Thorpe, was just about to be arraigned at the Old Bailey for conspiracy to murder. On this night at least, it would have been perfectly
reasonable to accuse me of gigantic naivety, or wild romanticism – or
even plain stupidity – but not, I think, of that kind of overriding ambition which regards principle as a necessary casualty in the battle for the
main chance.

The truth was that, in Yeovil, the Liberals had almost no chance.
My old friend and later House of Commons colleague, the much

loved and still sorely missed David Penhaligon, used to say that he won Truro for the Liberals because he was too naïve to know it was impossible. This was just as true of Yeovil. Over the next seven years, I would, in similar vein, remind my supporters of the famous (but perhaps apocryphal) Royal Aeronautical College examination question of the 1930s which gave students the full aerodynamic characteristics of the bumble bee, without naming it, and asked whether this creature could fly. The right answer was that it could not. But the bumble bee fortunately knows nothing of aerodynamics and manages to fly around quite adequately. One of my other favourite 'cheer up the troops' exhortations addressed to our small band of political desperadoes over the next seven years would be: 'Don't forget; Fidel Castro invaded Cuba with only eleven men!'

It was in exactly this spirit, and in high excitement, that Jane, Kate, Simon and I entered the Liberal Hall in Crewkerne that November night to submit ourselves to the judgement of Yeovil Constituency Liberals. I can still recall in almost perfect detail the scene that greeted us as we nervously entered the small hall. There were large gas fire panels suspended from the ceiling, which, though roaring away, did very little either to blunt the sharpness of the cold or to dispel the all-pervading smell of dampness. That smell, I was later to discover, is an endemic feature of all Liberal halls the country over, left behind from the Party's heyday in the nineteenth century. They were great hall-builders, those nineteenth-century Liberals, and I often wonder whether, in reality, the politics of the greatest empire the world has ever seen, was not in the end decided in little halls like this.

If I had been in a mood to see it, I might also have recognised that some in the audience before me had, begging their pardon, seen better days, too. There were some fifty or so people in the room, amongst whom were a very few younger faces of about my own age. The great majority were advanced – some well advanced – in the generation ahead of me. David Penhaligon also used to say that when he went to Truro the average age of the membership was deceased. There was a touch of that in Yeovil as well.

But I noticed none of this. They appeared before me as a veritable battle-hardened, shining army, booted, spurred and breast-plated, waiting only for the bright standard I was about to raise before them to begin our glorious, inevitable – and swift – march to victory. This was, moreover, my first political audience, and I was going to bring them to their feet in wild, stamping acclamation by the time I had finished my speech. This I had carefully prepared and still possess. It is of such earth-shattering banality that I can now scarcely bear to read it. One passage wasn't bad however:

> It is not the declining pound I fear, nor the appalling current level of unemployment, nor even our bankrupt economy. The disease [of our country] lies deeper. In the injustices of an antiquated social structure, in the inadequacies of a sham democracy and in the incapacity of our present leaders to abandon the pursuit of their own narrow party interests in favour of the radical policies we need to get us out of the mess we are in.

It did not, needless to say, bring them roaring to their feet, but it did elicit some polite applause, which nevertheless rang in my ears for days. After that there were some questions. And then they voted and – there being no other choice before them – concluded that I should be their candidate. The only hitch came when one of the Constituency notables – our only Councillor as it happened – said that they had, in my absence, decided that I should be known publicly as 'Captain Jeremy Ashdown, Royal Marines retired'. This was the only moment in the entire proceedings when my feet briefly touched the ground. I replied that, in that case, they had better choose another candidate, for I would be known only as plain Paddy Ashdown. Since there was no other candidate, they decided to follow the logic of another of the Constituency notables who, during the ensuing discussion, suggested that they should accept my proposition – it didn't really matter what I called myself, since we were never going to beat the Tories anyway.

The local paper, the *Western Gazette*, subsequently published the news of my selection as Liberal PPC in a small, three-column-inch article on page two, under the headline 'Jungle fighter chosen as Yeovil's Liberal Champion'. And *Liberal News* of 12 April 1976 published a small article on the last inside page, complete with a photograph, headlined 'He gave up FO for Yeovil'. It said:

> Yeovil has a new prospective parliamentary candidate. He is 35-year-old J.J. Ashdown, known to his friends as Paddy, who has given up a highly promising diplomatic career in order to nurse the seat.

In the car on the way back home that night, I was elated, the kids were confused, and Jane was ominously silent. The truth is I had not the slightest idea what I had let myself in for.

***

Four months earlier, on 16 July, we had driven home from Geneva across a Europe gripped by the worst heat wave for twenty years and arrived in Portsmouth to find Britain burnt to crisp. The glorious green fields we had longed to see were sere and brown, and even the trees were dying for lack of water. Before leaving Geneva we had commissioned work to be done in Vane Cottage, against solemn promises from the builder that all would be safely and surely completed by the time we got home. But when we opened our front door the scene which greeted us was absolute chaos. The floorboards were up, there was a cement-mixer in the living room, the air was pungent with the smell of anti-parasite treatment, and the water and electricity were both turned off. To make matters worse, our builder informed us – with that whistling sound through the teeth that builders the world over use to prepare the unwary for an incoming bill of painful proportions – that he had discovered dry rot under our sitting-room floor, which would all have to come up and be replaced by concrete. It was not an auspicious homecoming.

What made things even less auspicious was that, when I rang the Yeovil Liberal Association to tell them that I had cut short my tour in Geneva as they had suggested and was back, ready to be selected and eager to get to work, they informed me that there was a hitch. Party Headquarters had told them that they could not just select me as they had proposed. There had to be a competition in order for the process to be legal. They would now have to advertise for other candidates and give time for responses. This would mean that they could not possibly select until the early autumn at the earliest. I did not say that I wished they had told me this earlier. Nor do I recall feeling angry about it – just frustrated that I could not get started.

I had, anyway, a lot to do: dealing with our house, getting the kids into schools and all the paraphernalia of settling back into Britain. And, above all there was the need to get a job.

Here I hit a problem. I could probably fairly easily have got a job in London. But I knew that I needed to be local, and not just a visitor to the constituency at weekends. Between August and December I tried for dozens and dozens of jobs locally, but was always rejected. The problem was that I had made my political ambitions known publicly and did not try to hide them from prospective employers. And they, naturally, did not want to take on someone who, they not unreasonably suspected, might have more of his mind on politics than on working for them. In addition, as one of those to whom I applied has frankly admitted to me since, the local Tories, who counted nearly all Yeovil's major employers amongst their supporters, passed the word around that it would be unhelpful to give me a job.

I was not at this stage financially worried about my position – for we had come back from Geneva with a pretty substantial financial cushion (we had some £12,000 in savings – a considerable sum in those days). But these constant rejections did severe damage to my self-confidence. I had presumed that, given my (as I saw it) brilliant careers and talents, I would be eagerly snapped up by local employers and, after no doubt opening a strawberry cream tea or two, would inevitably and probably swiftly be elected to Parliament. I was beginning, even if only dimly, to understand the position I had landed my family in and the harsh realities of life as a challenger in a safe seat – and especially as a Liberal, in Britain's two-party electoral system.

I also filled some of this 'dead' time before (hopefully) being selected by trying to get some understanding and feel for the organisation to which I had now committed my life – Britain's Liberal Party. I visited the national Headquarters, at that time housed in the rather dingy attic of the National Liberal Club in Whitehall Place. There I met the then Secretary General of the Party, Hugh Jones (known affectionately in the Party as 'Huge Ones'), and the Candidates Officer, the redoubtable and delightful Janet Russell – who was to become a stalwart supporter and later told me (I suspect she was just being polite) that the moment I walked in the door she knew I was going to succeed in becoming an MP and would eventually lead the Party. Once again, my undiscerning eye glossed over what a sharper and more objective observer would have seen: that this was an underfunded and rather ramshackle organisation which compensated with commitment, dedication and enthusiasm for what it lacked in resources and efficiency. Much later I, in my turn, would come to rely on the extraordinary resilience and commitment of the Party's members and servants to make good our weaknesses in money and facilities. Though I did not realise it at the time, I was also discovering something else. That all my life I had, I thought, gained satisfaction from working among the elites – from mixing with those who were the best of the best of their profession. The Liberal Party and its members, then as now, do not pretend to be the elite. They are, for the most part, the very ordinary in the best sense of that word. And yet, somewhat to my surprise, I have felt a greater sense of privilege working with them, and been more humbled and inspired by what they were able to achieve through dedication, sacrifice and a refusal to accept the odds, than I ever felt amongst the elites of my previous careers.

A decade or so later, when I was Leader of the Party, I was to discover that, it is not necessary for a Party to love its Leader (think Blair) – to respect him or her is enough. But it *is* necessary for a Leader to love his or her Party – otherwise why would you put up with all that hassle?

My love affair with the Liberal Party and its successor, the Liberal Democrats, began during these months. It was greatly reinforced by travelling to Llandudno in September to attend my first Party Conference (we knew them as Assemblies in the old Liberal Party). This was David Steel's first Party Conference as Leader, too, and I still remember being electrified by his speech. He said that being a Liberal was not good enough if you rejected the possibility of influencing events by working with others. He had to fight against a very strong reaction from, among others, the Young Liberals. But his speech – in my view one of his very best: courageous, cogent, passionate – won the day and paved the way for the Lib–Lab Pact in the following year. Twenty years later, as his successor, I was to face the same choice between purity and power, and to face, too, the same opposition from those in the Party who believed we should only allow ourselves to be sullied by power when we had it on our terms, on the basis of an outright majority. It seems to me that every leader of Britain's liberal third force, if they are successful, has to face this dilemma sooner or later, and has to find their own way of playing the cards dealt them by our political system. Jo Grimond understood that; Jeremy Thorpe had to deal with it; David Steel had to face it, and so did I. And so will, I believe (and hope), our present Leader, Nick Clegg. Precisely how the cards are played depends on what the circumstances and the choices are. And these will always be different. But in the end the consequences of success in growing the Party and its support are that this is a hand that must eventually be played and cannot be avoided.

Back in Llandudno in 1976, however, these thoughts were very far from my mind. I was completely consumed by the joy of being in a hall with six hundred people who felt the same as I did and inspired by many of the speeches I heard. I remember listening to a speech from a young Peter Hain, then leader of the Young Liberals, and turning to a friend, saying that he was bound to be Leader of the Party one day. As for speaking myself, I never uttered a word. I was far too frightened to dare to stand up before all this political skill, wisdom and experience and expose my ignorance, inexperience and lack of ability.

<hr />

Back in Yeovil, after my adoption, I began to draw up an audit of our assets and assess the strengths and weaknesses of our opposition.

The outcome was not encouraging. Yeovil had been a rock of West Country Liberalism in the nineteenth century, marked by the fact that a summer gathering of Liberals from across the West Country, which had on separate occasions been addressed by Gladstone and Lloyd George, used to take place annually in an old Roman earth amphitheatre called 'the frying pans' on Ham Hill just above Vane Cottage. Later on, when I was an MP and doing my pre-Christmas rounds of old people's homes, I met an old man who told me that when Lloyd George attended these events he would always pop in to see a lady friend, the wife of a doctor, who lived close by. In the great Liberal landslide election of 1906 Yeovil had returned a thumping majority, with over sixty percent of the vote going to the Liberals. The Party in Yeovil even held on when the national Liberal vote crashed in the two 1910 elections. The Liberal MP for Yeovil (then known as South Somerset) at this time was Sir Edward Strachey, who had made something of a reputation for himself by being in favour of abolishing the House of Lords. He was then offered a peerage and took it, styling himself Lord Strachie (note the change in spelling) and causing a by-election, held on 21 November 1911, in which the Conservatives created a great national stir by winning with a majority of 374. I have a contemporary postcard celebrating the Tory win, which depicts an obviously Somerset chambermaid offering Lloyd George a full chamber pot with '374' written on the side, saying, 'Your Somerset cider, Sir.'

But it was not just the Tory 1911 victory in Yeovil which was remarkable. So, too, was the new Conservative MP. His name was Aubrey Herbert, and it was only by chance, and many years later, that I discovered that he had been the model for Sandy Arbuthnot, the hero of *Greenmantle*, John Buchan's famous tale of espionage and derring-do in the Balkans and the Middle East during the First World War. I also discovered that there were some intriguing parallels between our two careers, albeit, in my case at a much more prosaic level. Like me, he had been involved in the shadowy side of diplomacy, having been one of the British agents who helped organise and inspire the Young Turk movement that ultimately overthrew the Ottomans. And like me, he became passionately involved in the affairs of the Balkans.

An intrepid traveller and adventurer and a brilliant linguist, Herbert enthusiastically adopted the cause of Albanian independence, and, although a sitting MP, fought in that country's war of independence in 1913. As a result he was twice offered the Albanian crown, which he politely declined (rather a shame, I think; being known in the House of Commons as 'The Honourable Gentleman for Yeovil* and King of Albania' would have had a certain ring to it, I have always thought). During the First World War Aubrey Herbert took leave of absence from the House of Commons to join the Irish Guards and served with distinction in both France and the Middle East. He was wounded, taken prisoner and escaped during the Battle of Mons. But he was so horrified by the waste of young lives on the Western Front that when he returned home in 1917 he joined the Liberal Leader Herbert Asquith's anti-war campaign, for which he was reviled by his own Party and spat at in the streets of Yeovil.

Despite his unpopular opinions and somewhat eccentric actions (or maybe because of them?), Aubrey Herbert was re-elected as Conservative MP for Yeovil after the war, only to die (ironically of blood-poisoning as a result of dental surgery†) in 1923 at the age of 42, the same age as I was when I took his place as MP for Yeovil sixty years later. Aubrey Herbert was greatly admired and loved by his constituents, and the strong foundation he laid, together with the national decline of the Liberals, made Yeovil a rock-solid seat for the Tories, who held it with overwhelming majorities (with the single exception of 1966 when Labour ran them a close second), until 1983.

In her book *The Man Who Was Greenmantle* Aubrey Herbert's grand-daughter, Margaret Fitzherbert, writes: 'The electors of South Somerset are an independent people, with a strong non-conformist streak.

---

* The seat was renamed after its main town, sometime in the post-war years.
† He followed the fashion of the time and had all his teeth extracted, believing this would save him pain and dental expense later in life, but contracted septicemia after the operation.

Aubrey's lack of convention appealed to their sturdy, and sometimes surly, individualism.' This description of the voters of Yeovil remains as accurate today as it was in Herbert's time, and in due course this tradition of contrariness was one of the assets I came to rely upon in trying to win the seat.

But there were very few other assets. Labour was strong in the constituency, having come quite close to winning in 1966. In recent years we Liberals had been pretty consistently in third place, though in the February 1974 general election we had briefly and narrowly overtaken Labour, only to fall back to third place again in that year's second (October) election.

Meanwhile, since there had been a long interregnum when the Yeovil Constituency Liberals had been without a candidate, our funds were terribly depleted, our membership numbers were low, the membership itself rather elderly (with the exception of a few younger faces who had joined during the Liberal surge of the first 1974 election), and the organisation almost non-existent. It would all have to be rebuilt from scratch.

However, I did have one major asset to build on, apart from an ancient Liberal tradition which was still dimly remembered and what Margaret Fitzherbert called Yeovil's tradition of 'sturdy individualism'. That was my predecessor as Liberal candidate in recent elections up to February 1974, Dr Geoffrey Taylor. He was a devoted local GP who also made important contributions to public health, a lifelong Liberal, a unilateralist nuclear disarmer and a committed community activist. It was he who had built up the Liberal vote in the constituency, enabling the Party briefly to push Labour into third position in the first 1974 election. But, more than that, he had established a very wide and well-deserved reputation for community service and was much loved and admired, well beyond the circle of those who would naturally vote Liberal. It was on the foundation laid by Geoffrey and his wife Heather (the daughter of a Liberal Minister in the 1906 Liberal Government) that I built – and in large measure thanks to their work that I was, in due course, eventually elected.

There were two other relatively minor but useful factors I believed we could exploit. The first was that the Labour organisation, though much stronger than ours and with a substantial vote on the ground, was complacent. It took its support in the poorer areas of the Constituency for granted and was based too much on the trades unions and too little on community activism. And it always fielded a parliamentary candidate who came from outside the Constituency and usually only visited it at election time. There was a reservoir of votes to be tapped into here, if we were prepared to work at it.

The second factor was that the Conservatives, too, though outwardly all-powerful and monolithic, had actually become rather tired politically. They overwhelmingly controlled all the local Councils, had a branch in almost every village, could outspend us many tens of times over, and the sitting MP, John Peyton, though a survivor from a different, more paternalistic age in politics, was highly regarded in Parliament and enjoyed respect in the Constituency. But they had become much more a social organisation than a political one, were used, at the Council level, to being elected without opposition, especially in rural seats and also generally took their vote very much for granted.

It was from these scraps that, in the weeks after my adoption, I assembled a strategy for action.

It was only now that I at last, fully and with some horror, realised the depth of the hole in which I had put my family and myself. I was clearly not going to be elected to Parliament at the next election, as I had naively thought. I discussed my very gloomy assessment with Jane and put it to her that one option for us was to make use of the Foreign Office's promise of a 'safety net' and return to them. But she rejected this out of hand.

So what I needed now was a very clear long-term strategy based on the hard realities of the Liberals' position in Yeovil. Here is what I came up with and put to the Yeovil Constituency Liberals at a meeting in late December.

1. We should adopt a three-election strategy and should plan on the basis that I would probably not be in a position to mount a genuine challenge for the seat until my third attempt.
2. I would need to stay full-time in the constituency. So I had to get a job locally and could not afford to get distracted by anything other than the single task of winning Yeovil (i.e. I could not afford to allow myself to get interested in national Liberal Party affairs).
3. Our immediate aim at the next election was not to beat the Tories, but to beat Labour. Once we were the clear challengers for the seat, we would be able to squeeze the Labour vote in subsequent elections.

4. Our effort, therefore, should now be not in the rural areas, where we had traditionally concentrated, but in the towns – and especially in the Yeovil Council estates, where Labour's traditional vote was based.

5. We needed to build up our base from the bottom, concentrating first on local government elections.

6. We could not rely on any newspapers, either locally or nationally. So we would have to find other means to communicate directly with our electorate if we were to succeed in getting our messages across.

7. We would nevertheless need a strong Press effort – we should aim to get at least one story, with genuine news appeal and about a local issue, into the local Press every week.

8. The national Party's standing was not very high, so our key messages should be about local service not national politics. What was subsequently to be known as 'community politics' would be our battleground.

I am not sure that many of the rather thin audience to which I presented this grand plan understood the implications of the strategy I put to them, and I suspect that they had heard enthusiastic new candidates put such utopian plans to them before. Nevertheless, the strategy was formally agreed.

It was a little before Christmas, after four months and many tens of applications, that I finally got a local job. I was taken on in the contract department of Normalair Garrett, a subsidiary at the time of Westland Helicopters, which made high-grade engineering parts for the aircraft industry. My job was to help calculate the costings of engineering work for tenders. My salary was less than half what I had been earning with the Foreign Office, but I was glad to be back in a job. I knew nothing whatsoever about the work and had to learn very fast about my new world of commerce, the aircraft industry and the complexities of an engineering machine shop. I even joined the local branch of the trades union TASS and became involved in some of its activities. I cannot pretend that it was work I enjoyed, not least because one of the senior managers was a strong Tory supporter and did all he could to make my life as difficult and uncomfortable as possible. But my immediate boss, Wilf Baker, was a kindly and decent man who did much to ease my early days in the firm. And my workplace colleagues, especially the machine operators on the shop floor, for whose skills I developed a very high admiration, were in the main extremely generous and patient in protecting me from the consequences of my early ignorance. I owe them much and learned a great deal from them which was necessary for my survival and was to prove very useful later in my political career.

But if Westland occupied my time from nine to five, it was community politics which occupied my brain for most of my waking day. I was out canvassing almost every night up to Christmas 1976. And it was dispiriting work. We had almost no support, and no one had the faintest idea who I was. The rest of my time in these early months was spent making initial contact with the journalists from the various newspapers and getting to know what interested them as news stories, paying calls on past Liberal activists and seeing if I could persuade them back into active support again, and helping our branches to raise money through jumble sales and local fetes. But I had to concede by the end of the year that we were making very little progress. I could attract no attention in the Press, the amounts of money we were raising were paltry, and the Constituency's base of active members remained stubbornly few and mostly elderly.

Over Christmas I did a rethink and came to two conclusions. First, if I wanted to persuade people that I could be a good MP, I had better start acting like one – what I called 'the MP over the water' strategy. I would start holding weekly advice centres (which we called 'surgeries') on Saturday mornings in the Yeovil Liberal Club (which had become little more than a working men's club at the time). Second, we needed to get our messages across on our terms and not rely on the Press. To do this we needed regular leaflets through people's doors. Such an idea, though commonplace today, was completely radical at the time. Normally, the political parties only put out leaflets at election time. The idea of the year-round local leaflet, concentrating on local issues, had been pioneered by Liverpool Liberals with great success. I had seen a fellow candidate, Trevor Jones in neighbouring Dorchester, use this technique to win a string of local by-elections and learned how to implement it from him and two other Liberals, Richard and Phoebe Winch in Sherborne. But we did not have the money to have leaflets printed for us, so we would have to print them ourselves. This meant that I would have to get myself into the printing business.

Jane and I started our first 'surgery' in Yeovil on a bitterly cold Saturday in early January 1977, little realising that this would be the first of nearly a quarter of a century of Saturday mornings on which, from 9 a.m. to often 2.30 p.m., I would provide advice and help to people who came to see me, first as the Liberal PPC and then as Yeovil Constituency's Member of Parliament. The form was that Jane would make coffee, which we would sell much cheaper than anywhere else in town, while I made myself available to provide advice if anyone needed it.

At first, of course, no one came. Why should they? They did not know me from Adam. We spent several weeks setting up our stall and waiting all morning for no one to arrive. In the end, it was actually Jane's cheap coffee and biscuits which began to draw them in. Then we started getting regulars who came in every week. No one asked me for advice, but at least they knew who I was, and sometimes we even talked politics. And then one day a young couple came in and, in the course of our conversation, complained to me about the appalling state of their Council accommodation. I asked if they would like me to help. They said they would, and I paid them a visit a few days later, after which I wrote to the Council about the condition of their house and, with the agreement of the couple, invited the Press in to see it for themselves. There was a huge article in the local paper about it the following week, and the Council was forced to act. I had taken on my first 'case' and won it!

Gradually, over a period of about six months, more and more people came in to see me, and, in terms of custom, we were beginning to rival local MP John Peyton's rather less frequent surgeries. After some errors I gradually became quite adept at taking up my customers' cases with the various authorities, ranging from government ministries to the tax office and the local Councils. After we got home, I would dictate the letters on the cases which arose from the morning's surgery, and Jane would type them up. I found myself really enjoying these mornings which often also provided excellent material for human-interest articles in the local Press. My name was beginning to get known, not only as someone who could get things done, but also as someone who cared about local affairs.

It was not long before the Tory-dominated local Council tried to put a stop to my activities by instructing the Council officers not to deal with me – I was not elected, they argued (not unreasonably), and therefore had neither the right nor the legal locus to take up people's cases. I was in a quandary and could not see a way round this obstacle until a local solicitor who was one of our few younger supporters told me that in English law a citizen was entirely free to choose anyone they wished to represent them in dealings with the authorities. The chosen representative needed neither to be qualified (like a lawyer), nor elected. They just needed proof that they were the person chosen by the citizen in question to act on his or her behalf. With my next case, I enclosed a consent form which my 'constituent' had signed nominating me as their representative and an explanation of the legal position. The Council, on the insistence of their Tory masters, took legal advice before conceding that they had indeed to deal with me as a *bona fide* representative of the person concerned, even though I was not elected.

By the middle of 1977 there were queues to see me at our regular Saturday morning surgeries. I was getting coverage in the local Press almost every week on some local issue or another and had launched or got myself involved in more community-politics-based campaigns than I could comfortably handle.

One of these involved a campaign on council house repairs on the western side of Yeovil, which I launched with an appeal in the Press for people to contact me if they had problems with getting repairs done to their houses. I had a flood of applications for help and decided that I would visit each of the complainants personally to take details of their problems. It was winter, bitterly cold, and the nights were very dark. I managed to do about six houses a night, and on this particular night was invited in for a cup of tea at almost every house I called on. It was not long before I was cross-legged for a pee. As luck would have it, the fifth house I called on had a problem with the bathroom sink, which was hanging off the wall. But, the tenant explained, the taps still worked alright, and ran them to prove the point. This did absolutely nothing to make my condition more bearable. However, I saw, in the corner of the room, exactly what I was looking for: one of those old-fashioned loos with an elevated cast-iron cistern with 'Shanks' embossed on the outside. My request to use it was swiftly agreed, and my host left the room closing the door behind him. Perhaps the cistern, too, was hanging off the wall, or perhaps it was that, in sheer relief, I pulled the chain too hard, but as I did so the whole lot came crashing to the floor! My host, hearing the noise, rushed in, took in the wreckage with a sweep of his eye and enquired drily, 'I don't suppose you want me to vote Liberal as well, do you?' Covered in confusion and embarrassment I made a dash for the front door and reached for the handle, promising to get someone round in the morning. But he was quicker and grabbed the door knob before I could do any more damage, saying, 'I'll do that if you don't mind!' I still see him in Yeovil from time to time, and we still laugh about it. And, as it happens, I am pretty sure he did vote for me!

On another occasion I was visiting a house in a row which was laid out with the back doors facing the main road and the front doors facing a small *cul de sac*. I knocked on the front door, but there was no reply. I knew there was someone in, however, because the lights were on and I could see movement inside. Thinking the householder had probably mistakenly gone to the back door, I walked round the house heading for the back entrance. As I rounded the corner, the back sitting room window flew open and an entirely naked man, carrying his clothes in one hand and his shoes in the other, leapt out and legged it across the main road into the residential estate opposite, his little white bottom winking in the lamplight as he ran. I decided it would be in the best interests of my constituent to visit this house on another occasion.

I found I really enjoyed this work – and was getting some good Press coverage from it while earning something of a reputation for problem-solving. But it was not always the Liberals who benefited from this. One of my early cases involved a family living in a precast reinforced-concrete council house suffering from what came to be known as 'concrete cancer', when in the mid 1980s such buildings were all condemned. The house was literally falling apart, and I spent a long time persuading the Council to rehouse the family, which they eventually agreed to do. I subsequently visited the family in their new house, and they were delighted. As I left, the father said, 'Paddy, we are really grateful to you for what you have done for us – I can assure you we will never forget and we will never vote anything but Labour in future!' I did not have the gall to correct them, so perhaps they always did!

It soon became clear to me that our progress was being held back by our inability to finance our occasional campaigning leaflets (at this stage our leaflets were all related to specific issues – regular community leaflets would come later). We needed to find a cheaper means of printing. To start with, I used the services of my Liberal colleague in Dorchester, Trevor Jones, who had recently bought a small photo-offset litho machine which he ran in his spare back bedroom. It was from him that I learned the techniques of laying out a leaflet, how to photograph it with a plate-making camera and how to use the film to make a plate for the final printing process.

It was not long before I concluded that, if we were serious about winning in Yeovil, we too would have to obtain our own printing facilities. I first tried to persuade the constituency party that this was the way to go in May 1977. But the idea was rejected because we didn't have the funds (I recall our Treasurer announcing at around this time that we had the grand total of £12.60 in the Constituency bank account) – and anyway we had a duplicator, so what was the need? A month later the duplicator broke down, and I tried once more, again without success. But it was agreed that I could try to find a cheap second-hand electric duplicator. I bought this in December 1977 for £120.50, and it was on this mulish machine that a Liberal colleague from Chard and I printed our first regular community leaflet, *Chard Focus*, which had a run of 2,200 copies. It was murder to print, full of smudges and very primitive. But we were delighted with it. We produced two more issues of *Chard Focus* and some other leaflets on this machine before it, too, broke down. And just at the worst moment!

For I had by now launched a regular leaflet to be distributed in Yeovil every two months, called *Counter Point*. With our electric duplicator now broken, Jane and I decided that we would have to fund the first issue of *Counter Point* ourselves and have this properly printed on a friendly commercial printer's photo-offset litho machine, hoping this would persuade the constituency party to buy one of our own. The advantages of photo-offset litho printing over duplicated leaflets was that it allowed us to use photographs, to adopt a much more sophisticated layout and to increase the size from A4 to A3.* Jane and I did the set-up for the first leaflet in our printer friend's premises in February 1978. *Counter Point* was designed to be quite different from our other leaflets. It was intended as a community news sheet with attitude – a little like a local *Private Eye* – which would uncover local 'scandals' within the Tory-controlled Council, such as wasted money, undemocratic practices etc., while at the same time publicising the things which local Liberals were doing. By this time I had already concluded that, if they are to be effective, political messages have to have

* A3 is double A4.

both a 'push' and a 'pull' element: that is, your message has to give people a good reason *not* to vote for your opponent as well as a good reason *for* voting for you. *Counter Point* did both of these things. But it also took us into very dangerous territory, for it enraged the Tories by exposing things and people to the public in a way that made them feel very uncomfortable. Our very first issue produced the threat of an action for libel (which never materialised) from one of the Tory Council grandees. My friendly solicitor, Graham Hughes, who gave us his services at this time on a *pro bono* basis, gave me a tutorial on the laws of libel. He advised me that, on this occasion, I had nothing to worry about, but he also told me that, if I wished to keep *Counter Point* going on this basis, I had better take steps to protect my family. On his advice I transferred our house and our meagre bank account into Jane's name and kept publishing.

One of our other problems was finding the money to fund *Counter Point*. The Constituency party soon made it clear that they could not find the money to keep it going. And the traditional jumble sales and coffee mornings took up a lot of time while yielding very small returns. We had to find a better way to accumulate funds. One idea we hit on was to run 50/50 auctions. We advertised (in *Counter Point* and the local papers) that we would hold an auction on a given date in the Liberal Hall in Yeovil and that we would hand over fifty percent of the price of everything that was sold while keeping fifty percent to pay our expenses and for profit. We were astonished at the amount of goods of all sorts brought to us for sale. We had a team of helpers who provided transport for the heavier items, and another who 'lotted up' the items for sale, while Jane and her band of helpers made tea and refreshments. There were often well in excess of 200 lots for sale, fill-ing the Hall to bursting. I would then act as the auctioneer, usually starting at 2.30 and ending well after 5 p.m., after which we would have to transport the heavier items back to their purchasers. I really enjoyed the business of auctioneering (perhaps it was in my blood from my maternal grandfather, the cattle auctioneer of Rathfriland). But it was pretty exhausting and back-breaking. Still the returns were good – we usually made well over £1,000 for a single afternoon's work, enough for three editions of *Counter Point*.

Even so, we needed still more money, and we needed to make it with less effort. A Liberal friend called Clarence Drew hit on a new idea. What about running discos for young people? So were launched the

Norton Discos, which soon became a roaring success. We would hire the local village hall and a disc jockey (who quickly became one of our members) and engage the local pub to run the bar. We opened our doors at 7 in the evening and closed them at 11.30 p.m. The events became so popular with the young throughout the area that we had to turn people away because the numbers exceeded the limit set by fire regulations. We often made up to £500 a night. It was not entirely trouble-free, though. It was up to me to keep order in the hall, which was quite a challenge. But things were made easier after I got the support of a number of our regulars who were Hell's Angels, and they did much of the policing work themselves (I remember one occasion when one of their over-exuberant members drove his motorbike into the hall and straight through the heaving throng). Then there was the clearing up afterwards. Together with a team of helpers Jane and I were often busy until two in the morning clearing sick and other unmentionables out of the lavatories and returning the hall to its proper state.

Counter Point may have brought us problems, but it brought us benefits as well in the form of a lot of attention and some much-needed new blood. With our small band of helpers, we had to distribute the first issue ourselves to most of Yeovil. In it we appealed for help with distribution and soon had a team of over a hundred volunteers from all corners of the town. They were not members of the Party but they were supporters, and we treated them with great care. I would always do a letter telling them when the next issue was coming out and a thank-you letter afterwards. We also held two annual parties for them at our home, one in the summer and one in the winter. These were to become a reservoir from which we recruited both members and, in due course, activists. Most of the early candidates who stood for Council seats under the Liberal flag, some of whom would eventually lead South Somerset District Council and Somerset County Council, started their political lives as *Counter Point* deliverers in these early days.

Back in 1978 we still had to score our first victory in the polls. In July that year we had our first District Council by-election, in a Tory-held seat in the Preston and West ward of Yeovil. We had not fought this seat in recent memory, having largely conceded that Yeovil town local elections were a Tory/Labour battleground. This was, therefore, my first opportunity to put into practice our new strategy of focusing first on local elections and challenging Labour in its council-estate heartlands, while at the same time proving the effectiveness of our new leaflet-based campaigning techniques. It was now clear to all that a general election was very close. Most people thought that Prime Minister Jim Callaghan would go to the country after the Labour Conference that autumn. I persuaded the Constituency party that we should treat the July Council by-election as a dress rehearsal for a general election and throw everything into it. They agreed to dip into our very depleted funds to pay for three leaflets over the course of the campaign (unheard of for a local council election in those days), one of which was to be a 'good morning' leaflet, delivered to every elector at 5.30 a.m. on the morning of election day (even more unheard of at the time). There was some grumbling at this, but our small band of loyal activists duly turned up on time and, apart from tripping over an occasional milk bottle and rousing a number of sleeping dogs, had no trouble in ensuring that the leaflets were through the letter boxes by the time most people emerged for work. We then mounted our most comprehensive campaign ever for getting out the vote and, when the polls closed, felt well satisfied that we were about to score a famous victory that would justify both the strategy and our new campaigning techniques.

The result, therefore, was a profound shock. Labour, far from coming third, actually beat the Tories, and we came last.* I knew that what was at stake now was more than a seat on the District Council; it was also my credibility, my strategy and the new campaigning techniques I had hoped to convince the Constituency party to adopt. I went home that night in despair. Then, from the military history I had studied in the Royal Marines, I remembered a story about the Duke of Wellington. At one stage in the Peninsular War, Parliament was getting restive because the campaign was costing so much, while Wellington (at that time resting his army behind the fortifications of Torres Vedras), appeared to be doing nothing to take on the French. Wellington decided that what he needed was a victory – even a minor one. Unfortunately the next thing which happened was not a victory but a defeat, when one of his generals got badly mauled by his French counterpart. When he

---

* The result was: Dawson (Lab) 527; Jeffery (Con) 497; Roake (Lib) 345. Lab gain from Tory. In the District Council elections that took place on the same day as the general election a year later, following a full year of *Counter Point* and an intensive leaflet-based campaign, we swept this two-member ward, with two Liberal candidates being elected, winning a clear majority of all the votes cast.

heard the news next day, Wellington instructed the unfortunate General to ignore the defeat and 'write me a victory'. When the news of this 'victory' reached London, the bells rang all over the country, and Parliament gratefully voted more money for Wellington, who then marched on to eventual victory. There are, I presume, even to this day, some British regiments who carry this 'victory' as one of the battle honours on their regimental flag. I decided that if the great General could write victories, so could I. So that night I penned a press release which said how pleased the Liberals were with the result, without any-where mentioning either what it was, or the word 'Labour'. My head-line was 'Liberals enter the arena – Tories lose'. To my delight, in the following week's edition of the main local paper, the *Western Gazette*, the only report of the by-election was my press release, which they published, word for word, headline and all! In the folklore of Yeovil Constituency Liberals this defeat is still remembered as a victory.

As it happens this was to be the last local Council by-election we ever lost in my twenty-five years in Yeovil as Candidate and MP. But it could have been the last we ever fought, had we not turned defeat into victory through a press release, or if my tiny band of supporters had given up after this setback.

Instead we pressed our advantage and returned to the Constituency party with the proposal that we should now buy our own photo-offset litho press, with Jane and I putting up £400 of the estimated £600 cost. Finally, they agreed, and in August we found what we were looking for. She was an old 1930s Rotaprint 'bedstead' R30, which for years had been locked up, abandoned and unloved, in a shed near Fordingbridge. We christened her 'Clarissa' (I cannot remember why) and transported her proudly back to Yeovil strapped in a dignified upright position to a friend's diminutive trailer and towed gingerly behind his Morris 1100.

Little did we, or anyone else, know it at the time, but Clarissa was to become a much-loved family friend whose moods and inner work-ings I would get to know quite as well as (indeed probably rather bet-ter than) those of my own children. She also became the primary tool around which we now based all our political activities. Clarissa's low-key arrival in the Yeovil Constituency in 1978 may not have had the romance and drama of smuggling Lenin into Russia in a sealed train in 1917, but the political effect was the same. For she became instru-mental in the eventual overthrow of the best part of three-quarters of a century of Tory hegemony in the Constituency.

When Clarissa finally arrived at her new home, we discovered there were too few of us to lift her off the trailer, for she was a hefty old lady, clocking in at about three-quarters of a ton. So I walked a couple of hundred yards back to my local pub and asked for volunteers to lift her off. Among those who put down their pints to give us a hand was a young man called Andy Jacobs, who from that moment got drawn into the printing business, becoming in due course a fine printer, one of our most energetic activists and, eventually, the Liberal District Councillor for my own home ward.

Clarissa was first housed in the stable block of a friend who lived in an old Rectory in the village. (He was a Tory, and subsequently Chairman of the local Tory Branch – but I think he regarded our leaflets as a bit of harmless fun which would lead nowhere.) We marked this connection by calling the umbrella organisation set up to manage Clarissa's operations the Rectory Printing Society.

Now we had Clarissa housed, all that was left for me to do was to learn how to use her. This, with the help of patient friends and the expenditure of many hours, much swearing, gallons of ink and acres of wasted paper, I finally did. For the next seven years I became the Constituency party's chief printer and, even after becoming an MP, often turned my hand to a couple of hours' printing. I still think there are few tasks more satisfying than taking some images on a piece of paper and turning them into three thousand leaflets, all nicely stacked and wrapped and ready to go through people's letter boxes.

Clarissa underwent two further moves before ending up, finally, in 1981 in a specially purchased headquarters in Yeovil, where we held meetings upstairs to the sound of her chattering away on the ground floor below us. She printed all my leaflets in the 1979, 1983 and 1992 elections and literally hundreds of thousands of the regular community leaflets which were, by the early 1980s, springing up across the Constituency. She broke down rather frequently, but by the end I knew her every cog and cam and could strip her down as efficiently as I could a Bren gun in my Royal Marine days. Sometimes her ancient old parts broke and, being so old, could not be replaced. This was where my erstwhile friends in the machine shop in Normalair Garrett came into their own, for there is no part a skilled aircraft machine-tool operator cannot make, given a drawing or the original. I am not sure, however, that my old bosses in Normalair (mostly firm supporters of the local Tory party) knew how much the clandestine operations of their workers and undeclared times on their lathes were doing to help keep running the machine that was, by now, gradually eating up their vote.

In the days before computers and desk-top publishing, the process of first setting up and then publishing a leaflet was quite laborious and time-consuming. The set-up was usually done on our dining table and, as the number of our activists began to grow, poor Jane had to put up with more and more invasions of her house by groups of eager (and always hungry) Liberals from all corners of the Constituency, whom she, with great patience and often extreme strain on her limited housekeeping budget, would feed and water. We bought an electric typewriter, which enabled us to vary the font size and provide a more professional look. We became experts in the use of Letraset (for headlines) and Cow Gum for sticking the whole thing down. The next step was to photograph the artwork on a special camera in a dark-room and then develop the film (in the early days this was all done in our back shed, which I had light-proofed and fit-ted with red lighting). After this, the film had to be 'spotted out' to remove the stains, spots of dirt and lines you did not want to print, over a light table. This was usually Jane's task, and she became most expert at it. The film was then fixed with tape to a plate and exposed to ultra-violet light in a special plate-maker. The exposed plate was then washed with a light acid, revealing a positive image of the pages to be printed. I would then change into my printing kit – a pair of very disreputable and irre-trievably ink-stained jeans and a T-shirt so stained and threadbare it was known to all as 'the Turin shroud' – and strap the newly produced plate to Clarissa's big plate roller. We then inked her up, making sure that there was enough font liquid in the font bath to 'wash' the plate (so preventing it from gumming up with too much ink), loaded the paper, and we were ready to start printing. We could, if really pushed, produce a thousand leaflets from start to finish in an hour-and-a-half – and then continue pro-ducing them at a rate of about three-and-a-half thousand an hour.

Printing was largely a family affair. Jane got so proficient at it that she was often left to run Clarissa for a short time while I answered a phone call or saw some visiting activist in the next room. On one occa-sion I heard a terrifying scream from the print shed and dashed back in to find Jane's hair tangled up in Clarissa's flying rollers. She had had the presence of mind to knock down the lever which turned off the power – so preventing an even worse outcome. Nevertheless, quite a lot of her hair had been pulled out, and it took a long time to get the ink out of what remained.

The kids helped with packing printed leaflets and, from time to time, distributing them, too. But these were tough times for them. They saw very little of me, as I usually came home after my 'real work' at around 5.30 p.m. and then left an hour later for an evening's canvassing, or meetings with community groups or my Liberal activist colleagues. And, with the weekends largely taken up with surgeries and printing, I fear they had a pretty meagre time of it. The burdens of bringing them up fell disproportionately on Jane. The only time in the year when we were able to be wholly together as a family without politics intruding was our sacred week's skiing every winter, when we usually went back to Switzerland and stayed with old friends.

What made things worse for them was that, as I became better known, they became prey to much teasing and even bullying at the local comprehensive school they attended, where Simon became known as 'Paddy Two' and Kate as 'Padwina'. It was not unusual for them to come home with cuts and bruises, having been in a fight because one of their school colleagues had made some disparaging comment about me. Jane and I became increasingly concerned about the effects of this, especially on Kate, who had already had crucial parts of her education disrupted due to our return from Geneva.

In early 1978 we heard the terrible news that my mother had died of a massive heart attack in Australia. This, of course, hit me very hard – but it was especially difficult for Kate, too, for my mother was very close to her. Over the next year Kate became increasingly disturbed and difficult to deal with, and she and I used to have terrible fights.

I would never have succeeded even to the extent that I did in politics, had it not been for my children and the help and support they gave me. But this was given at a price, for politics can be very tough on the offspring of politicians, and the fact that both of them have become not only human beings to be proud of, but also our best friends, is a testimony more to their strength and Jane's skills as a mother than to my wisdom. In my first two elections, in 1979 and 1983, I used family photos in my election address. But I soon concluded that this was a mistake, and after that we always ensured that there was the widest gap possible between my politics and my children's lives. I only wish I had realised the importance of this earlier.

But this is to get a long way ahead of the story, for back in 1978 we were still busy trying to learn the art of printing and leafleting, our organisation was still very weak, our funds gravely depleted, and now there was a general election looming. At this stage we were lucky enough to gain another formidable weapon in our fight for Yeovil, whose effectiveness and influence was to prove even more powerful than Clarissa's.

In mid-1978, our voluntary and unpaid agent, Val Keitch, resigned. Our then Constituency Chairman, a trim and goatee-bearded smallholder called Fred Symes, announced that he had found a replacement: a Territorial Army Major called Nick Speakman, who had agreed to give one night a week – the same time as he gave to TA Drill Night – to the local Liberals. Inwardly, my heart sank when I heard the news. I had been assiduously trying to change the Constituency party from a largely middle-class organisation into one truly representative of all classes in the Yeovil community. Indeed, in comparison with the Liberal organisations of the neighbouring Wells, Taunton and Bridgwater constituencies, one of the distinguishing features of the Yeovil party at the time (and one reason, I believe, for our eventual victory) was its highly informal atmosphere and the fact that it was genuinely cross-class, with many of our members, key activists and officers coming from the council estates of our community. I used to joke at the time that, if you went to a constituency function in Wells you had to wear a dinner jacket, in Taunton, you had to wear a lounge suit, but in Yeovil, the right dress was open-neck shirt, sweater and jeans. So the last thing I thought we wanted in Yeovil was a TA Major. But I completely underestimated Nick, who has no side whatsoever and turned out to be not only a brilliant agent but also a solid rock of wisdom and advice, loved and respected by all in the Constituency. We often laugh about his promise of giving 'one night a week' to the Party, as he became the linch-pin and directing mind behind all our subsequent victories and served as my Parliamentary Agent in all my election campaigns from 1979 up to my resignation in 1999. He also, in due course, became the Chair of our local District Council and was awarded the MBE for his community work.

It is now generally acknowledged that Jim Callaghan made a grave error by not calling the election in October 1978; if he had, I think he would have beaten the Tories under Mrs Thatcher. But for us in Yeovil, it was a godsend. It was now clear he would definitely go to the country in the spring of 1979, giving us more time to plan and prepare for an election which would combine voting for both Westminster and local district Councils on the same day. I spent much of the remainder of 1978 and early 1979 finding local candidates, concentrating on the wards where Labour was strong in Yeovil. In the end we found ten candidates. I then went round with each of them identifying local issues in each ward – ranging across the state of a playground, litter, inadequate council house repairs, the absence of a convenient bus stop etc. In early 1979 we launched a series of leaflets in each target ward identifying these issues and introducing our candidates. I made it clear to the Constituency party that, in this election, properly resourcing the campaigns for these Council candidates should take priority over the resources for my general-election campaign.

And even when the general election came, I reminded them that our target was not to beat the Tories, but to push Labour into third place, the better to be able to squeeze them in the election to follow. At this time, towards the end of the 1978 Winter of Discontent, Labour was very unpopular. But so was the Liberal Party, which was being partly blamed for the industrial strife gripping the country, even though David Steel had ended the Lib–Lab Pact before the Winter of Discontent had started. So we decided to mount our attack on Labour chiefly on local issues – and particularly on the fact that their candidate, a rather decent man called Ian Luder, was not local, but came from Bedford. I fear we were pretty ruthless in getting this message across; no leaflet went out which did not attack 'Labour's absentee candidate'. When, after the election was called, it came to light that he was also fighting a District Council seat in Bedford on the same day, we published a leaflet asking, 'Which seat is he serious about – Yeovil, or Bedford?' and pointing out that in these circumstances a Labour vote was a wasted vote (which was very cheeky of us; this was normally the charge levelled at those who voted Liberal).

In late 1978 I received another boost to my campaign; my father decided to come back to England for good, saying that, now that my mother had died, he could return home for his last days. To start with, he hoped to live with his favourite sister, my Dorset Aunt Nan. But this did not work out, so he came to live with us. He threw himself into the organisational side of my campaign as well as filling in for me in doing the things with Kate and Simon (such as taking them fishing) which I was unable to do.

It is in the nature of political candidates, their supporters and their families that they have to suspend disbelief and radiate an iron confidence that they are going to win – otherwise how would they ever be able to put up with all the discomfort and embarrassments of campaigning? Despite having told others that 1979 would be a 'staging post' election before it started, once into the campaign I quickly fell prey to my own enthusiasm and a strong dose of 'candidate-itis', insisting to all that we were on our way to victory. I enjoy campaigning, so the election itself was fun. The people on whose doors I knocked, especially in country areas, were invariably very pleasant. I don't suppose I was the first inexperienced candidate, and I am certain I won't be the last, to mistake politeness on the doorstep for intended electoral support in the ballot box.

Additional drama was also injected into my campaign when someone dug up the fact that the new no-hope Liberal Candidate in Yeovil had once been on an IRA death list. Airey Neave MP, a war hero and one of Mrs Thatcher's closest lieutenants, had recently been assassinated by a bomb which blew up his car in the House of Commons car park, with the result that the election was conducted against the backdrop of heightened security and expectations of further IRA attacks. It was therefore decided at the start of the election that I should be accorded local police protection. This caused considerable puzzlement in deepest rural Somerset when I arrived to address village-hall audiences which could be numbered on the fingers of one hand to the accompaniment of police sirens – but it did my vote no harm!*

It was just before one of these meetings, early in our campaign, that I caught Nick Speakman carrying more chairs into the parish hall. This seemed curious, since there were about eighty chairs already in the hall, and the total audience who had turned up to hear me amounted to just three. I pointed out to him that our problem, it seemed to me, was not an insufficiency of chairs, but a distinct lack of people, and asked him what he was doing. 'Read the press release,' was his answer. When our meeting was duly reported in the Press it told the reading public that when Paddy Ashdown held his election meeting in such and such village hall, 'extra chairs had to be brought in'.

---

* This protection was withdrawn in, as I recall, the second week of the Election campaign, presumably on the grounds that someone exciting so little attention from Yeovil's voters was unlikely to be of much interest to the IRA.

By polling day I thought we had fought a good campaign and that the vote was moving towards us. On the last Monday of the campaign the *Sun* published a front-page article headlined 'Nuts in May' which, in brutal terms, warned people that the consequence of voting Liberal was to put the much-hated Labour Government back in power. Almost immediately I began to feel the vote, especially on council estates, starting to slip away from us. It was my first experience of a Tory card they almost always play on the eve of poll and which was to have a profound influence on my thinking when, less than ten years later, I was leading the Party towards an approaching general election. Nevertheless, I went into polling day feeling good and even just a tiny bit confident about what lay ahead.

So the actual result came as something of a shock.

In later elections, Nick Speakman used to keep me away from the count for as long as possible, having learned that my pessimism on these occasions is contagious and tends to spread alarm and despondency to all around me. For the truth is that I find election counts pure torture. The atmosphere is stuffy, and the smell of sweat and fear all-pervasive. The Council officials counting the vote have usually already done up to twelve hours manning polling stations. Those scrutinising the counting on behalf of the candidates are equally tired and uncomfortable at having to be in such close proximity to those they have just spent three weeks insulting. For me, at least, being a candidate at a count always reminds me of the people described in Hilaire Belloc's poem 'The Garden Party', who

> Looked underdone and harassed,
> And out of place and mean,
> And horribly embarrassed.

At the count, the piles of votes that have been cast for me seem as weightless and unremarkable as raindrops in an April shower. But each vote that has been cast against me resounds in the pit of my stomach as a thunderclap of disapproval, and strikes like a lightning bolt into my self-confidence and self-respect.

So the evening of 3 May 1979 was a most painful one. The full results were: Peyton (Conservative) 31,321 (47.9%); Ashdown (Liberal) 19,939 (30.5%); Luder (Labour) 14,098 (21.6%). I had lost to my Tory opponent by a massive and increased majority of more than 11,000 votes. I saw Jane's eyes briefly fill with tears, and I later learned that the children, sitting at home with my father in front of the television, had wept too. But I had to give the traditional candidate's speech of thanks, and I tried to mumble a few words. I hoped they sounded a little more dignified than those of the defeated Liberal candidate in the 1946 general election who, before stalking off the stage in disgust, having lost his deposit, declaimed: 'People of Yeovil, you have been handed the keys of liberty and you have dashed them to the ground!'

Afterwards I made a desperate attempt to cheer up my workers and supporters at the local pub, and then went home dejected, knowing that I would have to return to face them all again when the District Council results were counted the following morning.

It was, once again, Jane who brought me back to reality. On the way home she pointed out to me that we had in fact achieved almost everything we set out to achieve. True, we had not reduced the Tories' majority, but that was hardly surprising given the national landslide to Mrs Thatcher and the Conservatives. However, we had decisively beaten Labour into third place, scored what was, in percentage terms, the highest Liberal vote in Yeovil since before the Second World War, and were now the clear challengers. She said that Nick had done a calculation just after the count and had told her that Yeovil had moved up from the eightieth most winnable Liberal seat in the country to the seventeenth. Everything now depended on tomorrow's count for the District Council. If we had won a few of the ten seats we had contested, she pointed out, then all our strategic aims for this election would have been fulfilled.

She, my father and several stiff glasses of whisky did a little to cheer me up but not much. I was dreading the morning.

A 'celebratory' lunch was planned the following day at the house of our then Constituency Chairman, Sydney Harding, who had spent the morning attending the District count. He was late arriving back, so I spent the time before lunch doing what I could to cheer up our dejected workers. Suddenly Sydney burst into the room, his eyes brimming with tears, and announced, 'They've all won. Every single one of them has won! All ten of them have won! We have wiped the Tories and Labour out of every seat we fought and we are now the opposition on the Council.' What had become a wake swiftly turned instead into an instant and uproarious celebration. We might have been bloodied the previous night, but we were triumphant today – the strategy had worked – we were on our way!

I knew that the Labour candidate would return home and never be seen in Yeovil again. So that afternoon I issued a press statement saying that I would fight on and was starting the campaign for the next election the very next day, with a 'thank-you' leaflet to all who had voted for us. As I hoped, our local government victories and my declaration that my campaign for the next election would begin immediately received almost as much coverage in the local papers as the fact that Yeovil had once again (and with an increased majority) got a Tory MP.

The next four years were dominated for me by three developments on the national stage, three others that affected the constituency and two that personally and very painfully affected me.

The national developments were, first, the initial deep unpopularity of Thatcherism, counterbalanced in part by the second, the Falklands war, both of them played out against the backdrop of the third, the decline of Labour, the creation of the SDP and the formation of the SDP–Liberal Alliance.

The local developments were the redrawing of the Constituency boundaries, the announcement in 1982 that the Tory incumbent, John Peyton, would not stand again, and the rise and rise in strength and effectiveness of the local Yeovil Constituency Liberals.

The personal ones were that I lost my father, and then soon afterwards my job, and found myself unemployed again.

In 1978, shortly after he came to live with us, my father, who smoked more than sixty cigarettes a day until he was sixty, started to complain of pains in the chest. His GP said he thought it was an ulcer, but sent him down to Dorchester for a proper internal examination. After the examination, and before he came round from the anaesthetic, the surgeon called me in and told me my father (who only had one lung as a result of a wartime injury) had advanced cancer of the lung. They could not operate because he was too frail and because it was too deep-seated. I asked the surgeon when he was going to tell my father this. He said he wasn't; he was leaving on holiday and was therefore leaving it to me to tell him, after which he should have professional advice from his GP. That evening, in one of the worst moments of my life, I had to tell my father that he had cancer and was going to die. The doctors gave him a year to live.

Jane, once again, carried most of the burden of nursing him, along with everything else she had to cope with. In fact, he declined much faster than the doctors had anticipated. At one stage the visiting District Nurse recommended that he should be put into hospital or sent to a care home, but Jane and I insisted that he should stay with us. Above all things, my father was a most fastidious man, and we both knew how he dreaded the thought of others seeing him go through the humiliations of the failure of his personal functions, which (along with a lot of pain) attended his last days. In April 1980, shortly after my thirty-ninth birthday, our GP told me that the cancer had travelled up the arteries into his brain, but that he still thought my father had six months to live. In the third week of May, I decided that the time had come to call my brother Mark, who had returned to England and lived at the time in London, and tell him it was time to come down to say his goodbyes. This coincided with Jane and I having a terrible row, brought on by the fact that we were both physically exhausted (but Jane more so, for she carried more of the burden) and under great mental strain. I still plague myself with the thought that my father may have heard us rowing and, having said goodbye to my brother, concluded that he was a burden and the time had come to go. What I remember clearly was that, when I kissed him goodnight on that last evening, there was a full bottle of sleeping tablets and pain-killers on his bedside table. Jane and I woke together at 6 a.m. the following morning, 29 May, and immediately commented to each other that we had not been woken during the night to carry him to the lavatory. I rushed into his room to find him dead and, as I recall it, the bottle empty by his side. (Jane has no recollection of this story of the bottle and the sleeping tablets and is certain that he did not kill himself.)

I then went into my daughter Kate's bedroom (my son Simon was away at a scout camp), broke the news to her and asked if she would like to see her grandfather. She said she would, and I took her in to see his body.*

Although he had only been with us for eighteen months or so, my father had become something of a personality with our neighbours and

---

* There is an Ashdown 'legend' that when the senior male member of the family dies he 'visits' his eldest grandchild. I have a very clear dream of seeing my grandfather the night before the news of his death in Jersey reached us in Northern Ireland. Kate had a similar 'dream' in which she says my father walked into her room and sat on the side of her bed and said goodbye on the night he died.

amongst our friends, so there was quite a crowd at his cremation, after which we sent his ashes out to be scattered on the graves of my mother and their two children, Robert and Melanie, in Castlemaine in Australia.

Even if a death is expected, it does not diminish the impact, and I felt my father's death most painfully – as did Jane and our children. That we were able to nurse him to the end, and so prevent him having to endure the indignities of this kind of death in the company of strangers, gave us pride – and in some way enabled us all to be much more enriched by the process of his leaving us than we would have been if he had been cared for by others. But the fact that neither he nor my mother lived long enough to see me elected to Parliament has been a source of deep and still-felt sadness in my life.

Throughout the period of my father's last illness, the political pace, both nationally and locally, quickened. Normally there is something of a political hiatus after an election, especially one in which a new government is elected. During this period the opposition parties stand back for a bit and leave the new Government to find its feet during its early, honeymoon days. But the Thatcher revolution got under way almost immediately, with the brutal application of her monetarist doctrine. This soon produced a spate of closures and layoffs, with a sharp increase in unemployment and an equally sharp decrease in her popularity. It is often forgotten how swiftly she moved in these early days from the triumphant liberator who had freed the country from a hated Labour Government to the most unpopular Prime Minster since polling records began.

Meanwhile Labour, under the leadership of Michael Foot, was going through convulsions which looked at one time as though they might be terminal. The radicalisation of the Party and the rise of the militants had begun immediately after the 1979 defeat, leading in January 1981 to the 'Gang of Four' breaking away to form the SDP. The difficulties the other two parties were going through created fertile territory for me in the Yeovil constituency. The task now was to expand our base from Yeovil town to the other main centres of population in the Constituency, Chard, Crewkerne and Ilminster, and to begin to rebuild our campaigning structures in the countryside, which we had allowed to decay somewhat while we concentrated on Yeovil. Chard, where we had launched our first-ever community leaflet back in the electric duplicator days, was already a strong base. So I spent much of 1980 recruiting new teams of young activists in the other areas where we now needed to grow.

We were lucky with local government by-elections. There were seven of these in all corners of the Constituency between 1979 and 1983, and we won all of them, taking seats from Labour and the Tories in roughly equal measure. We were now clearly the coming force in the Constituency, and this brought us defectors, too. We gained two Tories on the local Council and one key Labour activist, Greg Jefferies, who would later prove a most gifted Chairman of Schools on Somerset County Council.

It was at this time that we unleashed an explosion of local community leaflets across the Constituency, most of them called *Focus*, but some with more imaginative names like *The Merriot Ferret* and *The Martock Bean*. Clarissa was busier than ever, and our dining room table was ever more frequently occupied by teams of activists setting leaflets for printing.

This caused us a problem.

Shortly before the 1979 election, I had been 'headhunted' (if that is not too grand a word) by Morlands Sheepskin Coats of Glastonbury to help them set up a subsidiary called Tescan in Yeovil. This was the brainchild of one of the Morland family, Richard Morland, who was a neighbour and friend in Norton and a Liberal supporter. The plan was to set up a separate arms-length subsidiary of the long-established Glastonbury firm, which would buy, process and sell 'raw' sheepskins (that is sheepskin purchased straight from the abattoir). We would be the main supplier of these products to the parent firm, but could also sell them on the open market to any customer. Richard wanted me to look after Personnel and Marketing for the new firm. This meant learning entirely new skills but I leapt at the opportunity, in part because it meant a higher salary, in part because it meant leaving what was essentially a clerical job at Normalair Garrett and taking on a management one – and in part because Richard believed in worker participation, a key tenet of Liberal policy at the time and asked me to create the systems and structures to put this into operation. After eighteen months he then asked me to take on a more senior job, managing the production department, which was at the heart of our business and which dealt with the treatment and grading of all our raw sheepskins.

What all this meant was that our family finances received a much-needed boost from the salary which came with the new job – just as well, as the financial cushion we had accumulated was now exhausted. But we still had to be very careful about money. So providing hospitality to all the hungry and thirsty activists who descended on our house put a lot of strain on our very meagre resources. To alleviate this we took on one of the village allotments, where we grew all our own vegetables, and I took up home brewing. I brewed all my own beer, which was kept in a large plastic pressurised barrel in a corner cupboard in our kitchen, from which everyone knew they could help themselves. This led to disaster one evening when one of our activists tried to inject more gas into the container, without knowing how to stop it, causing the barrel to explode with a large bang and distributing five gallons of beer all over the room and everyone in it.

I also brewed my own wine from almost any fruit, or even vegetable, I could lay my hands on. I have to confess that the results were of variable quality. My apple wine was, I thought, excellent. But I could not, in good conscience, recommend the carrot or the parsnip. The flower wines, too, could be good, though the sight of me tripping home from the fields in the spring with baskets of primroses led to much ribald comment and an occasional lifted eyebrow on the part of my village neighbours – who clearly wondered what such behaviour said about the nature of Liberalism.

Good, bad or indifferent, however, the one thing all my wines had in common was their alcoholic content. We used to have an annual summer party for all our activists in our garden, and more than once this resulted in people wandering off into the dark, to be found insensible in some field or hedgerow the following morning.

But my home-made wines were more than just fun. They were also a deadly weapon when it came to persuading reluctant candidates to stand for us in a forthcoming local election. I tried the technique out first on one of my closest friends, Dick Budd, who, thanks to the best part of a bottle of apple wine, was persuaded to fight and eventually win our first country by-election in a strongly Tory rural ward in 1981. Thereafter there was no stopping me, and there are today many people high up in the ranks of South Somerset District Council (as it is now known) and Somerset County Council, whose political careers were launched on a tide of apple or rhubarb wine in my sitting room.

The team we assembled over these years was an extraordinary one. They were all about the same age as me, came from all sections of society, were utterly committed, and remain to this day some of our closest friends. They were also exceptional campaigners and pretty ruthless when it came to winning a by-election. I remember seeing two of them leap out of a vehicle in which they were making a last-minute dash to get a voter to the polling station before it closed, in order to help a farmer herd his sheep into a neighbour's field because they were obstructing the road. On another occasion one of our activists called five times at a house to persuade a supporter to get to the polls, only to find the would-be voter absent. On the final, sixth call, with fifteen minutes to go before the polls closed, he met the voter coming down his own front path. 'Have you voted yet? ' the activist asked. 'No. I have just got back from hospital. I am very ill,' came the reply. 'Well you had better hurry, then,' was the response. 'It could be your last time!'

Despite the fact that our battles with the Tories were strenuous, our disagreements did not carry over into personal animosity, and there was very little bad blood between the two parties locally. Indeed, my next-door neighbour in Norton was an elderly lady who had some difficulty erecting the Tory posters on stakes in her front garden, which was immediately adjacent to mine with its generous crop of Liberal ones – so I always used to do it for her. Perhaps it was because of this that I adopted a policy of never voting for myself, which has always puzzled my colleagues and observers. To me, it somehow seems improper to vote for oneself – so I have always cast my vote for whichever of my opponents I believed on personal (i.e., not political) grounds would make the best MP.

Two other factors also helped our political battle for Yeovil in those years. The first was that in 1981 the Boundary Commission altered the boundaries of the Constituency, removing two strongly Tory areas which had previously been in Yeovil and placing them into neighbouring Somerton and Frome. *The Times* estimated that the effect of this would have been to reduce John Peyton's Tory majority at the last election from 11,0000 to around 8,000 at the next – still a hefty majority to overcome in a general election, but at least things were moving in the right direction. The second factor was the announcement, also in 1981, that John Peyton would not stand at the next election. The Tories pretty quickly got themselves a new candidate, David Martin, but I had a six-year start on him in terms of getting myself known locally.

By now my strategy of behaving like an MP, even though I wasn't one, was beginning to bear fruit. More and more people were coming to see me with their problems at my Saturday morning surgeries and now I was getting invitations, which would normally have gone to the sitting MP, to open village fetes and community centres. The Tories were furious about this, but there was nothing they could do about it, especially since their own MP was standing down.

I soon found, though, that behaving like an MP meant I had to take positions on local issues, and this meant risking losing support as well as gaining it. In 1980, shortly after the general election, there was much unhappiness in one part of Yeovil over a decision to locate a care home for youngsters with learning difficulties in the area; the residents said it would reduce the value of their properties. I visited the area, spoke to the residents, and quickly concluded that this was pure prejudice. So I published a leaflet referring to local opposition to the plan as 'Yeovil's shame'. Needless to say, there was a furious reaction from the affected area, but this did not appear to affect our overall support in the town at all.

In the same year I learned that Westland Helicopters, by far the largest employer in the Constituency and then going through a very difficult period for orders, was about to sell helicopters to Chile. One of the Chileans sent over to clinch the deal had, it was reported, been involved in torture during the Pinochet years – including the torture of women such as Sheila Cassidy, who, back in my Foreign Office days, I had accompanied when she gave evidence to the UN in Geneva on the abuses she had suffered. To the considerable anger of Westland workers and the trades unions, whose jobs were at risk if Westland did not get the order, I made a series of public statements and speeches, saying that we should not sell helicopters to this kind of tyrant or 'buy jobs with the blood of innocents'. There was quite a row about it for a couple of weeks. But, interestingly enough, when the election came round three years later I got overwhelming support from Westland workers, and one or two even came up to me and said that, though they were very unhappy with me at the time, they understood and respected the reasons why I had taken this line, as that was my job.

I learned an important lesson over these incidents. The dangers of putting your conscience and judgement before your popularity are often far less than we politicians realise. The loss of votes in the short term is often compensated for in the long term by the gain in respect. Many voters want their MP to do what is right and often respect those who do, even while disagreeing with them. The scope for a bit of courage in politics is far greater than we think it is, even in this age of spin and the dark arts of 'triangulation'.

I was beginning to get a wider reputation in the Party, too. I refused all requests to play a role in the National Party, believing that my job was to win Yeovil; the rest could come later. Nevertheless, at the 1981 Liberal Assembly in Llandudno I led the debate on a successful motion to oppose the deployment of cruise missiles, causing acute embarrassment to David Steel and the Party leadership. I still regard this speech as one of the best I have ever made, and it got me my first mentions in the national Press.* It also made me popular with the Party's radical element (though I remember warning them at the time that, not being a unilateralist or a member of CND, I would probably soon part with them on this issue when the situation changed). But it did not make me popular with the Party hierarchy, and I remember overhearing one of our senior peers asking, 'Who is this bloody boy scout, Paddy Ashdown?'

Llandudno was also the Assembly in which David Steel won support for the Party to join with the SDP in creating the Liberal–SDP Alliance. This enabled him to end his leader's speech with his famous exhortation: 'Go back to your constituencies and prepare for government!'

Increasingly, Yeovil was by now being picked out as an example of effective campaigning and a rising prospect and, together with other candidates from potentially winnable seats, I spoke on our successes so far to a crowded meeting at the annual Assembly at Bournemouth in 1982. Earlier that year David Penhaligon did a tour of potential target seats in the region and reported back that, in his view, the best prospect for a Liberal gain in the south-west was Yeovil. After this we started getting visits from VIPs and MPs, including Clement Freud, David Penhaligon himself, John Pardoe and, in late 1982, with the election coming into view, David Steel, who opened our newly refurbished (i.e., repainted by Jane, myself and some volunteers) offices in the Yeovil Liberal Club.

But, just as things were beginning to move forward strongly for us politically, they began to deteriorate sharply for us from a personal point of view. By 1981 the first Thatcher recession was beginning to bite sharply and was affecting Morlands, like many other small businesses. The pound was rising, causing the exports, which formed a major portion of Morlands' business, to become more expensive and

* *The Times*, Friday 18 Sep 1981: 'Paddy Ashdown, Liberal prospective parliamentary candidate for Yeovil opened the debate on nuclear weapons. . . . Mr Ashdown said that . . . the purpose of the resolution was to show a way out, to tell both superpowers that Europe would not continue one step more down that fatal road (of the nuclear arms race), that a united free and democratic Europe did not see its future as part of the super power conflict . . . (or) . . . mutually assured destruction'.

our foreign competitors' imports to become cheaper. In early 1981 I had to begin laying off workers, which I hated. But worse was to come. Later that year it finally became clear that the whole of Morlands was collapsing, and a few months after this I had to call all my workers together to tell them that Tescan would close and we would all lose our jobs. It was, needless to say, a terrible and painful day.

It also left our family with a real crisis. We now had no financial cushion left. I would have to live off unemployment benefit until I got a job. And getting a job during the recession of 1981–2 was going to be very difficult. I put in perhaps two-hundred-and-fifty applications for local jobs over the following months. All were rejected. I even looked into the possibility of training as a heavy goods vehicle driver (because the money was so good), but soon found I had absolutely no aptitude for the work. (In retrospect this was probably a good thing, for I am, by universal acknowledgement, a shocking driver and would have been, I am certain, lethal at the wheel of a large truck.)

I had by now persuaded the Constituency to sell one of its old Liberal Halls and buy a small town-centre property in Yeovil at 5 Waterloo Lane. In this we now housed Clarissa and another second-hand photo-offset litho to keep her company and share the work. I spent much of my unemployed time growing the printing business, which was now taking on work from constituencies all over the south-west and even commercial work from local community organisations. All the profits from this, however, were ploughed back into the Constituency party, so this was just a time-filler for me and not a money-earner.

Meanwhile, Jane earned us some much-needed extra cash by cooking produce for a local market and picking apples on the village fruit farm. In the autumn we used to go out as a family and gather what we could from the countryside to put in our deep freeze for the winter, especially blackberries, which seemed to half fill the freezer at times. Sloes were another favourite, from which we made sloe gin – when we could afford the gin! This was made in early October and, by family tradition, opened on Christmas Day. On one occasion, never forgotten by my family, I boasted that we could, if need be, live off the land and, to prove it, went out gathering a small fungus called 'fairy ring champignons' or *Marasmius oreades*. The French dry these and use them in stews, but I made the pile I had collected into a pie with potatoes. It was so indescribably awful that no one ate a bite of it, and I have never since been trusted with the family cooking.

These were very tough and dispiriting days for us all, but, as usual, the main burden fell on Jane. Things came to a head in late June 1982 when I reviewed our finances and discovered that we now had only £150 left in the bank. Something had to be done. Jane and I talked about the situation late one night after the kids had gone to bed. We agreed that we would spend £100 of our last reserves on sending the children to Switzerland to stay with friends for their summer holidays. And then, if I had not got a job by the time they came back, I would have to give up and return to my old employers.

Nothing changed until the very last day of July, when, with one week to go before our deadline, two things happened. The first was that I opened the post in the morning to find a cheque for a £1,000 from the Rowntree Trust, with a note saying that they hoped I would accept this and that it would help me keep going. It was only later that I realised that my good friend, fellow candidate and future Chief Whip, Archy Kirkwood, had played a part in this. He was working at the time in the Liberal Whips' Office in Parliament, had spotted my predicament and, together with Richard Wainwright, the Liberal MP for Colne Valley (who had not at the time met me, but in his supporting letter for the grant said he had been impressed by the chorus of support in my favour), had persuaded the Rowntree Trust Social Fund to help. Archy has since dug up my reply to this offer. It is dated 1 August 1982 and reads, 'I did not believe in fairy godmothers until I read your letter! Quite simply, this [offer] could not have arrived at a more opportune moment'.

The second event, which occurred later that same day, was that I heard that I had been successful in obtaining a post as a Youth Worker in Dorset County Council, funded by the Community Programme.* The salary was, of course very low, but it was a job, which meant a regular income coming in, and we were delighted.

I started my new job in September 1982 in County Hall, Dorchester and soon found myself totally engrossed in it. My title was 'Youth Initiative Officer', a new temporary post which was to last as long as the Community Programme funding did. The task was to work with the County's Youth Centres to devise schemes to help the young unemployed. I learned a huge amount from my colleagues in the Dorset Youth Service, who, like my colleagues in Normalair, were wel-

---

* A government-funded programme designed to get the long-term unemployed back to work.

coming and patient in introducing me to the complexities of youth work – not least to the lesson that successful work with young people depends on having the courage to listen to them, let them take responsibility and be ready to stand back when they make mistakes, so as to give them the space to learn. In the course of this work I devised a scheme that set up a fund, made up of contributions from local businesses, dedicated to helping the young unemployed to start their own businesses, with the local businessmen who had contributed acting as 'mentors' to help them get started. (A very similar formula was later adopted by the Prince of Wales in his Prince's Youth Business Trust – now called The Prince's Trust.) I was subsequently told by the Youth Service that in 1995 there were still some five thriving businesses in the County, employing several tens of people, which had started life under this scheme.

Shortly after I started my new job, Jane received a small legacy. We decided to use some of it to pay for a week's skiing holiday with friends in Switzerland.

Our trip out has become something of a family legend, as the journey from hell. Our car at the time was a small second-hand red Renault Five that had definitely seen better days, and into this the four of us crammed, together with all the kit we needed for a week's skiing and, unbeknown to all except Jane, an open apple tart – of which more later. The journey was cursed from the start. First the aerial broke just as we were leaving and had to be replaced by a bent piece of wire coat-hanger. Then, at the very moment we left Yeovil, it started to snow . . . and snow and snow and snow! That evening was spent battling through snowdrifts in Kent before arriving three hours late for the ferry at Dover. After a very rough crossing we were stopped at Calais by a French customs official, who had not unreasonably concluded that we were probably a family of illegal refugees on the move. He asked to see what was in the car and soon came across a bottle which was corked, labelled and full of a most suspicious-looking orange-coloured liquid. He asked me what it was that I was bringing into France. I replied that it was carrot wine. He looked at us with total incredulity.

'Du vin de carotte?? En France? Mais comme ils sont fou, les Anglais!'

Then he waved us through with a Gallic shrug to end all Gallic shrugs.

We drove off into a blizzard and soon lost our way in the white-out on the motorway, wandering off into the winding back roads of northern France and ending up at two o'clock in the morning in the little town of Abbeville. Here the poor old Renault finally baulked at getting up the steep hill out of the town, which was inches deep in snow. I announced that we would have to sleep where we were and try again in the morning. But ten minutes crammed into the Renault, getting colder and colder, soon changed all our minds. Reasoning that the car was a front wheel drive and that we might therefore get up the hill better in reverse, I put Simon on the bonnet, turned the car round and we backed all the way up to the summit of the hill without a hitch. A grey and snowy dawn found us on the outskirts of Paris, where we promptly lost ourselves again trying to find the Boulevard Périphérique. After an hour or so we rediscovered our route and headed south on the A6, thinking the worst was now behind us. But fate had other ideas. Passing Besançon, the exhaust pipe fell off and had to be tied back on using one of Simon's neck scarves (he was, at the time, following a pop group who were big on neck scarves). Then I left the petrol cap off at a filling station, and we had to plug the petrol tank with a plastic bag. Then, crossing the Jura in thick snow, we got a puncture, which meant unpacking the whole of the car. It was only at this stage that we discovered Jane's apple tart had spent the last twenty-four hours slowly leaking all over our clothes and ski kit. Finally, and foolishly, I tried a joke with a Swiss border guard at which he took offence – apparently shared by his very large dog, which made a determined attempt to eat me.

We arrived with our friends after 28 hours cooped up in a Renault Five at the end of a journey which should have taken fourteen. But then we had a wonderful week, with bright sunshine and glorious snow as compensation.

When we got back, Jane and I decided to use the remainder of her legacy to buy our (or should I say 'my') first computer. These machines were just appearing on the scene in Britain, and I was immediately fascinated by them and how they could be used in politics for better communication with the voters. My first computer was a Sirius, which used as storage two disk drives, each able to take a half-megabyte floppy disk. I used it to start with for correspondence, keeping the records of my surgery cases and managing our by now very complex and large-scale *Counter Point* distribution lists. But even in those early days I was very conscious of the potential of these new machines for communicating with the electorate and remember saying to a friend as early as 1982 that, alongside leaflets, computers would soon be used to send individually personalised letters through the post to each elector. I was subsequently the first MP to have a computer in the House of Commons. Later a friend, Gillian Gunner, and I wrote the first-ever election-fighting computer program: Polly. (To be precise, she did the programming, and I provided the political advice.) This software became widely used in the Party, gave us an early and important tactical advantage over the other parties in elections and was instrumental in our string of by-election victories in the early days of my Leadership of the Party.

We were now making steady progress in Yeovil. But we were not immune to the impact of political events on the national scene. The Labour Party was still catastrophically divided and floundering. Meanwhile the Liberal–SDP Alliance was enjoying a bubble of success. I was against the Alliance when it all started back in 1980, saying in a local TV interview that 'we should not sell our [Liberal] birthright for this mess of pottage'. But I soon saw I was wrong. The Alliance's popularity shot up at first, reaching a dizzying 50% in opinion polls at the end of 1981. But this hype could not be sustained, and soon we began to drift downwards again. Meanwhile the Falklands campaign burst upon us. I remember sitting on the Down above Weymouth, listening over my car radio to the debate in the House of Commons and wishing I was there. It is often believed that it was the Falklands campaign that turned things round for Mrs Thatcher. This is wrong. I remember very clearly feeling that the public mood was beginning to swing behind her several months before it began. The Falklands victory may not have created the Thatcher bounce-back, but it certainly consolidated and accelerated it.

It was clear to all of us that the general election would have to be called that year, and that Mrs Thatcher would wait to see the result of the 5 May District Council elections before deciding whether it would be a month later, in June, or whether she would wait for the autumn. In Yeovil we beat Conservatives and Labour alike in the local elections, winning a total of twenty-seven seats (twenty-four Liberal and three SDP) on the District Council and overturning decades of Conservative control. This gave us minority control of the Council, which soon became outright control, due to defections and by-election wins: a position never lost in the twenty-five years since.

But Mrs Thatcher was not looking at Yeovil. She was looking at the country at large, where the results confirmed that, in an early election, she would probably be returned with a handsome majority. The Alliance and Labour, meanwhile, were neck and neck in the national polls.

When, four days after the local poll, she called the general election for 9 June, and I said goodbye to my colleagues in Dorset Youth Service on temporary leave of absence to fight the campaign, I fully expected to see them again in a few weeks' time. I knew, of course that our position in Yeovil was much stronger than it had been in 1979, and that we would probably widen the gap with Labour and narrow it with the Tories – putting us within striking distance, I hoped, of being able to beat them at the next election. But I did not think we could actually win.

And the start of our campaign in 1983 did very little to encourage me. Nick sent Jane and me alone to Buckland St Mary (at the time a Tory stronghold) at the western extremity of the Constituency. In a whole day's canvassing we found no more than a tiny handful of supporters, and then, to top it all, at the first public meeting of the campaign in the village hall that evening, not a single person turned up. Dejected and cross, I rang Nick that evening complaining that it was a disaster and that no one had come out to help us. He calmed me down and got me back on the road the following day, saying that his plan was to leave our best areas to the last.

At first the Liberal–SDP Alliance did not do well. I remember being shocked by the discovery that Roy Jenkins (for whom I had, and retain, a very high regard) was so unpopular, especially in Labour areas. He was – most unfairly, in my view – seen by many, including potential supporters, as an upper-crust fat cat who had returned from Brussels (where he had been President of the Commission) and was completely out of touch with the realities of life in Britain. Our opinion poll ratings started to drift down dangerously. Halfway through the campaign, David Steel called a 'summit' at his house in Ettrick Bridge in Scotland and, in a move as deft as it was ruthless and necessary, sidelined Jenkins and took control of the national campaign. Our poll ratings began to recover immediately.

From this moment onwards our local campaign got better and better and more and more fun every day. Our daily and constant companion was Les Farris, then a relatively newly arrived activist, later a most effective regional agent for the Party in the south-west when I was Leader, and ever since one of our closest friends. He drove us everywhere in a long-wheelbase Land Rover lent by a friend, to which we became so attached on our dawn to dusk daily outings that, for some reason I cannot remember, we conferred on it a Party membership card under the name Trevor Dark Green. It was on this campaign that Les also invented a new political rule, which we called the Jack Russell Protocol. This asserted that everyone who owned a Jack Russell was a Liberal voter. And so it apparently turned out to be. For we tried the Jack Russell Protocol out on every owner of a Jack Russell we saw during the campaign (and there seem to be many in this part of Somerset), and it never failed us. On election day itself, we were driving down an especially bumpy and isolated country lane and came across a Jack-Russell-cross hunting in the hedgerow. I insisted that Les should stop so that I could search out the owner, who I found a few moments later and, in the presence of his half-Jack Russell/half-dachshund, I asked him how he intended to vote? He told me that he had half-decided to vote Liberal, but hadn't made up his mind yet!

A number of national newspapers visited Yeovil and did profiles on us, some saying (*The Times* in particular) that Yeovil was a possible Liberal gain from the Tories. We cut these out and put them in our last-minute leaflet to boost our momentum. On the eve of the poll, I met for an end-of-campaign pint or two with fellow campaigners in the Rose and Crown, a rural and very down to earth pub* we loved, right in the very centre of the Constituency. During our conversation one of our team complained that they did not have enough 'Good Morning' leaflets for the following day. I immediately went back to our headquarters, changed into the Turin Shroud, flashed up Clarissa and printed more for them before returning home at 2 a.m. I slept fitfully that night, worrying about what tomorrow would bring.

Despite the positive comments of the Press and the optimism of our campaigners, at the start of polling day I did not feel that victory was possible – though I did think we could come quite close. But during the day I was struck by a real sense of excitement on the streets. Children cheered us wherever we went, and so many people came up in the street asking for stickers that we soon ran out and had to call for more.

* We ended our triumphant 1997 national campaign in this pub with the narrow Somerset lane outside crowded with my national campaign 'battle bus', and the place heaving with television cameras and journalists.

Nevertheless, driving into the count at 11 p.m. that night I wondered to Jane whether I could keep it going for another four years to the next election. She told me not to be so silly: we were going to win. As I walked in, Nick Speakman came over to me and said he thought we were ahead, but it was narrow. Kate and Simon and one of our female activists who said she couldn't stand the suspense either, immediately retired with a packet of cigarettes to the ladies' loo and refused to come out. Jane and I, meanwhile, took ourselves off to a room set aside for the candidates, where we spoke to the Press and tried to look unconcerned. At a few minutes past midnight, Nick came to me and whispered in my ear that we had won. It was only at this stage that Kate, on hearing the news, emerged from the loo to throw her arms around the nearest startled stranger and tried to dance round with him, shouting, 'I can't believe it – he's won! He's won!', only to discover that her reluctant dance partner was the defeated Tory candidate, David Martin!

The rest of that night is a blur. I stumbled through my acceptance speech as best I could, after which my supporters took me outside and tossed me in the air (this was the picture which appeared on the TV, revealing that, in our hour of triumph, my enthusiastic friends very nearly bashed me to death on the overhanging concrete lintel of the counting hall).

When the news of our victory in Yeovil was announced on television that night it was misheard by someone in Liberal Headquarters who for some hours kept putting out statements saying the Liberals had won a stunning and wholly unexpected victory in 'The Oval'. The following morning, I heard Mrs Thatcher being interviewed about her victory. She was asked if she had ever thought she would lose. She replied that she had doubted victory only once – when, early in the night, she heard that the Liberals had won Yeovil. In the late afternoon David Steel rang to congratulate me, and Kate answered the phone. She asked who it was who wanted to speak to me, to be told that it was David Steel. She replied, 'Yeah! And if you're David Steel, then I'm Margaret Thatcher!' before I could grab the phone from her.

Looking back, I regard this night – the night of 9 June 1983 – as the night of my life and the achievement I am most proud of. Another new MP elected on the same night as me was Tony Blair. But the difference between us could not have been starker. He had walked into his constituency of Sedgefield and been selected as its candidate at the start of the general election campaign three weeks before. I had taken seven years to win mine. It was a matter we would, in due course, joke about when he was leading his party and I was leading mine – but it marked a difference between us, in our approach to politics, which I am not sure he ever understood. Jane and I were to become friends with Tony Blair and Cherie, and I always recognised him as a politician of exceptional gifts and talents. But his was a smooth, golden ascent to the top, which never involved either enduring personal hardship or encountering setbacks for what he believed in. I believe this was a weakness which sometimes caused him to be less anchored and more easily blown off course by storms got up by the Press than he should have been. It was certainly an impediment to our partnership before and after the 1997 election. He simply couldn't understand why I would never even contemplate a straight merger between Labour and the Liberal Democrats. I think he was never really able to comprehend why the Party existed at all, when its members could have taken the far easier option of joining one of the larger parties and taking an inevitable turn at power, instead of standing against the odds and putting up with so much for independence and what we believed in.

Shortly after our general election triumph the Yeovil Liberals repeated their success in the local Town Council elections, removing the Tories from power in all the politicised local Town Councils in the Constituency, and two years later, in May 1985, we took control of Somerset County Council as well, winning every County seat in my Constituency. In just over a decade we had swept the Tories away completely and ended the Conservative hold on Somerset which had endured for more than seventy years.

And these Council successes were not just technical victories. I believe they made a real difference to the quality of people's lives in our area, too – perhaps even more than getting a Liberal MP in Westminster. South Somerset District Council went on to become one of the flagship Councils for innovation and good government in the country and one of the leaders in rural decentralisation of services, bringing the Council closer to the people it served. It was also the first Council in which there were more women than men in the ruling group (i.e., the Lib Dems), and the first in which women outnumbered men in the key leadership positions. It was awarded the Council of the Year in Britain and has won a number of environmental awards as well. Somerset County Council has been similarly successful, winning Green Council of the Year in 2003, as well as receiving other recognition for the quality of its services, especially in environmental matters.

Nor was that the end. What we started in Yeovil spread throughout the south-west in what the Press later referred to as the 'orange tide'. When I was elected in 1983 my nearest Liberal neighbour was David Penhaligon in far-away Truro. Now three of the five Somerset MPs are Lib Dems, as are two in Devon and every single MP in Cornwall. The team we built in Yeovil over these years was very much part of this revolution. Of those who helped us take control of politics at every level in Yeovil Constituency, one (apart from me) is now in the Lords, one became an MP for Taunton, five fought their own Parliamentary seats, two (including my one-time Constituency Secretary, Cathy Bakewell, who had been present on that night in 1976 when I was selected) became Chairs or Leaders of Somerset County Council, and we have provided every subsequent Chair and Leader of the District Council, and almost every Mayor of Yeovil and the other major towns in the Constituency ever since.

On that cold and foggy November day in 1976 when I was selected as Yeovil's PPC I could have stood on Ham Hill, above the village in which I live, looking west over south Somerset, right into north Devon and north-west Dorset and not have seen a single seat controlled by Liberals, from parish and town level up. When I stood down as Yeovil MP in 2001 someone worked out that you could walk from Lands End to London without ever leaving territory held by a Liberal Democrat at some level or another.

But that was all still to come. My next stop, and our new adventure after 9 June 1983, was Westminster.

CHAPTER 11

Member of Parliament

NOT SINCE OUR NIGHTMARE winter journey to Switzerland had our little Renault Five, now significantly more dilapidated, been so overloaded. Kate, Simon and some of our overnight suitcases were jammed in the back, along with our dog Traddles, who, as always, was hanging out of the rear window, coat flying, ears flapping wildly in the wind, fulfilling his duty to protect the car by barking enthusiastically at every passer-by (much more fun here in London – hundreds more to bark at than in Somerset). His job was made easier because the Renault's back windows had become detached, and I had attempted to repair them with black tape, to keep Traddles in. But this minor impediment had long since been brushed aside, leaving a fringe of little flags of black tape fluttering in the wind, framing his barking head and giving the whole a faintly heraldic aspect.

For my part, I was doing my level best to pretend I was in no way connected with any of this, while trying to muster such as I could of the dignity befitting a newly elected MP on his way to the State Opening of Parliament. Jane, meanwhile, was trying to find her way through heavy traffic in London, with only a hazy idea of where she was going and pandemonium reigning around her. To be truthful – and to make matters worse – I had misjudged the time it would take us to get to Westminster, so we were not only lost, but also late. I could not banish from my mind the image of Her Majesty (who would have long ago left Buckingham Palace) turning up behind us – gilded coach, liveried footmen, Household Cavalry and all – and being forced to complete her Royal progress to Parliament behind our decrepit vehicle with Traddles hanging out the back window barking at the horses and having the time of his life.

Just as I was thinking that all was lost, and we should turn round and go home to Somerset, we burst onto the Embankment just short of Vauxhall Bridge. Shortly after that, we met our first police roadblock barring entrance to Parliament Square. We drove up, and I explained I was an MP (I think this was the first time I ever used the title) and needed to get to the House for the State Opening. The policeman took one look at the car and seemed disinclined to believe me. But I produced my newly obtained House of Commons pass, and he let us through, narrowly avoiding a savaging from Traddles as we passed. Now we were on Millbank, and the roads were largely empty, save for an ambassadorial Rolls Royce or two sweeping majestically past us and a few spectators. There was much laughing as we sped through and quite a few cheers, which I knew were not intended to be helpful.

Then another road block, another disbelieving policeman and another flash of my pass and we were in Parliament Square. Now there were many more spectators and much more cheering, to which Traddles responded enthusiastically – I was now trying to look as invisible as the front seat of a Renault Five would allow. Jane floored the accelerator and cut the corners of Parliament Square practically on two wheels, while Traddles (now three-quarters out of the back window) yapped as though his life depended on it. Finally, and with great relief, we dived into the safety of the House of Commons underground car park.

But if this day, 22 June 1983 and my first full one as an MP, began as farce, it ended in something that, for the six newly elected Liberal MPs, seemed very close to tragedy. That night, after all the pomp and ceremony of the State Opening was over, I joined my five new colleagues* at our first Liberal Parliamentary Party meeting, held in a windowless, airless underground room where the Liberal MPs, apparently by tradition, always held their meetings. We thought David Steel had fought a good campaign. He had certainly saved our bacon by deftly manoeuvring Roy Jenkins out of the limelight at the Ettrick Bridge summit. He had helped secure 26% of the vote for the Alliance, placing it only 2% behind Labour. And he had increased the number of Liberal MPs to 17, against the SDP's 6. And now we newly elected MPs were enthusiastic to start taking advantage of the turmoil in the Labour Party after its disastrous showing and the resignation, immediately after the election, of its Leader, Michael Foot. It therefore came as a profound shock to all the newcomers when, instead of being congratulated, our Leader was viciously attacked by some of our more experienced MPs in one of the most unpleasant and dispiriting meetings between colleagues I have ever attended – and all for very minor personal things.

* Michael Meadowcroft (Leeds West), Archy Kirkwood (Roxburgh and Berwickshire), Alex Carlile (Montgomeryshire), Jim Wallace (Orkney and Shetland) and Malcolm Bruce (Gordon).

Cyril Smith rounded on him because David's battle bus had got so held up by traffic that he turned up an hour late in Cyril's Rochdale seat, discommoding the brass band Cyril had arranged. David Alton attacked him because Steel and Alton had rowed over Alton's support for his neighbouring Liberal candidate. After choosing his own seat, Alton also backed the next-door Liberals, who did not want to cede their constituency (much of which had been in the constituency won by Alton's Liberals in the 1979 by-election) to an SDP MP from the other side of the city. Steel, not wanting to be seen to go against the nationally agreed deal with the SDP, therefore made only a very brief visit to support David Alton's campaign, which the latter seemed to regard as a personal slight. Others attacked David Steel because, as they put it, they were not deemed important enough to be asked to the Ettrick Bridge summit, and because, they alleged, his leadership style was too remote and high-handed. It was my first taste of what was to dog us for the rest of this Parliament and severely hamper our ability to capitalise on the historic opportunity of Labour's disarray. With a few exceptions (such as David Penhaligon, Russell Johnston, Richard Wainwright and our new Chief Whip Alan Beith), most of the older MPs were self-centred individualists: outstanding personalities in their own constituencies, but unable or unwilling to play as members of the team. The truth was that the Party had changed since the majority of these longer-standing Liberal MPs had been elected. Most of the 1983 new intake had a close relationship with Liberal local government groups and the Association of Liberal Councillors and knew both the habits and the importance of discipline and teamwork in politics; most of those who were elected before us did not. The point was graphically illustrated, when, after the meeting, Clement Freud invited Archy Kirkwood, Alex Carlile and me to dine with him and took us off to a club (a casino as I remember), where he spent the entire evening telling us how awful all his colleagues were, one by one.

Tantrums over trivial personal things were very frequent among the pre-1983 Liberal MPs, and I sometimes wondered how on earth David Steel kept his cool in the face of these provocations. In the case of Cyril Smith and David Alton, these most often took place in the full glare of publicity at the Liberals' Annual Assembly, presumably in order to achieve greater influence and attention. But others' ructions occurred in private. Stephen Ross, MP for the Isle of Wight, used to make a habit of resigning every other week at the Parliamentary Party meeting. Apparently on one occasion, when the weekly meeting was held in a new and unfamiliar room, Stephen stormed out with the usual display of drama, slamming behind him the door of what he took to be the exit, but which everyone else knew led into a broom cupboard. The rest of the meeting sat quietly waiting for him to emerge to a thunderous round of applause and much merriment from everyone (except, of course, him).

But it was not just tensions in the Liberal team that were depressing to newly elected MPs. Shortly after the election our partners in the SDP underwent a bout of squabbling, initiated by a visit David Owen paid to Roy Jenkins at which, in effect, he demanded his resignation as Party leader. Jenkins, not wanting the bloodletting of an internal election in the SDP, acquiesced and stood aside. Since both the other members of the Gang of Four, Shirley Williams and Bill Rodgers, had lost their seats, this left the way open for Owen to claim the Leadership unopposed in what David Steel has described as a 'bloodless coup'.* Unfortunately, Owen, in so many other ways the outstanding politician of his age, had a number of personal weaknesses, chief among them a powerful ego. But the one which wrecked us at this crucial time was that he was viscerally and often irrationally hostile to the Liberals, and frequently openly dismissive of David Steel – whom he regarded, I think, as just not having the stuff of real leadership in him (in the end, though, Steel proved much the more successful leader of the two). So, although the two parties had fought the election side by side as a single team, David Owen resisted any idea of their forming a single team in the Commons. The two parliamentary parties had to meet separately, and each appointed their own parliamentary spokespersons. This, in my view, was as tragic as it was self-indulgent, for it caused confusion, duplication and division between us, just when Labour was at its most vulnerable. Looking back on this Parliament, I believe David Owen's determination to be separate cost us the greatest historical opportunity we ever had to push Labour aside and become Britain's premier Party of the centre left. It became an issue over which some of us newly arrived MPs would criticise the SDP Leader increasingly openly during our all-too-rare joint Liberal/SDP Parliamentary meetings – something he plainly regarded as pure impudence from such neophytes. (This, I think, contributed a good deal to

* David Steel, *Against Goliath: David Steel's Story* (London: Weidenfeld and Nicholson, 1989), p. 249.

the personal tension between David Owen and myself when we had to fight a battle to the death in public after I became the Leader of the newly formed Liberal Democrats. But that was still a long way ahead.)

In 1983 our immediate problems of dissension and disarray were compounded by the fact that David Steel, exhausted by the election, fed up with the backbiting and still not over a very bad dose of flu, decided to throw in the towel and resign. We new MPs only heard about this afterwards, when our Chief Whip, Alan Beith, and other friends had persuaded him to withdraw his secret letter of resignation and announce, instead, that he was having a three-month 'sabbatical'. All this left us somewhat leaderless at a critical moment. The five newly elected Liberal MPs were not to be put off by such matters, however, and, under the highly able (if sometimes, for my taste, a little too conventional) leadership of Alan Beith, we mounted a guerrilla campaign in the House of Commons designed to show up Labour's weakness. This culminated on one occasion with my breaking the sacred conventions of the House and, during a debate on Trade and Industry, making my speech from the Official Opposition's Despatch Box, left unoccupied because Labour had not bothered to put anyone forward in the debate. (Alan subsequently mildly upbraided me for taking things too far on this occasion.)

To be honest, I was, even at this early stage, finding the traditions and pomp of the Commons pretty irksome. I am not at all a clubbable person, so the fact that the Commons is said to be 'the best club in London' held no attractions for me. The silly uniforms and strange names (such as the Gentleman Usher of Black Rod) are supposed to be quaint – but I just found them ridiculous. For my first three months or so as an MP I recall feeling that there was some dark, unnamed fear lurking in my mind. I finally concluded that the atmosphere and culture of the House was so redolent of my public school that my subconscious was worrying whether my mother had sewn name tapes on my all underwear! The hours, too, I thought ridiculous, permitting neither a normal life outside the Commons nor a reasonable life in it. I have never liked or mastered the Chamber of the House, and it has never much liked me either. In part this is because I am not very good at wit and repartee, which the Commons loves; in part it is because I find the style of Parliamentary debate offensively (even childishly) confrontational. But also it is because the Chamber of the House of Commons somehow or other – perhaps because of fear – brings out the worst in me, making me sound shrill and often rather self-righteous.

But what chiefly annoyed me about the House in 1983 was that it was so out of date. It took me six weeks even to get an office – though I did have a coat-hanger from day one. This not only had my name on it – in gothic script, no less – but also came complete with a red ribbon hanging from one corner. I asked what this was for, to be informed (in tones implying I must be a country bumpkin not to know) that it was to hang my sword from! I seriously considered bringing in my Royal Marines sword and hanging it from the ribbon, making myself perhaps the first MP for two hundred years to use this piece of apparently essential Parliamentary equipment for the purpose for which it was originally designed.

For six weeks I had to do my work and look after the affairs of my seventy-five thousand Yeovil constituents from four square feet of floor space in one of the covered cloisters of the House. As for my computer, this confused everyone. No one, apparently, had ever had one of these things before, and I was initially informed by the authorities that the House did not recognise computers and could make no financial or technical allowances for them.

Eventually, I got an office, taking over the desk of Bill Pitt, whose by-election victory in Croydon North West in October 1981 I had worked for, but who had been one of the Liberal casualties of the recent election. This meant that I shared an office with David Penhaligon, from which I benefited greatly (though I suspect he probably did not).

David was a remarkable man from whom I learned a very great deal. He loved to hide behind the bluff exterior of a simple Cornishman. But behind this façade was a most acute mind, buttressed by a real genius for speaking in a way which made even complex issues understandable to ordinary people. He was a natural comic, with superb timing, as well as a very decent man and a most generous colleague who went out of his way to help me through my first year in Parliament. One thing he was not, however, was organised. Another thing he was not was tidy. And the third thing he definitely was not, was an early riser.

None of these drawbacks would have been too serious for someone sharing an office with him, but for the fact that David did not just work in his (our) office: he also slept there – usually until around eleven in the morning. It seemed, moreover, that he only had two shirts (drip-dry), one pair of underpants and one pair of socks, which he would wash nightly and hang out on the office radiator to dry. This presumably had not mattered with Bill Pitt, since he, too, was a late riser. But I am an early riser and am invariably at my desk by eight at the latest and holding my first meetings shortly afterwards. Not that this disturbed David's sleep patterns in the slightest (he would, I am sure, have been quite capable of sleeping through a full-scale bombing raid).

It did disturb me, though, for I was acting as Liberal Parliamentary spokesman on Trade and Industry (David Steel asked me to do it because, he said, I was the only Liberal MP with any experience of running a business), and in this capacity had regular morning meetings with bankers and industrialists who wanted to be helpful. What these captains of British industry thought of meetings conducted to the accompaniment of David's stertorous snores from the other side of the office bookcase, while his shirts, socks and underpants hung in festoons around us, they were far too polite to say. I soon learned from bitter experience to avoid fixing meetings before 11.30. Before this, David could at any moment emerge, bleary-eyed, stubble-chinned and usually naked, but for a very skimpy towel round his midriff, and thread his way wordlessly through the assembly on my side of the office, heading for the adjacent Gents lavatory and his morning ablutions.

I found my first year in Parliament by turns dispiriting and frustrating, and also sometimes irksome. It proved quite exhausting, as well. In those days we received no training to be an MP and were more or less left to our own devices, to sink or swim with little help from the Party and none from the House of Commons authorities. Meanwhile, I had two complete offices to set up (one in London and one in Yeovil), together with staff to recruit and equipment to purchase for both. I was exceptionally fortunate on both fronts. My old Geneva Foreign Office Secretary, Sue Hedderwick (by then Sue O'Sullivan, married and with three children) agreed to come and set up my London office for me (in fact it was with her and her husband Rod, that we had all spent the night before the State Opening). And back in my constituency I managed to persuade the then Yeovil Constituency Secretary, Cathy Bakewell, to work for me. Both did an outstanding job. Sue O'Sullivan, who ultimately became a teacher, worked for me until expecting her fourth child, returning briefly to run my personal office during my campaign for the Party Leadership in 1988. Cathy Bakewell spent twenty long years working for me, first in the Constituency and then, after the 1997 election, running my Leader's Office in London. She later went on be elected a County Councillor, become a highly effective Leader of Somerset County Council and be awarded a MBE for her public work.

A person of fiery temperament, strong character and decided views, she and I fought regularly about many things, but never fell out for long over anything. I have discovered that secretaries to the 'important' generally come in two categories. There are the charming ones who present an ever-smiling face and dispense sweetness to all as they pass through the 'shining portals of power'. And then there are the 'dragons', who see it as their duty to lie across the front of the cave and give all, irrespective of rank or status, a sharp nip on the ankles as they pass. The formidable Cathy Bakewell (though no dragon in the conventional sense of the word, I hasten to add) definitely fell into the second category, and I knew several senior Parliamentarians who were so in awe of her that they would go to great lengths to make sure their visits to see me were at times when she was out of the office.

Even with the help of Sue and Cathy, though, it still took a good year to establish my two offices and get them working effectively. One of the causes of the system overload was, of course, me. I was like Billy Bunter in a tuck shop – I simply could not believe the number of things people suddenly wanted me to get involved in, and could refuse none of them. The result was that I took up speaking engagements from one end of the country to the other almost every weekend. By the time the summer Parliamentary recess came, what with the nervous energy of the election campaign and the hectic programme afterwards, I was exhausted. Jane and I decided to take three weeks in Switzerland, where we went to visit Kate, then working as an au pair in a village above Lake Geneva. After that we took two weeks with our son Simon and Les Farris and his wife Joan on a walking holiday in the Canton of Apenzell, using as our base a chalet belonging to some Swiss friends from our Geneva days. After one especially long walk I banged my shin, which, probably because of my run-down state, almost immediately went bad, spreading poison right up my leg and, after a couple of days, making me delirious with fever. We were a long way from a town and a doctor, but fortunately Joan Farris is a nurse, and she, with the help of a local pharmacist, managed to get me back on my feet again. The pharmacist said that I was lucky not to lose the leg.

In every other job I had done, I had found my energy had far outrun the needs of the job. But the job of an MP can be as big or as small as you wish to make it, and, being an enthusiast, I wanted to make it as big as possible. However, the lesson of my poisoned leg was clear: for the first time in my life I was going to have to limit myself to what I could do properly, rather than taking on everything that came my way. I swiftly decided that the first thing was to consolidate my base in Yeovil. With a majority of 3,600, it was anything but secure, so building it up into a safe seat was priority number one.

I discussed my frustrations with David Penhaligon, who pointed me in the right direction in Westminster: 'You want my advice? Specialise, boy,' he said. 'Choose something, preferably something eye-catching, and make yourself the acknowledged expert on it in the House.'

As it happened, just at this time I was being contacted by the newly emerging British computer industry about a rather obscure issue called 'extraterritoriality'. Though complex in its application, the issue was simple. Almost all British-manufactured new-technology goods at the time (and no doubt still) contained US-made components. The US had, however, passed a law saying that, where another country manufactured goods containing any US component, however small or insignificant, those goods could not be sold to a third country without a US licence. On the face of it this was a perfectly sensible precaution to prevent US technology falling into the hands of America's enemies (e.g., at the time, Russia and China), but the regulation was being used in a manner which was blatantly discriminatory: British firms' 'licenses' were held up by the US authorities while US competitors moved in and captured the market.

It was a great issue. It was of real importance, attracted a good deal of interest from the Press, was consistent with my position as Trade and Industry spokesman, incorporated my enthusiasm for the new technologies, and contained just a tiny hint of a fluttering Union Jack, which for a Liberal was always an added bonus. I was soon doing television programmes and writing newspaper articles on the scandal (which it was) of 'extraterritoriality' and the secretive and shadowy Co-ordinating Committee (COCOM) in Paris which ran the whole policy. I even got Mrs Thatcher to admit to me in a letter that, 'US claims to extraterritorial jurisdiction are offensive',* but she added that she could do nothing about it!

The expansion of my horizons had a human dimension as well as a political one. In the early years of the 1983 parliament I started to work in earnest with two people who were to become close friends and be crucial to me later, both as an MP and as the Party leader. The

* Letter to me of 11 November 1988.

first was Richard Holme, a fellow candidate (in his case, fighting Cheltenham). Richard, a man of outstanding gifts and extraordinary range,* was David Steel's principal adviser and would later play the same role for me. He was also one of the chief architects of the Liberal–SDP Alliance, of our eventual merger into one Party, and of the 1997 partnership between the Liberal Democrats and Tony Blair's New Labour that turned a Tory defeat into a Tory rout and was instrumental in leading to the greatest programme of constitutional reform in Britain since the early years of the twentieth century.

The second person was Alan Leaman, whom I had first met when he was a student at Bristol University and the *rapporteur* for a commission looking into youth policy that I chaired at the 1982 Liberal Assembly in Bournemouth. He would later play key roles, first in the merger between the Liberals and the SDP and then in my campaign to become the Liberal Democrats' first leader, before heading the policy unit in my Leader's office, writing many of my speeches and persuading me to take an interest in the war in Bosnia and Herzegovina.

It was also at this time that I started writing pamphlets and articles for the newspapers, especially the *Guardian* and, later, the *Independent* – something I really enjoy and still love to do when I get the chance. I find great satisfaction in taking a complex idea and squeezing it into a thousand carefully considered words for a newspaper, or into something a little longer for a pamphlet. In June 1983, only a couple of weeks after my election, Richard Holme and I wrote 'First Steps Back From the Brink', which proposed a multilateral freeze on all further deployments of nuclear weapons as the prelude to step-by-step, multilateral and verifiable reductions leading on to minimum deterrent holdings by both sides in the Cold War.

Perhaps as result of all this and other pamphlets, in mid-1984 I suddenly found I was often being invited to lunch by senior members of the Westminster Press Lobby and asked my opinion on the future of my Party and the Alliance. I long ago discovered my metabolism is just too weak to permit me to be more than a very occasional member of Westminster's lunching classes. Eating and (especially) drinking at midday inevitably sends me to sleep or gives me a ferociously bad temper –sometimes both – in the afternoon. My favourite lunch at this

* Richard eventually went to the House of Lords as Lord Holme of Cheltenham and died on 4 May 2008.

time was an hour in the gym and an apple at my desk, which must have made me quite insufferable to more normal inhabitants of the Westminster village. I also started to get invitations to appear on programmes like *Question Time* and its radio equivalent *Any Questions*.

In early 1985 I was on *Any Questions* with David Blunkett (then not an MP but still Leader of Sheffield City Council), who brought his guide dog Ted onto the set and settled him down under the cloth-covered table at our feet. Here he was invisible to the audience. But we knew he was there alright, for he farted heartily throughout the whole hour of the broadcast. Along with others on the panel, I found it nearly impossible to get through the programme because of a combination of near-asphyxiation and irrepressible laughter. The audience, who of course were oblivious of our suffering, must have been deeply perplexed. Jane told me when I got home that she could quite clearly hear suppressed giggling from the panel on the airwaves.

Shortly after this the US Government invited me to spend a month in the United States on their Foreign Visitor Programme to see the country as a guest of the US Government. I chose to go to Silicon Valley, near San Francisco, to look at their new-technology industry and then to visit some US defence establishments and finally to join a Congressman (Democrat Dan Glickman*) on his re-election campaign. The official part of the tour took three weeks, but I was allowed to bring Jane out for the last week, which we took as a holiday. We had a wonderful seven days touring New England, at the time dressed overall in the spectacular colours of the Fall, and visiting Boston (where I gave a lecture) and, on a moody day with drifts of sea fog, Hyannisport, to pay homage at the home of the Kennedys. It was good investment on the part of the US Government, for I have remained a great fan of the United States (even if not always of all its Governments) ever since.

Jane and I went more or less straight from our US trip to the 1984 Liberal Assembly in Bournemouth, where the key debate was on defence and nuclear disarmament. The US had just unilaterally deployed cruise missiles in Britain, with the consequence that the USSR had walked out of the disarmament talks. This was totally contrary to what Richard Holme and I had written in 'First Steps Back From the Brink' a year earlier, so I decided I would, once again, have to oppose the leadership and support an amendment to the Party's defence policy,

---

* Glickman became the Secretary of Agriculture in Bill Clinton's Administration.

calling for a withdrawal of the missiles 'forthwith'. This caused very considerable annoyance to most of my Parliamentary colleagues. David Steel himself took to the floor to argue in favour of a freeze on all nuclear deployments at present levels (i.e., with cruise missiles *in situ*) and then a negotiated withdrawal, adding that the amendment I supported would destroy the credibility of the Party's defence policy. But I responded by saying that you couldn't negotiate removal when there were no negotiations going on: the deployment of the missiles had stalled them! If we wanted to get negotiations going we would have to remove the block – and the block was cruise missiles. The issue was in danger of becoming a vote on David's leadership, and I recall saying in my speech that this was a motion about cruise, not our Leader and, turning from the podium in order to address him directly, since he was sitting on the platform behind me, and saying something like, 'David, this is not about you, it is about unnecessary nuclear weapons. We want to get rid of them. But we do not want to get rid of you.' This received tumultuous applause from the audience but a (wholly justified) look from him which was clearly intended to turn me to stone on the spot. It was, of course, the height of cheek from a new MP, and the newspapers next day reported it as a blatant attempt to mark out the fact that I wanted his job. Actually it was intended as no such thing. I was genuinely, if ham-fistedly, trying to diminish the damage I was doing to a Leader whom I respected. But then, in politics, more than in almost any other profession, the road to hell is paved with good intentions, especially if clumsiness and naivety are thrown into the mix. Steel, in his end-of-Conference speech skilfully dismissed the defeat, but added in an interview afterwards that he would step down as Leader after the next election unless he had some role in government, which did nothing to calm speculation about a possible Leadership election and likely candidates.

Though this incident generated a good deal of bad feeling towards me amongst my fellow MPs, I was once again lionised by the radical elements of the Party. Once again I warned them, though probably too feebly, that I was not a unilateralist, and if the disarmament talks did start I would be arguing that cruise should be put in the negotiating package, not unilaterally withdrawn. But, amidst the celebrations over the defeat of the Leadership (always a favourite Liberal pastime), no one heard these protestations – or, if they did, they paid them no heed.

In fact, though the newspaper reports were wrong in describing this speech as a bid for the Party leadership (the BBC Conference report at the end of the week even going so far as to say that 'perhaps the Liberals had identified their next Leader'), they were right in spotting that the horizons of my ambitions were beginning to widen, even if I was not yet fully conscious of this myself at the time.

When I was fighting Yeovil, I had only one ambition in life: to become an MP. That, I thought at the time, would be sufficient – I wanted nothing more. But now, as I began to feel my strength and observed others in the exercise of power, I felt my horizons start to expand and my ambition – never a quality I have been accused of lacking – start to grow. It was premature. They say pride comes before a fall (personally, I have always found that, when it comes to overestimating one's powers, vanity is the greater seductress).

Towards the end of 1984 Sue O'Sullivan, by now expecting another baby, told me she intended to stop working, but assured me that she wouldn't leave until a suitable replacement had been found. I was more than happy to leave the recruitment process to Sue, as she knew my whims and peculiarities as a 'boss' better than almost anyone, and was herself outstanding at the job. She advertised, conducted all the initial interviews and in due course presented me with a short list of recommended applicants, among whom was Tricia Howard. Tricia was clearly highly competent, had a relaxed and easy-to-get-on-with manner and was duly appointed.

Tricia started to work with me in 1985 and quickly justified Sue's confidence in her by becoming an excellent colleague and a superb personal secretary. But soon the fatal disease of the House of Commons caught us both. There is something both unhealthy and captivating about the Westminster combination of late nights, the loneliness of weeks away from the family and the ever-present and intoxicating proximity of the dramas and excitements of power. Sometime in 1985 Tricia Howard and I started an affair.

Jane, who is no slouch when it comes to observing humanity, knew what had happened straight away and bearded me with it. I, of course, took the easy refuge of denying it, in order (I argued to myself) to protect her from the truth. Many of my colleagues knew, too, though theirs were whispered conversations I was not supposed to know about. Worse still, Tricia's husband, from whom she had been estranged for some time, also knew. And he was seeking a divorce from her to marry again. I became obsessed with the danger that, even though long separated from his wife, he might cite me in divorcing her, and so I went to see my friend, ex-fellow-candidate and now personal lawyer, Andrew Phillips, to ask for his advice. He took notes, put them in his safe and advised me to relax – and that, we thought, was that. In early 1986 Tricia left and was replaced as my secretary by Alison Nortcliffe, who looked after me as MP and Leader until in 1992 she married Adrian Sanders, who also worked in my Office and was later elected MP for Torbay in 1997.

The great political event overshadowing the political scene through-out 1984 and 1985 was the miners' strike. This, being an industrial matter, should have been handled by Ian Wrigglesworth (for the SDP) and me (for the Liberals). But, since it was by far the major issue of the day, it was entirely taken over by the two Davids – and once again showed the yawning gap between them. David Owen, who had had an early reputation as a radical in the Labour Party, moved further and further to the right, seeking always to strike 'hard' attitudes (often indistinguishable from those of Mrs Thatcher), while David Steel adopted more modulated positions. The commentators picked up the differences between them immediately – and, worse, so did the writers of *Spitting Image*, the hugely popular satirical programme in which all the characters were played by latex puppets. From this time on they always caricatured Owen as a saturnine figure with a miniature David Steel poking out of his breast pocket. Normally politicians rather like their caricatures and even collect them (I have a large collection), for they are mostly fun and rarely seriously damaging. But there are some exceptions. Steve Bell's representation of Prime Minster Major in his underpants was one. And the *Spiting Image* representation of David Steel as Owen's poodle was another. It did real damage both to the public perception of David and, I think, even to his view of himself (I know it would have affected me). It was not the first time, and it would not be the last, when differences of tone and substance between the two men undermined the effectiveness of the Alliance.

By 1985, the issue of nuclear weapons, which seemed to run like a constant stream just under the surface of politics throughout this Parliament, suddenly broke into the open again. START (the Strategic Arms Reduction Talks) had finally begun again in Geneva. This pre-sented me with a very tricky problem, and one which every serious politician has to confront sooner later: how to conduct a U-turn with minimum loss of respect and maximum elegance. In asking, 'When cir-cumstances change, I change my views. What do you do, Sir?' John Maynard Keynes was only expressing a rational truth. But since politics

is often concerned less with rationalities than with personalities, changing one's views in public is neither easy nor comfortable. It did not
count for a row of beans that I had carefully warned my erstwhile fellow
disarmament campaigners that, if the disarmament talks did restart, I
would be saying cruise should be put into them, not unilaterally withdrawn. Nor were any of my one-time friends in the least impressed by
the carefully worded speech I constructed for delivery at the SDP
Conference that year in Torquay, announcing that events had now overtaken the campaign for unilateral removal of cruise, and that the
weapons should now become a subject for the talks in Geneva, not for
marching on the streets of Britain. Both Liberal and the SDP Party hierarchies were delighted and just a little smug. But those who had cheered
me loudest in the past were now the most furious in their denunciation,
christening me (the precursor of a later, much more hurtful, nickname)
'Paddy Backdown'. At the Eastbourne Liberal Assembly the following
year Bruce Kent, the head of CND, mounted a highly personalised and
acerbic attack on me, causing some newspapers to report that I had lost
much grassroots support and damaged any ambitions I might have had
for the Party leadership. Throughout these attacks I remained very confident that the position I had taken was the right one, but that did not
diminish the hurt or discomfort, for I am rather thin-skinned in these
matters. Perhaps this was why the Assembly speech I made, this time in
support of the defence policy proposed by David Steel and the Party
leadership, was one of the worst I have ever made. The vote at the end
of the debate was very narrow but the amendment was declared carried
by the chair, meaning another defeat for Steel (and this time, of course,
for me, too). There should have been a recount, but in the chaos of the
Liberal Assembly in those days there was no time for one, as the hall
had to be vacated for the evening's public entertainment in the
Eastbourne theatre (a farce, as I recall).

In early 1986, the first great cabinet crisis of the Thatcher years broke
over the Government. For the rest of Britain, the Westland affair was a
scandal about the actions of Ministers and the propriety of the
Government. For me it was about the survival of by far the most important employer and source of economic wealth in my constituency.

Westland was once again going through a very hard time, and its survival as a stand-alone helicopter-producer was seriously in question.

There were two options before the Company and the Government. The first was to accept a bid to team up with the US firm Sikorsky, which had been Westland's trusted and long-term partner since well before the Vietnam War (the course favoured by Mrs Thatcher). And the second was to fold Westland into a European helicopter consortium (the course favoured by Michael Heseltine). Given my position on Europe, I should have supported Heseltine. But when I looked at the European plan it was obvious that it would have meant dismantling Westland and turning it into a mere components manufacturer, which would have led to the break-up of its design and technology teams and the end of its capacity to design and build helicopters from the drawing board up.

For Parliament, the Press and the country, however, the Westland crisis was not about Westland; it was about Margaret Thatcher and Michael Heseltine. They were not interested in the bone – only in the dogs fighting over it. It is said that when Mrs Thatcher left Downing Street on her way to the Commons for the great Westland debate (in which John Smith first made his name as one of our generation's great House of Commons performers), she turned to a friend and said she was not sure she would be coming back as Prime Minister. In the debate I told Michael Heseltine that his European Consortium's approach to Westland was not so much that of a partner as of an undertaker and that, given his failure as Defence Secretary to support Westland in the past, his offer of help appeared to the people of Yeovil as though 'they are being offered a poison cup from the hands of the poisoner himself'.* Although my defence of the company did me no harm in my constituency, I fear it played little part in the final outcome (the Westland/Sikorsky deal went ahead), which was determined by the cannonade which went on far above my head. When Mrs Thatcher survived, so did Westland as an independent helicopter manufacturer.

Whilst it was, I suppose, inevitable that a great deal of my time should be taken up by Westminster matters in this Parliament, my Yeovil office team, under the stern guidance of Cathy Bakewell and Nick Speakman, made sure I did not forget my base in my Constituency. The Yeovil team had now been augmented by a new Constituency agent, Simon Thompson, and another key member, Sarah Frapple, who, like Cathy and Nick, had been there on that chilly night back in 1976 when I was first chosen by the Yeovil Liberals. They put in a huge amount of work

* Hansard 15 January 1986, column 1134.

strengthening the Constituency organisation and driving the Tories out of their remaining electoral strongholds, and this culminated in the 1985 County Council Election, in which we won every County seat in the Yeovil constituency. They made sure that the pace of my work in the community increased too, not just with regular weekly 'surgeries' (now busier than ever), but also with a full programme of other community events, including a 'roving surgery' every autumn, which consisted of Jane and me driving a large van to almost every village in our very rural constituency, parking outside the Post Office and holding a mobile advice centre in the back of the vehicle. I am not at all sure of the constitutional propriety of MPs operating in this way as a sort of universal social worker, as this undermines the role of local Councillors. But I loved this 'pastoral' aspect of my work and, right to the end of my time as an MP, I used to feel my heart lift on the train home at the weekend with every clack of the rails which took me further away from London and closer to Somerset, my family and my beloved constituency.

One of the innovations we brought in (borrowed from fellow Liberal MPs) was a series of visits Jane and I made before Christmas to care homes, hospitals, post offices, the police, fire stations, etc., to wish them all Happy Christmas, take them a present (usually a box of House of Commons chocolate or a bottle of House of Commons whisky) and thank them for their work during the year. It was on one such visit to Yeovil Hospital, on the frosty morning of 22 December 1986, that one of the Hospital staff came up to me and whispered that my secretary wanted to speak to me urgently on the phone (these were the days before mobile phones). I picked up the receiver to hear her in tears. Between sobs she told me she had just heard that David Penhaligon had been killed when his car skidded on ice on the way to an early-morning pre-Christmas visit to his local post office. Jane and I were poleaxed, and it was all we could do to stumble through the rest of our visits as best we could. David's funeral, on 10 January 1987 in the same church where he and his wife Annette had got married, was one of the most moving I have ever attended. The Party were there in full force and deep misery, of course. But so were the people of Truro, where he was loved with an intensity very few MPs or civic leaders could ever aspire to. Some MPs – though very few – not only represent their constituency but somehow personally embody its spirit too. David was one of these. But he was also a highly astute politician. By now I was pretty clear that, when David Steel stood down, I would probably try for the Leadership, and I had reckoned that David Penhaligon would do so too. I thought then (and still do) that, if I had had to fight him, he would probably have won.

Indeed, shortly before David's funeral I had been approached by a small group of supporters who said that, since it was now clear that David Steel would almost certainly stand down after the coming election, they would like to help me if I was intending to put my name forward for the Leadership. We started meeting regularly in January, and they helped to plan a programme of national visits to winnable seats which I would carry out in the forthcoming general election, which was now clearly in view. They also helped me write my speech for the pre-election Liberal–SDP Alliance rally in the Barbican on 31 January that year. (Max Atkinson, the author of the ground-breaking book *Our Masters' Voices** on how politicians make speeches, played a particularly important part at this time and later in helping to give my speeches greater impact.)

Shortly before the Election was formally called, the two Davids held a joint morale-boosting meeting of all the Alliance candidates. I don't think we were supposed to ask questions at this event, as it was primarily a rally. Nevertheless, I asked David Owen how he and David Steel had decided to answer the deadly, if hypothetical, question that was bound to come from the Press: which of the two of them would be Prime Minster, if we won? Owen said they had not decided on this and would sort it out after the election. To Owen's evident annoyance, I said that I thought this was madness. Surely, it was obvious? The Leader whose Party had the most MPs should lead. Owen – who, of course, knew that there were bound to be more Liberal than SDP MPs elected – dismissed this out of hand, calling it, if I remember correctly, 'immature'.

The 1987 Alliance election campaign began with television pictures of David Owen and David Steel jumping into their respective battle buses after their opening press conference and promptly driving off in completely opposite directions. As it began, so it continued, aided and abetted by the new technology of the day. The newest new technology quite often plays a key role in a general election. In 1987 the new thing was the mobile phone, and it did for the Alliance. 'Hunt the split' is the political journalist's favourite game and the basis of ninety percent of all political reporting. In 1987 the two Davids gave them what they

---

* *Our Masters' Voices: The language and body language of politics* (London and New York: Methuen, 1984).

wanted on a plate, all served up through the medium of the mobile phone – which every journalist had, but neither of the Leaders or any of their aides seemed to have heard of (or, if they had, they didn't think of using them to communicate with each other). All a journalist had to do was ask one David on his battle bus at one end of the country for his response to a given issue (defence was a favourite topic; Steel was nervous of it, and Owen had such a passion for weapon systems that he always left you feeling that, secretly, he could scarcely wait to use them). A quick mobile phone call to a colleague on the other David's battle bus suggesting that the same question be asked and, hey presto, five minutes later they had the Alliance split story of the day! For journalists this was money for old rope. For us it was deadly.

Added to all this was the fact that trying to co-ordinate two campaigns and project two leaders led to serious organisational and presentational problems. The two Davids each had to have equal space in every major interview, in which (if we were lucky) they both said exactly the same thing, only in different words. But even if the substance of what they said was usually the same, the style and body language was not. David Owen appeared much closer to Mrs Thatcher – and on one occasion (inevitably, the issue was again defence) in effect confirmed that, for him, Labour were less likely and less acceptable partners than the Tories. This generated almost immediate hostility on the doorstep, where our canvassers were asked what was the point of voting for the Alliance if the result was to let Mrs Thatcher back in?

The low point of the campaign came in what is generally accepted as the worst Party Political Broadcast in history, which gave star billing (at great length) to the then SDP MP for Greenwich, Rosie Barnes, and her pet rabbit.

And so we confirmed in the election what we had showed through the Parliament, that the Alliance was not a single force at all: just a framework for a squabble. That gave Labour the space to recover and begin to move forward again, and lost us our greatest chance since the early years of the twentieth century of becoming Britain's most powerful party of the Left.

After all the bright hopes and golden opportunities of the morning of my first election as an MP, just four years before, I found the general election of 7 May 1987 terribly depressing. Although I almost doubled my majority in Yeovil, the Alliance fell back in both popular votes and number of its MPs. It was clear to me things could not go on like this. The Alliance was over. The two Parties would have to merge.

CHAPTER 12

Leader I:
The Intensive Care Ward

O N THE DAY after the Election, I was on the panel of BBC
Radio 4's *Any Questions*, which was held, as I recall, in
Northampton. Naturally, the election results dominated the programme, including the performance of the Alliance. Freed from the
disciplines of the Election campaign, I let fly on the stupidities of
separateness and the absolute necessity of the two parties merging
without delay. I had not realised that, earlier in the day and, apparently, contrary to a tacit agreement with David Steel, David Owen
had held a press conference in his seat in Plymouth, at which he
fired what the *Independent* newspaper next day described as 'the
opening shots in his campaign against merger'. My pro-merger comments on *Any Questions* were immediately picked up by the BBC
news that night and then by the rest of the media the following day,
putting Owen and me head to head on the issue in all the Press coverage over the weekend. On Monday David Steel made a statement
in favour of merger (and was immediately accused by David Owen
of, 'bouncing him'!).

There is a rather good novel by Nicholas Monsarrat called *The Tribe
That Lost Its Head*. I have always been struck by the capacity of political Parties to lose their heads from time to time and, with single-
minded determination, ritually disembowel themselves in public.
Labour did it after the defeat in 1979. The Tories did it after their
defeat in 1997. And the Alliance spent a full year and more doing it in
spectacular style after the 1987 election, launching itself into an orgy
of self-indulgence, stupidity and internecine bloodletting, not just
between Owen and most of the Liberal leaders, but also within the
SDP: between those who supported Owen and those who wanted our
two Parties to merge.

At an early meeting of the group which had gathered round me and
started to prepare my leadership campaign, now known amongst us as

'The Ming Group',* we discussed all this. Someone quoted the old adage: 'He who wields the knife, never gets to wear the crown,' and recommended that, beyond placing myself firmly in the pro-merger camp, I should do my best to stay out of it altogether. I did not find this advice difficult to follow, as I have always believed that the best place for the ambitious to be when a coup is taking place, is somewhere else. Fortunately, I had good reason to follow this policy, too. The Government had just published 'The Great Education Reform Bill' as the centrepiece of its new programme, and David Steel had appointed me as the new 'Alliance' (that is the Liberals and the pro-merger SDP) spokesman on Education. This was a piece of real good fortune. The Great Education Reform Bill (or 'Gerbil' as it became known) was a strongly centralising measure which introduced crude measurement systems for schools and a test-centred regime for students and was deeply unpopular amongst teachers, educationalists and many middle-class parents who had voted for us. So, by taking the lead for the Party in opposing it, I placed myself centre stage in the main Parliamentary battle of the first year of the 1987 Parliament and gave myself a very good excuse to be too busy with politics to get involved in the blood-letting. And, by the way, it also provided a very good opportunity to build up my support amongst the Party's powerful education and local government sector and to make contact with key members of the pro-merger wing of the SDP, such as Shirley Williams and Anne Sofer.

In August 1987 the SDP voted decisively in favour of a merger. After this, David Owen dramatically ditched his Party and went off to start a rump SDP in his own image, taking with him some of the SDP's most gifted supporters, including a number of its key women activists, like Polly Toynbee and Sue Slipman (christened 'The Brides of Dracula' by anti-Owen SDP members, for their attachment to Owen and their penchant for wearing black).

Bob MacLennan, who had made clear his support for unification after the 1987 election, albeit on terms slightly different from those finally agreed, took over as leader of what remained of the mergerite SDP to oversee the merger negotiations.

---

* The origin of this is a little obscure – but as I recall Des Wilson, one of the key members, had made a rather extended joke at one of our meetings about the curious name of 'Ming' Campbell, one of our target-seat candidates who was regarded as likely to win at the forthcoming election. This had caused such mirth that for some reason the name became applied to the group.

While all this was going on, Jane and I decided that what we needed most was a good long break over the summer. So we booked a canalboat holiday with our Yeovil friends Les and Joan Farris and Lesley and Greg Jefferies on the Canal de Nivernais in northern Burgundy. The weather was not good, and the holiday fell a little short of what we had hoped for. But we fell in love with this area of France, and, meeting beside the Yonne river, in the little Place St Nicolas in Auxerre, for a last drink before returning home, we confided to the Jefferies that we were thinking of buying a house in the area. They confessed that they had had exactly the same thought. So, once again completely by accident, we took a decision that was to change our lives and those of our children completely. The following February (when I was up to my ears in the 'phoney war' phase of the Leadership campaign) Jane and the Jefferies went back to the Auxerre area, where they found and we jointly bought, for a total £10,000, a small tumbledown house in Irancy, a small north Burgundian village only a little more famous for making good red wine than it is for consuming it in large quantities. Irancy has since become not only our second home and refuge but also the centre of our second circle of friends and an integral part of the web and warp of our lives. My daughter Kate in due course married the son of the Deputy Mayor of the neighbouring village, settled in the region and brought up our French grandchildren as 'vrais Irancyquois'. And we have had some of our greatest pleasures from joining them every year, spending many roasting August days in the cool of our wine-making friends' *caves* and dining in our little courtyard under star-spangled skies and the canopy of our own Burgundian vine.

When we arrived back in the UK we found the blood-letting unabated and the merger debate raging away in both parties. In September we Liberals, in our turn, voted overwhelmingly for merger and entered into the protracted process of merger negotiations. Following this, in symmetry with Owen's action, a group of apostate Liberals, led by my 1983-entry Parliamentary colleague, Michael Meadowcroft (who actually took part in the first part of the merger negotiations), then broke away to establish themselves as 'true' Liberals. So, the new politics which we had all heralded with such unity and fanfares five years ago finally ended up like this: two rival SDPs and two rival Liberal Parties, with one of each still involved in something we continued to call 'The Alliance'.

I regarded myself as well out of all of this, and in November, with Alan Leaman, published a pamphlet called 'Choice or Privilege: The alternative great education reform bill'. Following this, while others were enmeshed in the next stage of the merger process and were drawing up a joint policy prospectus for the new merged Party, I toured the country attending education rallies and building support for opposition to Gerbil.

The policy negotiations between the merging parties were difficult and protracted, but finally, early in 1988, produced a joint policy prospectus. Its contents were radical and contentious and very soon began to leak, causing much vociferous unhappiness, especially amongst Liberals. The draft soon found its way to the Press, amid suspicion from the Liberals that the SDP had deliberately leaked it in order to bounce them. It quickly became known as 'the dead parrot'* (a soubriquet apparently invented by David Steel, in whose name it was supposed to speak!). Despite containing some lethal suicide pills (such as the proposition that VAT should be added to food and children's clothing), 'the parrot' was not as awful as it was painted. Its mistakes were, first, that it was excessively 'hair-shirt' for a Party within an ace of self-obliteration; second, that it was out of touch with the mood among both Parties' members; and, third, that it was just too far ahead of its time – though it proposed many items that were to become commonplace in the era of post-1997 Blairism.

The dénouement of the whole 'dead parrot' affair took place at a joint Parliamentary meeting in one of the Committee Rooms of the House of Commons on 13 January 1988, with a baying mob from the Press laying siege to the doors. There were tears and tantrums and revolts against the two Leaders (Steel and MacLennan), and even at one stage a near-physical incident, when Simon Hughes had to position his sizeable frame across one of the doors to physically prevent people leaving and falling prey to the baying mob of reporters outside. I was not there for the bulk of this meeting; I was visiting the Open University in Milton Keynes – clearly far and away a better place to be. But I did get back for the final half-hour, after things had calmed down somewhat, and the two Leaders had agreed to hold a joint press conference in the Liberal Club, rejecting 'the dead parrot' and promising to do better in future. My only contribution was to

* After the famous Monty Python sketch.

suggest that we all ought to be there, standing behind them to show our support. It was not a good suggestion. In the subsequent pictures MacLennan and Steel, with twenty MPs looking either menacing or melancholy behind them, didn't look much like two Leaders in charge of events – rather, they resembled hostages, dragged from some dark dungeon by a new group of radical terrorists in lounge suits and forced to read out a prepared text just before being subjected to something indescribably horrid.

At a meeting of the Ming Group in my flat that night, all agreed that David Steel would stand down almost immediately, in line with his earlier stated intention. But he seemed to waver for a bit; finally, in a speech to his Borders constituency on 12 May 1988, he announced that he would not be putting his name forward for the leadership of the 'Social and Liberal Democrats'. Bob MacLennan followed suit, making it clear just as nominations for the Leadership contest were closing that he, too, would not be putting his name forward.

A week after the 'dead parrot' debacle the Liberals gathered in Blackpool's Norbreck Hotel (which fully lived up its nickname 'the Colditz of the North') and agreed by a large majority to the merger, subject to a ballot of all members. The SDP followed suit in Sheffield a week later on 30 January, causing the final rupture with Owen, who purloined the old SDP name and used it for his breakaway party.

It now only remained to elect the new Party Leader, and then we could get back to business. Or so we hoped.

Everyone now knew there were going to be only two candidates in the race, Alan Beith and myself. But instead of getting on with it quickly, in order to minimise the damage, there was a protracted bureaucratic process which finally decided that the Leadership campaign would not start until June and would end on 28 July. The reason given was to try to avoid having an internal election at the same time as the local elections in May (in which we predictably lost over sixty council seats), but the consequence was a further period of rudderless drift for the Party. I felt the same frustration I had felt while waiting for Yeovil Liberals to adopt me back in 1976 – particularly since I could very plainly see that being without a leader was doing the same damage to the Party at large that it had done in Yeovil twelve years before. It was actually during this wasted six months that most of the real damage to the new Party's structures, finances, public standing and morale was done. We became the butt of every political joke, and we deserved it.

The result was that Alan Beith and I had, in effect, an exhausting six-month Leadership campaign. Most of the early part of it was spent scurrying round securing support from key figures; this often involved a kind of informal 'beauty contest', with each of us being 'looked over' by the grandees and institutions of both the old Parties.

It was in this spirit that, on 20 March 1988, the day after the new Party's launch rally in Westminster, Jane and I were invited to lunch with the grandee of all grandees (later a key pillar of my Leadership years) Roy Jenkins, at his house in East Hendred, Oxfordshire. We both realised that this was a job interview, even if it took the form of an elegant and amusing lunch preceded by some very good champagne and accompanied by some of Roy's outstanding claret. The assembled might of the SDP was there, including Dick Taverne, whose wife asked Jane where we lived in London. Jane said we didn't live in London, we lived in Somerset. But we did have a small flat in London. 'Whereabouts?' 'Kennington,' Jane replied, attracting a sharp intake of breath and the comment, 'Oh, *south* of the river'. Driving home afterwards she said that she didn't even know there was a 'wrong side' of the river.

However the occasion cannot have gone too badly, as, from that moment onwards, Roy and Jennifer, who hardly knew me before, gave me their unstinting and unfailing backing, not only in the subsequent campaign, but also throughout my Leadership years, and especially when I needed it most, at the darkest and most difficult times.

I launched my campaign for the Leadership at midday on 1 June 1988 in the Yeovil Liberal Club, after which Jane and I began an extended country-wide tour, taking in every corner of Britain and ending back in London on the day of the count, 28 July. The Ming Group's preparations paid off handsomely. Thanks to them, we were able to assemble a superb team and mounted a most effective campaign under the slogan 'The Ability to WIN – the VISION to Lead'.

The campaign itself was, by and large, a positive one, barring only a ten-point anonymous document, leaked to the Press just before the campaign proper began, which incorporated a series of pretty vicious attacks on me personally and professionally, including criticism that I was a loner, a poor communicator, a poor debater in the Commons, lacked a sense of humour and was short on real political and party experience, etc., etc. David Steel immediately criticised the tactic and called for a clean campaign, and Alan

Beith immediately wrote to me saying, 'This action was not in any way authorized by me or by any organized group known to me, and I would have been wholly opposed to the circulation or publication of any document of this kind.' I issued a response, saying that I admired Alan Beith's personal qualities and was grateful for his 'clear repudiation of both the style and content of the . . . document. For my part, I think we should now consider this rather unsavoury episode as closed.'

On the morning of the count I was walking through the House of Commons on my way to a farewell lunch for David Steel when I bumped into the veteran Labour MP, Tam Dalyell. He stopped me and wished me luck, adding, 'You will be elected today, Paddy. Here's a piece of advice. Keep a diary; you will find in a few years time it will be invaluable to you.' I took his advice and from that moment on kept a diary every day until I returned from Bosnia in 2006, since when my diary-keeping has been more sporadic, recording only events that seem to me of significance.

Afterwards we all went off to the rather dingy offices of the Electoral Reform Society, where the result of the election was announced: I received 72% of the votes cast, and Alan Beith, 28%. Alan was most generous in his comments, but I could see he was hurt – and understandably so, for he was much the more experienced of the two of us and had served the Party as an MP long before I had even joined. I asked him privately if he would be prepared to become the Deputy Leader to help me out, but added that there was no reason to make a quick decision, as the first thing we both needed was a rest.

And then to the Headquarters of the newly merged Social and Liberal Democrats (as we were then called) at No. 4 Cowley Street, where, after my acceptance speech as the just-elected founding Leader of the new Party predicting the certainty of a bright new dawn, there were photographs.

What neither the Press nor I knew at the time was that the event very nearly never took place at all. For, about half an hour previously, two men from the Inland Revenue had turned up at the front door of 4 Cowley Street with a writ to close the Party down for unpaid National Insurance contributions. Fortunately, they had been hustled into the building before the Press, the cameras and the accompanying circus arrived. Of all this, however, I and my Leadership campaign team celebrating that night, were blissfully ignorant.

Not for long, though. The following morning at a Cowley Street briefing I was told just what a catastrophic state the Party was in. We were heavily in debt, the Headquarters staff demoralised and leaving in droves, the Party in the country was in the midst of an identity crisis, and we were all punch-drunk from the succession of blows we had inflicted on ourselves over the last eighteen months. To make matters worse, we had saddled ourselves with a most ridiculous name, the Social and Liberal Democrats, or SLD – soon converted to 'the Slids', or just 'the Salads', by the Press and our opponents, who were, by now, accustomed to having wonderful fun at our expense. In a meeting three days after my election I told the staff that nothing mattered now but stabilising and unifying the Party and making sure that we won the battle with the Owenites for control of the centre ground; fighting the Tories and Labour would come later.

By now it was August, and everyone was ready for a break. Besides which, I needed time to rest and think. So I told them all to take a good holiday and come back refreshed, and then went off to Irancy with Jane, where I washed away my concerns and depression in some very hard physical work on our new house and a good deal of excellent red Burgundy. I am in fact a disaster at all things DIY-related. Jane says that, just as you can tell a piece of Chippendale by the standard of craftsmanship, so you can tell my handiwork by its complete absence: nothing is ever straight, and everything will have my blood on it somewhere. So I left the delicate work to others and immersed myself in some good hard navvying, pulling down ceilings and shifting tons of rubbish and earth from the garden. One day, covered in sweat and grime, I was called in to the *cave* of a neighbouring *vigneron*, whose dog had bitten an English lady visitor, and asked to act as interpreter. Afterwards the visitor and her husband, who I could see somehow recognised me, came back to our house for a cup of tea. Eventually the husband, who came from Bradford, could contain himself no longer. 'I know you', he said in a thick Yorkshire accent. 'You're a teacher from Bradford aren't you?' I said I was not. And then he clicked, 'Oh no you're not! I know 'oo you are! You're t'leader o' that party nobody knows t'name of!' I did not correct him, for it seemed a fair description and rather better than anything I could think of myself at the time.

But the holiday was not all work. I had time to think as well.

Since I was the first leader of the new Party, it now fell to me to take the lead in creating its shape, organisation and character. And I knew exactly what I wanted these to be. I wanted it to be a genuine synthesis between the Liberals and the SDP, incorporating the best of the two old parent Parties. We needed to keep the radicalism, community-based approach, campaigning spirit and dogged, bloody-minded determination against the odds, of the old Liberal party. But I wanted to ensure that we also incorporated the modernity, professionalism and intellectual rigour of the SDP (I recall saying many times, 'Just because we are radical does not mean we cannot be efficient'). I have always held the view that there are two competing strands in Liberalism. The first is social liberalism, which understands the importance of what we hold in common, seeks to heal the divisions in society and is dedicated to setting people free from the intrusions of an overweening state. The second is economic liberalism, which understands the importance of individual liberty, the free market and free trade. The two are often in conflict, and so the essence of the liberal debate is to find the appropriate balance between the two for the time and context in which we live. In my view, the old British Liberal Party had allowed social liberalism to become too dominant, and our policies had become far too aligned towards the producer interest, rather than the consumer or 'citizen' interest in society. The SDP, on the other hand, was much more avowedly a free-market Party, which put more weight on the interests of the consumer. I wanted to preserve that, so as to move the balance back towards a more free-market economic position than the old Liberal Party normally felt comfortable with.

I realised the name Social and Liberal Democrats would be an issue we would have to tackle, but I thought (wrongly, I soon discovered) that this could be delayed. I made it publicly known that I favoured 'Democrat', as I thought it gave the best indication that we were genuinely something new, and it would help knit in the SDP (I was wrong here, too).

I knew my first big task was to unite the two elements of the new Party into a unified whole and, if possible, draw back some of those very good people who had left for the Owenites or the apostate Liberals. So, in setting up my Leader's office, I was careful not only to draw an equal number of my key staff from both the parent Parties, but also to include amongst my closest advisers some of those who had opposed merger. Indeed, in the end, half my office was made up of people who had actually voted against the formation of the new Party.

Finally, I was very aware of just how limited were the time, resources and political capital that we had to put things right, and concluded that we had to ruthlessly prioritise what we did. The first task was to stabilise the Party's finances (we were heading for a deficit of half a million by the end of the year). This would mean staff cuts. Then we had to restructure the headquarters and start getting out our messages about why we existed and what we were for to a Party membership that was now deserting in droves. Only when we had done these two things could we begin to think about re-entering the wider political battle. Even then, our first battles were not going to be with Labour and the Tories, but with the Owenites for control of the centre ground. If we could not beat them, we could not survive.

I returned from holiday with a clear set of priorities and a detailed plan of what we needed to do – which was almost immediately overtaken by events. First, our financial situation was much worse than I had been told. I discovered that we would now be technically bankrupt by November, could no longer pay our bills, and even salaries were doubtful. Second, the Owenites were now making real progress. Owen had a very good Conference and was being treated seriously by the Press, while we were still the butt of jokes and derision (our opinion-poll rating at the time was 8%*). And third, the Tory Trade and Industry Secretary and former Home Secretary, Leon Brittan, a casualty of the Westland affair, had resigned to become a European Commissioner (where one of his leading staff members would be a young Nick Clegg), meaning there would be a by-election in Richmond, Yorkshire. This would bring us into head-to-head conflict with the Owenite SDP in one of the few areas in the country where they were strong. However much we may not have wanted to fight them yet, we were going to have to – and on ground that favoured them.

In September I had my first Party Conference to get through, at Blackpool. I get very nervous before all speeches, but my first Leader's speech was sheer purgatory. A Party Leader's Conference Speech is like no other speech a modern politician has to deliver. It is longer (forty-five minutes to an hour was my usual), minutely scrutinised, emotionally supercharged, critically important at the time and hugely nerve-wracking (or at least I found it so). I am not a natural speaker, like, for instance, Charles Kennedy. I tend to speak too fast, my voice has a habit of rising in register when I am nervous, I have a poor sense

---

* MORI/Times 26 Sep 1988.

of timing for jokes, and I tend to lose all light and shade in my delivery when under pressure. Later, in order to correct these faults, I went to a wonderful speech trainer who also happened to be an ardent Lib Dem. Margaret Lang taught me how to breathe properly, relax before a big speech and use the full register of my voice. Some senior politicians I know are embarrassed to admit that they have to have their voices trained like this. I don't know why. However good you are at the other aspects of politics, your voice is the essential tool you have to use to communicate your message – so learning to use it properly is no more strange or embarrassing than learning to use a saw in order to be a carpenter.

On this occasion, mercifully, my audience was so willing me to succeed that it was prepared to overlook a less than perfect performance. My aim was to try to provide a rallying cry for a demoralised Party, and I chose the environment as my central theme. The speech, entitled 'Starting the Journey', was not a great one but it seemed to do the job, and everyone left Blackpool a little more cheerful than they had been when they arrived.

Now it was time for the tough work to start.

Having discussed our dire position with the Chair of the Party's Finance Committee, Clive Lindley, I announced to the staff that we were cutting six posts; at the same time I put in place a secret financial package, borrowing enough money to keep the cash flow going against the security of the Party's buildings. These cuts were painful. But before long we would discover they were not nearly painful enough – I should have gone deeper.

At the time, though, I was concentrating on the crucial electoral struggle with the SDP that was looming in Richmond, which I knew we had to win. Chris Rennard had warned me that we desperately needed the financial resources to fight this by-election effectively if we were to have any hope against the Owenites, who were being heavily funded by the millionaire (and later Labour Government Minister) David Sainsbury.

Shortly after Parliament returned in October I had to get through the first weekly Prime Minster's Questions (PMQs) of my Leadership. This I found even more terrifying than giving the Conference Speech, partly because it is much more difficult for the third party leader in the House of Commons than for the other two. Labour and Tory leaders have the Despatch Box to put their notes on, but Parliamentary convention accords this facility only to front-bench spokespersons of the two major parties. So the third party leader has to speak from his normal seat in the Commons pews, which means he is not allowed to use notes at all and must memorise his question. Secondly, and crucially, although the Labour and Tory leaders have around three hundred opposition MPs on the other side of the House to contend with, they also have three hundred or so on their own side to help them. The third party leader has the full six hundred against him and (in my early days) only twenty or so in support. What this means is that, when you stand up (especially if the House does not much like you) there is a roar of hostility that quite literally drives all thought out of your brain. What *that* means is that, in memorising your question, you have to etch it so deep into your brain that nothing can drive it out – for one mistake or one falter in delivery, and the six hundred opposing MPs will eat you alive. (Actually, to be precise, you have to perfectly memorise two questions, because you always ask your question after the leader of the Official Opposition, who may well have covered the subject so effectively that the third party leader cannot ask another question on the same topic, and so must have something different up his sleeve.)

My other problem was that Mrs Thatcher was very good at PMQs, whereas I, at least until I got the hang of it, was not – as the papers pointed out at great length and with some glee. To make matters worse, though Parliament was not yet televised, it had just started to be broadcast on the radio, which faithfully reproduced my painful efforts for the whole country to enjoy. Of all the trials of that early period of leading the Party, the misery of being broadcast to the nation while being ritually handbagged by Mrs Thatcher was one of the most painful.

Meanwhile, there were other rituals to get accustomed to as well, including the duty of Britain's three main party leaders to act, when called upon, as part of the 'wallpaper of state', which provides the necessary backdrop to all great state (and especially Royal) occasions.*

---

* These occasions are not all Royal, though. They include, for instance, the Cup Final, Wimbledon, state anniversaries (like the Fiftieth Anniversary of D Day), etc. Because I have no interest whatever in sport, I found the sporting occasions boring and tried to avoid them whenever I could. The one exception was Wimbledon, not because I am at all a tennis fan, but because Jane is crazy about it and insisted that I attend this as my annual compensation for the things she had had to put up with on my behalf. On one occasion we were invited to the Royal Box for the semi-finals, to Jane's complete delight. However, I sat there for a few minutes and then fell fast asleep; so the next day's newspapers carried a most unflattering photograph of me in open-mouthed somnolent pose, accompanied by comments that might easily have graced a Bateman cartoon, entitled 'The man who fell asleep in the Royal Box during the Wimbledon semi-finals'.

The first of these occurred on Remembrance Sunday, when I had to lay a wreath at the Cenotaph. Beforehand Neil Kinnock (as Leader of Her Majesty's Loyal Opposition) and I (as leader of the third party in Parliament) were formed up alongside Mrs Thatcher and her Cabinet, ready to be led out to join the Queen for the Remembrance Service. Before we left, I watched with amusement as Mrs Thatcher went up and down her Cabinet like a mother inspecting her children before Sunday School, straightening the Foreign Secretary's tie here and tut-tutting over the state of the Minister of Defence's shoes there, etc.

Shortly afterwards Jane and I had to go to Downing Street for a formal lunch for the President of Senegal, after which Jane commented on the dead chrysanthemums, the worn carpets and Mrs Thatcher's strange handshake. She has a habit not so much of shaking a visitor's hand, as grabbing it and passing the unfortunate captive across her and away, much as one might a partner in a Scottish country dance.

Our next state event was the royal diplomatic reception at Buckingham Palace, which was attended by all foreign Ambassadors and their senior staff, held on 17 November 1990. While Jane was delighted to have an excuse for a new dress, I was shocked when I received the embossed invitation to find that I had to wear a white tie and tails, which of course I did not have. My Yeovil Constituency Chairman at the time* came to my aid, lending me his tails for the occasion. Unfortunately, although his waist and legs were roughly the same size as mine, his torso was significantly shorter, with the result that the waistcoat finished half way up my stomach, leaving a large expanse of exposed white shirt. To make matters worse I only discovered this deficiency when the taxi to take us to Buckingham Palace was ticking away outside. Jane, however, coolly solved the crisis by cutting the waistcoat in half at the back and then lowering the buttoned front halves down to the right position on a fragile halter of green gardening string looped around the back of my neck. She warned me that any intemperate movement would result in the whole fragile contraption ending up round my ankles, adding that, given my luck, this would be almost certain to happen just in front of the Queen. In the event, all passed off without incident until, at the end, we asked the Buckingham Palace attendants if we could now ring for a taxi to take us home. We were firmly told that you did not ring for taxis from Buckingham Palace,

---

* Canon Myles Raikes, now sadly dead.

leaving us with no option but to walk out of the front gates. This we did with the maximum aplomb we could muster, holding ourselves very erect as we sauntered nonchalantly through the great iron gates while Ambassadorial limousines swept past us. We then walked to the taxi rank in Victoria Station, where, as luck would have it, we arrived at the same time as a well-oiled group of Cockney sports fans. They, of course, thought my white tie and tails great fun, until one of them recognised me and shouted to his mates, ''ere, it's that Steve Davis – yer know – the snooker player!' After which they treated me with more respect.

In early February 1989 I had to go to Buckingham Palace again, this time to be sworn in as member of Her Majesty's Privy Council. Being a Privy Councillor actually means very little, except that you are entitled to receive privileged information of a secret nature from the Government of the day, can put PC after your name if you wish, are referred to as 'Right Honourable' in the House of Commons, will be consulted when the heir to the throne gets married, and when kissing the Queen's hand are permitted to actually touch it with your lips. Otherwise a Privy Councillor does not really do very much. But the ceremony is rather fun. It includes a good deal of kneeling on red cushions, holding special bibles, swearing a special Privy Council oath and, of course, giving the Royal hand your first, up-close-and-personal, genuine Privy Councillor's smacker. Meanwhile, at least when I did it, Her Majesty spent her time throughout this quaint and faintly preposterous ceremony shuffling rather impatiently from foot to foot like any bored housewife in a slow-moving queue at a Tesco checkout.

But these fairyland diversions into the kingdom of pomp were mere minor distractions from the immediate task at hand, which was to beat the SDP in Richmond and, if possible, beat the Tories, too. We had quite a good launch pad for the campaign, for a few weeks earlier in December the Party had come a respectable second, beating Labour, in the Epping Forest by-election (in which the Owenites won only 12%, which was, however, still enough to deny us victory over the Tories). We also had a good candidate in Richmond: Barbara Pearce (though, significantly, she was not from the area, whereas the Owenites had a local farmer). And the financial restructuring we had done earlier gave us enough money for me to tell the campaign team that we would bet our shirt on Richmond and they could fight a full-fledged campaign. It all seemed to go well until two days before the poll, when I was out campaigning with our candidate. At lunchtime our agent came up to me and whispered that he had just seen the latest opinion polls for Richmond, which would be published on the evening regional TV news and in tomorrow's eve-of-poll newspapers. These showed the SDP five points ahead of us and in second place, just behind the Tories. I knew exactly what would happen next, and I knew there was nothing we could do to stop it – voters who wanted to beat the Tories (who had a bright young candidate called William Hague), would now pile in behind the Owenites. And that is what happened. When the result of the count was announced at midday, William Hague narrowly squeaked in with a majority of 2,600, with the Owenites second and us third, 5,000 votes behind them. Now we were in real trouble! Owen was triumphant on every news outlet, and I knew that if I did not do something quickly we could be done for. I sensed that there was just a possibility I could change the story from Owen's triumph to the fact that, but for the divisions between our two parties, the Tory would easily have been beaten and that our joint self-indulgence had therefore enabled an unpopular Government to win where they should not have done. So I decided that, in that afternoon's interviews, I would be magnanimous to Owen and, without any wider consultation with the Party's members, call for the two Parties to immediately adopt a process of Joint Open Selection: by this method, candidates would be selected by a ballot of all members of the two local parties (in essence merging the Parties), resulting, I explained, in the fact that we would never again end up fighting each other and letting the Tories in.

This was a big risk and provoked a strong backlash from the Party, not least amongst some of our defeated workers in Richmond, who were very publicly infuriated that I would consider getting into bed with their hated rivals. But my calculation was that the risk was not as big as it looked, because Owen would never accept such a deal and that, if it was put to him, he would reject it outright, which would wrong-foot him and shift the story. And so it worked out. On my way north to a Councillors' meeting (where I got a very hard time about the line I had just taken), I turned on the five o'clock news to hear Owen being interviewed. The first question asked was not about his triumph, but about my call for a merger . . . there was a long silence, then the sound of him throwing the microphone down and stalking out of the studio, with the interviewer crying after him 'Dr Owen, Dr Owen . . .'. All subsequent news reports that night started off not with his triumph but with a question about why he was rejecting my offer.

And the following morning's papers followed suit, concentrating more on the fact that our divisions had enabled the Tories to win, than on the Owenites' 'victory' over us. Fast footwork had saved us from disaster this time, but I knew we were still standing on the last tuft of grass at the very edge of the precipice.

Some of my colleagues were, meanwhile, doing everything they could to propel us over the edge. My first problem had been to persuade Alan Beith to play a part in the parliamentary team, which he initially resisted. However, after a lot of persuasion, not least from David Steel, he finally agreed to come on board and take up the post of Treasury Spokesman for the Party (and in due course did an outstanding job, winning respect from all sides of politics and becoming a key ally in helping to establish a strongly free-market-based economic policy for the new Party). In January Labour, seeing our weakness, started to make overtures to some of our MPs (most notably Simon Hughes) and sending out messages to me that they were interested in some kind of a pact. I knew that, in our present weak state, this was a chalice of the most deadly poison, which would result in our losing first our identity and then our purpose. I told the Parliamentary Party that perhaps the time would come for this, but not until we were much, much stronger. This caused real annoyance to some of my MPs, who thought the offer should be pursued, and the opinion-formers in the progressive Press (the *Guardian* and the *Independent* in particular) expressed much the same view, criticising me for being unrealistic.

But the biggest issue, which threatened to destroy us altogether at the time, was the Party's name. The one thing which united everyone was that the name Social and Liberal Democrats (we were now regularly referred to by the Press as 'The Salads') had to be replaced. But there was deep division about what should replace it. The older Liberal MPs, especially those from Wales and Scotland, insisted that they should go on using Liberal and were prepared to do this unilaterally if necessary. At the Blackpool Conference I had said that my preference was for 'Democrats', which was also the preferred position of most of the ex-SDP. There was thus a real danger that we would all break off in different directions. The Parliamentary Party was especially deeply split on the issue, and the Press was full of reports of these divisions. On the night before the Richmond by-election Alan Beith got to hear of a letter the new Truro MP Mathew Taylor was going to publish in the *Independent* the next day, calling for unity behind my leadership. Alan immediately threatened that, if the Taylor letter went ahead, he would publish a counter-letter in the *Guardian* criticising me and our strategy. In a later conversation with our Chief Whip, Jim Wallace, he added, for good measure, that he was being put in an intolerable position and would resign the parliamentary Party whip over the name issue if he had to. I asked David Steel to see if he could persuade Alan to step back from the brink, which is what happened.

I was now dealing with four concurrent issues, any one of which could have swamped us: the Owenite resurgence; rebellion on all sides as a result of my fast footwork after Richmond; the name issue; and now, to add to all these, the fast-approaching local elections and European elections, followed by yet another by-election that had just been called in the Vale of Glamorgan, a place which, to put it mildly, was a desert for us.

I managed to persuade the rebellious Scottish and Welsh MPs to put the name issue to one side while we fought the coming elections – though it flared up from time to time, including in June when three of the Welsh MPs, backed by some of their Scottish colleagues, repeated publicly to the BBC that they were prepared to take unilateral action by calling themselves Liberal Democrats. Again, I managed to persuade them to withdraw, but it was clear that the boil had to be lanced, and quickly. The crunch came at a very bad-tempered meeting of all MPs in July (I should never have let it go on that long), at which Roy Jenkins and David Steel proposed we should let the name evolve naturally, and everyone could call themselves what they wanted in the meantime. I went home that night, poured myself a large whisky and quite quickly came to the conclusion that the problem was me – I was wrong and had to change course if I was not to destroy the Party completely. Being a relative outsider compared to the older MPs (something I later found I shared with Blair), I had, in my rush to create the new party, failed to understand that a political party is about more than plans and priorities and policies and a chromium-plated organisation. It also has a heart and a history and a soul – especially a very old party like the Liberals. Alan Beith and the other 'Name' rebels understood this better than me. They were right, and I had nearly wrecked the Party by becoming too attached to my own vision and ignoring the fact that political parties are, at root, human organisations and not machines. It was not difficult then to decide that the Jenkins/Steel proposition would only cause even more confusion when what we needed was clarity. I concluded that I should announce a referendum of all Party members, dare any MP to say that they would go against the democratic voice of the Party and announce at the same time that I would be voting for 'Liberal Democrat'. The row quickly subsided, a ballot of all members was arranged and, in the autumn, the Party agreed to 'Liberal Democrat' by an overwhelming vote.

But by then we had even bigger problems to deal with.

I had two abortive secret meetings with Owen to see if we could resolve the warfare between the two Parties. The first, on 16 March 1989, was at the house of his friend and financial backer David Sainsbury. This meeting, like the one which followed, foundered on the fact that Owen could not accept a process whereby local constituencies would decide their own local candidates, and I could not accept a nationally negotiated deal in which local constituencies played no part.

But by this stage the moment of danger was over and things were much easier, for the Owenites had done disastrously badly in the local elections (in which we had done surprisingly well, limiting our losses to a hundred). They then got a mere 2% of the vote in the Vale of Glamorgan, and in a later by-election in Glasgow Central came fifth behind the Greens. The *coup de grâce* came at a third by-election in Bootle, where they ignominiously trailed home behind Screaming Lord Sutch. They were now becoming the butt of all the jokes we had suffered from earlier in the year, and this, I think, David Owen found impossible to stomach. They finally packed up their tents and melted away on 14 May 1990,* to my great relief.

But, even before the Owenites departed the political scene, a greater and more deadly threat to us emerged. For the first time – and very suddenly – environmental issues started to become important on the national political agenda, causing even Mrs Thatcher to make pro-environment speeches (in one of which, to the great joy of the satirists, she promised single-handedly to 'save the world'). As traditionally Britain's most environmentally aware mainstream Party, we rather complacently believed we had a monopoly on this agenda. But

---

* Though they were not formally wound up until June the following year.

it was the Greens who suddenly caught the public's attention by launching a most imaginative campaign for the 1989 European Elections, in which they fielded an almost full slate of candidates across the country. Just before polling day I started getting reports of a strong Green surge and, indeed, could even feel it in my own Somerset constituency. But none of this prepared me for the shock of the morning of 18 June, when the Euro-election count revealed that the Greens had beaten us into fourth position in every single seat in Britain, except Cornwall (including in my own Somerset), getting nearly two-and-a-half times our national share of the vote. I went to bed that night tormented by the thought that the Party that had started with Gladstone would end with Ashdown.

The opinion-polling organisations run regular polls on how the party leaders are doing – measured by the public's answer to the question, 'In your opinion is Party Leader X doing a good or a bad job?' and then giving a figure based on the difference between those answering 'good' and those who say 'bad'. My rating at this time was a catastrophic minus 23%! This, I think, was the lowest moment of my entire Leadership.

I have always thought that the battle between the two major parties is like a heavyweight boxing match in which the two contestants slug it out, and the last one to remain standing wins. But third-party politics is much more like ju-jitsu: you have to take the momentum of forces you are given and turn them to your advantage. When faced with a political crisis, my first instinct, since I cannot alter the forces involved, has always been to try to find the means to turn them, or else find a way to ride with the punch. But on this occasion I could do nothing. It was a sudden and unforeseen disaster, and we just had to have the strength to hang on and sit it out.

The papers were full of the fact that this disaster was all the result of my leadership, and when I stood up at the next Prime Minister's Question Time, there were shouts from all around of 'Mr Six Percent!' (our poll share in the Euros) and 'Bite the cyanide capsule, Paddy'. To make matters worse, my postbag was now full of letters from members of the Party saying they were resigning and going to join the Greens, and the *Observer* published a report at the weekend that Simon Hughes was threatening to do the same, if things didn't improve.*

---

* Simon resolutely denied this.

And they didn't improve, for we were now facing another financial crisis. In early July Tim Clement Jones, a long-time supporter and close friend who had taken over the Finance Committee, told me that we were facing a £200,000 liquidity shortfall by the end of September and could not pay salaries after that date. Shortly afterwards, the bank threatened to foreclose on our loan, and the auditors announced that they were intending to qualify our accounts, in effect making us bankrupt. We would have to cut our costs – and that meant staff – again. Only this time, having recognised that we had been too timid previously, Tim and I were determined to cut deep enough to get ourselves back into the black, even if it meant reducing the Party's central staff to a mere skeleton and getting rid of our entire network of regional agents. I even asked my friend Archy Kirkwood to double up and combine his job as Deputy Whip and spokesman for Scotland with that of General Secretary of the Party in Cowley Street, in order to save costs. There was much opposition to this, with dire predictions about destroying the whole Party, but eventually we got the package through the Party's key committees. Even then, the bank would not agree not to foreclose unless the Officers of the Party signed a formal undertaking that our personal assets were, in the last event, on call if the bank could not recover the loan by any other means. One of the most moving experiences of my life was watching as each of my closest colleagues on the Executive Committee of the Party signed a form which, in effect, bet their personal assets on the Party's survival.

Our opinion-poll standing was around 4%,* and sometimes even lower. Indeed I think I am the only modern party leader who has had the distinction of presiding over an opinion-poll rating of an asterisk: indicating that the pollsters could find no detectable level of support!

There were, however, two tiny shafts of light amidst all this gloom. The first was the issue of Hong Kong passports. The Tiananmen Square massacre had taken place in June, and I had got immediately involved, visiting Hong Kong with Bob MacLennan and joining in some of the demonstrations.† On our return we persuaded the Party

---

* MORI/Times 27 June and 21 August 1989.
† Alastair Campbell, at that time still Political Correspondent for the *Daily Mirror*, wrote an excoriating article attacking me for getting personally involved in the Tiananmen Square affair, saying it proved I was just not serious. This he has subsequently and with great generosity apologised for, admitting that this judgement was wrong.

that we should adopt the highly risky policy of insisting that all the 3.5 million ethnic Chinese in Hong Kong who were British subjects should be given right of abode in Britain if they wished to take it up in an emergency after the Chinese took over in 1997. The Government had withdrawn this right, and the Labour Party had cravenly supported them. Needless to say, agreeing to allow 3.5 million Chinese to come and live in Britain was not a popular position, even with some of my MPs. But it was right and would, in my view, have greatly assisted with inward investment to Britain just when the country needed it most (instead, much of this investment went to the west coast of the United States and to Canada). Moreover, it was a policy supported by most of the left-leaning Press. But, most important of all, it was a clear and distinguishing radical position that was consistent with our Liberal Democrat internationalist traditions, gave us a *raison d'être* for our existence and some much needed pride in ourselves. Later we were to discover that our strong position on Hong Kong passports also had the unintended benefit of helping us raise funds for the Party from the expatriate Chinese community.

Secondly, though the benefits from this were to come much later, I had decided that I needed to put down on paper a clear policy prospectus outlining what it was that I believed the Party should stand for. In June, just after our devastating defeat by the Greens, I started to write my first book, subsequently titled *Citizen's Britain* and published in time for the Party Conference in September that year.

This was my first book, and the one that, in many ways, I am most proud of – for it sought to map a coherent new agenda for the liberal left in Britain based on shifting power from the state producer to the citizen consumer. It proposed that the delivery of public services, such as education and health, should be based on choice, and that the money should follow the citizen, not the citizen the money. It asserted that liberalism was different from socialism, because what it was ruled by was not equality of outcome but equality of opportunity, and that the job of the liberal state should be to provide this. And it thus established, long before Blair's famous 'education, education, education' slogan, that education was the key investment the nation had to make, paving the way for our later 1p on income tax for education, arguably the most successful policy the Party had in my time. In all these ways, it long predated the Blairite revolution. But it was different from Blairism in one crucial way. It was committed to deep constitutional change and the establishment of a strong bulwark of individual civil liberties, in order to create a Britain based around the powerful citizen, not the powerful state.

Having resolved the name issue, I was now determined to replace our old Party symbol, a dreadful diamond-shaped thing that was easily confused with the 'Baby on Board' sign that new parents put in the back of their car. In May the following year, after a very long process of consultation and against the background of some low-key criticism and a few rather good jokes at our expense from the newspaper cartoonists, the Party overwhelmingly adopted the yellow 'Lib Dem Bird of Liberty', which has remained our symbol ever since.*

The main national political issue of 1990 was the Poll Tax. On 8 March that year I was almost engulfed in one of the most violent of the anti-poll tax rallies when I went to speak at a protest meeting in Hackney, managing to escape through the back door of the Hall just before the Militant Left took over and the whole scene descended into violence. However, the really effective action that stopped the Poll Tax did not take place on the streets of London, but in a key by-election which had now been called.

On 30 July Ian Gow, the MP for Eastbourne and a close associate of Mrs Thatcher, was killed by an IRA bomb. Although we were second in Eastbourne, my initial instinct was not to fight the by-election, because I believed the IRA should not have the satisfaction of causing a potential defeat for the Government. We should therefore stand aside and let the Conservatives have a free run. Chris Rennard, now our director of campaigns, who was to prove himself a genius, much feared by the other parties when it came to by-elections, persuaded me otherwise, promising that we could win. I replied that I thought he was a hopeless optimist but agreed to back his hunch with every penny we could scrape together (most of it raised by Chris himself). At the Conservative Conference that year the Tories made sure that Ian Gow's widow was on the platform during a leader's speech, in which Mrs Thatcher dismissed the Lib Dems with the line that 'the

---

* This was originally designed for us by Rodney Fitch, probably the best-known brand consultant/designer of the time, who – together with others, like Peter Grender – helped us hugely in these difficult days.

soufflé never rises twice' and declared we were 'as dead as John Cleese's parrot'.* We concentrated our campaign on the hated Poll Tax and promised that, if we were to win, Mrs Thatcher would have to go. The election was held on 18 October and at 12.50 the following morning, Chris Rennard rang me to say that our candidate David Belotti had won a great victory, with more than 51% of the vote, turning a Tory majority of 16,000 into a Liberal Democrat one of 4,500. The *Evening Standard* headline that evening, over a harassed picture of Mrs Thatcher, shouted 'The parrot has twitched!'†

Our opinion poll ratings showed a marked jump after Eastbourne, and my personal ratings as Lib Dem Leader moved for the first time from the negative to a positive 9%. In March 1991 there followed another by-election victory in the safe Tory seat of Ribble Valley. These two by-elections had a huge effect on Party morale. For the first time since the merger our members began to believe that we could survive and perhaps even prosper again.

Less than a month later Geoffrey Howe resigned and, on his way out, gave one of the most effective House of Commons speeches I have ever heard. Wags said it took him half an hour to deliver the speech, but his wife (who, it was said, hated Mrs Thatcher) half a lifetime to write it. It was all the more deadly because it was delivered in Howe's usual flat, quiet monotone (he was nicknamed 'Mogadon Man' for his ability to send the Chamber to sleep). I sat opposite Mrs Thatcher and almost felt sorry for her as, one after another, Howe's sentences thudded into her like poison arrows. At one time I even saw her bite her lip in pain. A week after the Howe speech I was walking through Glasgow airport when it was announced over the public-address system that Mrs Thatcher had resigned, and the whole airport erupted into spontaneous applause.

A week after that, at a ceremony in the Savoy, the *Spectator* magazine voted me Party Leader of the year. We were back in business!

---

* According to legend, Mrs Thatcher (famous for having a rather limited sense of humour and even less contact with popular culture) had to be shown the famous John Cleese sketch three times before, still apparently rather bewildered at its relevance to this line in her speech, she nevertheless agreed to use it.
† This line actually came from one of Mrs Thatcher's own Cabinet colleagues, Kenneth Baker, who replied thus when a *Standard* journalist asked his reaction to the contrast between Mrs Thatcher's disparaging comment and our trouncing of the Tories at Eastbourne.

For me, the Major era in Downing Street began in January the follow-ing year, when, fulfilling one of my 'wallpaper of State' duties, Jane and I went there for an official dinner. The change from Mrs Thatcher and all that hyperventilating energy could not have been starker. I recorded my impressions of the new incumbents in Downing Street in my diary that night as follows:

> *Major is quite different from Thatcher (she was also there, very regal and gener-ally dominating the performance). He looks just like the man next door, who became Prime Minister to both his surprise and ours. Whenever I see him I think of those rows and rows of pre-war houses which line the South Circular on the way into London – he could emerge from any one of them, and you would think it absolutely normal. But he is effective in his own quiet way – a sort of suburban Baldwin of our times. Gentle, pleasant, courteous. Probably the most plainly decent man we have had in Downing Street this century. And I love Norma. She has a wonderful face, full of grace and poise. I hope they make a success of it.*

The new Prime Minster, however, didn't have long to get his feet under the table, for a mere six days later he was leading the country to war in the Gulf.

I have a theory about successful politicians, and especially political leaders: they start to make progress nationally when some event occurs that crystallises, in almost caricature form, the public's view of them. And, once he or she has been allotted this space in the public consciousness, the politician quite often starts to play up to it. Thus, after the Russians (foolishly) dubbed Mrs Thatcher the 'Iron Lady', that is what she became in the public's eyes – and she loved it.

For me the corresponding event was the Gulf War.

I formed a little team of war advisers made up of a friendly ambassa-dor or two and my old Royal Marine Company Commander (then General) Sir Jeremy Moore (of Limbang fame) and his colleague, my near-contemporary (also General) Julian Thompson, both of whom had been the key architects of the victory in the Falklands. Thanks to them, we always had a clear and usually correct line to take on most of the key events of the war. I also asked our press department to arrange a rota, so that somebody would be on duty round the clock, with instructions to get me first onto the air after every key incident, no matter what time of day or night. As a result, over the whole period of the war I was almost constantly on the airwaves as a commentator who appeared to know what he was talking about and seemed to make sense.

The crisis taught me three key lessons. First, that in opposition politics the important thing is to have a position. (In Government, of course, it is essential to have the right position; in opposition it is more important to have *a* position than necessarily to have the right one.) Second, generally speaking, the more difficult the issue, the clearer the line, the more you will carry others with you. And, third, it is much easier to perform well with a clear position, and much more difficult to do so with an ill-defined one.

My unequivocal position supporting the Coalition and the Government in the Gulf War contrasted with the more nuanced line taken by Neil Kinnock for Labour. But it also caused a good deal of unhappiness in the Party (including a few resignations) and even some concern amongst my most natural supporters, David Steel and Ming Campbell, in the Parliamentary Party.

It all came to a head on 13 February, when a US air strike killed a large number of civilians in a Baghdad air-raid shelter. At Prime Minister's Questions the following day there was real sense of shock, peppered with statements from some MPs that dripped with crocodile tears. Even Major seemed somehow uncertain and equivocal, evidently finding it difficult to show resolve for the war, as well as regret for the deaths. I struck a very different, almost bellicose note, saying that, however regrettable it was that innocent civilians had been killed, should we not remember that they were killed by accident, whereas Saddam Hussein had killed hundreds of thousands of his own citizens deliberately and as a matter of policy?* This became the line subsequently used by all at this crucial moment in the War.

When the War ended on 27 February, my fiftieth birthday, I suddenly found my personal poll figures as Leader rising sharply to +37%, putting me ahead of both Major (+11%) and Kinnock (−12%), a position I largely maintained until the 1992 election, which I entered with a rating of +40%.

In the local elections shortly after the end of the Gulf War, we made 520 gains and took control of 19 new Councils (which, in terms of

---

* Hansard 14 February 1991 Columns 994 and 995; 'Mr. Ashdown : Does the Prime Minister agree that, in considering the lessons of the terrible tragedy that took place in Baghdad last night, we should not forget that Saddam Hussein has, not through inadvertence, but through acts of deliberate policy, killed more Muslims than any other living person? Does he also agree that, as the terrible toll of the war rises, so should our determination to build a just and durable peace to follow it?'

gains, remains our best-ever local election result). We were now very well placed for the general election, which we all believed would come in late 1991 (but in the event did not occur until the following spring).

Some time previously I had asked my old friend and supporter Des Wilson to design and run our election campaign. Des, a New Zealander with a prickly personality and a strong ego, was probably the greatest single-issue campaigner of his age, having been responsible, amongst other things, for putting Shelter on the map after the seminal 1960s film *Cathy Come Home*, and for the campaign to remove lead from petrol. He had also run Friends of the Earth, been a key campaigner for freedom of information and had proved himself loyal to the Party in difficult circumstances. His style was not welcomed by my more delicate Parliamentary colleagues, but he designed a formidable campaign and prepared the Party to fight it better than we had ever been prepared before.

My concern was not just to do well in the campaign, though, but also to be prepared for what might follow: a hung parliament. I set up a small and secret team – Alan Beith, Bob MacLennan and myself – to begin to prepare for how we would handle this eventuality. We drew up papers on our bargaining positions, rehearsed who would play what role, and undertook training in negotiating techniques. Our bottom line was that we could not enter into any coalition unless proportional representation (PR) was part of the deal. Our reason for this was not just because we believed that PR would revitalise elections and lead to a more citizen-based politics; it was also – and perhaps chiefly – because we knew that when eventually a coalition government falls (as it must) it is always the junior party that suffers most. By accurately relating the number of seats in Parliament to votes won across the country, PR would have reduced the unfair share of the seats the big parties enjoy under Britain's present voting system and increased the number of seats allocated to the other, smaller parties (including the Lib Dems, of course). We saw PR, therefore, as the essential 'lifeboat' that would provide us, as the third party, with the insurance policy necessary to survive the end of a coalition.

But I was also beginning to think about what would happen if, unexpectedly, the Tories won. Privately, I viewed this as perhaps the most beneficial outcome for us. I judged that a coalition with Neil Kinnock and Labour in its current form would have been very difficult to handle and almost impossible to make a success of. On the other hand, a fourth Labour defeat could open up the road to a historic realignment of the Left, which would heal the rift that had occurred when Labour broke away from the Liberals in the early years of the twentieth century. In early July 1991 I asked a very close and trusted friend, William Wallace, to start thinking about what we could do to push this forward as soon after the election as possible, if the Tories won again. I asked him, in particular, to look at the wisdom of my giving a speech, perhaps as early as the week after the election, which would propose a deal between us and Labour, based on a broad programme of constitutional reform, beginning with a joint Lib/Lab convention on a Scottish Parliament.

It was also about this time that some newspapers started to report trouble in Yugoslavia. I asked for a briefing and had to be shown where the various 'countries' of Yugoslavia were, after which I dismissed it all as too complex and, anyway, not something for me to bother about, because it wasn't going to amount to anything important.

Reviewing progress at the end of the year, I felt rather self-satisfied. We had made real advances, taking a third Tory seat (Kincardine and Deeside) in November of that year. The reckoning was that I had had a 'good' Gulf War. The Parliamentary Party was united and purposeful. And my personal ratings in the polls were consistently higher than either of the other two party leaders. I thought us well placed for what everyone recognised would be a very tight election in a few months.

It was in just this upbeat mood that I was enjoying a late-night glass of whisky with Des Wilson in my flat after a long but successful day, when the phone rang. It was Tricia Howard saying the *News of the World* had been round to her house. I made an excuse to bid Des goodnight and rang her back. Apparently a woman reporter had called on her and related the full story of our relationship when she was my secretary back in 1985. I felt my stomach sink into a black pit. I asked her if the reporter had given any indication where they had got the information from? None. I promised her all the support I could provide and said I would ring her again in the morning after I had time to think. I then rang my solicitor and old friend, Andrew Phillips, to tell him what had happened. So began the worst week of my life.

The following morning I briefed my close advisers, who were, without exception, supportive. It was in the course of this briefing that

Andrew Phillips told us that a few days previously the safe in his office (where he had put the envelope containing the notes of my conversation with him about my affair with Tricia) had been broken into, and the notes had been taken. What this meant was that the *News of the World* was using stolen private documents as the basis for its story, something that was plainly illegal. We agreed that, on this basis, it was worth trying for an injunction to prevent the *News of the World* and other newspapers who might follow its lead from publishing, or at the very least buy us a little time to make our dispositions. Andrew put the relevant papers together and, that afternoon, obtained an *ex parte* injunction in very short order.

Meanwhile my brother Mark, who is himself a solicitor in Bristol, collected Tricia, who was living alone and had no one to help her, and brought her to London, so she could get some advice from Andrew Phillips and we could provide her with the support she needed. After this I returned to Yeovil and went through the excruciatingly painful process of telling first Jane, and then my Constituency officers what had happened and discussing with them what action we should take next.

Over the next few days rumour started to spread like wildfire around Westminster, and articles hinting at 'a senior politician in a sex scandal' started to appear in the newspapers. The *Independent* published just such a blazing headline, juxtaposing it with a separate report and full page photo of me at a minor meeting they would never normally have given two column inches to. Moreover, it was clear that, although the injunction would stop English newspapers publishing, it would have no effect on Scottish or European ones, and the moment one of them ran the story, the English Press would be free to follow suit.

On 4 February (actually in the middle of a private reverie during a pre-election dinner with the BBC) I took the decision that I was not going to wait for the papers to break the story; I was going to grab the initiative and break it myself. I phoned Jane that night to tell her. She agreed it was the right course of action and said she would come up to London the following day to be with me. The following morning I called in my key advisers and informed them what I was going to do and, at a packed and highly charged press conference at noon, made a clean breast of it all.

The following couple of days were terrible in the Press, with the *Sun* coming up with the headline, 'Paddy Pantsdown', which is still sometimes shouted at me from a distance by drunks or young men wanting a bit of fun. Even the *Guardian* went to town, with a lead story spread over ninety percent of the front page and the whole of pages two and three, plus the main leader and another three pages with articles on the subject. Some of my political enemies enjoyed this greatly, especially because, although I have never either commented on or criticised anyone on matters of private morality, I did have a habit (chiefly springing from nervousness) of sounding a bit self-righteous and even priggish in the House. Indeed, the current joke about me was that the message on my answering machine was 'Hello. This is Paddy Ashdown. Please leave your message after the high moral tone'. So this fall from grace caused a good deal of quiet satisfaction for some. But the Lib Dem MPs in the House of Commons, and especially my front-bench colleagues were outstanding, as was John Major, who wrote me a private letter expressing his sympathy and support.

And the British public at large seemed to be extraordinarily forgiving, too – my opinion poll ratings actually went up as a result! I was in no doubt, though, that this did not mean that they approved of what I had done, only of the way it had been handled. So often in these matters it is the public lying that does the most damage.

But nothing could lessen the shame I felt, especially at bringing such pain to Jane, my family and, indeed, to Tricia, quite apart from letting down so many in the Party who were preparing for a vital election. Indeed, the damage from my actions spread even wider, for the Press were determined to try to find other scandals to uncover, and for months up to and including the Election, there was barely a female friend who was not approached and accused of having an affair with me, and barely a day without some rumour or other being relayed to me. Jane, meanwhile, received a string of most unpleasant letters and phone calls which gave further 'details' of my supposed indiscretions, while in pubs and phone boxes in my Constituency anonymous flyers were circulated purporting to be a personal message from someone claiming to be my 'love child', complete with a picture, saying that I had abandoned her. All this made life for my family even more difficult, and seriously undermined my self-confidence too. That, it appears, was precisely what was supposed to happen – as we discovered after the Election, when we learned* that some Tories had imported a group of US activists called 'The Nerds', whose job was to manufacture

* See *Sunday Times*, 17 May 1992, back page.

and spread malign rumours and make unfounded personal accusations against senior opposition MPs to undermine their effectiveness. Perhaps this was done without official sanction from the top of the Conservative Party. But perhaps not. After the election Kelvin Mackenzie, then editor of the *Sun*, revealed that at least one Cabinet-level Tory Minister had approached him seeking to retail scurrilous and untrue allegations against a number of senior opposition MPs.

None of this, of course, made for an easy general election campaign – though it had its moments. John Cleese helped us a lot during the campaign with appearances, advice and some very useful speech suggestions. Jokes (which I am not good at) are as valuable as gold to politicians, and they are always on the look-out for good ones – especially one-liners which can defuse a tricky moment. On one occasion, at a crucial point in the campaign, the Tories announced that David Owen was going to vote for them. I knew that the first thing I was going to have to do on the news that night was to give my reaction to Owen's defection. Lost as to how to respond, I rang John, who gave me, seemingly without a moment's thought, the perfect response. Sure enough, the first question I was asked that evening was 'Mr Ashdown, what is your reaction to the fact that Dr Owen has announced that he will be voting Tory at the Election?' To which I responded, with appropriate concern on my face, 'Well it's only fair. It *is* their turn.'

Des Wilson's brilliant campaign was later acknowledged to be, by a clear margin, the best of the general election. All the same, we did make one major tactical error, which was more my fault than Des's. We had both agreed beforehand that the aim of the campaign would be to make a hung parliament, and our role in it, the key issue of the last week of the campaign. In this Des succeeded brilliantly. By the last weekend, all the polls were pointing to a hung parliament, and I was on every news broadcast being asked what my price for a coalition would be. I tried to pretend that I could go into a coalition with either Party, but everyone knew that, after thirteen years of an increasingly unpopular Tory Government, I could never in reality have helped them in through the back door of Downing Street if the public had kicked them out through the front.

However, what neither Des nor I had spotted was that, as the campaign wore on, the public were getting increasingly concerned about the prospect of Neil Kinnock moving into Downing Street. Meanwhile in my weekend interviews before polling day I compounded the error by sounding far too strident and cocky in my demands for proportional representation – I made it look as though I was more interested in what was good for the Lib Dems than in what was good for the country.

John Major caught the public mood much better when, on the Monday before the election, he pulled out his famous soap box and recast himself as the underdog, a decent man fighting against the odds and against a conspiracy between Kinnock and me. And then, at the infamous Sheffield Rally, Neil let his guard slip and indulged in a most unwise bout of loud-mouthed triumphalism, so confirming all the public's fears about him. I once again felt the votes move massively away from us in the last days of the campaign.

On polling day, 9 April 1992, John Major, against the odds and all predictions, returned to Downing Street with a majority of 65, surprising the nation and, I think, himself as well. We had privately hoped to end up with 30 MPs, but we won only 20 seats, one more than when I was elected. Still, at least we had survived, which was more than almost anyone had predicted after the horrors of the first two years of the Party's existence.

CHAPTER 13

Leader II:
Back on the Field

I T IS 2 AUGUST 1992, the Election is behind us and I am on my way to Sarajevo. Far below us the Adriatic shines with a deep ultramarine blue never seen in northern waters. Here the grain of Dalmatia runs parallel to the coast, leaving a necklace of islands and submerged inlets strung along the shore, where the great mountain ridges of the Dinaric Alps vanish under the Adriatic. After an hour's flying we pass over the ancient town of Split, its red roofs a splash of colour against the slate grey of the hills which encircle it. This was the birthplace of the Emperor Diocletian, who drew, only two hundred miles to the east of us, the line that divided the Eastern from the Western Empire, around which blood and turmoil have swirled for two millennia and do so still today.

Suddenly the aircraft banks and gently dips, as we swing away from the coast towards the east and begin the long, slow incline downwards towards a distant rim of mountains, etched in a darker blue against an azure sky. 'Now it gets more tricky,' explains the pilot, sitting just in front of me. 'Sometimes they fire at us. It happens rarely. But it does happen, and it can be a bit hairy at times.' I notice that the RAF Special Forces team flying this *Hercules*, with its thirty tons of aid, suddenly put aside the relaxed atmosphere of our journey so far and begin preparing the aircraft for our approach.

We are now flying across north–south ridges, watered by lively streams and sprinkled with small alpine hamlets. It appears idyllic – until I look closer and see that the land is abandoned: very few houses have roofs, and many are little more than blackened shells.

Ahead, the rim of mountains starts growing into a row of formidable 6,000-ft peaks, at the base of which I can now dimly see a dark grey smudge spread like a stain across a broad open valley between the peaks. As I watch, this resolves itself into the outlines of a great city with a blanket of smoke hanging in the still air above it, fed by several columns rising up from the buildings below.

Now I can see the airport, perhaps ten miles ahead of us. As we cross the final ridge, the pilot tells me that if I look down I will see a Serb radar-controlled anti-aircraft battery tracking us in – and, sure enough, there it is, swinging gracefully with us as we pass overhead. The aircraft sensors pick up the hostile radar, and suddenly there are missile alarms screaming in our ears. The pilot flicks a switch to turn them off and then, it seems almost at the same time, the ground tips wildly up towards us, as the aircraft's nose dips down at a suicidal angle, pointing straight at the threshold of the runway fifteen hundred feet below. The pilot has forewarned me that, because of the danger of ground fire, we will be doing a 'Khe Sanh' landing (as used by planes resupplying US forces besieged there during the Vietnam war), which means a very fast descent from fifteen hundred feet. But this in no way diminishes my concern that the ground is now rushing towards me on a sharp collision course, while just behind my head thirty tons of stores are straining against their lashings to break free and obey the law of gravity. The co-pilot is now counting, 'Twelve hundred, a thousand, eight hundred, seven hundred . . .' When he announces four hundred feet the captain lowers the flaps; again the ground tips crazily, this time back up into the right position, and G forces push my legs into the aircraft floor so hard that my knees are forced to bend involuntarily. Then, with little more than a whisper and as gently as thistledown, we are on the ground and taxiing towards the end of the runway, where I can see a ruined tank sunk at a crazy angle in a ditch, its gun pointing aimlessly at the sky.

'Welcome to Sarajevo,' the captain says.

Looking around, I see a collection of wrecked and burnt-out airport buildings, some sand-bagged foxholes, a terrace of ruined tenements pockmarked by bullet and artillery fire, and a large, cheery man wearing a flak jacket, a crazy sunhat and the most enormous white beard I have seen outside a Santa Claus grotto at Christmas.

'Hi. I'm Larry Hollingworth,' he says and sticks out a great square, work-calloused hand to greet me.

———◆———

Larry, the head of the UNHCR (Office of the UN High Commissioner for Refugees) operation in Sarajevo, would become a good friend and wise counsellor on everything to do with Bosnia. He would also become famous, in this region and in the world of humanitarian assistance, as the man whose personal courage and dogged determination kept the great city of Sarajevo alive during its terrible three-year siege and, in so doing, undoubtedly saved many thousands from starvation.

Later that afternoon I went into Sarajevo and called on the Bosnian President, Alija Izetbegović, at whose huge funeral in the city I would speak more than a decade later, describing him as 'the father of his nation'. We had a long conversation on the agony of Sarajevo and the tragedies of Bosnia, as a noisy Serb mortar and artillery barrage fell into the streets outside the shattered windows of his Presidency.

Later, when the bombardment had stopped, I walked briefly around the centre of the city, carefully taking Larry's advice on which street junctions to run across, so as not to give the snipers in the hills surrounding the city too easy a target. I was shocked at the tired, frightened, grey faces of my fellow Europeans, for whom death was now an everyday accompaniment to the daily business of collecting water and rummaging for food in order to stay alive. Afterwards, at the local hospital, I stood at the bedside of a young boy of ten whose stomach had been ripped open by shrapnel, and wept as he died before my eyes.

Our final visit during that day was to a local park, now turned into a makeshift cemetery, where they were already excavating the graves for people not yet dead, but who would be among the inevitable harvest of those the snipers would cut down in the coming winter, when the ground would be too frozen for digging.

That night I spent in a small underground bunker Larry and his team had dug on Sarajevo airport. A particularly heavy bombardment made it difficult for either of us to sleep, so we sat outside on the sandbags, drinking our way slowly through the best part of a bottle of whisky I had brought with me. We talked about this senseless horror, and the culpability of those who had the power to stop it but didn't, while watching the shooting stars above and their mirror-image of tracer arcing around us, much as one might an especially noisy firework show.

<hr />

And so it was that in 1992 the threads of my life first became intertwined with the fate and future of the little country of Bosnia and Herzegovina and its extraordinary people.

It began, as have all the most important events of my life, completely by accident. One day in mid-July, two months after the general election, I was walking back from a television interview (on the shelling of Sarajevo, as it happens) with my friend and close adviser Alan Leaman, bemoaning the fact that politics was always so dull after an election; the Government were entitled to their honeymoon period, and the Opposition could only sit tight, watch and wait for them to start making mistakes again. Alan, quite casually and I think not really meaning it, said, 'You know a bit about wars, Paddy. If you are so bored, why don't you go out and have a look at the one that has just started in Yugoslavia. You've always said that your style of politics is to get out of the House of Commons and see what is happening on the ground for yourself. Well, Sarajevo is where it's happening – why not go there?'

And so, two weeks later, I was touring refugee camps in Croatia,* experiencing for the first time my uncontrollable Balkan affliction of unbidden tears as desperate people told me of their plight and the horrors they had suffered, while witnessing something that I had never dreamt we would see again on European soil, the use of railway wagons as instruments of 'ethnic cleansing'. That evening, in a bar in Zagreb where I was having a drink with the local head of UNHCR, Tony Land, I managed to persuade the Special Forces RAF Squadron flying aid into Sarajevo for the UN to take me with them – largely, I think, because I remembered some of the names of the Special Forces guys who used to fly me in my SBS days.

At this point I must backtrack briefly for the benefit of those too young to have followed the Balkan crisis of the 1990s, or whose memory of events has become blurred.

The trouble had started in 1991, when Tito's Yugoslavia began its violent disintegration. The Slovenians were the first to go, managing their exit largely peacefully. But, as Croatia moved to follow Slovenia, conflict broke out between Belgrade and Zagreb, with Yugoslav jets bombing the Croatian capital and severe fighting between the Yugoslav National Army (JNA) and Croatian forces, including the bombardment of Dubrovnik. Under pressure from Germany – which had its own

* I had a guide and an interpreter with me that day. The guide was Gurkha Col. Mark Cook. Later that day Mark, who was just about to retire from the Army, showed me an abandoned orphanage in the little Croatian town of Lipik, which he said he was going to open after he retired as the first venture of a new charity he and his wife intended to launch for orphans of war. He was as good as his word. The charity, Hope and Homes for Children, now operates worldwide, and I am one of its patrons. Our interpreter that day was Lidija Topić, who would later become Deputy Foreign Minister of Bosnia and Herzegovina and then its Ambassador to the EU, when I was High Representative in the country from 2002–2006.

reasons for favouring Croatia's independence – Britain* and other European nations recognised Croatia. This lit the fuse, and the Muslim majority in Bosnia and Herzegovina immediately moved to follow their Croatian neighbours, with their President, Alija Izetbegović, calling for a referendum. In response to this the Bosnian Serbs, under the leadership of Radovan Karadžić, started to mobilise in the hills.

The flashpoint in Bosnia came on 5 April 1992, when a sniper in the Holiday Inn in Sarajevo shot dead a Muslim woman, Suada Dilberović, who was on a peace march. This was followed by further slaughter when Serb gunmen shot a number of Sarajevo citizens demonstrating in a park opposite the Bosnian Presidency building. These events, and others, provided the trigger for all-out war between the three communities – Bosniak Muslim (known nowadays as 'Bosniak'), Croat and Serb – which quickly spread to all corners of Bosnia. By June, Sarajevo was under siege by Serbian forces, the UN airlift (which would keep the city alive for almost four years) had started, and Larry Hollingworth had been sent there to organise the distribution of the aid it delivered. On 30 June 1992, following a UN Security Council Resolution, a battalion of Canadian troops wearing the UN's blue berets took over Sarajevo airport to facilitate the delivery of aid to the city and other parts of Bosnia. At the end of June, about a month before I flew in to the city, the Canadian UN forces left Sarajevo, and their role was taken over by French troops.

When I arrived back in UK after the Sarajevo trip, I wrote an article for the *Guardian*, a letter to the Prime Minster and a speech which I delivered to a meeting in London – all with the same message. This was definitely a war crime, probably the beginnings of genocide, would certainly lead to greater instability, could be stopped and should be.

A week later, while Jane and I were visiting Monet's garden in Giverny outside Paris, Radovan Karadžić, the Bosnian Serb Leader, contacted me with a message: 'You have seen the Muslim side, I invite you now to and come and see ours.' I could not, of course, refuse and on 8 August caught a plane to Budapest, where I met my Lib Dem colleague Russell Johnston, and we took a car for the long journey

---

* It has subsequently been claimed that John Major did a deal with German Foreign Minister, Hans Dietrich Genscher, exchanging German acquiescence in Britain's EU Social Opt Out, for Croatian recognition.

across the flat, fertile plains of Hungary to Belgrade, the capital of Serbia proper. All the way our driver listened to a radio station blasting Serb turbo-folk, interspersed with news. At one stage, just after we had crossed the border into Serbia, our interpreter burst out laughing. I asked him why, and he replied that the radio news had just announced that the successor to Gladstone (me) had entered the country on his way to see the Government! The Serbian President, Milošević, was apparently out of town, so the following day I was taken to see the Yugoslavian President, Dobrica Ćosić,* in the Soviet-style government buildings in Belgrade. I had not the first idea what he looked like, so was somewhat flummoxed when the great doors on the reception room were opened and I was confronted with a long line of men, all with seemingly identical granite Slav faces, all in identical suits. Fortunately, I chose the right hand to shake. (On a later occasion, in Montenegro, when meeting a Government minister, I enthusiastically shook the hand of his astonished driver instead!) After what was not a very illuminating meeting, we were bundled off to a nearby helicopter pad, loaded onto an armoured Russian helicopter flown by a Russian (who told me the helicopter was made in a factory outside Moscow that also made tractors: 'Helicopters one end, tractors the other') and took off on the most frightening helicopter flight of my life over the mountains of Bosnia to Karadžić's headquarters in Pale, from where he was directing the siege of Sarajevo. The events of the following two days, when we visited the prison camps at Manjaca and Trnopolje, have already been described in the Prologue.

Shortly after I returned, with the images of these two visits still freshly burning in my mind, I sat at the dinner table next to an extremely elegant and distinguished man in his mid-sixties who spoke in that languorous, easy manner of upper-class Britons born in the early years of the last century. He courteously asked me what I thought of Bosnia and what should happen there. I told him that I had just been there and seen things for myself, so I knew *exactly* what should happen – we should intervene. He said gently that he didn't altogether agree. But I would have none of it and told him that I had been there and seen

---

* Yugoslavia made something of a speciality of having lots of presidents. There was one for each of the component states (e.g. Serbia, Croatia, Bosnia and Herzegovina, etc.) as well as a Federal President, the post that Ćosić held at this point.

things for myself, so I knew what I was talking about, etc., etc. After I had spent a good fifteen minutes digging this massive hole for myself, someone across the table sought to attract my dinner companion's attention by calling out 'Fitzroy!' Only then did I realise I was sitting next to Fitzroy MacLean, one of my all-time heroes, who had parachuted into Yugoslavia and fought alongside Tito throughout his great guerrilla campaign against the Germans across the mountains of Bosnia in World War Two. Needless to say, he brushed aside with infinite politeness my stumbling apologies and pathetic expressions of admiration.*

As a result of these two trips Bosnia became, even some of my friends would say, something of an obsession. What happened there, I saw – and still see – as the greatest crime on European soil since the Second World War. And Europe's failure to intervene I saw – and still see – as the greatest act of moral failure and deliberate, culpable blindness of our time. I also saw the Bosnia war as, in some way, our generation's Spanish Civil War: a time when ordinary people understood better than their leaders what was happening, and what needed to be done, in a conflict that was not a hangover from the past but a predictor of things to come.

During the almost four years of the siege of Sarajevo I visited the city twice a year – once in the summer and once in the winter – making a point of staying for several days with Bosnian friends, and not just dropping in for an hour or two, as most visiting dignitaries did. During these visits I smuggled in aid and medicine for the relatives of Bosnian refugees in Britain, carried letters in and out between distraught relatives and arranged for the secret transport of detonators to enable the blasting of coal from an open-cast mine in nearby Kakanj to continue, so as to keep a local power station going and the city's lights on, albeit intermittently.

In the House of Commons I asked so many Prime Minster's Questions on Bosnia that they used to shout 'The Honourable Member for Sarajevo' when I stood up. My party (including some of its MPs, I have

---

* I seem to have made rather a habit of this kind of thing in my life. Once, on a train to Poole one very cold January day during my SBS days, a fellow traveller, seeing my Royal Marines uniform, asked me if I was in the SBS, and what was it like nowadays? I told him, perhaps rather brusquely, I couldn't tell him anything because of security. It was only at the end of the journey that I realised that my companion was none other than Blondie Haslar, the leader and one of the only two survivors of the great 'Cockleshell Heroes' raid on Bordeaux in the Second World War – the event which, in effect, founded the SBS.

to admit) grumbled that I spent too much time on the subject; many of my constituents seemed to agree, judging from my postbag, and Labour MPs, though they prefer not to remember it now, used to shout 'war-monger' when I repeatedly called for the West to intervene and stop the carnage.

Looking back, I think there is probably some substance in these criticisms. As Leader of the Liberal Democrats I should not, perhaps, have allowed myself to get so obsessed by a single issue. But I still regard this as the best work I ever did in the House of Commons and a cause in which I was privileged to be involved.

Nevertheless, although Bosnia was a constant backdrop to all five years of the 1992 parliament, there were other big things happening too, as Britain moved towards the twilight of the Conservative years, and the Left began to reshape itself for government.

In my first meeting with Party officials after the 1992 election I told them that the Party's survival phase was now over. We were now no longer spectators. I was determined that, in this Parliament, we would prove that we were back on the field as players.

On 9 May, exactly a month after polling day, I gave what I believe was my most important speech as Lib Dem Leader, and one I had been thinking about for almost a year. It became known as the Chard speech, after the little town in my Constituency where it was made. It proposed, in essence, a new coming together of the Left to form a pro-gressive alliance dedicated to ending the Tory hegemony and bringing in radical reforms to the British Constitution, beginning with a Scottish Parliament.

This speech was received with hostility by some of my MPs and by a large swathe of the Party at large, although it had actually been watered down during successive consultations with parliamentary col-leagues. It proposed that we formally start to align ourselves with opposition to the Tories and end what had become a pretence – the Party's traditional policy of being equally opposed to both Labour and Tories. This paved the way for the long, slow process of shifting our position and ended, three years later, with the Lib Dems' historic deci-sion to abandon the Party's traditional 'equidistance' from the other two main parties, so enabling us to be an integral part of the tidal wave of change which was to sweep the Tories from power in 1997.

To start with, however, there was no response from Labour, who were at the time in complete disarray after their general election defeat and preoccupied with electing John Smith as their new Leader. My first meeting with Smith was not until October, when we met over a whisky (actually several) in his Commons office. He made it very plain that he would continue to pursue a 'go-it-alone' strategy for Labour, didn't think that creating a broad coalition for constitutional change (which he was genuinely committed to, far more than Blair) was necessary, didn't want to upset the equilibrium of Labour, and didn't believe there was room for anyone else in the battle to beat the Tories. We might work together if he needed us, he told me, but not if he didn't. 'Let's develop the habit of friendship, even if this is not the time for formal co-operation,' he said as I left. I was depressed that his vision was so narrow but well satisfied that this now left the space for the Lib Dems to lead in the process of creating a wider consensus for radical constitutional change, which I knew many of Labour's natural supporters agreed with.

Our relations with John Smith's Labour Party were, moreover, not improved by our position on the biggest political issue of the day, the passage of the Maastricht Treaty through the House of Commons in early November. This came just six weeks after the fiasco of 'Black Wednesday': Britain's humiliating exit from the European Exchange Rate Mechanism and the devaluation of the pound (which occurred in the middle of our Party Conference in Harrogate in September). Both these events terribly weakened Major's Government and presented the Opposition parties with a most tempting opportunity to vote with Major's Euro-rebels and defeat him in the Commons. But if we did this we would destroy Britain's future in Europe at the same time. After much debate and some arm twisting, especially with Charles Kennedy, who was very uncertain on the issue* (I wheeled out Roy Jenkins to help me here), the Lib Dem Parliamentary Party finally agreed we would stand by our European principles and support the Government. Labour, on the other hand, though in favour of the Bill in principle, said they would join the Tories' Euro-rebels in order to damage Major and perhaps even, as they saw it, bring his Government down.

When it comes to deciding what you should and should not do in Opposition, I have always believed in the policy of George Lansbury,

---

* Charles Kennedy, *The Future of Politics* (London: HarperCollins, 2000), pp. 6–11.

Labour's forgotten leader before the Second World War, who said it is usually wisest for opposition parties to reject the temptations of easy opportunism and act as they would do in government. For that is the best way to show the electorate that they can be trusted with power.

There was some further wobbling amongst Lib Dem MPs (Charles Kennedy and Simon Hughes were especially worried), accompanied by anger and even resignations amongst Party members at large, who fell for Labour's line. (Our Cowley Street headquarters was receiving some 150 phone calls and about as many letters a day from Party members opposed to our line, about half of whom said they were resigning over this.) As the Maastricht vote approached, hostility towards us from Labour and the left-wing Press for 'supporting the Government' grew sharply. But in the end we voted together according to our European beliefs, with the result that both the Government and Britain's future in Europe survived. This was the vote I am proudest of having cast in my time in the Commons. There was huge, but largely synthetic, anger from Labour afterwards. But sticking to our principles, while Labour abandoned theirs, did us very little harm in the end and may even have done some good.

For John Major, however, this was only just the beginning of his torture on the rack of Europe at the hands of his Euro-rebels – later in the Parliament he would famously refer to them as 'the Bastards' – and in the end this issue would cripple his Government and bring him to the point of resignation. At his request, I met with Major secretly on several occasions to co-ordinate our actions in order to save Maastricht from the treachery of his rebels and the cynicism of Labour. This had to be carefully and discreetly done, for by early 1993 we had, in Newbury, the first of two key by-elections in seats the Tories held by huge majorities, and I could not afford to be seen to be too close to the Government.

We had an excellent candidate in Newbury, David Rendel, and fought a very strong campaign, once again under the direction of Chris Rennard. At 4.20 a.m. on Friday 8 May, the day after the Newbury Poll, the Party General Secretary rang to tell me that David Rendel had won by 22,000 votes. I said that I didn't want to know how many votes he had got, I wanted to know what his majority was. 'Paddy, that *is* the majority!' he said. Newbury, which saw a 28% swing to the Liberal Democrats, did much to help us recover from the disappointment and lost momentum after the 1992 general election.

However, for me, 1993 was about more than Europe and by-election campaigning. I was by now deeply involved in writing another book: *Beyond Westminster*. After the 1992 election I had decided I needed to get out of the fug of Westminster and start refreshing my knowledge of the way ordinary people across Britain were living their lives. To be honest, it was something of a relief, for I never much liked Westminster, and the feeling was, I think, mutual. Some MPs take the view that politics is a purely Westminster affair. For me politics is what happens in people's lives, and Westminster was just the place where I had to work. In 1983, when I was elected, I discovered that the things I had done in my previous 'real jobs', from soldier, to 'diplomat', to businessman, to youth worker – even to being unemployed – had greatly helped me with the job I now had to do in Parliament. Indeed, though my trajectory through these jobs had been entirely accidental, they all combined to form a very useful apprenticeship to being an MP. But, after ten years in Parliament, I felt jaded and increasingly caught up in the Westminster game. I needed to refresh the reservoir of my enthusiasm and personal experience, and *Beyond Westminster* was the way I hoped to do this.

I spent much of the early months of 1993 in a series of visits, living and working with people across the country. The format we hit on was for me to work for maybe two or three days with individuals in their workplace, spending the evenings with them and their families. The Press were not invited and only informed of my visits afterwards. My first visit was in January, to Britain's deepest coalmine at Monktonhall in Scotland, where I worked a shift with the miners. Other visits included two days fishing with Cornish trawlermen in the Irish Sea; working with a businessman in Omagh, Northern Ireland; spending Ramadan with a Muslim family in Peckham and living with a black family in Moss Side, Manchester, which at the time was so under the control of drug gangs that it had become practically a no-go area for police. It was during my Moss Side visit that Jane got an early-morning phone call from Manchester police saying that they had just carried out a drugs raid, in the course of which they had stopped someone observing from the sidelines who claimed to be me and, indeed, looked very like me. But they couldn't believe it was me. 'Can you tell me if it is your husband?' the caller asked. 'Yeah, yeah,' Jane replied, 'that's him!'

I made copious notes on each of these visits and then wrote *Beyond Westminster* in my courtyard in France, getting up at 5 a.m. every morning so as to be able to do four hours of writing in the cool of the day.

The book was published in paperback in time for the Party's Spring Conference in 1994 and, even if only briefly, reached the *Sunday Times* top ten paperback list – thanks, I think, to the loyal Party members purchasing it *en masse* during Conference week.

The central message of the book was that the Government was becoming dangerously out of touch with the lives of ordinary citizens in Britain and was fast losing their confidence. Unless we tackled this democratic deficit, I concluded, the gap between government and governed would only widen and perhaps even, in time, threaten the democratic process itself.

At the end of July 1993 we overturned a 23,000 Conservative majority in the Christchurch by-election, where our candidate, Diana Maddock, won by more than 16,000 votes. My press release after the result said that this was 'a shout of anger from the heart of Britain'. At 35%, this was the biggest swing against the Tories in a by-election in more than fifty years and temporarily catapulted us above the Conservatives in national opinion polls. The day after the by-election I left for my fifth visit to Bosnia.

Having made the previous three trips through Croatia and across the Dinaric Alps into Bosnia with the help of British troops serving in the UN force, I decided that this time I would again go in through Belgrade. I crossed the Drina River, which marks the border between Serbia and Bosnia, at Zvornik, where my car was stopped by a Serb frontier guard sporting a fearsome beard and an even more fearsome machine-gun. He wanted to know who I was, where I was going and why, and seemed to be on the point of refusing to let me pass when another fearsomely bearded Serb stuck his head out of the machine-gun bunker he was manning and shouted, according to my interpreter, 'Let him pass. His lot has just smashed Major in some British election!'

It was on this trip that I met General Mladić for the second time, when he attended a dinner for me given by Karadžić on the night of my arrival. Mladić spent much of the time boasting about his army. But I knew that, shortly before my arrival, a Bosnian Serb assault on Sarajevo from the East had been bloodily repulsed by the Bosniaks, with heavy losses. So I asked Mladić, somewhat mischievously, why, if his army was so superior, he had not taken Sarajevo already? His reply was chilling:

I can take Sarajevo any time I like. But I was Russian-trained. And we were always taught that, if you have a choice between shooting an enemy in the head or shooting him in the balls, always shoot him in the balls. It takes only two people half an hour to bury a dead man. But it takes many tens of people many tens of weeks to keep a wounded man alive. I am very happy to leave Sarajevo as it is. The West is now spending so much of its time and energy keeping Sarajevo alive, that you have none left to deal with me. While you have to go on doing that, I can go on doing what I want.

Its frontal assault having been driven back, the Bosnian Serb army was, however, now in the middle of a major offensive in the mountains above Sarajevo whose aim was to extend the Serb ring around the city by capturing Mount Igman, which dominates and protects the west end of the city. The day after our dinner I went to the area and met Mladić again, this time directing fire from a battery of 130mm howitzers high in the mountains above Sarajevo. His guns were parked, openly visible, on the side of the mountain and without either camouflage or concealment. I said to him, 'You have never experienced air attacks or counter-battery fire, have you?' He asked me why I had asked the question. I replied that, if he had, he would never have placed his guns in such an exposed position, with their ammunition piled alongside them. He replied that if NATO aircraft ever dared to attack he would knock them out of the sky long before they got to his guns. He was to get a very nasty surprise when, in the end, NATO did intervene two years later.

Just a few minutes after we left the gun site, a stick of Bosniak mortar bombs landed just where we had been standing, killing an Associated Press cameraman who had stayed behind to take pictures and terribly wounding his reporter colleague.

———◆———

In mid-1993, following our by-election victories, our opinion poll ratings were beginning to rise quite sharply, reaching 28% in July and August, while Labour's were languishing at a level insufficient to guarantee a Tory defeat at the next election. Indeed, John Smith was proving a much less decisive Leader than Neil Kinnock. He was taking Labour back to its old, socialist positions and was widely criticised for failing to carry through some of the reforms that Neil Kinnock had initiated, especially in modernising the Party and reducing the influence of the trades unions. There was, I knew, quite a lot of unhappiness about this amongst newer Labour MPs.

On 14 July 1993, just before the Christchurch by-election, Jane and I were invited to dinner by my colleague Anthony Lester, who had just joined the Lib Dem team in the Lords, having been one of those who had left Labour to found the SDP. He and his wife Katya had also invited a young Labour MP called Tony Blair and his wife Cherie, whom I had never met socially before. Blair had been elected at the same time as me in 1983 and had been making quite a name for himself as Labour's Shadow Home Secretary. We spent much of the evening talking privately in a corner, while the Lesters kept the others away in order to give us space. We discussed the need to realign the Left and the necessity for root-and-branch reform of the Labour Party. He said, however, that he was very concerned not to get himself too far out in front. He was especially worried about getting into a head-to-head with either the unions or Labour's Left too soon – it would have to be done carefully, at the right time and step by step. 'The history of the Labour Party is littered with nice people who get beaten, and I don't intend to be one of them,' he said. Before the evening ended, I suggested that he and his wife might like to come to dinner with us sometime before the end of the year, and he agreed. Commenting on our meeting afterwards Anthony Lester said that he thought Blair was very good – but doubted he was brave enough to do what needed to be done.

Our next meeting with the Blairs was on 1 December 1993, when they came round to dinner at our flat. We agreed on much, including the need for a new attempt at a realignment of the Left in order to beat the Tories and keep them out of power, perhaps for a generation; the belief that this should be based on a new relationship between the citizen and the state, and the fact that the modernisation of Labour had to go much further than Smith had so far committed himself to. The most revealing comment of the dinner came from Cherie, who confided that her husband was rather low at the moment, worrying that, if Labour under Smith didn't change more, then they wouldn't beat the Tories, and he didn't intend to waste his life in permanent opposition. My diary for that night records that he appeared to have arrived at the same view of the new politics of the Left as I had, but from a different direction.

My assessment of our position at the end of 1993 was, therefore, an optimistic one. The Lib Dems were getting stronger and stronger. Our membership was rising, as were our poll ratings, and our funds were as secure as they could be for a third party. Moreover, the by-elections of the last year had proved that we were able to beat the Tories in places Labour could not reach. Most important of all, John Smith was proving a very conventional Labour leader, retreating to old socialist positions and failing to institute the internal reforms which were essential if they were going to win. Meanwhile, I had a very clear view of where the open ground was on the Left of politics, and it was empty and waiting for us to occupy it. And, moreover, in Blair I had made a very useful contact amongst the new forward-looking Labour MPs with whom, I felt certain, we could do real business when the time came.

At the end of each year I wrote a 'position paper' for my MPs over the Christmas holidays, describing where I thought we were and what the challenges for the year ahead would be. Here is what I wrote in 1993:

> We have real opportunities ahead of us, not just from the early unpopularity of the Government, but also, and perhaps more significantly, from the perceived failures of Labour and their new Leader.
>
> We must do everything we can to capitalize on this opportunity.
>
> This means winning when we have the chance.
>
> It means re-establishing a sense of impetus within the Party and clarifying the message we give outside it.
>
> It means showing Labour up where we can and capturing territory from them where this is possible.

It is sometimes said that espionage is the Great Game, but politics has a better claim to the title. For in politics things are constantly changing, and you have to be constantly reviewing your choices, especially in a third party, in order both to avoid being squashed and to advance your aims. If you make a mistake you usually pay the price very quickly. It is this that makes it more exciting – and often more terrifying – than active service. For on active service nothing happens for ninety percent of the time. But in politics, things happen all the time, and the bullets can start flying just when you least expect them. In most things you can look at the momentum and direction of forces and predict reasonably accurately what the outcome will be when they collide. But in politics there is the ever-present, ever-changing variable of the human factor, which has a habit of altering everything just when you thought it was fixed. Who could have predicted Michael Heseltine's sudden walk-out from the cabinet over Westland, which brought Mrs

Thatcher to the edge of the precipice? Or the precise moment when Geoffrey Howe's patience with her would snap and cause her to be finally pushed over? Or that, in a few months' time, quiet, long-suffering John Major would finally turn the tables on his tormentors by briefly resigning in the rose garden of No. 10 Downing Street, challenging them to 'put up or shut up'?

John Smith's death on 12 May 1994 was one of these events. It shocked everyone, of course, for he was much loved and respected, especially by rank-and-file members of Labour, who, in those times of turmoil and change, felt that socialism and the Party they loved were safe in his hands. But it changed almost everything else, too.

His death resulted – as I knew it would as soon as it happened – in the election of Tony Blair as Labour leader. And from this moment onwards the ground on which I had sought to position the Liberal Democrats was progressively undermined. It did not matter that we were there first, or that Blair's vision of what had to be done was seriously deficient in some areas (for instance, civil liberties and constitutional reform). Such was the clamour for him in the Press, the clarity of his vision and his formidable powers of salesmanship that we were in severe danger of being run over by Blair and his New Labour bulldozer.

The Press knew it and goaded me with it. And I became grumpy and bad-tempered and showed it. I found this altogether one of the most difficult periods of my leadership. For the truth was, I did not know how to react to the fact that the ground had suddenly been cut out from under me by the arrival of the phenomenon of Anthony Charles Lynton Blair. Indeed, I seriously thought about resigning. Here is what I wrote in my diary for 8 August 1994:

Richard Holme arrived at Vane Cottage at 3.00. We set off over the hills. . . . I led off, saying that I had been very depressed. I seem to have completely lost direction. I have been building the Party to fill a certain gap in politics, which I know is there and which would give us real electoral pull. But then along comes Blair with all the power of Labour behind him, and fills exactly the space I have been aiming at for the last seven years!

I was seriously wondering whether I wanted to continue in this job; whether I had the energy and the ideas; and whether I was the right person to take the Party forward. He said that of all the leaders he had known, I was the one who he really felt could get us somewhere; kind flattery, of course, but it cheered me up for a couple of days.

Left: The 'day job'. Signing a World Intellectual Property Organisation agreement. UN, Geneva, 1975.

Above: With my brother, our guide, David Martin and Simon Cornwall on the summit of Mont Blanc, June 1975.

Right: Maison Kundig (on the right), Lake Geneva, 1975.

With Simon, Jane and Kate on our allotment in 1978; I am wearing the 'Turin Shroud'. (This photograph was used on my 1979 Election address.)

Yeovil Constituency Liberal Association Executive Committee, 1982.

The winning of Yeovil (note the look of relief and shock on our faces), 9 June 1983.
(Photo: Western Daily Press)

My first Leader's speech at the first conference of the new merged Party, with Jane and Ian Wrigglesworth, Blackpool, September 1988. *(Photo: The Guardian)*

Arguing with Karadzic, August 1992. *(Photo by Lord Russell-Johnston)*

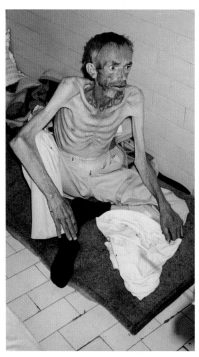

Above: One of the old men at
Trnopolje, August 1992.
(Photo by Lord Russell-Johnston)

Right: Sarajevo graves, winter 1992.
(Photo by Nick South)

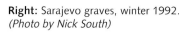

The goldfish joke. With Major and Blair, August 1995. *(Photo: Press Association)*

On a trawler during my 'Beyond Westminster' tour, autumn 1993. *(Photo by Paul Reas)*

Comforting Fadila at her brother's graveside, Srebrenica, July 2005. *(Photo: Kate Holt/eyevine)*

The goldfish joke. With Major and Blair, August 1995. *(Photo: Press Association)*

On a trawler during my 'Beyond Westminster' tour, autumn 1993. *(Photo by Paul Reas)*

Comforting Fadila at her brother's graveside, Srebrenica, July 2005. *(Photo: Kate Holt/eyevine)*

Jane and the widows of Sutjeska above Srebrenica, autumn 2002.

With Ahmed Sitkić, his sister and Jane above the Drina Valley, June 2003.

With Simon, Kate, Lois, Jane (with Annie Rose on her knee) and Matthias outside the Lord Nelson pub in Norton sub Hamdon, July 2008. *(Photo by Stephanie Bailey)*

He tried to persuade me to make the break from equidistance* now. But my instincts are against this, since I think it's still too early. It will look like a panic move, responding to Blair, without knowing what he will do.

I would much prefer to prepare the ground with the Party in September and move in the spring.

The effect of all this was not just theoretical. New Labour was beginning to challenge our dominance as the main opposition to the Tories in the south of England, too. Although our candidate David Chidgey won another by-election in Eastleigh in mid-1994, we had had to fight very hard to hold off a challenge from Labour, who beat the Tories into third position in this southern Conservative heartland.

What I was wrestling with was the unpleasant fact that this was another 'ju-jitsu' moment. I could not prevent New Labour's surge in the polls or protect us against the fact that this could do great damage to both our policy positions and our electoral appeal. I would have to find a way to turn the Blair phenomenon into something from which we, too, could benefit. I concluded that, if he was to lead the wave of change that would unseat the Tories, we had to be part of that. Fortunately, the Chard speech back in May 1992, and the work I had done repositioning the Party since then, would help. But all would depend on whether Blair, now that he was actually Labour leader, was sincere about exploring the possibilities of a realignment of the Left along the lines we had spoken of at my flat before John Smith's death.

I met Blair again just before our respective 1994 Party Conferences, when Jane and I went round to a family dinner at their house in Islington. It was then that we laid the foundations of the next five years of close and mostly secret co-ordination between the two of us and our parties. We agreed that we could not stop our parties fighting each other where they had always traditionally done so (i.e., where we challenged each other). But in the public comments we made we would each show respect for the other's party. There would be no question of withdrawing candidates. However, in places where one of us was the principal challenger to the Tories it made no sense to 'station tanks on each other's lawns' by putting resources into each others' principal target seats. This agreement eventually culminated in the two parties secretly exchanging a list of Tory key seats in which the one that had little chance of winning would not invest resources in contesting the seat, so as to give the other

* Which I had been planning since before John Smith's death.

the best chance of beating the Tory. Chris Rennard subsequently (and secretly) met Peter Mandelson at a dinner and persuaded him that the most useful thing that the Labour Party could do to help us defeat the Tories in our key target seats was to arrange for a third party to publish a list of where Labour voters should back the Lib Dems in order to beat the Tories. Eventually, at Mandelson's behest, the *Daily Mirror* published a list of twenty-two seats which had been secretly negotiated with us, and we won twenty of them in the subsequent general election.

Blair's office and mine also regularly co-ordinated our key lines of attack at Prime Minister's Questions and started to draw up a list of some policy areas, particularly constitutional reform, where we could work together – though even at this early stage Blair made it clear that he was 'not yet convinced' of the case for proportional representation. It was from this discussion on our joint constitutional agenda, elaborated at a dinner at Derry Irvine's house a few months later, attended by teams of key advisers from both sides, that the Cook/MacLennan Commission was born. This would, in due course, produce a framework for co-operation between the two parties on the issue of constitutional reform and lay the basis for the constitutional reforms which formed the centrepiece of the first Blair Government's legislative programme.

But creating the framework for a long-term partnership was only part of my task. I knew very well what Blair would do next. He would very ostentatiously pick a fight with the unions, abandon socialism and the Left and move his party onto the centre ground. My chief worry was that the Lib Dems would vacate this ground and move to the left. This was not because the Lib Dems are, at heart, socialists – far from it. It was just because the natural tendency of a third party, faced with a constant struggle for survival in a two-party system, is to look for the empty ground and occupy it. Blair was a master of the 'cuckoo strategy': occupying other people's territory and forcing them to move to other, usually more extreme ground. In government he was to do this to the Tories, who made the fatal mistake of ceding the centre ground to him and moving to the right, until, after ten years and under David Cameron, they finally realised their mistake. I was determined that he should not do this with the Lib Dems in 1994, and so I once again turned to writing, producing a pamphlet, which I called *Making Change Our Ally*. The aim of this publication was to stake out for the Party our own modernising agenda before Blair produced his, and to prevent a retreat to the easy grazing of the pastures of the Left. I published *Making Change Our Ally* just before the start of our Party Conference in Brighton that year and sent a copy to Blair.

The 1994 Brighton Conference, however, was not one of my finest. My worst fears seemed to be realised when the Party debated two motions: one, mildly controversial, on the monarchy, and the other proposing a more liberal approach to drugs. In normal times I would have regarded neither of these issues as anything to get too aerated about – but in the context of an ascendant New Labour I knew they would be misrepresented, especially by the Press, as a shift to the Left, and that would be deadly for us. In truth, I reacted to both grumpily, and this was compounded by the fact that it looked as though I stalked off the stage in disgust when the drugs motion passed, so making it more of a story*. My predecessor, David Steel, and my successor, Charles Kennedy, would have shrugged their shoulders and said it didn't matter, which would have been infinitely the wiser policy. But I suppose I am just not that kind of person.

The rest of the autumn of 1994 was spent deepening the relationship with New Labour and carefully widening the circle of those in the know on both sides. As a result, by the end of the year, all Blair's closest advisers and all mine were in the know and discreetly involved in some way or another in developing a part of the co-operation agenda.

A curious episode took place in October, when I received an approach from Mohamed Al Fayed, who, through my colleague Alex Carlile MP, passed us evidence of a Government minister, Neil Hamilton, accepting money. The ensuing scandal resulted in Hamilton's resignation and unleashed the era of 'sleaze' which so damaged the Major Government. One upshot was that Al Fayed offered me a million pounds 'for the Party, with no strings attached'. We were now beginning to prepare for the next election, and a million pounds amounted to around a half of our projected election costs – so it was a very great deal of money to us. This was, moreover, before Al Fayed had the reputation he has today. I consulted all my closest advisers and the senior MPs in the Party, saying that I did not believe we should accept the money, not least because, whatever was said, there always would be strings attached. With very few exceptions, they advised that, given what we could do with the money, I was mad not to accept. There was real anger amongst some when I turned the offer down.

---

* In fact I had to leave to attend a previously arranged engagement.

On 6 May 1995, the Government held a great banquet lunch in the Guildhall to mark the fiftieth anniversary of VE (Victory in Europe) Day in 1945. Some bright spark at the Foreign Office who had responsibility for the table plan concluded that, since I knew a bit about the Balkans, I should sit next to President Tudjman of Croatia. I had, in fact, met Tudjman before and concluded that he was one of the most unpleasant people I had ever come across. Slobodan Milošević, his contemporary as President of Serbia, was basically an opportunist, but Tudjman had a creed, and it was, as far as I was concerned, fascism in modern guise. So I decided to be a little mischievous. I made sure that his wine glass was never empty and then, towards the end of lunch, and after he had drunk a good deal, asked him as innocently as I could what he thought would be the future for the Balkans? He reached for the printed menu and on the back of it drew a rough outline of ex-Yugoslavia and then an S-shaped line dividing it in two, explaining that this would be the future. There would be no Yugoslavia. In its place there would be two countries, Croatia and Serbia. But what about Bosnia, I asked? Where is Bosnia? 'No Bosnia,' was his reply. What about the Bosnian Muslims? 'They are welcome to live in Croatia, if they obey our laws. Otherwise they can go home to Turkey,' was the response. But what about the enclave of Serbs who lived in the Krajina in south Croatia? Tudjman said that he would launch a war very soon and drive them all out. I said that could be very costly for his troops. He replied that he could do it with less than a thousand casualties, and I found myself betting a bottle of good Croatian white wine that it would cost him more.

Suddenly I realised what he had told me. The map on the back of the Guildhall menu was the secret deal for the division of Yugoslavia which was known to have been cooked up between Milošević and Tudjman at a remote royal hunting lodge in 1991.* I sent a confidential copy of my diary notes, together with the map on the menu, to the Foreign Secretary, Douglas Hurd, next day.

True to his threat, Tudjman launched *Operation Storm* three months later, in August. And, true to his predictions, Croat casualties were light, though the suffering and brutality caused to ordinary Serbs, both in Croatia and in the west of Bosnia was terrible. To start with, the West, and especially the US, appeared to take a hesitant approach to

---

* It was known as the 'Karadjordjević agreement', after the royal family who had originally owned the lodge.

Tudjman's aggression, probably because Tudjman's army had been largely trained by the US, and also presumably because they believed that if the Serbs suffered a defeat, that might be helpful in creating better conditions for a negotiated peace in Bosnia. But as I read the reports of the Croatian advance I became worried that this could easily get out of control and result in the carving up of Bosnia which Tudjman had sketched out on the back of his lunch menu. So I deliberately leaked the menu and the story to *The Times*, which ran a large piece on it. Shortly afterwards, the US finally acted and stepped in to pressure Tudjman to halt his advance. In March 1998 I gave evidence on the basis of the Guildhall lunch and 'The Map on the Menu',* in The Hague trial of one of the Croatian Generals (Tihomir Blaškić) who led *Operation Storm* and who was charged with war crimes.

Three weeks after the 'map-on-the-menu' incident, Jane and I were at our house in France, having a rather boisterous dinner with some French friends, when the phone rang. I answered, to be told it was Downing Street. They had the Prime Minister on the line, was I available to speak to him? Just as he came on, Jane walked in from the kitchen and said something extremely salty, in a very loud voice, about the job always interfering with our lives and couldn't they leave us alone for one minute, to gales of laughter from our French friends. I tried, meanwhile, to be as serious as a lot of red wine and the riotous company would permit.

The subject of the Prime Minister's call was serious enough. British troops had come under lethal attack from Mladić's Serbs in Goražde, one of the 'safe havens' which had been set up under UN auspices to provide refuge for the Bosniak Muslims, and some had now been taken hostage. The Prime Minister said that he was recalling Parliament early to announce that he was sending 6,000 more British troops out as reinforcements. Acting purely on a hunch, I suggested that, in fact, the generals were telling him that the safe havens were now indefensible and that he needed to think about withdrawal. The extra troops he was proposing to send were, I suggested, actually intended to fulfil a double purpose. First, they were a show of force. But, second, they were an insurance policy, so that there were enough forces on the ground to carry out a withdrawal, if the show of force did not work. Major replied: 'Exactly.'

* This map became quite famous as '*Mappa na servjetu*' (literally 'the map on the napkin') in the Balkans.

At a private meeting with the Defence Secretary Malcolm Rifkind on 31 May, just before the House of Commons debate on sending British reinforcements, Rifkind admitted to me that the Government were now in fact beginning to draw up contingency plans for a withdrawal from the safe havens as, in their view, these had indeed become indefensible. I warned him that it would not, then, be long before General Mladić, a past master at probing the will of his enemy, would know about this change of policy. What would Britain do then to protect the Muslims who had taken refuge in the safe havens – now to be exposed after our withdrawal – if they were attacked? He replied that they would be provided with the means to protect themselves and rejected the idea that this would inevitably lead to tragedy.

I have subsequently come to believe that a few days before Major's phone call to me there had been secret discussions between representatives of the main UN troop-contributing nations and the UN force's military commander in Bosnia, the French General Bernard Janvier. At this meeting Janvier had, it appears, declared he could no longer defend the safe havens, and it was therefore agreed that they would, in the last analysis, not be protected in future.

Little more than a month later, just before Mladić's troops took Srebrenica, Dutch aircraft tasked with driving back the Serb attack were ordered back to base at the last minute, and the Dutch troops stationed in the enclave were commanded to withdraw with the women and children, leaving the entire male population of the 'safe haven' to the mercy of Mladić and his Serb army. The subsequent slaughter of 8,000 Muslim men and boys, by hand, over four days, has become one of the most iconic moments of evil of our time – and a lasting stain on the reputations of those who let it happen. Both the UN and the Dutch soldiers on the ground have, justifiably, been blamed and criticised for this. But the Western powers, whose decision I believe led to the safe havens not being fully protected, have never come under either scrutiny or criticism for their part in this tragedy, even though their decision also contributed to a chain of events which led, almost inevitably, to the Srebrenica massacre.

On the very day that Srebrenica was falling and, unbeknown to us all, the massacres were starting, I met in Stockholm with some Bosnian friends who had come out of Sarajevo specially to see me. They told me that things in the city were now getting desperate. The Serb ring around the city had tightened, and the only way in now was over old logging tracks through the forests on Mount Igman, south-west of the city and then through the tunnel under the airfield that had been secretly dug by the Bosniaks. They begged me to pay another visit, saying that this would help draw attention to their plight. But this time the UN refused to help me get in, saying that it was now too dangerous. The Foreign Office, too, put me under strong pressure not to go, citing the hazard and claiming that 'if anything happened [to me] it would worsen a fragile situation'. (I omitted to say it could spoil my whole day too.) I talked it over with Jane, and in the end we both agreed that I could not say no. So I arranged to meet my Bosnian friends at 2 a.m. on the morning of 16 July in the little Bosnian-Muslim-held town of Jablanica, some twenty miles south of Sarajevo, and then drive with them in their Renault Five across Igman in the dark. We would then hope to make use of the mist which usually covers the mountain at first light to run the gauntlet of the Serb guns down the last exposed portion of the track into the southern enclave of the city which was still in Bosniak hands. Thence we would go into the city through the secret tunnel.

This was going to be by far and away my most dangerous trip into Sarajevo, and I had a terrible sense of foreboding about it. On most of my previous trips to Bosnia after the first, I had taken a member of my staff. But this time I decided that it was just too dangerous, and so I should go alone. Just before I left, I wrote a short letter to Jane and left it with a friend in case anything unpleasant happened. It contained all the usual things that couples say to each other in these circumstances and ended:

> Some will say (and I think you believe) that I am going to S'jevo out of bravado. This is not so. I would not risk my life for bravado – and certainly wouldn't risk my life with you and my beloved kids for it. I am doing this because I think it has to be done. There are, you know better than anyone, two things which drive me (both will sound pompous) – justice – and I genuinely believe a great injustice has been done to the Bosnian people – and my liberal beliefs. Internationalism is the core of the latter and, if our Party will not stand up for this, who will?
> See you!
> XXXX
> P

In the event my journey into Sarajevo was even more difficult than we had anticipated. My Bosnian friends were two hours late, and we got a puncture crossing Igman. This delayed us so much that, when we came to the most dangerous bit of the journey – descending the last part of the track into the city – it was broad daylight, the hoped-for mist had burnt off, and we were fully exposed to the Serb guns below us. We rocketed down the track at full speed, past still smouldering hulks of shot-up lorries lining the route. The Serb gunners must have been asleep, for they ignored us, and we were able to reach the safety of the Bosnian-held enclave with only a minor dent from a collision with a fast-moving UN aid truck going in the opposite direction.

There followed a mile or so's tramping through communication trenches in order to reach an isolated house whose basement formed the control point for access to the tunnel that ran under Sarajevo airfield and into the city. When we arrived we were led through a curtain made of heavy material into a waiting room lit by three low-wattage bulbs and some candles. I could hear the sound of a generator gently thumping away somewhere close by. As my eyes grew accustomed to the dark, I saw we were not alone. The room was full of people waiting to go into the city. Some soldiers, together with a wounded colleague, were smoking and swapping soldierly jokes. Judging from their haggard, hunted look, I guessed, they were returning at the end of their shift on the front lines protecting the city. There was also a disabled man on his way back home after a leg amputation, a young mother with her two daughters, and some old men and women with baskets of vegetables sitting hunched in the corner. There were perhaps twenty-five of us, together with two piles of cases containing ammunition and cigarettes, all waiting to take our turn in the tunnel. The air was full of cigarette smoke and rancid with the smell of bodies. On the right of the room we could see the tunnel running away from us, lit by the same dim electric lights, and to the left of the tunnel entrance, sitting behind a table on which two candles guttered, sat an official who checked the papers of my friends. He asked for my passport and when I produced a British one, asked angrily what I was doing here. My friends explained who I was, that they had permission from the Government to bring me in and that I had taken my chances thus far, just like any other Bosnian. The official produced a torch and shone it my face, and then motioned us to wait in the darkness until our turn came to enter the tunnel. In due course, from deep in the tunnel, we heard the sound of people approaching. Suddenly their shadows leapt ahead of them into the room, followed by their dark shapes moving through us towards the door. They seemed little more than bulky black forms, like the dark spaces in Goya's paintings of the 'Horrors of War'. But as each of them pushed aside the curtain and broke into the sunshine, they leapt briefly into Technicolor life, like a picture taken with flash, before vanishing to the world outside. I counted around thirty in all, including fully armed soldiers, some old women carrying panniers for vegetables, one young man on crutches and a father and mother with two young sons of perhaps eight and ten.

The last man through said something to the official, and we were waved into the tunnel. It was very narrow, lined with planks and supported with wooden pit-props every two yards. The ceiling soon dropped down sharply, causing us to stoop uncomfortably as we walked. Bare electric light bulbs were positioned in recesses in the walls every ten yards or so, and every fifty yards there was a passing place. On the floor of the tunnel were two lines of upturned angle irons which acted as rails along which we pushed or pulled makeshift trolleys, loaded with our packs and suitcases. Other trolleys were piled with vegetables, cigarettes and ammunition being taken into the city. Somewhere in front of me the wounded man had been bundled onto a trolley and was moaning quietly as he was pushed along by fellow soldiers. To start with, there were occasional air holes in the ceiling through which we could see snatches of sunlight, but after a while, as the tunnel dipped downwards under the airfield, these stopped. After about half a mile, I noticed that the floor had stared to get wet. Soon we were carrying our packs again and wading through a foot or so of water. This, I surmised, was the lowest point, where the tunnel passed under the runway and I couldn't help thinking of the *Hercules* laden with aid that I had first flown in on, taxiing over my head. After about a hundred yards of wading the tunnel started to turn upwards again towards the entrance about a quarter of a mile further on. Here we were at last able to straighten up, before emerging, to the accompaniment of bird song and the crump of distant shells, into a bleak city square surrounded by ruined houses.

I spent three days in Sarajevo, visiting my old friends, including Larry Hollingworth (who told me of his worries about the city running out of food), calling on President Izetbegović and spending some time with new UN commander in Bosnia, General (now Sir) Rupert Smith, who emanated a new energy and determination to break the Serb siege once and for all. I was shocked to see how much Sarajevo had deteriorated. The people seemed to have lost hope and appeared as scarred and dejected as their shell-shattered homes. We were now entering the fourth year of the siege, in which it has been estimated 10,000 people, including 2,500 children, died from starvation, cold, shells and snipers' bullets. Conditions in the city were now deteriorating sharply again. As I departed over the Igman logging tracks, this time under cover of darkness and fog and in a British Army Land Rover, I wondered how this great city could possibly survive another winter. We had to act soon.

On my arrival back in London I put in my regular report on conditions in Sarajevo and Bosnia to the Foreign Secretary, appealing once again for action soon. Afterwards I caught the train north for two days' campaigning in the Littleborough and Saddleworth by-election, where the Tories, who had held the seat, were plainly going to come third, leaving us and Labour in a head-to-head struggle. Despite my previous agreement with Blair, Labour's campaign was a very dirty and personalised one against our candidate, Chris Davies. Furious about this, I rang Blair on my way back home to Yeovil and said, 'We really cannot pretend that we are creating a new kind of politics based on respect for each other's parties and then spend three weeks character-assassinating the other's candidates like this.' Blair, in his usual disarming way, said he was unaware that things were this bad (this was not to be the last time he either couldn't, or didn't want to, restrain his attack dogs at a crucial moment) and anyway we were going to win. Which we did, though Labour came within a hair's breadth of causing us to lose.*

Shortly after I returned from this trip, I started to run a very high fever and relapsed into delirium. Jane called the doctor, who diagnosed a severe lung infection (contracted, she said, during my time in Sarajevo) compounded by physical and nervous exhaustion. I was forced to take a week off work, the only period of absence through sickness I had to take during the eleven years of my Leadership.

This was my last trip to Sarajevo under the siege. Shortly afterwards the international community finally decided it had had enough and, in the kind of swift action that could have been taken years and tens of thousands of deaths earlier, broke the Serb siege and, with it, the Serb army – so paving the way for the Dayton Peace Agreement and the end of the war.

---

* Lib Dem: 16,231 (38.5%); Lab 14,238 (33.8%); Con 9,934 (23.6%).

One way and another, 1995 was turning out to be a very busy political year. But neither politics, high and low, at home, nor wars and other dramas abroad interrupted the rhythm of ceremonial state events, which also had to be fitted into the programme.

On 20 August John Major, Tony Blair and I had to interrupt our summer break to attend the celebration of the fiftieth anniversary of Victory over Japan Day (VJ Day) and the end of World War Two, which took place on Horse Guards Parade in London. The three of us were in position a little early and found ourselves free of our advisers in a corner of the spectators' stand, as we waited to be shown to our seats. It had been a wonderful summer, so we were all quite tanned. I remarked on this to Major and asked him whether he had had a good holiday. He said he had been at the family home in Huntingdon and had a great time, except that the sun had been so strong that his goldfish had got sunburn. He had taken them out, one by one, and put sun cream on them. But to no avail; the very next day the local heron raided the pool and ate them all. 'Most distressing,' said Major, in his typical, clipped way. Blair and I obviously had the same mental image of our gentle, Pooterish Prime Minister anointing his goldfish, only to find that his sun cream had simply helped a heron's breakfast to slip down more easily, and burst into peals of laughter (joined, it must be said, by Major himself). The next day's papers were full of the pictures of the three of us roaring with laughter – though it was only much later, when I made an injudicious comment to a journalist, that anyone discovered what had caused the outbreak of hilarity.

In early November Yitzhak Rabin, the charismatic Israeli Prime Minister, was assassinated, and Blair and I joined Major, the Chief Rabbi and the Prince of Wales in the Prince's private jet for the flight out to Jerusalem and the funeral. This was my first experience of a 'working funeral', as it is known in the diplomatic trade. The primary purpose of these events is, of course, to bury the unfortunate great man or woman. But the other great men and women who attend do not miss the opportunity for doing business over their departed colleague's grave. So the solemn processes of funeral, service and burial are interspersed with the lively business of bilateral contacts and negotiations of international business. Blair and I watched fascinated as Major was wheeled from 'bilateral' to 'bilateral' with other key heads of government, one after the other. As we were waiting in the cemetery, I noticed that Major's officials seemed to have fixed a meeting with

John Bruton, the Irish *Taoiseach*, as the two were waiting in the long queue to go to the graveside. I watched with admiration as the two sets of Prime Ministerial officials deftly manoeuvred their charges into the same place in the long queue and then hovered around them taking notes as the discussions began. But then the unexpected happened. Both Prime Ministers obviously came to the same conclusion. They could not last another long ceremony without first having a pee, and so, with the officials scurrying along behind them, they headed off together and at some speed for a nearby Portaloo, where they continued their animated conversation in an almost equally long queue, while their harassed-looking officials tried to elbow their way close enough to make notes of their masters' conversations. Finally, John Major's turn came and he went in, leaving poor John Bruton hopping from one foot to another, though whether from embarrassment or as an aid to bladder control, I can't say.

Later that month, Jane and I were invited to a Downing Street lunch for, I think, the Spanish Prime Minister. After the formalities were over, and the guest of honour and his party had left, a little informal circle remained, consisting of the Prime Minister, Norma Major, Kenneth Baker, his wife Mary, Jane and I. There had been some Press comment recently about a remark Norma had let slip that her husband was feeling very tired. I, however, thought he looked rather well and said so. He turned to me and said, 'I *am* well. I wish Norma hadn't said that to the Press. You know what they are like. Jane would never say a thing like that about you, would she?' To which my wife, who has a barrack-room turn of phrase, not uncommon in an ex-soldier's wife but not usual in a politician's, retorted, 'No, I wouldn't say Paddy was tired. I would say he was bloody knackered!'

There were other events happening 'off stage', too. Back in Yeovil I had become aware of a bunch of white racists who were trying to drive a local Indian restaurant out of town. I visited the restaurant and met its dynamic and courageous young Bangladeshi owner, Luthfur Rahman. I asked him why he hadn't been to see me, his local MP, about his problem – after all his restaurant was only fifty yards from my office? He replied that he didn't think that, as an Asian, he was entitled to ask a British MP to help him. I launched a campaign against the racists and on 29 November paid a late-night visit to the area with the local vicar, Mark Ellis. As we were standing across the road from the restaurant we were approached by several of the local gang, shouting abuse. One, a man called Chris Mason who was notorious in the area, looked to be the chief trouble-maker, so I engaged him in conversation, drew him away from the group and persuaded him to walk with me round the block, hoping to calm him down, while Mark Ellis spoke to the others. By the time we came back, things seemed to be calmer. But suddenly, Mason came up behind me and, stretching his arm over my shoulder, placed the blade of his flick knife against my throat, threatening to cut it if I didn't 'F**ck off'. I knocked the knife to one side and the police, who had two undercover officers in the area and had been watching the incident, moved in to arrest my attacker. After three hours in the police station I returned home to find the *Sun* newspaper, which had clearly been alerted by someone local, camped outside my door asking for a comment. The story caught the imagination of the national Press for a full three days. But Mason would now have to face the court on a charge of attempting grievous bodily harm – so the matter, though closed for the moment, was by no means over and done with.

None of these diversions and amusements, however, could hide the uncomfortable fact that both the Lib Dem vote and our ability to get any attention from the Press were now being seriously squeezed by the national love affair with Blair and New Labour. Our poll ratings were dropping again, and the Press was once more asking what the purpose of the Lib Dems was, now that Blair was occupying our ground. Meanwhile, many of the old SDP were expressing support for New Labour, and one or two of the more ambitious ones, with an eye to the main chance, were quietly redefecting to them.

They say that God tempers the wind to the shorn lamb. So it was on this occasion. For just as I was beginning to despair about how we could get ourselves back into the game, we got what a third party struggling for attention hopes for most after a by-election victory – a defector. Or, to be precise, two of them.

In late September we started getting messages from Peter Thurnham, the Tory MP for Bolton North East, that he was fed up with the Tories and was thinking of joining us. Andrew Phillips entered into secret negotiations with him, in the middle of which, to great fanfares, another Tory MP, Alan Howarth defected to New Labour. Thurnham, a most decent man, was wracked with guilt, not at the thought of leaving the

Tories, but at the prospect of letting his constituency party and its workers down. Jane and I invited him to a secret dinner at our flat in late November. Warming to the spirit of the occasion, he turned up dressed in a trench coat with the collar turned up and wearing a most sinister looking hat. Over dinner he confirmed that he wanted to come over to us, but he needed to take his time – perhaps first resigning the Tory whip and then joining us some time later, much nearer the elections. He also expressed an interest in standing for us at the next election for the nearby and winnable seat of Westmoreland. But he insisted that, if this were done, it could only be with the agreement of the current Lib Dem candidate, who had to be treated properly. There could be no question of his being imposed against the will of the local Lib Dems.

The black arts I had learned from my time in the shadows had given me a good insight into defectors. They usually fall into one of three basic categories. The first are the 'mid-life crisis' defectors, who, realising their current careers are not going to end in the triumph they had hoped for, are seduced by the prospect of five minutes of fame, perhaps combined with a chance to start afresh and see if they can do better the second time around. Some defect to a new life and a fresh start, others make their change by remarrying, and a few do both. This category is the most difficult to handle, for they need patience and care and constant reassurance that they are doing the right thing.

Then there are the venal. They can be bought – and their price is usually money, position or other pleasures of a more illicit kind. In politics the currency is not cash, but usually the promise of positional goods, such as a ministerial post or a place in the House of Lords. These are initially the easiest defectors to handle. You simply have to find out what their price is and then decide if you are prepared to pay it. But when they have pocketed their reward, downloaded their information, and there is nothing left in the kitty, then they can get bitter and disgruntled and often redefect, if the option is still open to them.

And finally there are the 'true believers'. They are the ones you always hope for, because they defect for ideological reasons. And since there is no one more committed than a convert, these are the defectors who will be most bitter about their erstwhile friends, because that provides them with a form of self-justification. They tend to be what we used to call 'walk-ins', who knock on your door, rather than hoping you will knock on theirs. They want nothing except to serve the cause and so, provided their self-respect is protected, are the easiest to handle. Peter Thurnham believed passionately in what he was doing and sought nothing in return, beyond the possible chance of standing as a Lib Dem in future elections. For this reason – although I badly wanted him to defect as soon as possible, because we needed the publicity – I told my colleagues that we had to respect his needs and do things at a pace that suited him not us, which meant later rather than sooner. Forcing the pace could mean losing the fish. In the event Peter Thurnham resigned the Conservative Whip shortly afterwards but did not formally join us until a year later, in October 1996.

Very soon after Peter Thurnham's approach, I started to hear about a much bigger fish. On 5 December our Chief Whip in the Lords, John Harris, reported a rumour that Emma Nicholson, the Tory MP for Torridge and West Devon and previously a vice-chair of the Conservative Party, was fed up and wanted to come across to us. I was at first very suspicious. It seemed to be too good to be true. And anyway, if she really wanted to come over, there were much more secure ways of passing a message to us than through the rumour mill in the House of Lords. I suspected a trap that was designed to make us look foolish. So I primed her Lib Dem next-door neighbour Nick Harvey with a carefully prepared script and asked him to breeze up to Emma at an appropriately discreet moment and say, 'Emma, last year there were rumours about me joining the Tories. It was nonsense of course. Now I hear that you want to join us. Is it true?' To which he received the somewhat startling reply, 'I might if you asked me.' I was now even more suspicious, because this put the onus on us to make the approach and could be the prelude to a very public rebuttal. So I looked for what I would have called, in earlier days, a 'cut out': someone who knew her personally but was unconnected with us, although of course sympathetic. This would enable us to have complete 'deniability' if accused of making the approach. Richard Holme found just such a person, a business acquaintance of his called Jonathan Taylor, who also had business contacts with Emma's husband, Sir Michael Caine, and could easily probe her intentions under cover of a purely social conversation. Taylor duly made contact and reported back that Emma was indeed very unhappy and wanted to join us.

There was almost no technique I had learned in my 'Foreign Office' days which Emma and I did not use over the following three weeks to clinch the deal, except secret writing and the use of dead-letter boxes. It all culminated in a meeting at a 'safe house' just before Christmas at which we agreed that we would announce her defection on 29 December in order to dominate the news over the New Year period, when the three Party Leaders traditionally publish a political New Year's message. The actual day of the defection was planned down to the last detail and went like clockwork, giving us complete domination of the news agenda for nearly a week, putting the Party back in the news and getting 1996 off to a flying start.

Emma stood aside for a Liberal Democrat, John Burnett, who was elected in Torridge and West Devon at the next general election. She then went on to fight and win a seat in the European Parliament and subsequently joined the Lib Dem team in the House of Lords, where she has been a doughty and courageous voice for liberal and internationalist causes, especially on the suffering of Iraq's Marsh Arabs and on matters of human rights and international justice. In due course she was followed by other Tory defectors, chiefly on the issue of Europe, including Hugh Dykes (whom I persuaded to join us in the course of a very bibulous evening drinking Burgundy at our house in Irancy) and John Lee, both also now playing very active roles in the House of Lords as respected members of the Lib Dem team there. Others also followed.*

Though we entered 1996 on a higher note politically, ominous clouds were beginning to gather as a result of the police action prompted by the knife attack in Yeovil in November. The police informed me that Mason, my attacker, was claiming to the local Press (which, of course, duly passed it on to the nationals) that I had been a 'customer' of a local 'massage parlour' with which he and his associates were connected, and suggesting that this would come out if the trial went ahead. I suppose Mason thought I could be frightened into dropping the charges. Just before Christmas, the *Mail on Sunday* correspondent in the Commons approached me saying that he had heard that I was withdrawing my charges against Mason, was this true? I said it was certainly not true, adding that I was utterly determined to see this man, whose associates had held our friends in the Indian restaurant (and so many others in the town) to ransom using violence and threats, was brought to justice.

---

* Including Bill Newton Dunn and James Moorhouse, both MEPs.

I thought that was where the attempts at intimidation would end, although the police said they thought there was more to come. On 2 February, just before 4 a.m., the phone rang by my bed. It was my next door neighbour Steph Bailey, saying that our car, which, on police advice, had been parked in one of her outside sheds, was on fire. The local fire brigade arrived swiftly, followed by the police equally swiftly, followed by the national Press, which published blaring headlines on the incident the following day. *The Times* article was accompanied by a hilarious Nick Newman cartoon showing two Somerset yokels chewing straw, one of them was saying to the other, 'Red sky at night, Paddy's Vauxhall's alight.'

Over the following weekend Yeovil was flooded with national journalists, which gave Mason's associates an even greater opportunity to spread their lies. Once again, some elements of the national Press seemed all too eager to believe their words and published a number of articles full of innuendo. In the end this proved more painful to Jane and me than the fire-bombing of our car. We were both deeply upset that the Press would allow itself to be used by people who they must have known were trying to intimidate me into withdrawing charges. But we decided that, whatever happened, we were going to see this thing through. So we sat tight, believing that the worst was over.

But it wasn't. On the Monday after the fire-bombing of our car, the *Western Daily Press*, our regional newspaper, which should have known better, published the whole farrago of lies on their front page, without having even approached me for comment or denial first. Normally, I believe politicians should avoid taking legal action except as a very last resort. But this newspaper must have known exactly what sort of people Mason's associates were. They had not even tried to check these completely false claims, which were made, as they must have known, with the specific intent of getting me to back down so that one of this fraternity could escape justice. The tale Mason's associates had been retailing to the Press, and which was at the centre of the *Western Daily Press* story, was that I had been a customer at the Yeovil massage parlour/brothel. They even supplied the name of the prostitute whose client I had allegedly been, adding considerable verisimilitude to their story. As it happened, this brave lady had left the area some time previously, having been threatened with extreme violence. She read the newspaper stories and, despite the risk to herself, asked her solicitor to contact Andrew Phillips and confirm that the story was a complete fabrication. Jane and I were very touched by her courage.

We took legal action that night which forced the *Western Daily Press* to print a full, front-page retraction the next day and an apology the following one, as well as facing other substantial penalties for what I still regard as one of the most egregious breaches of decency and professionalism I have ever come across in the profession of journalism.

The car-burning incident also produced a sackful of very kind letters of support, but also others much less salubrious.

We also received a number of phone calls threatening to burn our house if I went ahead and gave evidence at the trial, shortly after which the local Chief Superintendent asked us to go into the police station to see him. He had some information he wanted to talk to us about and did not wish to do this over the phone. When we got there we found two or three other officers in the room, including one from the CID. They told us that they now had reliable information that there was a contract out to fire-bomb our cottage over the coming Easter holidays, when it was known that we would be away in France. The police proposed a plan for installing a series of covert alarms round the house and asked us if they could secretly move in while we were away for Easter.

On 8 February I went to Yeovil crown court to give evidence at Mason's trial. The Press gallery was packed with reporters from the national Press and broadcasters, all hoping for some dramatic revelation. But they went away disappointed, and Mason was duly found guilty and imprisoned.

The police alarms caused us some problems to start with. They kept on being set off by everything from the cat to branches waving in the wind – and sometimes, it seemed, by nothing at all. This resulted in the whole village being disturbed by screaming sirens and armed police being scrambled to our house at all hours of the day and night. On one occasion Jane returned from walking the dog to find the house and garden full of armed police, one of whom was yelling 'Freeze or we fire' at her and a bewildered, but angry, dog. On another I had friends round, and turned off the electricity in order to repair a lamp. About a minute later, there was a screech of police tyres outside the house, all the roads in the village had been sealed off, and, we were told, a helicopter had launched to the area. The police patiently explained that their alarms were run off our electricity and were triggered if it was turned off. All in all, Jane and I decided that we were not very good at being the subject of close protection.

When we left for our Easter holidays, Jane shed some tears at the prospect of our house being reduced to a burnt-out shell. But she is extraordinarily resilient and while we were away planned out the changes she would make to our rather small cottage if we had to rebuild it.

In the event, nothing happened, and in due course the police decided that the threat had passed and left us alone again. But we carried out Jane's redesign plans anyway, and they have given us a lot more space and greatly improved the way the house works. I, meanwhile, managed to persuade some wealthy Indian supporters to invest in my Bangladeshi constituent who ran the restaurant that had been at the centre of all this drama. He now runs a chain of outstanding Indian restaurants in the West Country, and the one in Yeovil was recently voted among the best one hundred Indian restaurants in Britain. So at least we all got something positive out of the whole wretched business.

◆

Meanwhile, the pace of politics continued unabated. In late February Major was saved by a single vote at the end of a debate on the Scott Report on the selling of arms to Iraq. A month later the BSE crisis broke and was catastrophically mishandled by the Government.

Blair's rise and rise, however, continued unchecked, and our secret talks on co-operation quickened both in frequency and substance. In March we agreed to launch a joint Commission on constitutional change under the joint Chairmanship of Robin Cook and Bob MacLennan, and this was formally announced later in the year.

Thanks in large part to the growing public perception of a partnership between the Lib Dems and New Labour, we were now, to my relief, no longer being seen by Press and public as irrelevant to the coming wave of change in Britain, but as part of it. And this showed both in our opinion-poll ratings and in votes cast in the May local elections, when we increased our national share of the vote and, with 150 gains, our number of councillors, too. These advances gave us an excellent springboard for the general election, which everyone now knew would be in the spring of 1997.

At the end of August, my daughter Kate got married in Cravant, the next-door village to Irancy. She had met her French husband, Sébastien, while working in the area, so the wedding was a very bibulous,

Burgundian affair which went on until the very small hours of the morning. Sébastien's mother was the Deputy Mayor of Cravant and therefore able, under French law, to conduct the civil ceremony. Afterwards, as is the local custom, I walked with my daughter on my arm at the head of a procession of all our guests through the village from the *mairie* to the church – one of the proudest moments of my life. My first grandson, Matthias, was born, after a terrible 72-hour labour, right in the middle of the general election campaign in April the following year.

By the end of 1996 Blair and I had a clear plan about how the relationship would develop after the election, which everyone now knew would result in a Blair government (though Blair would never allow himself to admit it). Our preferred option was for the two of us to form a partnership government, even if there was a Labour majority. And we agreed that one of the first elements of its programme would be to bring in a series of constitutional changes, including providing Wales and Scotland with an element of self-government based on the Cook/MacLennan proposals, which were published on 4 March 1997. We also discussed how we might work together on our agreed constitutional agenda.

John Major finally called the general election two weeks after the Cook/MacLennan report was published, and fixed the date for 1 May. Throughout the ensuing campaign there were secret contacts between Richard Holme and Peter Mandelson to ensure that we limited the damage we did to each other, concentrated our fire on the Tories and prepared the way for the partnership between our two parties after the election was over.

On polling day I had a phone conversation with Blair from the Headmaster's study of a local school I was visiting:

PA: I hope you now recognise that you are going to win.
TB: Yeah. I suppose I accept that I will, now. How many (seats) are you guys going to get?
PA: Thirty at the low end; thirty-eight tops.
TB: Look, I have more or less decided what to do. However, I want to speak to John Prescott and Robin Cook first. Then I will come back to you later. I am sorry I cannot speak to you in more detail now, but I do want you to know that I am absolutely determined to mend the schism that occurred in the progressive

forces in British politics at the start of this century. It is just a question of finding a workable framework. But we are now in a position of strength, and I intend to use that.

PA: Well, that is what we have always agreed. But I want to make three points to you. Firstly, please do not bounce me in the press. Don't put me in a position where you make me an offer in public which I have to refuse. I am perfectly happy to sit on the opposition benches. Under those circumstances I would want to see if we can open up a new salient of co-operative opposition, so we could support you when you needed it. And in my view, with a large majority, this may be your best opportunity.

TB (interrupting): No, curiously, with a large majority I can do things I couldn't otherwise have done. If you sit on opposite benches of the House, then the natural process of politics will mean that the parties will move apart rather than together.

PA: I agree. But then you must understand my second point. We could not accept simply having Liberal Democrats administering a Labour programme. With a large majority you will want to implement your programme in full. But if we are to do something that is really a combination of both parties' ideas, then you must be prepared to amend that. We don't need anything big; something relatively small and symbolic will do. Otherwise it simply will not work. When you make me the offer you intend, please remember that. Lastly, please ensure that this is kept secret until you and I want to bring it out. I may have to put my whole political career on the line here. So it mustn't become public until after we have agreed a common position. We must not be seen to negotiate in public. And we mustn't be seen to disagree in public, either.

He said that was all fine and that after he had talked to Robin and John he would come back to me, perhaps that afternoon, perhaps the following morning.

PA: Finally, I want you to consider one other option. On the basis that I still think is the most likely – that we sit on the opposition benches – there is a position we can adopt based on Parliamentary precedent. Perhaps Jonathan* would look it up for

* Powell, Blair's Chief of Staff.

you? It comes from Baldwin's Premiership. Then, opposition parties worked with the Government on a Cabinet Committee. If we were on the other side of the House there is no reason why we should not progress constitutional reform through such a committee. This would allow us, on the one hand, to stay on different sides of the House of Commons, but on the other to institutionalise the relationship, which, if it worked, could bring the two parties closer together in a gradualist way.

TB: That is very interesting, and I will get someone to look it up for me.

PA: Good luck tomorrow.

TB: You, too.*

---

* Paddy Ashdown, *The Ashdown Diaries*, vol. 1, *1988–1997* (London: Allen Lane, 2000), pages 555–6.

CHAPTER 14

Leader III: The End Game

O N POLLING NIGHT we left my count in Yeovil almost as soon as the results were announced and were driven to London, accompanied by the Special Branch escort that had been with me throughout the four weeks of the general election. No doubt it was their presence, blue lights flashing in front and behind, which justified us driving so fast across the early-morning, empty roads.

Out of the car window I could see the great stones of Stonehenge and the graceful sweep of Salisbury Plain sharply etched against a dull, red-ember glow spreading across the eastern horizon. Slowly colour was seeping, by half-tints, back into the greys of night. It was going to be a peerless May day of blue sky and hot sunshine.

Jane, was asleep, her head on my shoulder, exhausted from the campaign and the nervous energy of the count. But though my body cried out for sleep, my mind, swirling with what would happen next and my conversation with Blair the day before, would not let me nod off.

Despite my earlier fears, my majority had increased to 11,400 votes, nearly three times what it was when I was first elected. Yeovil was now a safe seat which I could hand over to my successor, just as, some months earlier, I had promised Jane I would. In truth, she did not need to persuade me to make this decision. We had both agreed when I was elected that doing the job of MP for Yeovil properly required the energy of a young man. From the start I had told close friends (though I don't think they believed me) that I did not want to be an MP beyond my sixtieth birthday – now only four years away. I had, moreover, been Leader of the Lib Dems for nearly ten years and judged that I had done my best work for them, and it would soon be time for someone else to take over. Most importantly, I had always planned to stand down on my terms and at a time of my choosing, so that I could plan a smooth handover to my successor, both in Yeovil and in the Lib Dems. Too often political careers, even for the greatest, end in tears. One of the skills of life is to know when it is time to go. And I was determined that I would finish when people would still ask, 'Why is he going?' rather than 'Why isn't he?'

But the question was – when? I was now engaged in a new kind of partnership with the man who would shortly be Prime Minister, and this had great potential to deliver things which I had stood for all my political life and which I believed were not only right for the country but also good for my Party. Finally, all this was built on a very personal relationship – Blair and I had learned to trust each other. I had no alternative but to see this through to its natural conclusion before standing down.

The problem was, I could not yet see what form that end point would now take.

Blair had talked of forming a coalition government, something he had very clearly alluded to in our last conversation – even going so far as to say that the bigger his majority, the easier this would be for him. Listening to the car radio as we sped down the M3 on the last leg to London, it was already clear that his majority was going to be huge. We were going to do well, too. Richard Holme had just called on the car phone to say that, though our share of the national vote would be largely unchanged from 1992, we were probably going to nearly double our number of seats in Parliament. Far from being squeezed, as I had originally feared when Blair arrived on the scene, our relationship with New Labour had delivered huge dividends for us. We had helped turn a Tory defeat into a Tory rout, and we could now establish the Lib Dems as the strongest liberal force in Parliament for more than half a century, giving us a voice and vote that could no longer be ignored.

But ours was a minor sub-plot in the drama of the night. The main story was New Labour's landslide, which had exceeded everyone's expectations. It was already very clear, even this early in the day, that the new Labour government was going to completely dominate the new Parliament – and would probably have a majority over all other parties some three or four times bigger than the total number of Lib Dem MPs. Could Blair still go for a coalition government? Would he? Would it not now, somehow, be an affront to democracy to add perhaps forty Lib Dem MPs to his maybe four hundred, creating something close to a one-party system and leaving the Tory Official Opposition as a mere rump, with neither the power to challenge the Government nor a significant influence on events?*

I had always believed that the best relationship between parties in partnership was to be in government together – to form a coalition – because this made both sides subject to the disciplines of power. But would Blair pay the price of proportional representation, without which a coalition would mean the near certain decimation of the smaller party at a future election, when the Government started to get unpopular (as it inevitably would)?

The alternative, I mused, would be for us to co-operate with the Government from the opposition benches. This might work for a bit. But it could never last long; we Lib Dems would soon find it too difficult to resist the easy pickings of opposition and too frequently damaged by being blamed for the actions of a Government over which we had little influence and no control. This would also mean, as Blair himself had said in our last conversation, that we would forfeit the historic opportunity to heal the schism on the Centre Left which had made the Tories the natural party of government in Britain for three-quarters of a century. Furthermore, with a Commons force only a quarter the size of the Government's majority, what bargaining power would we have? Why should Blair pay any attention to us, when he didn't need us at all? A loose partnership in Opposition might be an option, but it would be one which it would require a lot more skill and a huge amount more leadership to handle.

By the time we reached London it was full daylight, and the Special Branch escort[†] had peeled off. The Lib Dem celebration at Pizza in the Park, however, was still in full swing. They gave me a great welcome, I made a short speech, drank a few glasses of champagne and then went off to catch an hour's nap before what I knew was going to be a demanding and historic day. The last image I saw before falling into an exhausted sleep was of Tony and Cherie Blair being greeted by cheering crowds at Labour's victory rally at the Royal Festival Hall.

---

* In the event Labour won 418 seats and the Lib Dems 46. If we had combined in a coalition government, this would have increased the Government's majority over all other parties from 179 to 269, leaving only a total of 195 MPs from the Tories and minority parties sitting on the opposition benches. If this had happened, it would, incidentally, have been impossible to accommodate all the Government MPs on the Government side of the House, probably necessitating a redesign of, or at least a reallocation of seats in, the Commons Chamber.

† All three party leaders are given full-time Special Branch protection during a general election, and those involved are outstandingly professional. But, as soon as the result is known, protection for the defeated leaders is withdrawn more or less instantaneously, leaving the team with the new Prime Minster in place for as long as he or she is in post.

By eleven o'clock I was back in my office for the phone call with Tony Blair that my advisers had arranged with his staff the previous day. He rang exactly on time, saying he was just off to see the Queen, but wanted a word before he left. He would spend the afternoon making his major Cabinet appointments and now had in mind a 'framework of co-operation' with us. There was no mention of a relationship with us in government.

The first thing that struck me was how his tone had changed since yesterday. Thinking about this afterwards, I have concluded that something happened overnight to change his view of the previous day that a coalition was a good option. Some months later a private conversation with Robin Cook confirmed this. He told me he had met Cherie just before they had gone to Downing Street on the morning of the election. She had said that, as Blair listened to the results roll in, he had been taken aback by the size of his majority. She had told him that he really must go ahead 'with the thing with Paddy', as he would never get another chance. According to Cook, he had agreed. But then, in the early hours of the morning, probably while I was travelling up from Somerset, he had either met or spoken with Prescott and Brown, and both had made clear their virulent opposition to this – leading him to conclude that, if his Government was to get off to a smooth start, he had to begin by taking the easier option of a loose relationship across the floor of the House of Commons, rather than the bigger gamble of a tighter one in government.

In my early-morning conversations with my advisers I had reached the same broad conclusion. A partnership in Opposition was probably marginally better for us. But I had decided that, if Blair had wanted to go for a coalition, I would take the risk, providing PR was in the package.

So it came as something of a relief to me when, during our phone call later that day, he said he wanted to take up my suggestion of using a 'Cabinet Committee' as the context for a relationship outside government, adding, however, 'I am absolutely determined to change politics with you and heal the schism. If we allow ourselves to get into a position where we play conventional politics, the schism will just reopen.'*

---

* Paddy Ashdown, *The Ashdown Diaries*, vol. 1, *1988–1997* (London: Penguin, 2001), p. 559.

It is my experience that far more mistakes are made in life by being too careful, than by being too bold; the SAS motto, 'Who dares wins', is not just an exhortation to show courage, it is also a statement of wisdom. I have come deeply to regret the decisions both of us took that morning, and I suspect that Tony Blair has too. For what we lost in the very early hours of 2 May was, I think, a unique opportunity to do something really historic: to enter into a partnership government at the optimum moment – not because we had been forced to do so to command a majority in the House of Commons in the aftermath of a hung parliament, but on the high ground of principle and in the aftermath of a great victory. This could, in my view, have led to a complete realignment of the Centre Left in British politics, keeping the Tories out for the best part of a generation. It would, using the old language of the heyday of the Liberal–SDP Alliance which so captured the public imagination, have really 'broken the mould' of British politics, which is what I came into politics to do. And a partnership with the Lib Dems might, I also allow myself to believe, have prevented some of the worst aspects of the Blair government, not least some of its early follies, such as its egregious attacks on the fundamental civil liberties built into our democratic system – and maybe (but perhaps not under my leadership) even its later tendency to embark on military action without properly thinking through the complexities of peace-building afterwards.

Most of the fault for this failure to seize the moment lies, of course, with the two of us. But some also lies with that unique and much vaunted, but in my view overrated, British constitutional institution, the Downing Street removal van. In many countries there is a gap between an election and the new Government taking office. In the US a President is elected in November and doesn't move into the White House until the following January. But in Britain the removal van turns up at the back door of No. 10 Downing Street as soon as the result of the election is known, usually around 9 o'clock on the morning after polling day. The outgoing Prime Minister is then bundled out, bag and baggage, so that the place is empty and ready for the next Prime Minister to take over as soon as he has 'kissed hands' with the Queen. From that moment the new Prime Minster, exhausted from four largely sleepless weeks and probably still awash with the adrenalin of the campaign, is instantaneously faced with all the key and complex decisions necessary to set up a new Government, while at the same time running the country. This is just not sensible. It would be far better if there were an interregnum, as in the US, but briefer, while the old Government continues to govern and the new one has time to get a rest after the exertions of the campaign trail, before preparing itself for office.

I know that, from a purely personal point of view, I felt relieved when it became clear that I could go home to Somerset, my garden, some holiday with my children and a good rest. But, although I did not recognise it at the time, the truth was that this decision, so quickly taken, meant that over the next three years both Blair and I would spend huge amounts of time and energy, initially trying to recover the opportunity lost that morning and then, when it became clear this was impossible, trying to blow as much heat as we could into the dying embers of a partnership that had lost its fundamental purpose: to 'change politics and heal the schism,' as Blair himself had put it.

My first meeting with Blair as Prime Minster took place a fortnight after the election, just after the State Opening of the new Parliament. On my way in through the back entrance to Downing Street (which runs from the Cabinet Office through a passageway, one of whose walls is the edge of Henry VIII's Royal Tennis Court, still constructed of the red brick of his time) I met the Cabinet Secretary, Robin Butler. He told me that he was much impressed with the start made by the Blair government; but, he added in a confidential whisper, accompanied by a slightly perturbed Civil Service look, 'Do you know, they don't eat lunch!' On balance, I thought this rather a good sign, though he seemed faintly offended by this break with Whitehall tradition.

Blair agreed that we should set up a Cabinet Committee along the lines of our discussion on polling day, and that this would have the primary function of overseeing the constitutional changes which were agreed in the Cook/MacLennan agreement. Though stressing he was still 'unconvinced by the case for proportional representation', he also undertook to set up a Commission to look at electoral reform for Westminster, which was, for us, the *sine qua non* for the kind of closer relationship in government to which he said he was still committed.

One thing was becoming increasingly clear to me, however, even in these early days of the new Government. Blair's heart was never really in the constitutional reform agenda. Before the election he had told me many times that it was his aim to change Britain permanently, as Mrs Thatcher had done. It is ironic, therefore, that it was arguably only in the field of constitutional reform that he really succeeded in achieving this, because constitutional change was a subject that evidently bored him, and which I think he saw as a distraction from the business of 'real' government. He went along with the Cook/MacLennan reform agenda, I suspect, not because he really believed in it, but because it was a legacy from John Smith that he felt duty-bound to honour and a framework within which to build a closer relationship with us. It was, if you like, the entry ticket he knew he had to offer to get us to enter his 'big tent'. A few days after the election I had concluded that the best time for me to step down as Leader would be the end of the year. But now, after meeting Blair, I realised that I would have to stay until as much of the constitutional reform agenda was delivered as possible; for, if the relationship ended before then, there would be much less chance that the elements of the constitutional reform agenda which were important to us Liberal Democrats would be incorporated in the Government's programme, in the way Blair and I had agreed.

Our meeting of 15 May 1997 was, I suspect, one of the first to be held on the famous sofa in his little office off the Cabinet Room in No. 10, which was destined to become the nerve centre of his later style of 'sofa government'. What neither of us realised at the time, however, was that this was merely the start of a complicated gavotte that we would dance over the next two years. Ultimately, it would deliver most of the Cook/MacLennan agenda, including a Parliament for Scotland and an Assembly for Wales, the incorporation of the European Convention on Human Rights into British Law, a Freedom of Information Act and, for the first time, the introduction of PR into British elections at the European, Scottish and Welsh levels. But when the dance ended, with it would also end the chance for voting reform for Westminster, the opportunity to break the mould by creating Britain's first peacetime partnership Government, and my leadership of the Lib Dems.

Mercifully, the end of May brought the Parliamentary Whitsun holidays. Jane and I spent them in glorious spring sunshine at our house in Burgundy, where we ate too many of the local cherries, drank too much of the local wine with our French friends and slept a lot. But none of this could stop my brain churning as I pondered what to do next. By the end of our holiday I had concluded that the Cabinet Committee could only, at best, be a stop-gap. Its effectiveness would be bound to erode over time as a result of the inevitable temptations of opposition for the Lib Dems, and the inevitable mistakes which were bound to be made by the Government. Before I left I wrote a letter to Blair telling him this and saying that, if he was serious about creating a partnership Government, as he had claimed to both Roy Jenkins and I, then it had better be done soon, or he would lose the opportunity.

Shortly after my return from holiday Roy Jenkins and I joined the Blairs and Peter Mandelson for a private dinner in the Blairs' new apartments in Downing Street to discuss the situation and, especially, how to handle the issue of PR. When we arrived, Blair explained that they had taken over the apartments normally used by the Chancellor, because these were larger, and the Blairs needed the extra accommodation for their family, while Gordon (then still single) could do with the rather smaller Prime Ministerial flat upstairs. The rabbit-warren passageways of Nos 10 and 11 had caused some confusion amongst his new ministers, Blair told me. He said that the new Foreign Secretary, Robin Cook, couldn't find his way out of No. 10 after a meeting in the Blair's new flat and had to be shown out by Euan, the Prime Minister's eldest son.

We had dinner in their dining room, which was still decorated in the most garish red-flock wallpaper, making it look like an Indian restaurant. This caused some mirth as we speculated which past Chancellor was responsible. We concluded that it could have been John Major, but was probably Norman Lamont.

At this dinner, we agreed on four outline 'decisions in principle'. First, that we would go ahead with the joint Cabinet Committee, probably in July. Next, the Government would agree proportional representation for the European Elections, and then Blair would set up a Commission on Electoral Reform for Westminster. Lastly, all this would be treated as a process which would lead to the Liberal Democrats taking up ministerial posts in what would then become a coalition government, probably by the autumn, when Blair said he was anyway planning a reshuffle of his Ministers.

On 30 June I flew to Hong Kong for the ceremony handing over the Colony to the Chinese. Blair asked me to fly back with him in the Prime Ministerial aircraft, so that we could have a chance to talk. There was also a posse of journalists and a Tory MP (Alastair Goodlad) on the plane, so, to be able to speak in privacy, we went off to the Prime Ministerial sleeping space. There we sat cross-legged on his bed, with our backs on opposite aircraft bulkheads and a bottle of claret precariously balanced between us, as the aircraft bumped through a rather violent thunderstorm. At one stage, Cherie, in night attire, put her head round the curtain and instructed me not to keep him up too late. A few moments later Alastair Campbell did the same, shook his head and said, with a smile, 'VERY cosy'. The discussion was chiefly about the timetable of events which would be needed if we were to make the announcement of our intention to move to a formal coalition on the basis of a commitment to electoral reform for Westminster and an agreed programme of policy. This would happen in October or November, leaving me time to take this to my party and seek its approval (I knew it would be far from easy to convince my fellow Lib Dems, and, if I failed, it would mean the end of my Leadership). The conversation ended when the bottle was finished at about 3.30 a.m., and I went off, dog tired, to find a seat to sleep in.

I woke with the dawn and looked out of the window to see the wastes of Siberia slipping by below us. I went forward to chat with the RAF crew, arriving just in time to watch them land for refuelling at the bleak and semi-derelict airport at Novosibirsk. As soon as the Russian ground crew came with the aircraft steps I went out to get a breath of fresh air, blinking in the early-morning Siberian sunlight. Shortly afterwards, Blair appeared, tousle-haired and bleary-eyed, at the top of the aircraft steps. We continued our previous night's conversation on the tarmac, wandering away from the plane so as to get out of earshot. We had gone no more than thirty yards, however, before a very determined Russian border guard rushed up to us and, waving his weapon, told us that we were illegally trespassing on Russian soil and would be arrested if we didn't return immediately. Using sign language he pointed to a circle in red paint drawn round the aircraft and said that we could walk around inside this, but must not cross it on pain of arrest for illegal entry into the Russian Federation. We continued our conversation in these somewhat surreal circumstances for the next twenty minutes or so, walking round and round the aircraft. Finally I said, referring to the chronology we had worked out the previous night, ending in a coalition Government in October, 'I am assuming we have now taken the formal decision to go ahead.' He nodded and replied: 'Yes.' (It was at this stage that the Press finally woke up and, emerging from the aircraft, spotted us deep in conversation. John Hibbs of the *Daily Telegraph*, commented, 'Ah the Lib/Lab Novosibirsk Pact!', little knowing just how close he was to the truth.)

Later in July we took the first step in the programme mapped out at Novosibirsk, when Blair announced the formation of a joint Cabinet Committee, tasked, among other things, with co-ordinating the implementation of the constitutional reform agenda. Shortly afterwards Jane and I left on our annual holiday, where, sitting in my daughter's garden in France, I wrote the first draft of the policy programme for the intended coalition government and sent it to Blair, as promised. He rang me a few days later from Chequers saying that he broadly agreed with the policy document and that, the more he thought about 'all this', the more important he believed it was – though he had some doubts about whether he could do it in October or November and thought it might have to be left till later. I replied that the longer he left it, the more difficult it would be – the gloss was already coming off the Government. It was very important to do this during the Government's honeymoon period, before it made too many mistakes and events started to erode his popularity.

But no one could have predicted the next event, which shook every one of us and came very close to toppling one of the fundamental pillars of the whole British constitutional establishment: the Royal Family.

On 31 August, at 4.30 a.m. the phone by my bed rang, and a bleak voice told me that Princess Diana had been killed in a car crash in Paris.

I met Blair again on the day before Diana's funeral. His mind was, quite understandably, preoccupied with the nasty public mood which had developed over the fact that the Queen had stayed too long in Balmoral before coming to London and that the flag on Buckingham Palace had not been lowered to half-mast. He told me how uncomfortable it had been to have to explain just how dangerous the public mood was to the Queen and advise her to come to London. I thought he had very skilfully embodied the public mood and done himself a huge amount of good in the process, and told him so. Inevitably, our discussion of the Novosibirsk plans on this occasion was sketchy. But he did reveal that he had spoken to Gordon Brown about them and was now beginning to believe that we had to delay things a little to give him more time to convince his colleagues. I again warned that the longer he left it, the more difficult it would get. If he really wanted to do this, he had to do it soon or risk losing the opportunity.

In the autumn I had to face a rather difficult Lib Dem Party Conference, as rumours and some well-sourced reports began to emerge about my talks with Blair. One of the techniques I had learned from my days in the Royal Marines was to fire off a few rounds in the general direction of an enemy, so they would fire back and reveal their positions (the French call it sending up *un ballon d'essai*, a trial balloon). I decided that I needed to gauge the extent and location of Lib Dem opposition to what Blair and I were planning, so just before the Party Conference I gave an interview to the *New Statesman* in which I deliberately, if rather obliquely, mentioned the word 'coalition'. It worked all too successfully, producing a furious reaction from many of the new MPs and a lot of our activists. I had quite a struggle to fend off a determined attempt to close the door on any deeper relationship with Labour at the Conference, but in the end concluded that, while there was no doubting how strong the opposition would be in some quarters of the Party, if it came to it I could still (just) win overall support for a coalition, provided there was a firm commitment to PR and a proper policy agreement, including lots of things Lib Dems could support.

It was about this time that I decided that, if we did go ahead with a coalition Government, I would not take a Cabinet position in it, so that I could argue the case with the Lib Dems without being seen to have something personal to gain. I also believed that, in the early days of such an enterprise, it would be better for me to manage the relationship from outside government rather than involving myself in the day-to-day action. This would, in addition, leave me freer to step aside when the relationship between the two parties in government had been properly stabilised.

By October, however, it was clear that Blair wanted to delay again, this time until the spring, because, he said, opposition from within the Cabinet, especially from Brown and Prescott, was too strong. To make matters worse, in mid-October, in a famous leak made in the *Red Lion* pub in Westminster, Charlie Whelan (Gordon Brown's spokesman) made it clear that his boss was not prepared to let Britain join the Euro 'in this Parliament'. This effectively undermined one of the key planks of the policy agreement I had drafted in my daughter's garden in France over the summer holidays. What followed was the establishment of the Brown criteria for entry into the Euro, which in effect passed control of this key element of Blair's European agenda from No. 10 Downing Street to No. 11, where it remained until Blair left No. 10 and Brown moved in.

Though I did not realise it at the time, I can now see that the best (perhaps the only) chance of creating the conditions for a coalition government along the lines Blair and I had discussed ended in October 1997. For this was the last moment when the Blair government was still sufficiently popular and unsullied by mistakes for me to have been able to argue to the Lib Dems that it was to our advantage to join with them. It was also, probably, the last moment when Blair's personal authority in his own Cabinet and Party was high enough for him to have been able to carry them. Roy Jenkins had it right when he warned Blair, at a dinner we attended with him at the end of October, 'If you seize the moment, you can shape events and not have events shape you.'*

This is not to say that I should have abandoned the relationship at this point – there were still too many things of benefit to be gained from it, not least in relation to Scotland, Wales, voting reform, a Bill of Rights and Freedom of Information. But I should have realised in October that the last chance to resuscitate the opportunity we had lost on 2 May effectively died with Prime Minister Blair's decisions to delay until the spring of 1998.

In a conversation with Tony Blair some months before he became Prime Minister, he had told me that if he succeeded in being elected, then his greatness or otherwise as a Prime Minster who genuinely transformed the landscape in Britain, as Mrs Thatcher had done, would depend on three things. First, on whether he was able to change the fundamental political geology of Britain by reuniting the Centre Left. Second, on whether he could reconnect Britain to Europe and make us central to the conduct of European affairs. And, third, on whether he could, by spreading opportunity, narrow the chasm in the country between the very rich and the very poor. Whilst Blair was in my view a good Prime Minster, he did not fulfil any of his self-established criteria for greatness. By the time he left Downing Street the best opportunity we shall ever have to reunite the Centre Left had gone. The country was not more pro-Europe but more anti-Europe than when he came to power. And the gap between rich and poor has not narrowed; it has widened to an unprecedented level. I also believe that, despite his formidable abilities, basic decency, courage and a remarkable clear-sightedness on many things, nearly all the faults that were eventually to undermine public confidence in Tony Blair's government were there and plain to see by the autumn of 1997:

* Paddy Ashdown, *The Ashdown Diaries*, vol. 2, *1997–1999* (London: Penguin, 2002), p. 104.

1. The hesitation on domestic affairs, which prevented him from seizing the moment when he needed to (curiously, this did not apply to international affairs, as we shall see);

2. His fatal attraction to the 'spin agenda', which I am sure was why, for example, he insisted on going ahead with the disastrous Millennium Dome project, inherited from the Tories, even against the overwhelming opinion of his Cabinet;

3. His overestimation of the power of his charm when it came to moving his most senior colleagues;

4. The susceptibility of his Government (and Blair himself) to the influence of those who were successful and had money, as shown in the affair of Bernie Ecclestone and Formula One; and

5. His ambivalent relationship with Gordon Brown, in which he always sought to smooth over rather than confront. When I complained about this at around this time, he told me that the key relationship in any government was that between a Prime Minster and his Chancellor, and therefore, whatever Gordon did, he had little option but to keep him sweet.

By the autumn of 1997, however, none of this was evident, except perhaps to the most discerning. And I was far too close to a relationship which still had much to deliver, including perhaps the ultimate prize, to be one of these. I was acutely aware that I was presented with the best opportunity any leader of Britain's Liberal Party had had for the last fifty years to do what all of them had wanted to do – initiate a process of deep constitutional reform and realign the Centre Left around a broadly liberal agenda. I had no option but to take every last chance and go every last mile to do this, while being very conscious that, if I failed to achieve it all, my useful time as leader of the Party would be over and I would have to stand down.

At the end of December we took the next step along the road we had set out on Novosibirsk, when Blair announced the Independent Commission on Electoral Reform under the chairmanship of Roy Jenkins, which was to report within a year. It was also at this time that Blair asked me to see Gordon Brown and John Prescott, explaining that they were the biggest obstacle he faced in moving forward, and that if they could hear some of what we were planning from my lips, it might help.

I saw Brown in early December. He seemed comfortable with the general idea of a coalition, but, whereas Blair's interest was chiefly in how this would affect the positioning of the Government, Brown's obsession was with matters of policy. We spent much time talking about the concurrence of ideas between New Labour and the Lib Dems, about the need for an intellectual framework for our joint approach and about what the policy portfolio for any partnership would be.

Prescott, whom I saw in February in his tiny and chaotic Commons office, surrounded by cardboard boxes, was much more down-to-earth. He thought that what Tony and I were discussing was 'airy fairy' and beyond Blair's 'room for manoeuvre'. He was completely opposed to PR for Westminster and would say so publicly if it came to the crunch:

> I am a tribalist, pure and simple. I think the tribe we have is the tribe we must hang onto, and I think the business of reforming and becoming part of a larger and broader tribe carries huge dangers which will only give our enemies opportunities. I want to preserve the Labour Party for my children, not break it up.*

In March of 1998, Blair said he needed to delay again – this time until the following November, after the Jenkins Report had been published. Again, the reason was opposition from Brown and Prescott. It was at this meeting that I told him that if full coalition government went ahead then I would stay on as Lib Dem Leader to see it bedded in. If it did not, then I would resign immediately, so as to give my successor time to prepare for the next election, at which I would also stand down as an MP.

But by now external events were also beginning to impose themselves both on Blair's agenda and on mine. In a conversation with Blair in January 1998 he told me that he was getting very worried about the threat posed by Saddam Hussein in Iraq. He had seen some weapons inspectors' reports which led him to be 'quite convinced that there was some very nasty weaponry hidden away in [Saddam's] presidential palaces'† and that military action would probably have to be taken to stop him. I cautioned against this, saying that I didn't think he had made the case to the public for war, that there were no clear aims for this action and that all diplomatic routes to restrain Saddam had not yet been exhausted. He told me that if I had seen what he had seen in the intelligence reports I would understand the threat.

My attention at this time, however, was focused not on the Middle East, but back in the Balkans.

---

* Ibid., p. 169.
† Ibid., p. 159.

The Bosnian war was now over, and a peace treaty had been signed at Dayton. Meanwhile the UN had established a special war crimes tribunal, the International Criminal Tribunal in former Yugoslavia (ICTY) in The Hague, charged with bringing to justice war criminals from all the wars in ex-Yugoslavia. But, despite these steps, peace was far from secure in the region. Milošević, thwarted in Bosnia, had turned his attention to the Serb province of Kosovo, where the majority Albanian population was being increasingly persecuted and denied basic human rights, such as access to health care and schooling for their children in their mother tongue. By early 1998 I had become convinced that war in Kosovo was inevitable, and that I should go there to see for myself what was happening.

My original intention was to go in the spring, but the trip had to be delayed because of key Parliamentary debates. And a good thing it was, too, for in April 1998 another crisis broke much closer to home, when a newspaper leaked the information that the police had placed a well-known self-confessed paedophile, Sydney Cooke, in Yeovil police station for safe-keeping. Angry and threatening mobs, mostly of local people, but with some outside agitators and even criminal elements, started to gather outside the local police headquarters, followed by a feeding frenzy of rage and sensationalism in the national and local Press. I privately appealed to the local paper to calm things down and rang key members of the local clergy, asking for them to give a moral lead. Then I made a public statement calling on the crowds to disperse and leave the issue for the police to handle. To my horror, our chief local paper the *Western Gazette*, far from calming things, published a highly inflammatory editorial that, among other things, included an attack on me for not understanding the public mood. I rang the editor and, I am afraid, rather lost my temper with him, following this up with a highly critical letter for publication.

There was a vociferous public outcry against me for defending a paedophile and a flood of very angry letters from my constituents. One local school, whose spring fete I had promised to open, even asked me to reconsider the invitation, because parents had said they would not attend if I did. All this, the police told me gratefully, had the effect of making me, rather than them, the lightning-conductor for public anger, and I received very nice messages from Home Office ministers thanking me for standing up to the mob, etc. But this did little to diminish my discomfort or the anger of my constituents, as I discovered at a public meeting I called with the protesters: one of the most unpleasant and difficult I have ever attended. (What hurt most is that some of these people were my friends, most had been supporters, and a few had even worked to get me elected.) After a while, though, reason prevailed, and public anger subsided enough for the police to move Sydney Cooke, who had by now become seriously frightened for his life, quietly away to another secret location.

In May, Blair asked me to go to Northern Ireland to join the campaign for a Yes vote in the referendum on the Good Friday agreement. Apparently William Hague, the Tory Leader, had insisted on going, and Blair was worried that he might come across as 'too English' and 'establishment'. On the other hand, he argued, my Northern Ireland background might mean that I was listened to a bit more. I replied that I rather doubted it but would go nevertheless. Campaigning in the Protestant heartland of the Shankill Road in Belfast a few days later, I stopped one man on the street and asked him for his opinion on the Good Friday Agreement. He replied in a very thick Belfast accent, 'The Good Friday Agreement? The Good Friday Agreement? I've just got two words for that: RID-DICULOUS!'

Later that day I went to see an old Northern Irish friend, Ronnie Flanagan, then the Chief Constable, and expressed puzzlement as to why the Protestant community were opposed to the Agreement. Ronnie reminded me of the old Ulster story of two men walking down the street, and one saying to the other, 'I like yer coat!' The other replies, 'Well, I'll give to you,' to which the first responds, 'Ach I'll not have it if you give it to me!' It was an attitude which, I was to discover, was by no means unique to Northern Ireland; I was to see it again and again when, in due course, I found myself trying to help bring peace and stability to Bosnia.

I finally found space in my programme for a trip to the Kosovo area in June 1997, embarking on a six-day tour of the region with one of my staff, Roger Lowry. Our trip took us first through Macedonia, on to Tirana, the capital of Albania, and then by helicopter over the mountains to Bajram Curi, in the Albanian badlands on the edge of the 6,000-ft mountain ramparts that mark the Albanian/Kosovo border. At the time this was the headquarters of the Kosovo Liberation Army (KLA) as well as the jumping-off point for their main supply route for arms into Kosovo. I was warned, both by the Foreign Office before leaving and by the British Embassy in Tirana, that it was a very lawless area and could be dangerous. But we were looked after by some Albanian friends, so I knew we would be safe enough. During my visit I had the chance to speak to Kosovar families, including young children who had been driven across the mountains by Serb attacks on their villages. Many of them had been wounded by small-arms fire and artillery bombardments, which the Serbs had concentrated on the high mountain passes through which they had had to travel. We also visited one of the Albanian 'weapons bazaars' where local and international arms traders sold weapons to the KLA, who, as we watched, loaded them onto mules and donkeys for the long, hazardous journey over the mountain passes into Kosovo. One day, in the company of some official European military observers, we followed the KLA arms trail up the mountain onto a high ridge overlooking the plain of Kosovo, from where, after crossing over the border a short way, I was able to observe, just below me, Milošević's tanks, mortars and infantry attacking what seemed to me completely defenceless Kosovar Albanian farmsteads and villages.

On our return I put in a report to Blair and the Foreign Office, saying that it was obvious that a war was coming unless we acted quickly and proposing a plan which included sanctions on Milošević's Government if he continued to use force to drive out the Albanian Kosovars; helping Albania to cut off the KLA arms supply; and stationing a token EU or NATO force along the Albanian/Serbian frontier to seal it. A few days before leaving for this trip, at Blair's request, I saw Ibrahim Rugova, the rather other-worldly Kosovar Albanian leader, who was visiting London and asked him if such a deployment would help calm the situation. He said it would – very much. But nothing happened, as usual. As I was to find later, the international community finds it easier to reach an agreement to fight a war than to act early to prevent one.

Over the remaining summer months Blair continued to swither back and forth, not only on the question of timing, but now also on his attitude to the central question of PR. Meanwhile I continued to warn him that delay was deadly. If we waited beyond November, the opportunity would be lost.

I also managed to grab a little time off to go and see my daughter Kate in France. Sitting at a pavement café in Paris with a carafe of wine and a book watching the world go by, I suddenly realised, after eleven years of leading the Lib Dems, how attractive ordinary life could be.

Meanwhile, of course, the Kosovo situation steadily deteriorated towards war.

In September, just before the Lib Dem Party Conference, I drove to Chequers for a very long private meeting with Blair to resolve the remaining issues blocking the way forward. In the course of this I told him that we had reached the crunch moment – if we did not go ahead with his plan for a coalition Government after Roy Jenkins produced his report on electoral reform in October, then I would conclude that this part of the project had failed, and I would stand down as Party Leader early in the New Year. Blair, for his part, made it very clear that the price he wanted for agreeing to the Jenkins proposals was a full merger between the two Parties. I said I could not countenance an imposed top-down merger, because I did not think it would work and would never get the support of my members. I had been involved in one forced marriage (with the SDP) and had no desire to try another. But I would not discount an eventual 'organic' merger of the two parties after a period of partnership in Government, if that was what the members of both parties wanted. We eventually agreed a form of words, based on his agreement to put the Jenkins proposals to a referendum coupled with his personal tacit support for electoral reform. We also discussed Kosovo. I told him that I would make another visit soon, and he suggested I should carry with me a personal letter from him to Milošević, urging restraint. I left once again believing that the log jam was broken and that we had, at last, reached an agreement to move forward.

On 26 September, just after a pretty difficult Lib Dem Conference during which there were more determined attempts to close off my options with Blair, I left once more for Kosovo. This time I went with the official support of the British Government and carried Blair's personal letter to President Milošević warning him not to misjudge the resolve of the West to act if his aggression in Kosovo continued. We went into Kosovo itself, passing through the mountain crossing from Macedonia. My first night in the Kosovar capital, Pristina, was spent in the Park Hotel, which had until recently been the city's premier brothel and was still fully equipped with lurid black-and-crimson nylon sheets on the beds and a plain-glass bathroom window, positioned precisely at genital height, overlooking the whole of town.

In Pristina I met up with Britain's outstanding Ambassador in Serbia, Brian Donnelly, and also with the redoubtable head of UNHCR in Kosovo, Morgan Morris. On our second day we drove from Pristina to Kosovo's western city Peć, passing long columns of Serb tanks and armoured vehicles which were pulling back after a major operation in the Drenica region against, they claimed, KLA forces. Already stories of the horrific massacres of civilians were emerging from this area. We could see tall columns of black smoke rising as we passed. Brian Donnelly commented that the armoured columns did at least appear to be moving back to base, which was consistent with Milošević's recent promise to the international community that all military operations in Kosovo had now ceased.

From Peć, we turned east again, skirting the Albanian border under the mountains on whose peaks I had sat a few weeks earlier. We briefly visited the little jewel-like twelfth-century Serb Orthodox Monastery of Dećani, where we were shown round by Father Sava, later to become famous during the Kosovo war as the 'cybermonk' because of his mastery of the internet. We then continued through the shattered villages I had seen being bombarded in July, following the roads parallel to the Albanian border and visiting the site of a massacre of Serbs by the KLA on the way. Around midday, we started to hear the sound of distant artillery fire and shortly afterwards crossed a low ridge to see laid out before us the whole of the Prizren valley running south to Macedonia, its little villages burning in the sunshine, and high columns of smoke rising in black palls into the summer sky. Now we could also see bursting artillery rounds and hear the crack of the guns as they fired somewhere off to our left and the crump of their shells echoing round the horseshoe valley in front of us. Brian Donnelly immediately pulled out his satellite phone and got through to London to report that, far from ceasing, Milošević's military operations had now shifted from the Drenica area to the Suva Reka/Prizren region, where artillery and tanks of main battle units of the Serb Army were being used to bombard defenceless Kosovar villages. In the course of his conversation he held the telephone receiver up so that his colleague in London could hear the sound of the barrage.

We managed to speak to a frightened man who ran a roadside garage nearby. He explained that the Serbs were targeting each village in turn. First, the police would arrive, demanding that the village give up its weapons. If the villagers said they didn't have any, they were given a deadline to deliver some, on pain of being shelled. Frequently villages had to resort to raising money to buy weapons so that they could hand these over before the deadline. In this way, he claimed, a circular black market in weapons had been established, run by the Serb police. Arms that had been purchased from the black market by one village were duly handed over to the Serb army, who then passed them on to the police, who sold them back into the black market, ready to be purchased by the next village threatened, and so on. I was inclined not fully to believe this story, particularly since I had seen the quantity of arms being shipped over the mountains from Albania a few weeks earlier. But Morgan Morris said that UNHCR had evidence that there was truth in it. The arms I had seen had chiefly gone to organised units of the KLA, she said, and not to village defence forces, though no doubt many of these did have some shotguns and old rifles.

I asked our informant whether the villages we could see being bombarded had somehow resisted the demand to turn in weapons and if this was their punishment? He replied that they had fully co-operated, but were still shelled. He said that the routine was always the same. First, the demand for arms; then, after they had been collected, the soldiers came and told people to leave, as the shelling was about to start; then, after the village had been evacuated, organised army looting teams came in with lorries and carried everything of value away; then the shelling and burning began. He said that Milošević's plan was to drive them all out. Again, I was inclined to treat this as exaggeration at the time. But it was subsequently proved to be correct – what we were seeing that day, though none of us knew it at the time, was the beginning of Milošević's *Operation Horseshoe*, which reached its climax during the subsequent Kosovo war and whose aim was a 'final solution' for the Kosovo problem based on the expulsion of the entire Kosovar Albanian majority population from the province.

It was now getting late, and we risked not being able to get back to Pristina before the start of the curfew imposed by the Serb authorities if we did not leave immediately. Brian Donnelly decided to return to Belgrade, so that he could brief his fellow ambassadors on what was happening and co-ordinate further moves with London. Morgan Morris and I decided that we had to get into the area being shelled to see conditions there for ourselves.

So, very early the following morning, under a light but persistent drizzle and in the company of the BBC's David Loyn and a camera team, we retraced our steps to where we had been the day before and then dropped down off the ridge into a nearby village, where we met with the elders. They told us that they had just been visited by the Serb police who had demanded weapons. They had clubbed together and raised some money to buy enough weapons to hand over. I asked to see these. Mostly they were very old and very rusty Russian-made rifles, which were clearly unusable, and some very unstable-looking but fully armed hand grenades weeping with condensation. I warned them to be very careful indeed of the latter, as they looked as though they might go off at any moment – and one of them told us some hand grenades had indeed exploded recently, killing some Serbs who were handling them at the time. The BBC filmed the weapons and broadcast the film in their report that night. Much later, Milošević, then on trial in The Hague for war crimes, was to dig up this footage and use it to support a claim that I had, on behalf of the UK Government, been involved in secretly arming the KLA.

Morgan Morris and I then continued our attempt to get into the area being shelled by the Serbs, but we were soon stopped at a Serb military checkpoint, where we were ordered out of the area. We pretended to obey their instructions, driving off in the direction they pointed us in. But then, as soon as we were out of sight, we turned off the road and made our way back over very bumpy farm tracks towards the villages that were being shelled. Before we could get to the first one, however, we found our road blocked by a miserable convoy of refugees, including women, very young children and the elderly, sheltering from the rain under canvas sheeting and heading away from their village and out of the area on foot, old farm carts and decrepit tractor-drawn trailers. They told us that they had been given a deadline of midday to leave their village, after which it would be shelled. The deadline was now fifteen minutes away, they explained, and they were keen to leave as soon as possible. We wished them luck and pressed on deeper into the area, passing through the deserted village and moving towards the sound of the shells which were now, we estimated, not too far ahead of us. But before we could get right into the area being bombarded we ran into another Serb checkpoint. Here the Serb officer in charge was very aggressive and completely unimpressed with my attempt to pull rank by saying that I was an emissary of the British Prime Minister and would be seeing his President Milošević the following day. What was worse, he started threatening our Albanian interpreters, two local women who were well known to the Serb authorities. Morgan and I agreed that to press on against their orders could place our interpreters in jeopardy if the Serbs caught up with them later – and, besides, we now had all the evidence we needed of what was going on. So we acquiesced to being escorted out of the area under Serb armed guard.

Later that day I met a senior Serb commander and told him that what I had seen was a clear breach of the Geneva Convention, for which he and other commanders could be indicted. He seemed to me much more concerned about the prospect of being indicted at The Hague than about the threat of NATO bombing.

That night I drove to Belgrade and stayed the night at Brian Donnelly's ambassadorial residence,* ready to see President Slobodan Milošević the next day. In the morning I first met with the US Ambassador, Christopher Hill, who told me that his people had done some research which confirmed that what Brian Donnelly and I had seen was indeed a clear and flagrant breach of the clauses of the Geneva Convention laying down the rules governing armies' treatment of civilian populations. He gave me a marked-up copy of the relevant paragraphs to take with me when I went to see Milošević.

When it came to the tragedies of the Balkans many Western statesmen saw Milošević as part of the solution. I had always seen him as the source of the problem. So our meeting was a rather tetchy one. I handed over the Blair letter, stressing that he should not underestimate the West's resolve to act if the appalling scenes I had seen yesterday continued. He denied any such acts had taken place and said this was all got up by the Press. I told him his officials were lying to him; these disgraceful acts were indeed taking place, because the British Ambassador and I had seen them with our own eyes the previous day. He said that, as a politician, I didn't understand what had to be done when fighting terrorists. I replied that, as a soldier, I had fought terrorists several times in my life and lost good friends to them. And I knew that what his army was doing was not the way to beat terrorists, but instead to multiply their numbers. What was more, the actions I had witnessed were a clear and flagrant breach of the Geneva Convention for which he and his army commanders could be held accountable. Indeed, now that I had, in the presence of the British Ambassador, informed him of what was being done by his army and was leaving with him the relevant passages of the Geneva Convention, he himself could no longer claim to have no knowledge of what was happening or its implications, and could therefore end up being held responsible for these actions before the court in The Hague. The next time I saw Milošević *was* in The Hague, where he was

---

* This villa, set in splendid grounds, was given to Britain by Tito after the Second World War in recognition of the help given by the United Kingdom, Fitzroy Maclean and SOE during his guerrilla campaign against the German and Italian occupying forces in Yugoslavia.

on trial for war crimes, when I gave evidence about the events I had witnessed. I reminded him of this conversation with the words, 'I warned you, Mr President, the last time we met, that this is where you could end up – and here you are.'

Back in London I wrote a report for Blair proposing, among other things, that the court in The Hague should be encouraged to initiate immediate proceedings by indicting the Serb commanders of the operation I had witnessed. I still believe that, if this had happened, *Operation Horseshoe* might just have been stopped in its tracks, and the whole tragic course of the Kosovo war might just have been avoided.

Events were now moving steadily towards two concurrent climaxes. The first was the wider international crisis over Kosovo, the second, the narrower personal climax in the relationship I had established with Blair more than six years previously.

At a long meeting on 27 October, two days before the publication of Roy Jenkins' crucial recommendations on electoral reform, Blair told me that he would have to draw back from our Chequers agreement, because he did not feel he could overcome increasing opposition from within the Cabinet, and could not risk splitting the Government.

> *Look Paddy, I don't want to let you down. We have come a long way together. But you must understand that there are limits beyond which I cannot go at the moment. I remain committed to the long-term process, but I can only do what is possible now.**

I replied that I would try to think of a way through but could not easily see one. If this failed, I would have to stand aside in due course. All would depend on his reaction to the Jenkins recommendations. If he could be warm about these, there might still be something to play for. If not, it was all over.

When the Jenkins Report was published two days later, Blair's response was entirely neutral. Later that day Robin Cook (a long-time supporter of electoral reform) rang me and, in a conversation which he said I should treat as 'never having taken place', told me that there had been a discussion about Jenkins at Cabinet that day.

---

* Paddy Ashdown, *The Ashdown Diaries*, vol. 2, *1997–1999* (London: Allen Lane, 2001), p. 311.

Mo [Mowlam] and I won the argument intellectually. But, since Tony hadn't taken a firm lead, the debate swung the other way, and the best Mo and I could get was that the Cabinet's position should be neutral.

Blair had been uncharacteristically silent, Cook complained, adding that he was really worried about Blair's lack of leadership and inability to make decisions sometimes.*

The *coup de grâce* came on BBC *Newsnight* that night, when Jack Straw, then Home Secretary and so responsible for the whole constitutional agenda, was anything but neutral, rubbishing the whole Jenkins Report in the most contemptuous terms. Blair rang me in apologetic mood next day. I told him that I was fed up with finding ways round his retreats from what we had already agreed and how angry I was about Jack Straw's comments the previous night. If he did not now make some statement that would counteract the negative spin Straw had put on Jenkins, then everyone would know that Jenkins was dead, and, if that was the case, then so was our project.

No such statement ever came. Britain's best chance of getting much-needed electoral reform for Westminster was dead, and my time as Leader of the Lib Dems was coming to a close. Two days later I told my closest adviser, Richard Holme, that, though we had achieved much, the ultimate aim of my strategy was now unachievable, and I had concluded that my usefulness to the Lib Dems as their Leader was over. I had therefore decided to resign at the earliest opportunity, which would enable me to do so on my terms and hand over to my successor as smoothly as possible.

In November there was one more attempt to revive things, this time initiated by Blair, but it came to nothing. The long dance was over. We had failed to recover the chance we lost on the night of 2 May 1997. Perhaps it would have been different if Labour's majority in 1997 had been smaller. Perhaps not.

Looking back, I have concluded that there were several reasons for the failure of our plans. Way back in 1997 I asked Richard Holme, 'Do you think Blair really means it?' His reply was, 'Yes. But then the best seduc-

---

* These words, used by Robin Cook (now sadly dead), are taken from my diary for that day. They were included in the first draft of volume two of my published diaries, but were then omitted at Cook's request and replaced, with his agreement, by a brief statement that he rang me and was depressed about the outcome.

ers always do!' So, did Blair mean it? In the end, I must leave others to decide. But I do not believe that, as a new Prime Minster facing huge challenges at home and abroad, he could have afforded to spend as much time as he did on something he had no intention of carrying out. And his most senior colleagues in the Cabinet, such as Brown, Straw and Prescott, who were surely in the best position to know, certainly believed he meant it – which is why they opposed it so strongly.

I think the fault lies elsewhere.

Tony Blair has many extraordinary qualities: an outstanding ability, second only perhaps to Mrs Thatcher, to locate and stimulate the erogenous zones of the British public; and very considerable personal courage. He also has an exceptional ability to recover when on the back foot. It used to be said of Gladstone that he was terrible on the rebound – Blair is, too. He has, too, an unfussy, unpompous and straightforward approach to problems and people, an ability to take criticism without rancour (in 2001, when the Government was going through a bad patch, I warned that many people in Britain saw him as a 'smarmy git', and he never turned a hair) and a mind interested solely in the practicalities of politics and unencumbered by its creeds.

I remember being particularly struck by the contrast with Mrs Thatcher here. If you took a proposition to her you could see that the first question she asked herself was whether this was something consistent with her personal creed. Then the second was, 'Will it work?'. Most politicians are like that. But with Blair the only question was, 'Will it work?'. This was a weakness as well as a strength, for in politics beliefs, creeds and principles are the sheet-anchors that hold the ship's head to the sea when the storm blows. The fact that Blair had abandoned socialism but never really found something else to replace it meant that he was far too often blown around by the prevailing winds – especially, in his latter years, those blowing from the direction of Fleet Street.

But, whatever his formidable and many strengths, Blair had weaknesses, too. First, although I think he spoke the truth when he said the partnership with the Lib Dems was the big thing he wanted to do to reshape British politics, it never was the *next* thing he wanted to do. Hence the delays, which in the end killed us. In politics waiting for 'the ripe time' is important – but you have to be able to spot the ripe time when it arrives. A leader's powers are always greater on Day One than on Day Two, in the first month than in the second, and so on. The early days are the golden period of leadership, when almost anything is possible. After that, the capacity to do is eaten away by events and an inevitable decline in support which comes from the necessity to make decisions. I fear that, in Tony Blair's case, these early 'golden hours' of leadership were wasted, as his Government appeared to decide that the most important achievement of his first term would be to get elected for a second one.

The second problem lay in Blair's overestimation of the power of his most formidable weapon: his charm. This was indeed a most prodigious instrument in his hands: I remember, like St Augustine, who pressed a rusty nail into his palm to resist the temptations of the devil, preparing myself for our meetings with the armour plate of a clear set of objectives in order not to succumb to his persuasiveness. But the problem was that Blair believed that he could overcome all obstacles through personal charm and did not see that, with hoary old warhorses like Prescott and Brown, this was simply not enough.

Thirdly, Blair and I shared a major deficiency. We were both, to some extent, strangers in our parties. Unlike Brown and Prescott (and there were many equivalents in the Lib Dems), we were outsiders not steeped in the cultures of the organisations we led. This caused both of us, I think, to conclude that, because something was logical, it was therefore achievable. In consequence, we perhaps underestimated the task of persuading organisations held together by a necessary tribalism to abandon this for the risks of partnership with others.

Do I feel deceived by Blair?

No. We always knew that whatever deals we made, both of us were governed by *force majeure* and the law of the possible. As it happens, it was Blair who had, in the end, to tell me that he could not carry his Cabinet on PR. If he had been able to do so, then it might very well have been me who would have had to tell him that I could not now carry my Party for a coalition. The fault here was not one of sincerity, but of underestimating the scale of the obstacles that we faced and an overestimation of our ability to overcome them.

Do I regret making the attempt? No, not that either. I do blame myself for focusing so much on what was possible that I did not spot how much more improbable it had all become after the end of 1997. But I do not regret trying.

Someone once said that, in big things, it is enough to have tried. I do not agree. It is precisely because a thing is big that trying is not enough; it is all the more necessary to succeed. And, though much was delivered along the way, we did not succeed in our stated aim of reuniting the

Centre Left. Politics has returned to its same old shape and its same old ways. The best I can do is take some comfort from the fact that not to have tried in these unique circumstances would have been a dereliction of duty by both of us, but especially by me as the Leader of a third party whose *raison d'être* has always been to be the centre of a broad movement to bring liberal values into the Government of Britain.

◆◆

At the end of November I started actively to plan for my resignation. I had decided to announce this on 20 January the following year and to remain in post for five months as a caretaker Leader, while the Party fought the local elections in May, after which it would get down to the business of electing my successor.

In December I paid another trip to Kosovo, this time with Shirley Williams. The international community had finally persuaded both sides into a ceasefire and installed a 'Kosovo Verification Mission' (KVM), which was unarmed and had little or no power. I never believed this would work and had said so, but I wanted to see things for myself on the ground. Shirley and I came away convinced that the ceasefire could never hold, and the KVM was too weak to enforce it. Before long, we said in our report to the Government, Kosovo would slide back to war.

On 13 January, a week before my planned resignation date, Ming Campbell invited me to dine with him at the Reform Club. I knew he was thinking of standing as Leader when the time came and would probe me about my intentions. Sure enough, during dinner he asked me directly about my intentions. I fear I deceived him. I know that this upset him greatly later and led him to believe that I had somehow betrayed the bond of friendship between us. Ming was, and remains, a very close friend and was one of the key pillars upon whom I relied during my leadership years. But the duties of friendship, though great, do not in my view override the duties of leadership. The plain fact is that, if I had told Ming the truth that night, I would in effect have given him an advantage over others who might have wanted to stand for Leader in the coming contest, and this, I fear, I was just not pre-pared to do, even for a close and much admired friend.

The announcement of my resignation on 20 January took everyone by surprise, including, I regret to say, one of my own MPs. Ed Davey, who was speaking in the Commons when the news broke (an hour or so prematurely), and, when asked by a Tory whether he knew I had resigned, replied that he didn't, but that, even resigned, I was still a better Leader than the Tories had!

Blair put out a very generous statement on the public announcement of my resignation, as did others. I also received a flood of kind letters and phone calls. Inevitably, some were less so:

Dear Mr Ashdown,
I will be sorry to see you go, but at least it will save me from the constant frustration and ever-mounting anger of listening to you talking perfect sense about the Balkans and being ignored by everyone that matters.

Reluctantly I have come to the conclusion that you have been ignored because, although you talk sense about Bosnia and Kosovo, you talk bollocks about nearly everything else, particularly Europe and PR.

Now that you are free and don't have to pretend to embrace these dangerous notions, I hope that you will put some guts and gumption into British and European policies in the Balkans.

Presumably the new House of Lords will be the correct place from which you will lead the world?
Yours sincerely, etc.

Dear Sir,
Having found out that Paddy Ashdown is retiring, I wish to apply for the position of Liberal Democrat Party leader. Please grant me an interview. Attached is my CV.

I want to start up the World Space Agency (WSA); the World Army (WA); UK's National Union of Unions (NUU); school governors introducing the space industry; the UK space industry's non-periscope submarine fleet which when permanently submerged will carry, launch and land mini-submarines; safer and economical improvements to NHS hospital treatment to babies and more District Council jobs;
Thank you.
Yours faithfully, etc.

Dear Paddy,
When you started you were third out of three. You finish third out of three. In the Jobcentre in Barrow St Helens, Merseyside, they are looking for bin men and street-cleaners.
Yours, etc.

The remaining five months of my leadership were very relaxed. Ever since 1976, when we left Geneva, it had become a fixed family ritual that, no matter where we were or how limited our financial resources, we would always get together as a family and with friends for a week's skiing, usually during February. This year we had one of our best ever weeks in one of our favourite resorts, Val Thorens. The weather was wonderful, the snow was perfect, and I was more relaxed than I had been for the last ten years.

I also had time to make two further trips to Kosovo, and had one final 'wallpaper of State' function to fulfil. On 7 February, the international 'graveyard' circus descended on Amman for the funeral of King Hussein of Jordan. This turned out to be the very acme of 'working funerals'. To start with the whole international community were closeted for several hours in one of King Hussein's palaces. Although Prince Charles was given a small suite, very few of the other Heads of State or Government seemed to have been accorded the same luxury, and I found little groups of Kings, Prime Ministers and Presidents huddled in corners and having urgent conversations sitting on the stairs. While Blair was being wheeled around a series of bilaterals, I took a wander round and counted, on the ground floor alone, the Queen of the Netherlands, the Kings of Norway, Sweden and Spain, the Secretary General of the UN, a very ill-looking Yasser Arafat, a very touchy-feely President Clinton, a very sunburned ex-President George H.W. Bush, a very sozzled-looking President Yeltsin, the German Chancellor, the French President and more Prime Ministers than you could shake a stick at. After a while we were all ushered outside and up the hill to the Palace where King Hussein's coffin was lying in state. Then, pushing and shoving as only world leaders can, we filed off to a small square where a Jordanian army Corporal, obviously trained in the British tradition, bawled at the assembled multitude in a voice that would have been the envy of my Royal Marines drill sergeant, Bert Shoesmith:

RIGHT YOU LOT. LINE UP FOR THE GRAVESIDE.
ALL HEADS OF STATE TO THE FRONT!

The Heads of State meekly obeyed and filed forward, leaving the rest of us in a most terrible crush under the boiling sun. Unfortunately, a small group of Gulf Arab Heads of State, being of diminutive stature, got caught in the general mêlée, and I was quite concerned that harm might befall them in the crush. So, placing my arms on a wall in front of me, I pushed back against a collection of Japanese notables who obviously believed that, when it came to pushing, the Tokyo rush-hour had made them world champions, and they were going to prove it. I made an arch with my arms, under which passed sundry gorgeously attired Bedou royalty on their way to the grave of their Arab neighbour.

Six weeks after King Hussein's funeral, the Kosovo War started with US air raids on Belgrade. It did not go well. As many of us had suspected, the US air raids did little to damage the Serb forces but a lot to unite the Serbs behind Milošević, who continued the expulsion of the Kosovars with renewed vigour, this time blaming the international air strikes. Inevitably, bombing from fifteen thousand feet led to mistakes and the loss of innocent lives among both the Kosovars and the Serbs. The Allies were losing public support, and the cohesion of NATO was coming under great strain. To make matters worse, the Government seemed to believe that bombing could create what they called a 'permissive environment' in which ground troops would be able to occupy Kosovo without having to fight. Robin Cook went so far as to say that ground troops would never be used 'in a hostile environment', and other ministers echoed the same line. I spoke to Blair, saying that this was folly. Even if they did not feel that they could send ground troops into action, they should not say so: you do not tell your enemy what you are not going to do. And anyway, in my view, NATO could not win unless Milošević was convinced that the alternative to a peace on the international community's terms was an invasion that we had the will and the means to push through, if needed.

Blair over time clearly came to the same view, as the Government's policy started to subtly change. But the Clinton Administration was still strongly opposed to committing US ground forces. Just before Blair went off to see President Clinton in Washington, I set off on another trip to the region with one of my close advisers, Julian Astle. We went first to Kukës on the Albanian/Kosovo border, not far from where I had been on my first visit a year previously. Here, amid the rain and the mud, we saw thousands of wretched Kosovar refugees flooding over the border as Milošević's *Operation Horseshoe* increased in violence and intensity. Then we went to Macedonia to visit the NATO commander, General Mike Jackson, who was gathering a formidable force on the Kosovo border. Over a good deal of whisky (a favourite Jackson accompaniment to late-night talks), it became clear that NATO's commander had no idea what his political masters wanted of him. He had heard the Government say that troops would only be used in a 'permissive environment'. But, being an intelligent General, he was also looking at alternatives if it came to a forced invasion. And here all the options were difficult to the point of being almost impossible. Mike Jackson told me, with concern, that apparently some, especially on the US side, were even thinking that the best way into Kosovo was to launch an invasion from Hungary, crossing the plains of Serbia and entering Kosovo 'through the back door'. This would have been the height of folly. It was going to be difficult enough pushing the Serb Army out of Kosovo, which, though it may have been a religious centre, was now no longer regarded by most Serbs as part of their real homeland. But a full-scale invasion of Serbia proper would be resisted inch by inch by the whole Serb population – not to mention also probably starting a World War at the same time.

I flew back to London very worried indeed that we were on the brink of defeat in Kosovo, or something much worse if some of the military follies being considered were not brought under control by political leaders. I was also very concerned that, if Milošević could just hang on for another six weeks or so, the internal cohesion of NATO would break up and the will to do anything at all would vanish. My report to Blair concluded that NATO had to decide soon that it would be prepared to use ground troops in a hostile environment, or it would lose; that the US had to get involved; and that someone (preferably Blair) had to brief General Jackson very soon on what precisely was required of him, as at present he had no clear instructions worthy of the name.

On the day after I got back, I received a call from Jonathan Powell who was in Washington with Blair. He asked for my conclusions from the visit and I told him. He replied that Blair was about to go and see Clinton. Could I please fax my report through immediately, so that he could read it before the meeting? I did so.

It was, I believe, at this meeting that Blair finally persuaded Clinton, against the counsel of his closest advisers, that he should be prepared to risk putting US troops in harm's way and start preparing for an opposed invasion if necessary. This was an extraordinary achievement on Blair's part. If he had failed to persuade Clinton, then I have little doubt that Milošević would have won in Kosovo, and NATO would have lost – with incalculable consequences for the region and for the credibility of NATO in the future. Tony Blair is to be credited with playing the greatest role in ensuring that this did not happen.

Someone once said that when history repeats itself it is either as tragedy or as farce. In my view one of the chief reasons for Tony Blair's miscalculations over the Iraq War arose from *hubris* in the wake of Kosovo, which led him to believe that he could have as much influence over President Bush junior on Iraq, as he had over President Clinton on Kosovo.

On 3 June, finally convinced that NATO was serious about an invasion if it proved necessary, and after the Russians had made it clear that they would not support Belgrade in the case of an invasion, Milošević threw in the towel and agreed to the international community's terms for peace. These included the total withdrawal of all Serb forces from Kosovo. On 12 June Mike Jackson led his NATO army across the mountain passes from Macedonia, and a few days later I flew to visit him in Pristina for my last visit to Kosovo, now peaceful and under the protection of NATO, and another punishing late-night whisky session with the General.

A few days later, returning from a conference in Paris, I was rung by the outgoing High Representative in Bosnia and Herzegovina, Carlos Westendorp, asking me to put my name forward to be his successor. This was the first of several calls from senior international officials in Bosnia and elsewhere asking me to do the job. I told them all the same thing. I already had a job as MP for Yeovil and I did not believe in starting one job before I had finished the previous one. After I had stood down as an MP, perhaps. But until then, my answer was no.

Gordon Brown also asked me to head a Government-backed enquiry into cigarette-smuggling, which was costing the Treasury millions in lost taxes. I gave him the same answer.

On 9 August, the Liberal Democrats elected Charles Kennedy as my successor.

My diary for that day concludes:

I left the [Charles Kennedy] celebrations quietly and walked back to the House feeling just a tinge of sadness that I am no longer a leader of one of the great British political parties. But this was more than offset by the feeling of having cast off a very heavy burden.

It has been a day of showers and rain, but the evening light has a wonderful luminescence. Some purplish clouds over County Hall and white cumulo-nimbus, like great confections of cream, in the far distance. The air is rain-washed, the Thames is blue and buffeted by evening winds, and I feel very contented.

CHAPTER 15

Bosnia and Herzegovina

AFTER HANDING OVER the leadership of the Lib Dems I was hit by severe withdrawal symptoms and took it out on my back garden. We bought a strip of adjoining land from our neighbours, which more or less doubled the size of the small garden behind our cottage. In this I created a new vegetable plot, complete with compost heap, greenhouse, shed, fruit cage and a small orchard. I then redesigned our old garden, laying a herring-bone brick path and building over it a wooden pergola, which is now covered with honeysuckle, wisteria and roses. Next, I rearranged Jane's flower garden and laid a paved hard standing, over which I built a vine covered lean-to, in whose shade I am writing this. So deep was my boredom that I even threatened to learn to cook – until Jane put her foot down and said she would leave me if I didn't get out of her kitchen. I also, with more self-discipline than I knew I possessed, restrained myself when I found my fingers itching to get back into the action and tried to be as good an ex-Leader for Charles Kennedy as David Steel had been for me.

There are, I observe, three kinds of ex-Leader in politics, and, I suspect, in wider life, too. The first believes no one can be as good a general as they were, and, to prove it, they wreck the place before they go and seize every opportunity to lob in a hand grenade afterwards. What they are trying to do is enhance their own reputation, but they almost always end up doing exactly the opposite. Both Margaret Thatcher and her predecessor Ted Heath were this kind of ex-Leader. Those in the second category leave the battlefield and never return, even when they are needed.

The third kind retire to a place nearby where they keep quiet and stay out of the way unless asked for, when they do all they can to help. I aimed to be in this category and, when I resigned, said my motto would be the words Mark Twain relates were posted in the wheel-houses of the old Mississippi steamboats: 'Don't speak to the helmsman; don't spit on the floor.'

Before long I found that this actually suited me rather well too. For as soon as the withdrawal symptoms passed I found I had plenty of other things to do. I could be present for the first days in the life of my new granddaughter, Lois, and began to teach my grandson Matthias to ski. I turned back to writing again, too, publishing two volumes of my diaries in February 2000 and September 2001.

I also began to prepare for retirement by getting back into private enterprise, joining the International Advisory Board of *The Independent* newspaper, which I loved. I especially enjoyed working with its mercurial and engaging proprietor, Tony O'Reilly. On one occasion, our Board meeting was at his home in Ireland, Castle Martin House in Kilcullen, Co Kildare. This is a splendid eighteenth-century mansion once occupied by the Rolling Stones. Shortly before we arrived for the meeting, Tony had managed to purchase an original Monet painting – and not any old Monet either, but one of the very few of his iconic thirty or so canvases of Rouen Cathedral in different lights to have remained in private hands. For this he was rumoured to have paid $22 million. The painting was duly delivered under the strictest security to Dublin airport, whence it travelled to Castle Martin House in the back of a local taxi, which Tony had despatched from Kilcullen for the purpose. When it was finally safely unpacked and hung on the wall, Tony invited the cab driver in for a viewing. The little Irishman, cocked his head to one side, squinted at it through one eye and declared, 'Bejaisus, for 22 million dollars, don't you think it's a little smudged?'

I got involved with a couple of other commercial enterprises, too. But since I have always believed that MPs should not receive incomes beyond their Parliamentary salaries, my earnings from these activities were paid into a special fund I set up in my Constituency for the use of my successor when he was adopted as the new Lib Dem Candidate.

My involvement with the Balkans did not finish when I stood down as Lib Dem Leader, either. I paid several visits there in 2000 and 2001, mainly to Montenegro, which at the time looked as though it might go the way of Bosnia and Kosovo and become a cockpit for conflict. I had retained one member of my old Leadership staff, Ian Patrick, who had joined me as a temporary employee aged 19. Ian, a young man of exceptional ability, soon proved himself indispensable for his good judgement, his ability to make organisations work and his skill at bringing order to my otherwise turbulent and chaotic life. I took him with me on these Balkan trips, and he went on to become one of the key pillars of my staff when, a year later, I went to Bosnia.

In March 2001 Ian and I happened to be on a tour which included Kosovo and Skopje, the capital of Macedonia, when the western Macedonian cities of Tetovo and Gostivar, where the Albanian minority in the country was concentrated and where the Kosovo Liberation Army had been born, suddenly burst into flames. Albanian rebels took to the mountains, and there were sporadic clashes and some deaths. On 21 March the Macedonian army started to mass for a full-scale assault on the rebels. Many (including me) believed there was a real danger that the situation would ignite a general war in Macedonia, into which Greece and Turkey (both NATO members) would be drawn on opposite sides, so launching the third and potentially most dangerous act of the Balkan tragedy. I was visiting the British Ambassador in Skopje when we suddenly received a call from Downing Street. The Prime Minister was at a crisis summit of EU and NATO leaders trying to find a way back to peace. He asked if I would do what I could to broker a ceasefire on the ground and prevent the Macedonian army assault on the rebel positions, which was planned for dawn the following morning. So I visited the leaders of the Albanian rebels in the hills above Tetovo and got them to agree to a ceasefire and negotiations with the Macedonian government and then drove back to Skopje to try to persuade the Macedonians not to launch their assault. The Macedonian Prime Minister and Foreign Minister were prepared to consider the proposition, but only on condition that I could obtain the agreement of the Speaker of the Macedonian Parliament, a granite-faced hard man called Stojan Andov.

Together with the British Ambassador, I spent most of the night trying to persuade Andov, over considerable quantities of Macedonian beer and Scotch whisky, of which he seemed to be able to drink prodigious quantities without visible effect. I threatened him; I cajoled him; I told him that the Macedonian army assault was doomed to failure, all of which had not the slightest effect. The only time he wavered was when the Ambassador, a very good man who loved Macedonia deeply, got so emotional about the bad things that would happen if the attack went ahead that the tears started rolling down his face uncontrollably. Andov was used to threats – they come two a penny in Macedonia. He was completely immune to international pressure – he had seen that all before, too. But the British Ambassador weeping was something he was not used to. It checked him for a moment, before the old obduracy returned. Eventually, in the small hours of the morning and much the worse for too much beer and whisky, we gave up. The Macedonian army attacked next morning, and it was, as we predicted, a disaster. They were easily beaten back by the rebels. I was now sure that Macedonia would descend into civil war. But as a result of some very skilful diplomacy, George Robertson, then Secretary General of NATO, and Javier Solana of the EU, backed by Chris Patten, then a European Commissioner, succeeded in negotiating an agreement which pulled the country back from the brink at the very last minute and which has, in essence, lasted and kept the peace in Macedonia ever since.

Meanwhile, back in Parliament, I discovered to my surprise that I was now suddenly regarded as an elder statesman and accorded a respect in the House of Commons that I was not used to, having never experienced it before. This I found perplexing and amusing in equal measure, because nothing had changed in my opinions or behaviour, except, of course that I was now safely part of the past, rather than a potential threat for the future. The House of Commons can be a generous place from time to time, but only to the politically dead or those regarded as irretrievably moribund.

My occasional Downing Street meetings with Blair also continued. At one, on 6 March, he asked me if I was prepared to allow my name put to be put forward for the post of international community High Representative in Bosnia and Herzegovina, which was shortly to become vacant. The Government had previously put forward my name to be the international supremo in Kosovo. At that time I had made it clear that, although I would prefer to finish my time as an MP, since Kosovo was an emergency, I would do the job if asked. I subsequently had a meeting with Kofi Annan, the UN Secretary General, to discuss the post, but in the event he appointed Bernard Kouchner.* Blair went on to explain that this offer was different, since the Bosnia post would not become vacant until after the general election, so I could do it after I had finished as MP for Yeovil.

I went home to discuss the suggestion with Jane, who said that she was really looking forward to settling down, but thought, nevertheless, that I should do it and that, if I did, she would come with me. On this basis, I wrote to Blair saying that I would accept the job, provided the Government could get the necessary support from the international community.

In December I met him again to outline how I planned to undertake my Bosnia mandate and to warn him that, if I was to make

---

* Bernard Kouchner was a founder of Médecins Sans Frontières and is now the French Foreign Minister.

progress there, I was going to have to make some quite big waves, both in Bosnia and possibly in the wider international community too. I would then need his support. He readily gave it and was as good as his word later when I needed him. But his mind was chiefly on the aftermath of 9/11, and especially on Afghanistan and the coming invasion. He insisted: 'We will have a very limited operation you know. It will be confined to Kabul, and then we will get out early. I don't mind a deal that has us going in early providing we can get out early.' I said I thought this very wise – Afghanistan was a country in which it was very easy to get bogged down.

My last major project, before standing down as MP for Yeovil, was to get my Lib Dem successor elected. MPs get very proprietorial about their constituencies, which they tend to regard as a cross between a unique fiefdom whose complexities only they understand and a personal possession which cannot safely be entrusted to anyone else. So handing them over is always a very tricky moment, involving a wide gamut of usually base emotions, ranging from the pain of giving up a much-loved possession, to jealousy of the youngster whose beginning is your ending. I was spared all this. Whilst I scrupulously took no part in the selection of my successor, my constituency party was wise enough to choose someone quite exceptional. David Laws had been a close adviser and a safe pair of hands to whom I could leave even the most difficult tasks during my leadership, so I never doubted he would be a skilled Westminster MP. But what I hadn't realised was that he would also be one of those rare MPs who can combine ability at Westminster with genuine dedication to his constituency. I had not a moment's hesitation or discomfort in handing my precious Yeovil over to him, and I felt real pride when he won the seat in the general election of 7 June 2001 with a majority greater than mine had been when I was first elected in 1983.

Before I left the Leadership of the Lib Dems, Blair had asked me if I would like to go to the Lords. I said that I didn't much believe in the place, but would go there when the time came so that I could argue for, and cast my vote in favour of, replacing it with an elected second chamber. In July that year I was duly introduced into the House of Lords, with Roy Jenkins and Richard Holme as my proposers, in a ceremony which involved getting dressed up in ridiculous robes, swearing ancient oaths of loyalty to the Queen and doing a great deal of bowing. They asked me afterwards if I would like a photograph of myself in my peer's robes. I replied that I certainly would not and would much prefer it if they burnt the negatives, so none of my friends could blackmail me with one afterwards. The best part of the ceremony was that my daughter, who happened to be over from France with our two grandchildren, was able to attend and watch the performance. According to House of Lords tradition at the time, the eldest son (but significantly *not* the eldest daughter) of a Peer was allowed to sit on the steps of the Queen's throne in the Lords Chamber, to watch the ceremony. I was shocked at this piece of sex discrimination and asked why my daughter could not do the same. It was finally agreed that peers' eldest daughters could be accorded this 'privilege', too. Kate was, I believe, the first peer's daughter ever to be able to do this, while Jane and our grandchildren watched from the public gallery above the Lords chamber. Unfortunately the Lords' authorities had not reckoned with the republican tendencies of my two-year-old French granddaughter Lois, who, completely unfazed by all the monarchist mumbo jumbo, pantomime costumes and medieval pomp going on below her, spotted her mother sitting amongst the gilt, gold and crimson of the royal throne and started shouting in a voice which rose to a climax loud enough to drown out the ancient oaths: 'Maman! Maman! Maman! – JE VEUX FAIRE PIPI!' It was all I could do to suppress a fit of giggles, and I noticed some of my fellow peers watching from the Lords benches didn't even try.

In the middle of 2001, the international community decided that I should take over as the new High Representative and European Union Special Representative in Bosnia and Herzegovina* in May of the following year. A senior member of the Foreign Office told me he was present when Tony Blair sought support for my candidature from his fellow European leaders. One of them asked who I was and whether I was really up to such a difficult post, to which Blair replied, 'Look, this guy led the British Liberal Democrats for eleven years. After that, Bosnia will be a doddle!'

---

* There had been three previous international-community High Representatives in Bosnia: former Swedish Prime Minster Carl Bildt (now Swedish Foreign Minister), Spanish diplomat Carlos Westendorp and my immediate predecessor Wolfgang Petritsch, a senior diplomat from Austria. In 2001, however, the EU decided that, to reflect its growing role in stabilising Bosnia, it would create an EU Special Representative there and asked me to 'double-hat' my role to fulfil this function, too.

In September Ian Patrick and I set up a small office in the attic of the Foreign Office. Here, over the next few months, we assembled the core team who would help me in Bosnia and started to put together a plan for what I would do when I got there.

I also started to try to learn what used to be known as Serbo-Croat, my sixth language, with the help of an outstanding Bosnian teacher in the Government language school, Edina Kulenović. In fact, the term Serbo-Croat is never used nowadays, and the language is known as Serb in Serbia, Croatian in Croatia and Bosnian among the Muslim population of Bosnia – even though the three languages are, for all practical purposes, exactly the same. But, whatever people chose to call it, this was by far the most difficult language I have ever attempted: partly because I was only able to do it part-time for a short period, partly because of its grammatical complexities, but mostly, I suspect, because my brain was far less supple and agile at sixty than when I had learned Chinese as a twenty-seven-year-old. I cannot say that I became fluent, but I learned enough to understand most of what was being said and to converse on simple, everyday matters.

Over the next few months, three others joined us to complete what would become my personal office. Julian Braithwaite, who was to handle my relations with the Press, came to me from a spell as Alastair Campbell's assistant in No. 10 Downing Street, having been a diplomat in the Belgrade Embassy before that. Edward Llewellyn, who turned down the opportunity to work for the Prince of Wales in order to join us, was a committed Conservative who had worked for Chris Patten when he was Governor of Hong Kong and, later, a European Commissioner. He also had experience in Bosnia, and now joined the team as my Chief of Staff and head of my political department.* The third of the triumvirate, Julian Astle, who would look after all my relations with the domestic political structures in Bosnia, had worked in my Lib Dem Leader's Office as a speech-writer, policy adviser and manager of, amongst other things, our secret negotiations with Blair and No. 10. Together with Ian Patrick, Deana Brynildsen, who was lent to us by the

---

* Ed Llewellyn's commitment to the Tories was an integral part of his life. Towards the end of my time in Bosnia, with the 2005 Election approaching, I suggested to him that this was an opportunity he should not miss and encouraged him to take a month off on unpaid leave in order to take up the offer from his friend, David Cameron, who was clearly one of the rising stars in the Tory party, to help him during the election campaign. A few months later, when Cameron was elected the new Tory Leader, and Ed's tour with me was coming to an end, he joined Cameron's team, putting his formidable talents to use as Chief of Staff.

Canadian Government for confidential duties, our two secretaries, Amela Zahiraǧić and Sandra Radosavljević, and three drivers, Dragan Grahovac, Sejo Palo and Mirsad Tufo, all of whom we recruited from the staff of the OHR in Sarajevo, they formed the most gifted and able team of close advisers I have ever had the good fortune to work with.

During the seven years since Dayton was signed, my three predecessors as High Representative had overseen a huge and successful effort to stabilise Bosnia, with the international community pouring into the country more aid per capita than the Marshall Plan for Europe after World War Two. As a result, much of Bosnia had been reconstructed, refugees were now returning home in large numbers, and there was freedom of movement across the country, all under the secure peace established by a massive NATO presence, numbering at one time some sixty thousand troops.

It was clear to me that the stabilisation phase of Bosnia's return to normality was over. Our job during my mandate was, therefore, not to create peace – that had already been done – but to begin to build a functioning state capable one day of joining Europe. Slowly, over the ensuing months, we put together a detailed plan of what we would do, concentrating chiefly on building the basic framework of a lightly structured state, with most power decentralised. We gave special priority to three areas: establishing the rule of law, getting the economy moving and beginning to tackle high-level corruption in the country.

In the middle of all this, I was suddenly confronted with one of those events that people in public life half wish for, but half dread at the same time. On Saturday 20 October, at Ian Patrick's insistence, I somewhat grumpily agreed to interrupt a weekend and drive up to London to do a BBC interview at their White City studios. As I was checking in at the BBC reception desk, Michael Aspel emerged from behind a curtain with a cameraman and uttered the famous phrase, 'Paddy Ashdown, This Is Your Life.' It was a considerable shock, but a marvellous one, which ended in a very emotional evening with many old friends and some long-lost relations, including, to my joy, my brother and sister from Australia whom I had not seen for more than thirty years.

As soon as I had waved an emotional goodbye to my Australian siblings at the end of a memorable week together, I found myself flying off in the opposite direction, to the United States to try to win the support of the US Government for the Bosnia plan we had assembled. There I saw Colin Powell, the Secretary of State, who gave me his unstinting backing and said I could call him up any time if I needed his help. It was a most generous offer and one I was to take up only once during my four-year mandate.

In the early months of 2002 we visited the other key capitals, mostly in Europe, whose support would be crucial if we were to push through what was by now a very detailed and ambitious plan to begin creating the effective institutions of a Bosnian state and tackle high-level crime. Now we were ready to go. Jane had packed all our stuff, the plan was finalised and my little team was eager to start.

But I had one more thing to do before we left. On 12 March 2002 I was summoned to The Hague to give evidence in the trial of Slobodan Milošević on the bombardment of villages in southern Kosovo and my subsequent meeting with him in September 1998. Milošević had proved a most effective advocate in his own cause and had often showed that he knew more about specific events and places than those who were giving evidence against him. He had also developed a devastating line in sarcasm and had often established a dominance over witnesses, especially simple Kosovars, which had effectively destroyed their credibility. He was able to achieve this because he was completely uninterested in the judgement or procedures of the court, whose legitimacy he contemptuously rejected. His audience was not in the courtroom at The Hague, but amongst his own people in Serbia and Bosnia. I knew our televised encounter (which was heavily publicised beforehand) would be widely watched, including in Bosnia, and if he succeeded in making a fool of me or intimidating me then my authority in the job I was about to do would be fatally undermined. Our meeting therefore became something of a battle of wits in which I tried to keep him tightly confined to the events I had seen and not let him wander off into generalised diatribes about western politicians and the west's 'illegal' actions in the recent war. In the end he proved far less effective than I had feared, and the prosecution and my Bosnia team seemed, overall, satisfied with the outcome. For my part, I was just relieved it was all over. (This was not my last visit to The Hague. At the end of 2002, I was back in the Tribunal courtroom for my third visit, this time giving evidence about what I had seen at the Serb-run Manjaca and Trnopolje camps during my first visits to Bosnia, back in 1992.)

Finally, our preparations complete, the six of us flew out to Sarajevo on 27 May 2002. There Jane moved us into a modest house above Sarajevo old town, and I started my mandate as the new High Representative.

At this point I need to do three brief introductions; first to the Balkans; then to the star of this chapter and these years of our lives, the little country of Bosnia and Herzegovina, and finally to the job I had to do there as the international 'High Representative'.

The best description of the Balkans I know is in Cy Sulzberger's 1969 book *A Long Row of Candles*:

> The Balkans, which in Turkish means 'mountains', run roughly from the Danube to the Dardanelles, from Istria to Istanbul, and is a term for the little lands of Hungary, Rumania, Yugoslavia, Albania, Bulgaria, Greece and part of Turkey. . . . It is, or was, a gay peninsula filled with sprightly people who ate peppered food, drank strong liquors, wore flamboyant clothes, loved and murdered easily and had a splendid talent for starting wars. Less imaginative Westerners looked down on them with secret envy, sniffing at their royalty, scoffing at their pretensions and fearing their savage terrorists. Karl Marx called them 'ethnic trash'. I, as a footloose youngster in my twenties, adored them.*

I was neither footloose, nor a youngster, when I arrived in Sarajevo airport in May 2002, but that in no way immunised me against the fascination and romance of the Balkans that Sulzberger evokes so well. For the truth is that what began as an interest in Bosnia turned, over the next nearly four years, into a love affair with this remarkable country and its people, which for Jane and I has now become inextricably woven into the pattern of our lives.

Some countries are defined by their unity. Bosnia, about the size of Wales, is defined by its divisions. Even the land is divided into three.

Northern Bosnia is flat, alluvial and lies in the flood plain of the Sava River, which marks the country's northern border and is one of the great tributaries of the Danube. Here they grow corn, wonderful plums and other fruit, as well as superb vegetables

Then there is middle Bosnia, which I especially loved. This is a country of high, snow-capped mountains reaching up to 6,000ft, deep valleys, primeval forests, vertically sided ravines and raging torrents. Here are bears and wolves, ibex† and mouflon,‡   not because they

---

* C.L. Sulzberger, *A Long Row of Candles: Memoirs and diaries*, 1934–1954 (London: Macdonald, 1969; New York: Macmillan, 1969).
† Wild goats.
‡ Wild sheep.

have been recently imported, but because they have never left. Here are alpine villages, cut off for three months of the year, where things haven't changed for a hundred years. And here is a phenomenon so extraordinary that, as someone from flat, boring northern Europe, it always seemed a wonder to me. The Bosnian call them *vrelos*, which just means 'springs'. But these are completely different from the little gurgling things that I am used to. These are whole rivers that leap, fully formed, crystal-clear and ice-cold, from the foot of mountains. Bosnia stands on the world's largest limestone *karst* plateau, which runs from southern Austria to the Adriatic. All the rain and snow that falls on its mountains sinks vertically down through the limestone, and it often takes several years for the water to make its way down into underground rivers and out into the sunlight again. Each *vrelo* in Bosnia is different, but all are magic. The *vrelo Bosne* seeps as quiet as a prayer into limpid green pools on the outskirts of Sarajevo, before flowing away north as the Bosna River (from which the country gets its name) to the Sava, the Danube and the Black Sea. The *vrelo Bune*, near Mostar, swims like a sinuous green fish out of a mysterious black cavern over which sits an ancient Dervish monastery. It forms the Buna River, which joins the great Neretva near Mostar and flows south to the Adriatic. Near Livno in the south of Bosnia is the *vrelo Bistrice*, which, after rain, roars out of the base of a cliff like a lion, flows quietly for a couple of kilometres and then vanishes underground once more, never to be seen again.

And finally there is southern Bosnia – a land of great rolling hills and wide, open valleys – which looks like a scrub-covered version of lowland Scotland. Quite suddenly, as you cross into this part of Bosnia the vegetation shifts from northern European to Mediterranean. This transformation can occur in the space of a few yards, across a single mountain ridge line, with wild raspberries and northern Alpine flowers on one side and sage and wild thyme and *maquis* scrub a few steps away on the other. Life is tough on these great ridges, where a myriad limestone sink-holes steal away the water as soon as it falls, and where the people are as hard as the stones from which they make their living.

Bosnia, with a population of some 3.5 million, is also divided into three ethnically. The largest group (about 45%) are the Bosnian Muslims, or Bosniaks as they are called today. Then come the Bosnian Serbs (about 35%) and finally, the Bosnian Croats (about 17% and dropping). There are also a wide range of smaller groups, such as the

Jews* and the Roma people (gypsies). Almost every community in Bosnia is multi-ethnic to a greater or lesser extent, with minorities living in almost every town. Generally speaking, though, the Serbs are a majority in the north, the Bosniaks are a majority in the middle, and the Croats are a majority in the south.

I have often been struck by the similarities between those countries whose fortune (or misfortune) it is to find themselves at the junction of the tectonic plates of race, culture and religion. Countries like Switzerland, Afghanistan and Bosnia are all of them mountainous regions, incredibly beautiful, the battlegrounds of conquerors and the cockpits in which, from time to time, terrible inter-ethnic conflicts break out (before the Treaty of Ticino in 1516 the famously peaceful Switzerland of today was the Bosnia of the middle ages when it came to internal war and ethnic conflict).

Bosnia sits four-square on just such a fault line. It was no accident that the Roman Emperor Diocletian divided the Eastern from the Western Roman Empires along the line of the Drina River, which now marks Bosnia's eastern border with Serbia. Two thousand years later history has made this region an even more complex meeting point of cultural, religious and ethnic differences. Today Bosnia marks the south-western frontier of the Slav people (Yugoslavia literally meant 'the country of the South Slavs'), the easternmost outpost of Orthodox Christianity (most Serbs are Orthodox), the furthest north-western foothold of the Turkish empire and the religion of Islam (the religion of most Bosniaks), and the eastern boundary of the rule of Roman Catholicism (most Croats are Catholic). In Bosnia, east meets west, face to face and over the garden fence.

Nowhere is this better seen than in Bosnia's capital, Sarajevo, sometimes referred to as the westernmost city of the East and the easternmost city of the West. Lying in a great bowl dominated by the snow-capped peaks that surround it, Sarajevo has a setting which, along with those of Hong Kong and San Francisco, is one of the most spectacular and beautiful in the world. It is, essentially, a garden city, with each house in the old *mahalas* (neighbourhoods) sitting in its own garden or courtyard. It used to be called 'the Geneva of the East' for its famous spirit of tolerance, which, along with its buildings was damaged but not obliterated by the siege. It was here that the adherents of the Albigensian heresy came,

* A very large proportion of Sarajevo's Jews (especially the younger ones) emigrated to Israel during the 1992–95 war.

fleeing the Inquisition in the thirteenth century.* They are believed by some to have been the carvers of the strange and beautiful 'bogomil' tombstones that can still be found even in the remotest places and on the highest of Bosnia's mountains. And after them, came the Jews, driven out of Spain by Ferdinand and Isabella† in 1492. They finally found refuge here, after being persecuted all across Europe, and their ancient language, Ladino, is still spoken by the older members of Sarajevo's now fast-diminishing Jewish population. When the Jews came to Sarajevo, they brought with them their most precious sacred text, known as the Sarajevo Haggadah, now the city's most prized possession, carefully hidden from the Germans during the Second World War and securely protected from Serb bombardment during the 1990s siege.

Sarajevo was famous the world over for its jumble of religions and cultures. From our house I could count the minarets of seventy-three mosques. Sarajevo mosques are, in the main, not great, ostentatious affairs but little and ancient and beautiful, each fitting into its community as comfortably as an English church sits in the heart of its parish. Below our house, a stone's throw from the great Bey's mosque built in the 1530s, stands the Catholic cathedral, its straight, strong bell-tower pointing with confident affirmation towards its God. And a hundred metres away the Serbian Orthodox cathedral stands, distinguished by its onion domes and characteristic architecture. Here is how Bosnia's greatest writer, Ivo Andrić, winner of the 1961 Nobel Prize for literature, captured the sounds of Sarajevo which I could hear lying in my bed every night:

> Whoever lies awake in Sarajevo hears the voices of the Sarajevo night. The clock on the Catholic cathedral strikes the hour with weighty confidence: 2 a.m. More than a minute passes (to be exact, 75 seconds – I counted) and only then, with a rather weaker but piercing sound does the Orthodox church announce the hour and chime its own 2 a.m. A moment after it the tower clock on the Bey's mosque strikes the hour, in a hoarse, far-away voice that strikes 11, the ghostly Turkish hour, by the strange calculation of

---

* The Albigensian or Cathar Crusade (1209–29) was a military campaign initiated by the Roman Catholic Church to eliminate the Cathar heresy, which was centred on the Provençal town of Albi in France.

† Queen Isabella I of Castile and León and her husband King Ferdinand II of Aragon, married in 1469 in Valladolid. They were responsible for the Christian reconquest of the Iberian peninsula from the Moors and for uniting Spain under a Catholic monarchy.

distant and alien parts of the world. The Jews have no clock to sound their hour, so God alone knows what time it is for them by the Sephardic reckoning, or the Ashkenazic. Thus at night, while everyone is sleeping, division keeps vigil in the counting of the late small hours and separates these sleeping people who, awake, rejoice and mourn, feast and fast by four different and antagonistic calendars and send all their prayers and wishes to one heaven in four different ecclesiastical languages.*

George Bernard Shaw, writing with terrible accuracy about his people (and mine) once said, 'If you put two Irishmen in a room, you will always be able to persuade one to roast the other on a spit.' There is much of this quality about the people of the Balkans, too. This is the dark undercurrent that lies unseen, but deeply sensed, beneath the seemingly placid surface of life. And it is capable of re-emerging in evil times with terrifying rapidity. This darkness of spirit may be unspoken in ordinary conversation, but it is there, clear enough, in the black humour and the everyday aphorisms which are common across all the ethnic communities of the Balkans. The most famous of these is, '*Da Komšija crkne krava*' – 'May my neighbour's cow die.' Another illustrates something of the same sentiment with a little more humour and a lot more vulgarity; '*Lako je tudjim kurcem gloginje mlatiti*' – 'It's easy to beat thorn bushes with other people's pricks.'

The problem, I think, lies in the question of identity, which is all the more important because all three peoples come from the same root, speak the same language and look identical. The Croats can't really decide whether they are part of the Germanic races to the north, as they would like, or of the brotherhood of Slavs to the east, as they fear. The Serbs know who they are so well that they are prepared to do terrible things to those who aren't them, and terribly brave things against the whole of the rest of the world, when someone convinces them that is necessary for national preservation. The Bosniak Muslims, meanwhile, have yet to find their true identity. They did not exist as a recognised group during most of the Tito years. Their identity was forged in the crucible of the recent 1992–5 war, whose aim was their extinction and during which they were abandoned by the rest of the world. They are gifted, artistic and hospitable to a fault. But their most powerful identity remains that of

* Ivo Andrić (ed. Celia Hawkesworth), *The Damned Yard and Other Stories* (London: Forest Books, 1992).

victims. Constantly alert and often suspicious, they are fearful of the future, always worrying that it will repeat the past again, especially since 9/11, Iraq, Afghanistan, al-Qaeda and the 'war on Islamic terror'.

Actually, it is this very fact which ought to lead Europe and the West to value Bosnia's Muslims as a powerful bridge in the dialogue of the deaf currently under way between ancient Christendom and newly militant Islam. For Bosniak Muslims are not the new Islam in Europe, which we have suddenly and frighteningly found planted in our inner cities. They are ancient European Islam, which is four hundred years old. Alija Izetbegović used to say that he was a Muslim and a European and could see no contradiction between the two. Walk down Sarajevo's main street, the Ferhadija, during the *corso** and you will see the same for yourself. For Muslim though most will be, there is here as much fashionable finery, as much exposed flesh and as many short skirts as can be observed in any self-respecting European capital of a fine summer's evening.

Or drive up a Bosniak valley on a still day in late October and note the thin columns of smoke rising through the clear blue air to a God who frowns on alcohol. At the foot of each you will invariably find one of the communal village stills which provides each Muslim family with the ten litres or so of fierce plum brandy (*šlivović*) without which none of them would dream of entering the long nights and deep snows of the winter months.

Bosniak Muslims wear their religion very lightly. Which is lucky for Europe, for, even though we abandoned them in the recent war of extermination, they remained resolutely unradicalised. And they resolutely remain so still, despite continued, determined and expensive attempts by Wahabi extremists to make them into militant Islam's European fifth column.

Bosnia's history, just like everything else, has been sharply and often bloodily divided, too. It is an old country, which sent knights to the crusades and until the thirteenth century had its own kings, who despatched embassies to most of the courts of Europe. Then in 1463 came the Turks. They ruled for four hundred years. Contrary to popular perception, though, Muslims had special privileges under the Turks, there were very few pogroms against other religions, which were, in the main, tolerated. As the Turkish empire sickened and then died in the last

---

* A Balkan and Italian tradition in which everyone comes out between 6 and 8 p.m. and promenades in their finery through the city's main streets and squares.

decades of the nineteenth century, the Austrians moved in and brought good government, splendid railways, impressive new state institutions and buildings to match. I remember an old man, curious about what being a member of the European Community would bring, once asking me, 'My grandfather used to tell me that when the Austrians ruled us, if you paid too much tax, they actually gave you some back! Will joining Europe be like that? If it is, then the sooner we get there the better!'

But Austrian rule had only been in place some forty years when a young Bosnian Serb nationalist, Gavrilo Princip, assassinated their Archduke, on a street corner in Sarajevo (a plaque still marks the spot where the fatal shot was fired and set the world alight). After the First World War the 'wise men' who divided up the world could not work out what to do with three untidy spaces left over when the bartering was finally complete. So they drew lines round them and called them countries: Czechoslovakia, Iraq and Yugoslavia. After that it was just a question of bundling Bosnia and Herzegovina into the last of these, along with its inconvenient neighbours who didn't have a king powerful enough, or major state interested enough, to stand up for them. In World War Two, Tito used the mountains of Bosnia as the centre of his great guerrilla campaign against the Germans, aided by the British SOE, afterwards reuniting Yugoslavia under his special form of communism. Only his *cvrsta ruka* (strong fist) could hold the country together, however, and in the aftermath of his death came the terrible years of Milošević and Tudjman. After them came the Dayton Peace Agreement in 1995, the engagement of the international community, and the time of the High Representatives, of which I was the fourth.

So what exactly was this job – with its title out of Gilbert and Sullivan and powers that ought to have made a Liberal blush – which I suddenly found myself doing in this deeply complex country about which I knew so frighteningly little?

The task of the international High Representative in Bosnia and Herzegovina is to look after the implementation of the civilian aspects of the Dayton Peace Agreement – in other words to build on the peace that Dayton created. In effect, this meant that my job could be as broad as I wished to make it, ranging from education, to human rights, to the conduct of government, to the operation of the economy, to the restructuring of the transport system, to the reconstruction of houses, to the reform of the media, etc., etc. In this job, I could interfere in anything and get swallowed up in everything if I wanted to.

And to help me interfere in everything if I wanted to, I had a staff in the Office of the High Representative (OHR) of approximately 800 and a budget of some €36 million. And to make interfering in other people's business even more fun, I had an array of formidable powers called 'the Bonn Powers', under which I could impose laws, subject only to their eventual endorsement by the domestic parliaments, and remove officials and politicians who were blocking or undermining the implementation of the Dayton agreement.

At first sight, this sounds altogether too tempting, especially for someone who would really like to have been Prime Minister. But I soon discovered that it was, on the contrary, extremely frightening to have so much power in a country about which I knew so little. I soon realised, too, that any law I passed, or any decision I took to remove an official rested, as the law in any ordinary country does, on public consent. My first conclusion, therefore, was that I could only do this job successfully if I saw myself as the servant of the people of Bosnia and Herzegovina, and that, if I ever lost their support for what I did, then my job would be finished overnight – and me with it.

The other way to fail at this job was to try to do everything. I insisted that we needed to be clear about what we would *not* get involved in. We had to avoid getting distracted by the things it would nice to do, in order to concentrate on the things it was vital to do. So we made a plan which focused on the essentials, and I gave instructions that, as these were completed, we would hand our responsibilities over to the Bosnians and start cutting the size of the OHR.

But I was also, formally, the servant of the international community, and had to get their agreement for any action I took, as well. One of my key tasks as High Representative was to 'co-ordinate' a veritable alphabet soup of UN and other bodies, ranging from the UN High Commission for Refugees (UNHCR), through to the UN Development Programme (UNDP), the UN Mission in Bosnia and Herzegovina (UNMIBH), the World Bank (WB), the International Monetary Fund (IMF), the European Commission (EC), the European Union Monitoring Mission (EUMM), the Organisation for Security and Co-operation in Europe (OSCE), the International Criminal Tribunal for ex-Yugoslavia (ICTY, better known as The Hague Tribunal), the International Commission for Missing Persons (ICMP) and so on *ad infinitum*. The problem was that, although I had a formal duty to co-ordinate all these bodies, I had no formal powers to do so. For, as I very soon discovered, they all had their own mandates, reported directly to their own headquarters and paid little heed to what I said or did. If I was to succeed in this part of my job I had to do it through force of personality and with a clear plan in my back pocket.

To add to this potential confusion, there exists alongside the OHR an entirely separate and parallel military structure responsible for the security and military aspects of the implementation of the Dayton Peace Agreement. (For most of my time this was the Stabilisation Force, SFOR, commanded by a three-star US general who reported directly to NATO in Brussels.) There was, however, no formal structure for co-operation between me and my military colleague, and before my arrival relations between the two headquarters had traditionally been cool to the point of hostility. One of my early decisions was to mend this division, so that the local NATO commander and I lived in each other's pockets, felt each other's heartbeat and acted always as one.

It is sometimes said that the High Representative in Bosnia is accountable to no one. The opposite was the truth. I was directly accountable to the Peace Implementation Council, made up of those countries most engaged in stabilising the peace in Bosnia, whose key Ambassadors formed a Steering Board with which I met every week and whose broad agreement I had to obtain for any major action I intended to take. I was also charged with reporting to the UN Security Council twice every year. In addition, as European Union Special Representative, my boss was the European 'Foreign Minister' in Brussels, Javier Solana. I also had to account to the European Commission (for the early years of my mandate the responsible Commissioner was Chris Patten) for the very considerable sum of money allocated to my mandate.

Before I left the UK to take up my new post, a very old friend with much experience in the region warned me that getting things to happen amid the complexities of Bosnia was 'like herding cats'. What I very soon discovered was that the cats that were really difficult to herd were not the Bosnians I was working with, but the members of the international community behind me. Relations with them were much more difficult and much more complex, and in the end swallowed up much more of my time, than dealing with events in Bosnia. But I knew that the time I spent on this was worth it. Because they were the key. If the international community remained divided, as it was when I arrived, there was little I could accomplish. But if I could get them to work to a single plan and speak with a single voice, then there was nothing we could not do. And that was how it worked out.

There is an old Foreign Office saying; 'He is a good man to go tiger-shooting with,' meaning that the recipient of the compliment does not flinch in the face of danger. With only few exceptions, the nations and multilateral organisations which made up the international community in Bosnia proved just such partners. Some, like the governments of the US and the UK and the institutions of NATO and the European Union, were outstanding, giving me unwavering and generous support when I needed it (even, sometimes, when they thought I was wrong) and providing the resources to get things done when I required them.

But all this meant spending a lot of time visiting capitals and seeking their support for what we were proposing to do. Which meant far too much time spent on aircraft and in airports that should have been spent in Bosnia getting on with my job.

The travelling was not just one-way, though. Bosnia was also at the top of the list for many VIP tours of eastern Europe. Over the four years we were visited by the UN and NATO Secretary Generals, most of the EU's Commissioners, President Clinton, many of the Prime Ministers and Presidents of Europe (but, significantly, not Tony Blair) and countless Admirals and Generals. One of the latter I especially remember. He was a US Air Force General straight out of central casting, with a body built like a bull and one of those heads that passes straight into the chest without the intervention of a neck. I opened our conversation with small talk, asking him whether this was his first time in Sarajevo, to which he replied, 'Yup. First time I've been on the ground. But I bombed it a good deal!'

Inevitably, as with every other job I have done, Jane was involved in almost all I did and carried a very considerable burden of her own, not least because our house during the summer seemed always to be full of visitors and because, as in Geneva, she chose not to employ caterers to handle the diplomatic entertaining my job required but to do it herself. Here are extracts from a few of her emails to friends and family back in Britain, which give a flavour of our life in Sarajevo from her perspective:

2 Aug 2002
On Tues I did a farewell dinner for the US General commanding SFOR (NATO's force in BiH). We will be sad to see him go, but at least the evening here wasn't sad!! That's one thing about being posted to a place for 2 yrs, you get to make friends, then they leave, & you'll probably never see them again.

24 Sep 2002
Hi,

We've been quite busy. Had a supper at our house for some returned refugees, which terrified me. I wanted them to feel relaxed & easy with us. I hope they did. Then we had Chris Patten to stay the night, which meant another dinner, then last night another 10 to supper. Thing go on apace. Paddy is as busy as ever. We had hoped to go walking over the w.e. but the weather prevented that. The 1st plan was that P. should go rafting down some gorge or other with a few mad friends, but they decided that as the temperature of the water was minus 4, it was too cold!

25 June 2003
P's well, but tired. I still cannot persuade him to take more than 10 days away from here. He has just had a pretty tiring trip to New York, Washington, London & Thessalonica. Back home now for a little, I hope. We had our annual reception last night. I do thank God there is a lot of the Lib Dem in the average Bosnian. The Lib Dems seem programmed to go home as soon as the raffle is drawn. Here, after about 1hr they just seem to melt away

28 April 2005
Poor old P. has been negotiating all week. Left on Sunday, comes home today. I shall be glad to get him back. At least he will be tired & pleased at the unexpected success they had, better than tired and unsuccessful!

Well, have a couple of journalists round to supper, so must off and make a cottage pie.

Clarissa Eden once said that at the time of the 1956 crisis she felt that the Suez Canal was flowing through her drawing room. Jane must sometimes have had similar feelings.

8 October 2002
This weekend was another to zoom past unnoticed, filled with meetings in smoke-filled rooms in our house, impromptu meals & dashing out for more beers, etc. I guess more of the same until a new government is formed. Last time, I am told, it took 3 months.

21 Jan 2003
Last w.e. came and went, without really being noticed. There was a crisis & wall to wall meetings downstairs in the dining room, with lots of tea & coffee consumed. However P. did manage 3 hrs skiing yesterday, between meetings and hair-tearing!!

Over the next nearly four years, despite the crises and the difficulty of herding diplomatic cats, we did manage to make some progress. We took Bosnia's three armies, which had just fought a vicious war of annihilation against each other, and combined them into one army under the control of the state and on its way to joining NATO. We dismantled the entire complex, fractured and broken taxation system of the country and replaced it with a single VAT system, all in less time than any other country has ever brought in VAT. We got rid of the country's three secret services and created a single unified intelligence service, under the control of Parliament. We got rid of corrupt judges, created a state-wide judiciary and put together a body of modern law, consistent with Bosnian tradition and European standards.

We made the state government more effective and somewhat better able to govern the country. We stripped out many of the old communist business-destroying laws and liberalised the economy, so that by the time we left in 2006 Bosnia's economic growth was five percent a year, the fastest in the Balkans – albeit from a very low, war-shattered base. We unified Bosnia's two customs services into a single service, created a Bosnian equivalent of the FBI at state level and set it to work tackling high-level crime and corruption and arresting or neutralising some of the leaders and crime kings of Bosnia's corrupt structures, in Government and outside it. We broke the logjam of non-cooperation from the local Serb authorities in capturing war criminals, sending a total of thirteen indictees to The Hague, including some of Karadžić's and Mladić's closest lieutenants. And we reunited the divided city of Mostar, whose great bridge was also finally rebuilt and opened in my time. In the process, we handed whole chunks of things the internationals had been doing to the Bosnian authorities and cut the staff and budget of my own organisation, the OHR, by a third.

In case I am giving the impression that either I or the international community did all these things by ourselves, we did not. Nearly all the great changes made in my time were not done by me or using my powers – they were passed through the democratic processes and Parliaments of Bosnia, so that the country could qualify to start the process which, hopefully, will eventually end with full membership of the European Union. It is fashionable in international circles to criticise the dysfunctionality of Bosnia's institutions and the ineffectiveness of its politicians. But Bosnia's structural dysfunctionality is not of the Bosnians' making. It was the international Dayton Peace Agreement which gave this poor and war-shattered country of 3.5 million people, eleven mini-states made up of cantons and entities and no less than twelve Prime Ministers, each with their own mini-government. I am not criticising Dayton here. The compromises and complexities of Dayton were necessary in order to get peace – and there is no responsible person I know, in Bosnia or out of it, who would not have preferred even a very untidy peace, to the continuing slaughter. But this left Bosnia with a huge problem when, with stability and peace achieved, it became necessary to build a functioning state. And that was our task in 2002: to start to build the institutions of effective government. And this meant beginning slowly to dismantle the structures of Dayton, to which most still clung for security, in order to build a state which many had fought and died to prevent coming into existence. The fact that we managed to make some progress down this road depended, not on the wisdom of the international community, but on the political courage and ability to compromise of many Bosnian leaders, whom we often insisted should take the kind of risks with their popularity which very few of our Western democratic leaders would ever have countenanced. The heroes of Bosnia's slow and painful rebirth are not the High Representatives or the international community, but the Bosnians themselves, and especially the long-suffering ordinary people of this remarkable little country, who, in the main, just want to try to live again as neighbours.

One of the most frightening aspects of my job was that, in order to get things moving, I often had to challenge the opinions of elected representatives – and sometimes use my powers to overrule them, where I believed that what was at stake was in the best interests of *all* the citizens of Bosnia and Herzegovina, rather than the sectional interests of the ethnic groups they represented. This is, on the face of it, an undemocratic thing to do, but the alternative would have been to let progress be vetoed at every step when the representatives of one or other of the three peoples of Bosnia chose to do so. It is also a very scary thing to do. Because, when a politician representing an ethnic interest threatened that his people would be out on the streets if we did X, we had to have sufficient confidence in our own judgement about what the people of Bosnia really wanted, or at least were prepared to tolerate, to be able to push ahead nevertheless. So we spent a very great deal of time measuring and gauging public opinion and building up public support.

My policy was to make myself as visible and available as I could, both to ordinary Bosnians and to their political representatives. I gave instructions that my drivers were not to use the flashing blue lights and police escorts which were (and still are) beloved of international diplomats and important Bosnians alike, but instead to drive around in as normal a way, and with as little disruption to the lives of ordinary Bosnians, as possible. I insisted (against some opposition from our security people) that the gates of my office building should be left open, so that it looked less like a fortress. I instituted regular speeches to Bosnia's Parliaments, followed by an open Question Time, and made it clear that any decision I took as the international High Representative could be challenged through the Bosnian Constitutional Court, and that, though not legally required to under international law, I would nevertheless abide by its judgements. And I walked to work through the Sarajevo streets and markets almost every morning, instead of using the armoured BMW thoughtfully provided by Her Majesty's Government. On one of my early walks I came across an old, destitute man selling plastic lighters for one KM* on the corner of Sarajevo's Cathedral Square. I pressed a 2 KM piece into his hand, wished him 'Dobro Jutro' (good morning) and walked on. To my surprise he ran after me shaking his white stick and shouting angrily. I stopped so he could catch up and, puzzled, asked what I had done wrong. 'What's this?' he said with real anger, as with force he pushed my coin back into my hand. 'What do you think I am? A beggar? Well I'm not. I'm a lighter-seller!' After that I bought a lighter from him every morning I found him there, bitter winter and boiling summer alike, accumulating a collection of more than two hundred before I left Sarajevo.

---

* KM or Konvertibilua Marka, the Bosnian currency was set up in pre-Euro days and was based on the German Deutschmark at the rate of just a fraction of a cent below 2 KM to the Deutschmark. In our time 1 KM was worth just a little over 30p.

To the great annoyance of the Sarajevo *carsia* (coffee-house society), who thought my job was to be there for them, Jane and I also spent a great deal of time out of the city, living and working with ordinary Bosnians, especially the poorest and most disadvantaged, much as I had done when researching *Beyond Westminster* or in my old constituency. These visits gave me a vital understanding of what life was actually like for ordinary people. I am a great believer in the African-chief theory of leadership. African chiefs accumulated cattle in their *kraals* in order to sell or trade them so as to achieve things they wanted to achieve. That's how I see popularity: not a bubble bath to be wallowed in, but a store which is accumulated to 'trade in' when you need to get things done.

These visits out of Sarajevo also gave Jane and me some of our most moving and unforgettable experiences. Here is one detailed extract from my diary which gives a flavour of one of our trips.

Tuesday 10 June 2003

It took us a good two hours to drive to Visegrad [in eastern Bosnia], with much lightning and rain as we passed over Romanija mountain. But we burst into the Drina valley in glorious sunshine, having followed the old Austrian railway line that runs down through the tight little gorge from Rogatica. Here the road skirts the Drina, plunging through cliffs in a series of dramatic tunnels. . . . Then sharply left and dizzily up the mountain rampart, skirting along the edge of a steep slope, with the Drina thousands of feet below us as we climbed and climbed. Finally we arrived at the little hamlet of Rogrohica, with barely half a dozen houses, all but one of them burnt out.

We stopped by one blackened and roofless ruin, alongside which was placed an extremely decrepit and disintegrating tent with the faded letters 'UNHCR' still clearly visible. This was the home of our hosts, Ahmed and Sebiŝa Setkić, who had lived in this tent on this spot, fierce Bosnian winter and boiling summer alike, for the last two years.

Ahmed, brown as a berry with a nose as sharp as a hawk's and eyes to match, is seventy-seven and Sebiŝa seventy-four. They have lived here since the war, eking out a living by growing vegetables, chiefly potatoes, paprika and onions on the little patch of land by their house and waiting for a foreign donation to help them rebuild their burnt-out home.

We sat round a rough table outside the tent and chatted, as I idly watched some clouds beginning to gather in the distance and silently marvelled at the Drina sparkling in the sunlight thousands of feet below us and the tumbling cliffs pouring down the mountains into the valley below. This is where the Emperor Diocletian in the third century drew the line to separate the Eastern and the Western Roman Empires.

Ahmed's life story, as he told it to me in the slanting sunlight on his little patch of land on the mountainside, was just a modern version of the fate of so many particles of human dust caught up in the conflicts spawned by this great fault line down the march of the centuries.

A Muslim, he had been born in this house, as had his father and his grandfather before him. His grandfather had lived to a hundred and twenty-five, and his father to over a hundred. The land round here and the special air of the Drina valley, was the best in Bosnia, he said.* Everybody here lived to a ripe old age – unless they were killed in the mindless storms of war which, generation after generation, swept over them for unknowable reasons in far-away places.

Then, their lot was not peace and the quiet enjoyment of simple lives, but burnt houses and blood and the swift exodus to the hidden, traditional places in the caves and forests where father, and grandfather too, had hidden before. And then always the sly return when the madness had passed and the back-breaking job of rebuilding their houses, reclearing their land and replanting their crops.

It had happened to Ahmed three times in his seventy-seven years. First the Germans burnt his house in 1941, then the Partisans in 1943. Then, in 1992, Arkan came.† He had been the worst. He killed everything, father, son, mother, daughter, sheep, cats, dogs – nothing was left alive.

As Ahmed told his story, a small crowd of his neighbours materialised around us. One, Šemso from a neighbouring village, showed me the wound in his jaw where he had taken a bullet fleeing from Arkan's troops as they had swept through the mountains to his village.

Ahmed told us many had died. Every house had been burnt. He had stayed behind with his son to try and defend their homes. They had held Arkan up for a couple of days, but his troops had heavy weapons, and the villagers only had only hunting rifles. In the end they had been forced to flee. He and his family had spent the war years in besieged Sarajevo.

---

* I found this was the eternal claim wherever you go in Bosnia and Herzegovina where an obsession with health is a national pastime. Everyone believes they have the best air, the best grass and, above all, the best plums and *šlivović*.

† Arkan (real name Željko Ražnatović) was the most infamous of the Serbian warlords. He personally commanded the notorious Arkan's Tigers, who brought systematic terror to Croatia in 1991 and Bosnia from 1992 to 1995. He was indicted by the ICTY in the Hague in 1997, but was assassinated in Belgrade in 2000, and so never stood trial.

But three years after the war ended he decided to try and return. At first they had just come back for the weekend, braving hostility from the local Serbs. Then, two years ago, they had received a tent from UNHCR, which they had put up alongside their burnt-out house and come back for good – except if the winter got really bad, when they returned to Sarajevo to stay with relatives until the better weather came.

At about 6 o'clock the skies suddenly opened, and it started to rain fiercely. We took shelter in a nearby empty house. Soon the rain changed to hailstones, which got progressively larger and larger until they were the size of a gob-stopper marbles, dancing in wild profusion on the grass and rattling cacophonously off the corrugated roof of a nearby shed. We watched as showers of unripe plums were knocked off the trees and Ahmed's vegetables took a severe battering. After about twenty minutes it stopped, and we wandered out to inspect the damage.

To my horror I saw that the hailstones had gone right through the rotten fabric of Ahmed's tent, in which Jane and I were to spend the night. The tent now looked as though a host of shotguns had been fired at it, and there were large puddles of mud where we were to sleep.

Ahmed and I decided to go off for a walk while the ground dried, picking our way along the mountainside on an old track, until we came to an ancient graveyard of stećaks* *positioned on a prominent saddle overlooking the Drina valley. Ahmed told me that he thought that the* stećaks *were left by the Romans, but I told him that historians believe them to be from the time of the Bogomils, who were originally heretic Christians who had come to Bosnia in the thirteenth century.*

He told me that there are other, older graves nearby and pointed out a collection of broken stone sarcophagi poking out of the ground about fifty metres away. These appeared, to my uneducated eye, to be much older, perhaps even Neolithic.

We then wandered back along the track, chatting about history, the ancient settlement of this land, of life, of war, of our children, of women and of plum harvests and the countryside. By the time we got back to the tent, a large fire had been lit and the sać† *was steaming away on the fire, smelling delicious.*

---

* *Stećaks* are a kind of gravestone or marker peculiar to this area of the Balkans. They consist of huge blocks of often intricately carved limestone.

† Pronounced 'satch', this is the traditional form of Bosnian cooking vessel: a circular metal dish, into which the meat – usually lamb – is put with water, potatoes, onions and vegetables. This is then covered with a metal hood and placed on the embers of a fire, with embers also piled over the hood, so that the whole cooks very slowly from top and bottom simultaneously.

We all sat down under the gathering twilight, drank beer, ate lamb and chatted by the glow of the fire until it grew dark, and the stars came out, and the moon shone in a watery sky above us.

At around ten o'clock everyone started to drift off home.

It had been agreed that Jane and I should sleep in the tent, so Ahmed and Sebiša went off to a neighbouring house, which had recently been rebuilt, while we settled down for the night.

Before we went to bed Ahmed told us to watch out for snakes. When they first moved back they had lived in a nearby stable and had been constantly plagued by snakes. Several had come in each night, and they used to hear them hissing and fighting with Ahmed's dog (a stocky little terrier of uncertain breeding, but courageous as a lion. Ahmed said he had been out seeing off a wild boar which had come to forage in Ahmed's vegetables the previous night). Neither of these stories was especially conducive to settling down for a good night's sleep.

Nevertheless, dog tired, we fell asleep fairly quickly, lulled by the sounds of the night and the drip of the wet canvas above us.

The next morning we were up at 5.30 and washed at a tap fed from a nearby mountain stream. Everything damp and musty. This morning the clouds were lying in the valley below covering the Drina. But as the sun came up these gradually cleared to reveal an astonishing view down the valley, of the Drina sparkling in the early morning sunshine below us.

In due course we all gathered around the embers of last night's fire, which Ahmet fanned into a roaring flame again and on which he soon had a pot of strong Bosnian coffee bubbling away, waiting for us. We all sat down, some ten of us, to a breakfast of cold lamb, kajmak* pura† and boiled eggs before saying our farewells and returning down the valley.

Jane's emails recorded her own impression of other visits we made together to all the four corners of Bosnia during our years there and of some of her work with those who had suffered most. (On these visits out of Sarajevo, we were careful to ensure that we visited and stayed with families from all three of Bosnia's communities, equally – although, coincidentally, all the descriptions quoted here relate to visits to Muslim families.)

---

* Bosnian cottage cheese from the mountains.
† A kind of polenta, much favoured by the poor in the Balkans.

11 Aug 2002

Paddy is well, in fact he surprises me as to how well he is , when you take how hard he works, the stress he is under, the pressure of the job, etc. He still loves the job, & the ordinary people seem to really appreciate him, too (though I don't think you could include the politicians in that!). I really am very proud of what he has done here. It's as if his whole life has been an apprenticeship for this job. On Friday P and I went to Srebrenica. I can't describe it on 'paper', the story tells its own tale, but we went to all the sites, the football field where 1,500 men & boys were murdered, then to visit people who had returned, all women of course, except one village where we spent the night, where they are clearing the rubble of their destroyed homes. The women had lost husbands, sons, grandsons. It was extremely moving, and very humbling
XXXX
Jane

8 October 2002
Last week took us to some lovely, & not so lovely, places.
Tuesday started gloomy, with low cloud and rain – so no helicopter, which meant an early start driving to Vitez, which used to be a thriving steel town. The only thing the war seems to have done to its (Vitez') advantage is that the air is now fresh, & there are fish in clean rivers, but no jobs & no thriving town any more.

Then to Tuzla, where we stayed in a hotel which was so cold I had to put on P's socks. We visited a newly built centre where they try to help traumatised women. Several Srebrenica women there. P is arranging that there will be a grave for each Srebrenica victim, even if no remains have been found, so that everyone has somewhere to mourn. To the cemetery next day to see the war memorial for all who died between 92 & 96. Over 2,000 names on a Vietnam-style marble memorial. Then a beautiful drive over the hills to Bijeljina, the trees are turning, and the countryside is spectacular. In Bijeljina we visited the hospital. I went to see the children's 'ward', which was worse than some condemned buildings in the UK. The staff were wonderful, though – but only one bath (no shower) between all patients, parents & staff.

23 Oct 2003
The countryside looks superb. The trees are the most wonderful colours, seeming to turn from the tips first. We went off to Goražde to make

šlivović on Sunday. They (Muslims all) had this great machine, belching out steam & 'slivo' one end, being fed by water, wood & fermented plums at the other! Of course it was an excuse for a party. All the friends of this couple seem to bring round their fermented glop of plums, sit about, drink & eat, whilst this machine turns it into firewater.

16 March 2004
Must off. Have 10 women from an organization called 'Women Victims of War' for whom I am doing lunch at our house tomorrow, which I am dreading. All rape victims, some of even worse atrocities. I don't know what I can do for them. I am told that it's best just to listen. Seems good advice to me, but if I had those awful experiences, to go to lunch with this old granny in her posh house would only make me more angry. But I am told they want to come . . . so a quiche-making session ahead.

21 March 2004
My meeting with the Women Victims of War went much better than I could have wished. I was extremely nervous. There were 12 of them – 2 in their 20s, so they must have been in their teens when all this dreadfulness happened. One woman was raped 130 times, & another had 7 family members killed in front of her. How one can go on after that, I just don't know. However, 1 of the young ones, in bright shocking pink, smiling throughout (well nearly), who gave me hope for them She had a job in a plant nursery & therefore can see a future.

There are 1 or 2 things we can do immediately, like register their vehicle. It will cost 400 KM, but too much for them to find all at once. Also they have 7 women who are protected witnesses, but live in a flat without a telephone, which we can sort out for them.

21 July 2005
Just got back from Žepa. Another so called 'safe haven' which wasn't. It is the most beautiful place, snug in a mountain valley, surrounded by mixed woodland. The weather was wonderful, but the life there isn't. We stayed with some elderly refugees. The village has no employment, no school, no medical facilities, no senior school for the kids. The road in is so rough, no one wants to invest. All very sad in a place of such beauty.

I had many partners, national and international, without whose help I would have achieved nothing in Bosnia. But two require special mention. The first was the Bosniak Muslim state Prime Minister, Adnan Terzić. He is less devious than perhaps it is necessary to be in politics, especially in the Balkans, but he is a genuinely good man and a brave one. He was also one of the very few Bosnian politicians I knew who was motivated not by nationalism but by what was best for his country as a whole. The second was the President of the Serb-dominated Bosnian entity the Republika Srpska, Dragan Čavić, whose public acknowledgement of Serb involvement and shame in Srebrenica, involved an act of political courage of the same order as Willy Brandt's statement of atonement at Auschwitz. To my deep regret and pain, both of these men, who were my partners and friends, and who took many personal risks to put their country on the road to a stable peace and the EU, paid with their political careers at the elections after I left. I hope it will not be too long before Bosnia will again recognise that what it needs is more such leaders, not fewer.

One of the policies I instituted when I arrived was to open all positions in the OHR, which had up to then been dominated by internationals, to Bosnians. They proved to be just as able, and in many cases more so, than the internationals who had been sent to Bosnia to do jobs that they could easily have done – with the added and priceless advantage that they knew the country and its customs and traditions. They were a wonderful team to work with, and I was very sorry indeed to have to part from them when my mandate was over.

Nevertheless (and despite their help), I made many mistakes too, of course. I probably devoted so much time to trying to persuade the Serbs that they could not be a state within a state that I may have overlooked the importance of the Croats. I cannot pretend, either, that every decision I made about the use of my powers to make things happen faster was wise, for some were not. Towards the end I probably got a little too impatient to get things done quickly. Indeed I did not realise just how frustrated and impatient I got in the last days of my mandate as I pushed forward the final reforms, especially to Bosnia's fractured and politically dominated police forces. But Jane did. Here is her description of this time, in an email to a friend:

8 June 2005
Why is it that one goes through periods of one's life when everything
seems to turn to shit? We are passing through one of these periods.
The Republika Srpska government have now turned down police
reform, therefore shutting off the Bosnians' path to Europe. The P.M.
(Muslim) has just sacked the Foreign Minister (Serb), & Mostar
have problems with this year's budget [sic]. I have a husband in the
deepest despair. Just to add to the sweetness & light, it has been rain-
ing since Sunday, with no sign of a let-up in the forecast until next
Thursday!! Snow has been reported somewhere in Bosnia (can't
remember where, & I doubt I could spell it if I could!) Flaming June
eh! And we have our first 2005 guests arriving this eve! Watch this
space. Lots of love from us both,
Jane XXXXXXXXX

With hindsight, I think I should not have left Bosnia until this last
great reform – the reform of Bosnia's police force – was properly
secured. To my regret, much of this has been allowed to unravel by the
international community (and especially the EU). For this, I fear,
Bosnia will pay heavily in the future.

And there were failures, too. The biggest was that Radovan
Karadžić and Ratko Mladić remained at large when I left – despite a
determined attempt to capture them that was conducted with my
partners, the US Generals commanding the NATO force in Bosnia
and the British General leading the European Union force (EUFOR)
that took over in 2005. One look at Karadžić, when he was eventually
captured, with that long beard and unkempt hair, confirmed to me
what I suspected at the time, that he was almost certainly protected
during many of his years as a fugitive, not by his 'cover' as a 'doctor of
alternative medicine', but by being disguised as a monk in the Serbian
Orthodox Church. I am delighted that he is now, at last, in The Hague
– where, I am told, I may have to return for the fourth time, to give
evidence at his trial.

But General Mladić, who is accused of having the blood of
Srebrenica more directly on his hands, remains at liberty, protected in
his case, I am sure, by renegade elements of the Serbian state security
structures. There cannot be a stable peace in the western Balkans
without justice in Bosnia, and justice will remain incomplete until

these two primary architects of the Bosnian horrors both end up in The Hague where they belong.

Some things with which I was engaged in Bosnia were not strictly speaking part of my job, but being involved in them gave me a great sense of privilege, nevertheless. Perhaps none more so than leading the international fund-raising effort to establish the memorial graveyard with room for eight thousand Muslim men and boys at Srebrenica, opened by President Clinton on 20 September 2003. This beautiful and moving site with its thousands of simple white headstones,* built on the very spot where the Serbs gathered their victims before they were taken away to be murdered, will in time, I hope, become one of the world's iconic symbols of remembrance and a testimony to what happens when the international community remains silent in the presence of great evil.

It was my involvement in this project that brought me into contact with a little group of Bosniak Muslims who lived at a place called Sutjeska, in the mountains immediately above Srebrenica. When the Serbs stormed through in 1995 they all fled. But in 2002, on my first visit to the town, I heard that some had moved back and, with Jane, drove through the forest and along the vertiginous mountain tracks to find them. What we discovered when we got to Sutjeska was a small community of women led by one of the very few men to have escaped the massacre, called Hasib Huseinović. He had been the first to return, with his wife Fatima and his daughter Fadila. Jane and I were very moved by the courage of these women who had moved back into the area where they had lost husbands, sons, fathers and grandfathers and settled down to rebuild their burnt houses, clear their land and live amongst their Serb neighbours again. We both felt humbled by the fact that, faced with the same experiences, we would never have had the courage to do what they did. During our visit we discovered that they had some goats, but desperately needed a cow, for milk and cheese and for calves with which they could start a new herd. So we bought one and arranged for it to be sent to them. When we visited them a last time before leaving Bosnia, and Hasib 'spun a lamb'† in our honour, we were delighted to find that our cow had had produced two daughters, and the little community was thriving. Jane's email home tells it all:

---

* There are about two thousand there at the moment – the number of bodies which have so far been identified from the Srebrenica remains.
† A Bosnian tradition in which a whole lamb is roast on a spit over an open fire, often as a welcome tribute to a guest.

1 April 2004
We had a great trip to Srebrenica. We went to the village we first vis-
ited when we first got here. They now have another 15 odd houses
rebuilt, with animals, ducks, chickens, dogs, & of course, the cow we
gave them last time is pregnant again, they also have another calf too.
So slowly, slowly and step by painful step. Best of all was the young
girl who had lost all her brothers & Father, and then her Mother died
of a broken heart. She now has a new house, was working out in the
fields, & ran towards us, grinning from ear to ear. They have a huge
green house, & electricity at last. There were tears, of course, but of joy
this time.

The story is not all happiness, however. In 2005 the remains of Hasib's
son were identified by the International Commission for Missing
Persons, using DNA identification techniques, as one of those killed in
the Srebrenica massacre. I attended the Srebrenica memorial service on
11 July that year when Hasib's son was buried. Here is my diary entry
for that day:

Before the ceremony I bumped into Hasib in the huge crowd. He told me
that his son was amongst those to be buried today. He was trying to be
stoic, as a man should, but his big round eyes filled with tears that
wouldn't keep back. And Fatima and Fadila, who were with him, were
weeping uncontrollably
  After the ceremony, I asked Darko [my interpreter] if he would go and ask
Hasib and Fatima if they would mind if I came down and helped him fill in
their son's grave.* He came back and said that I would be very welcome. So,
as the VIPs dispersed around us, we broke off and made our way across the
mud, pressing through the vast crowds of mourners. Everywhere there were
small groups standing by open graves waiting for the coffins to arrive. People
were amazingly kind, stretching out and shaking my hand, asking for my
photograph, and saying how much they wanted me to stay. One woman said
that I was their Tito; please would I not go? Although another, a lawyer
from Travnik, gruffly told me I should be doing more to catch war criminals.
  We made our way down through the mud and the crowds to the end of the
graveyard where Hasib's son was to be buried. By now the coffins, each cov-
ered in green cloth [the Muslim colour of mourning], were arriving, passed
from hand to hand in a long column over the crowd's heads to the terrible

---

* It is Muslim custom that male friends at a funeral help to fill in the dead person's grave.

shrieking and wailing of the women. When I came up to grave number 83, there was Hasib standing erect, his arms around Fatima, and Fadila, who were pressed against him as tight as wrecks cast up on a rock. As the coffins came, dancing on outstretched hands towards the little tableau, like frail green barques tossed on a sea of grief, I watched Hasib, his big brown face now broken with sorrow and streaming with tears, craning his neck for the first sight of coffin number 83, which would bear the remains of his beloved son to him at last. I thought of what he had told me the first time we had met; he had parted from his son there, at the corner of that field, Hasib had said, pointing. He had told the boy that he would go through the woods. His son had replied that he would take his chances with his friends and flee along the roads. They had then shaken hands, wished each other good luck and parted. Hasib had watched the boy until a bend in the track hid him from view and had replayed this last image in his mind a thousand times since. He had only come back to Sutjeska because he knew that, one day his son would walk over the hill and join him again in the place where they had parted. And now, instead of scanning the horizon for his son coming over the hill, he was searching for coffin number 83, which would bring him the last few shards of bone that were the only remains of his beloved boy.

As coffin 83 was born up to him, Hasib leapt into the grave, in Muslim fashion, to prepare the bed on which the coffin would lie and, with infinite gentleness, guided it as it was slowly lowered in. I moved towards the mound of earth to help the friends fill the grave, only to find Fadila already there, spade in hand. I gently took the spade from her (women aren't supposed to do this), and started digging furiously to hide my tears. In due course someone came and took the spade from me so that they could take their turn at filling in the grave. I pressed past the mourners to put my arm around Hasib and mumble something unintelligible about there being no words to express my sorrow, and Jane's too. He mumbled some reply between bitter tears.

As I looked back there was Fadila on top of the mound again. I was afraid she was going to throw herself into the grave, so I moved back towards her and, as I approached, she threw herself at me, crushing herself in my arms, and weeping uncontrollably as great waves of sorrow mixed with anger wracked her body. So, I confess, did I. I just cannot imagine what it must be like to have to bury your own kith and kin in such circumstances.

We made many, many good friends like Hasib in Bosnia.

But I made quite a lot of enemies, too. The Serbs mostly disliked me because they knew I was trying to build a state, and this meant reducing the powers of the state within a state which they had created in Republika Srpska. The Bosnian Muslims liked me for much the same reason, but they also disliked me because I refused to allow them to name Sarajevo International Airport, which represented all ethnicities in the country, after their wartime leader (and my friend) Alija Izetbegović. The Croats disliked me because they knew I would resist their attempts to create a breakaway mini-state in the south and because I removed their directly elected President when he was indicted for corruption. The crime kings and war-criminal-protection networks of Bosnia, of whatever ethnicity, all hated me because we mounted a determined attack on their structures and businesses.

Nevertheless, and despite many really frightening moments when I feared I had got it wrong, I am proud of the job we did in Bosnia. By and large, the Bosnian people showed incredible patience with my faults and unwavering generosity and hospitality to both Jane and I, and for this I am very grateful to them.

We also had some very good times and made many good friends. Here are some more of Jane's emails home which give a flavour of our daily lives, our Bosnian friends and the rhythm of the Sarajevo seasons:

17 June 2002
Hi,
We really are now settled in. You can get everything here, except mango chutney (even Marmite and Branston Pickle).

Our home is now complete with curtains scrounged again from the Brits; they seem to have a cavern filled with things people may need. Anyway I now have their curtains, lengthened, shortened pulled and persuaded to hang at the windows. The weather is hot & sticky, but pleasant. We have a family of magpies in our garden. I think they will be the only 'pets' as yet. P is very well. Relaxed but working hard. I still have no wheels, which is frustrating, and have blisters from walking to market!!

23 March 2003
I am sitting at Paddy's desk, overlooking the bowl of the city of Sarajevo. On the mountain opposite there is just a smidgin of snow lying. It has all gone very quickly this year, probably due to the fantastic weather we have

been having in the last 2 weeks. The winter pallor seems to have left people's faces, the tables & chairs have appeared on the streets, & people are now strolling around enjoying the warmth, sitting out drinking coffee – which is a really serious thing here, & can last for hours.

24 April 2003
Well, the gentle rain falleth from the heavens, now all we need is for a little bit of sun & warmth & we will be O.K. I am slightly encouraged today, as I found that some of the feverfew seeds I bought from home had germinated. Now I shall have a garden full of them!! This w.e. we are going to be able to plant the bottom bit of the garden at the house we have just purchased on the shores of Lake Jablanica about an hour from Sarajevo. I have decided to plant ground-covering roses & conifers. I'm also going to try to find some grass seed with wild flowers which I am told you can get, for the bottom of the garden, which is planted out with fruit saplings. Plums for šlivović, of course.

3 June 2003
The countryside is looking absolutely fabulous. The blossom received a kick in the teeth late in April, with a series of late frosts, which did no good to the poor fruit-growers in Herzegovina. But since then things have got greener, & what with the false acacia trees, of which there are many, the gorse & the 40 shades of green the countryside looks fantastic. The snows have melted on the mountains, & the lakes have all filled, nearly to their summer levels, & the rivers have swollen a good deal, with all the rain we've had.

21 September 2003
Life continues at a pace, Paddy is still herding Bosnian and international cats with a vengeance. Sometimes he looks so tired I want to weep, but nothing that a whisky & a good night's sleep doesn't put right.

 Last evening we spent with friends in an orchard they own, overlooking Sarajevo. It was really lovely. I got there about 5, & Suzanne & I picked apples, of which they have 1,000's. Then when Paddy arrived, about $^1/2$ hour later, we settled down to pre- barbeque gins & tonics, under the trees. Mirza, who owns the land with his 2 uncles & a cousin, has a workshop on the land, & the uncle lives in the small house. It's quite a spread, right down to the big cemetery on the edge of the city. The uncle *explained that the neighbours (the cemetery) were very good, quiet neighbours, & caused no problems!! Mirza was here through the war, caring for his sick mother, who has since died. He said most of his friends now live all over the world, as they left during the war, & he is rather warier of making new ones, as all they do is leave. He sounded sad & a bit lonely. His wife & child (daughter) went to UK & now still live in Cambridge. but that's the way of it here.*

21 October 2003
Dear Sally,
We woke up to snow, on the ground & falling from the heavens on Monday morning. I hate Mon. morn any way, but that made it worse. It fell nearly all day, but today (Wed) it's nearly all gone, & it's really lovely out, bit misty. The trees are something else. The colours are absolutely breathtaking. I felt like a small child with its first Christmas tree, with all the ohhs & ahhs!!

8 January 2004
We are back in Sarajevo, where we have heavy snow, & a temp. of minus 9!! All the cats are fluffed up, and determined to find a perch which gets their feet off the cold ground. Looking out on the white city, it seems hard to imagine the heat of summer. Bare trees with shivering birds in the tops of them, white roofs, & general grey & white. My poor little garden looks dead, but when you come I hope it will be full of roses! I'm off to Mostar with P tomorrow for a bit of an adventure. Actually I'd better not use that word to him, as I told him I'd had enough of adventures!!
Love from us both, Jane XX

29 January 2004
I will swop your sprinkle of snow for our large dump any day, though I can't say P. will agree. It's feeeeeet deep on everything. Balancing in heaps like icing on trees, chimney pots, phone lines, & TV aerials. I do not like it one bit, though I have to confess it looks quite pretty!!!!
XXXXXXXXXXX

8 February 2005
Hiya! Cold bloody greetings from Sarajevo, where the temperature is hovering around a cool minus 20!! Minus 25 last week! After about 10 mins outside you begin to realise just how bloody cold it is, as the cold

intrudes between the seams of your clothes, & settles in the most unexpected of places! Hard to believe we were sweltering in 43 in the shade not 6 months ago. We have been back but a few days to the snowbound wastes (actually rather beautiful in the evening light, as long as you're inside!) of Sarajevo, after a lovely break at home.

Jane and I were the first members of an international organisation to invest in the country, buying a house on the edge of the very beautiful Lake Jablanica outside Sarajevo, where we spent many weekends and where our children, grandchildren and friends came to visit us each summer. My other summer passion was walking on Bosnia's incomparable mountains. Together with friends and with the help of a Bosnian mountain guide, Fikret Kahrović, I climbed all Bosnia's highest peaks, as well as Durmitor, the highest mountain in neighbouring Montenegro.

In the winter we skied. Winter sports in Bosnia, the home of the 1984 winter Olympics, are rather more rugged than most pampered Alpine skiers would be prepared to accept. But it was good fun and challenging in equal measure, especially when combined with a long Bosnian lunch and a hefty helping of *šlivović*. Her Majesty's Government decided at the start of my tour that I should have full-time protection while in Bosnia, and this was provided by a team of (usually eight) Royal Military Police, who came out for six months at a time. They went everywhere with me and even lived in our house, where they became, for Jane, a rotating collection of sons and daughters who joined our family every half year. They were outstandingly professional, and I grew to rely on them utterly. When it came to the winter team, however, they had to be able to ski, or learn very quickly indeed. This they did with variable success and some casualties along the way. During the 2004 winter season no fewer than three of them broke bones while skiing with me, and I was abruptly instructed by their headquarters that they were running out of replacements, and please would I be more careful with their soldiers in future.

Nor was their job unnecessary, for there were, I was informed, three death threats against me which the teams took seriously. One was apparently a contract let out to the Chechens for two million Euros – which I thought insultingly cheap, all things considered. The upshot, though, was that, when we came to leave after nearly four years, I was strongly advised that we should sell our beloved house on the lake; there would be no means of protecting it after we left, and it would be bound to be blown up or burnt. It broke our hearts to do this (and didn't help the bank balance either, for we had to sell at a heavy loss) but there was no alternative.

Mostly, events in the outside world passed us by during my years in Bosnia. In part this was because my position as an international civil servant precluded me from getting involved in politics, but the main reason was that all my energies and all my focus were directed on my Bosnian mandate. There were two exceptions, though.

The first was the Iraq war, which placed me in a delicate situation in Sarajevo. My job was to hold together an international coalition upon which all the resources and all the support I needed to get things done in Bosnia depended. The problem was that this coalition (which included, of course, all the major European countries and the US) was deeply divided over the wisdom of launching an attack on Iraq. I decided that my duties to Bosnia had to come before my desire to make my views on the subject public, so I kept silent. But I did write a private letter to Tony Blair on the eve of the conflict, saying I thought he was right to go ahead. Supporting the Iraq war now looks like a major error of judgement on my part – and one not much diminished by the fact that, like most others, I believed what I had been told about weapons of mass destruction, nor by the excuse that the war phase of the Iraq intervention was actually a success. It was what happened afterwards which turned it all into a catastrophe.

With a few months to go before the end of my tour, the Liberal Democrats swam back into my life again, too. Jane and I had gone home to the UK for Christmas 2005, returning to Bosnia by car on the very day my son's partner had our second granddaughter, Annie Rose, born on 30 December 2005.

While we were in the UK, there was much gossip and chatter about Charles Kennedy's leadership. Back in Bosnia, on 5 January 2006 I was telephoned by my successor in Yeovil, David Laws, speaking, he said, on behalf of a number of MPs especially from the new intake after the 2001 elections. Things were becoming intolerable with Charles. If he did not stand down by the following Monday (i.e., in four days' time), then David and twenty-two other key MPs would sign a public statement resigning from the front bench. They would then support Ming Campbell as the new Leader. Did I have any thoughts on this? I told David that I thought the timing was wrong – it would be mistaken by the Press and public as a panic reaction to the recent successes of David Cameron (by then elected leader of the Tories). Better to wait till later in the year. Moreover, I was not at all sure that this would be right for the Party, or for Ming. His age would be a real problem. I was, as he knew, a great Ming fan and had hoped he would stand when I had stood down. But the Press would now have a field day with his age, which would make it very tough for him, and probably uncomfortable for the Party too. It would be better, I suggested, to skip a generation and go for Nick Clegg. David replied that, if Nick stood then a number of the other younger MPs would stand as well, and this would lead to an unholy mess. They needed something clean, and Ming would make an excellent bridge to the next generation of younger MPs with ambitions (of which David made it clear, he was not one), giving them time to sort themselves out. I thought, but did not say, that this appeared to me to be a classic example of the old political adage that young Cardinals always vote for old Popes. 'Bridge' leaders hardly ever worked, I commented, unless they used the position to make themselves permanent (like Mrs Thatcher), and Ming, for reasons of age, could not do this.

In the next few days it became clear that delaying was not an option, and Charles stood down as Lib Dem Leader very soon afterwards. On the day of Charles's resignation, I spoke to Nick Clegg and told him that, if he stood, he would have my backing, adding that this was the one time in his life that he could lose without losing; he was young enough not to win without that damaging him, and, even if he lost, he would still have succeeded in marking the card, showing that he was ambitious for the job in the future. If he did not stand, however, then I would back Ming. Nick decided not to stand, for reasons I fully understood and which, with the benefit of hindsight, I think were probably right. (Though I do wonder whether, if he had stood, he might not have won – for in the end the contest between Ming and his opponent Chris Huhne was a very close one.)

After my conversation with Nick I rang Ming and offered him my support if he decided to stand, but warned that, for the reasons given above, I was not at all sure this was the best solution for the Party, and that it would be neither easy nor fun for him either.

As the end of my mandate in Bosnia approached, the international community made a determined attempt to persuade me to stay on (they had already persuaded me to extend my time in Bosnia twice, from two years to nearly four). By now, however, Jane was increasingly keen to get home, and I was certain that my effectiveness was decreasing, that I had done my best work and that it was time to hand over to someone else. But our international masters delayed and delayed about finding a replacement, so prolonging the final date for our departure. Once again, Jane's emails illustrate our feelings as we drew closer to our departure date:

6 Oct 2005
Still waiting for our departure date. The 'Powers that Be' want P. to stay. They explain that there is no consensus over a replacement. Well hard bloody cheese, I say. P has done nearly twice what he said he would. Why do they want blood out of the stone? P. says much the same, only in a more polite way!!

5 December 2005
Hooray ! The packers come in on Thursday.
Getting a date for us to leave out of Paddy's masters has been a story in itself, but they have now come up with the end of Jan 2006. His successor, according to well placed rumour, will be a German gentleman of 75 summers!! I can only think they have decided that they have had enough of the whirlwind Ashdown, & want a quiet time! One of the drivers thought he was so old he was dead!!
Paddy has been dragging himself round taking leave from his colleagues & signing off in the past few weeks. So now we will be home by the middle of Feb, as we want to spend some time with the French family skiing before getting back to Blighty. Our new grandchild will be one month old by then. Paddy says he is going to have a whole month doing nothing. I don't know if I quite believe him, but would be really delighted if it were true.

And so, in deep snow on a bitterly cold day at the end of January 2006, after nearly four years in Bosnia, Jane and I flew out of Sarajevo airport on our way home. Jane cried as we left, and I felt very miserable. But I could not complain. I had been exceptionally lucky to have done such a fascinating job, in which every decision I took had a direct and often immediate effect on people's lives. I felt regret at leaving, of course. But I also felt exceptionally privileged to have been involved, for a few years, in the life and future of Bosnia and Herzegovina, which I am confident, despite recent setbacks, will one day be a member of the European Union and prized as one of its little jewels.

CHAPTER 16

Pretending to Be Retired

B LAISE PASCAL, contemplating space, wrote: *Le silence éternel de ces espaces infinis m'effraie* – the eternal silence of these infinite spaces frightens me. I felt much the same about the prospect of retirement. But, once again, I needn't have worried, for it turned out there was plenty to keep me busy.

Before we left Bosnia, Jane and I had teamed up with our children, Kate and Simon, to buy a small chalet in the Savoie region of France, to which we went for a few weeks' skiing holiday straight after leaving Sarajevo. It had always been a lifetime's ambition to have a chalet in the Alps, and this one has given us huge pleasure when, as a family, we gather with our grandchildren, twice in the winter for skiing and once in August to walk in the beautiful Beaufort region close to Mont Blanc.

As soon as we got back to Britain, I started on my next book, *Swords and Ploughshares: Bringing Peace to the 21st Century*.* By now it was plain that the US and Britain had made a number of wholly unnecessary mistakes in the post-conflict reconstruction phase in Iraq. Afghanistan was already looking increasingly difficult, too. I became (and remain) concerned that the pain of burnt fingers in both these places may lead the West to conclude that we cannot make a success of intervention and should never try it again. In fact, the lessons from Iraq and Afghanistan should not be 'never again intervene', but 'never again do it like this'. The history of our efforts in both countries has been one of *hubris*, nemesis and above all amnesia. *Swords and Ploughshares* was an attempt to examine past interventions and from them to identify the lessons which, if applied in future, would make it more likely we would succeed, rather than more likely we would fail. I started writing articles again, too, particularly on Iraq and Afghanistan, and was asked to present a two-hour television documentary on Jerusalem for Channel Four, learning in the process some of the skills of interviewing, rather than being interviewed.

In the spring of 2007 Peter Hain, then the Secretary of State for Northern Ireland, asked me if I would chair a small group of people

* London: Weidenfeld & Nicolson, 2007.

drawn from across the sectarian divide, to see if we could find a long-term solution to the vexed and still explosive issue of parading in Northern Ireland. I agreed, but stipulated that the group I would work with should be selected from people who had real influence on the streets, rather than from among the great and the good. One of those chosen to represent the nationalist viewpoint in our talks was a committed republican activist in the Ardoyne area of Belfast when I was a soldier there in 1960. Walking together through the corridors of Stormont, as our work drew towards its conclusion last autumn, he joked 'I bet you never imagined that one day you would be walking through here with a member of Sinn Fein!' I replied 'You are right. If I had seen you here thirty years ago, I would have arrested you on the spot.' 'Ay,' he replied, laughing, 'I suppose I had better not mention what I would have done to you, if I had seen you first!' My Sinn Fein colleague remains what he always has been, a determined and intelligent advocate for those he represents. But now, along with all the others in our working group from across the Northern Ireland sectarian divide who remain equally committed to their separate viewpoints, we have all found the way to put our different pasts behind us and, through dialogue and compromise rather than the gun, try to build a new future for Northern Ireland.

At the start of our work I went to see Ian Paisley and Martin McGuinness. Though Mr McGuinness, too, was previously active in the IRA, he was now, in partnership with Ian Paisley, heading the Stormont government in Northern Ireland as an effective Deputy First Minister. He started our conversation with the words, 'You know, Mr Ashdown, my people don't trust you, because you were a British soldier.' I replied, 'We were both army men, Mr McGuinness. But that doesn't stop us trying to build the future.' He smiled and wished me good luck.

Right from the start we all agreed that, if we were to succeed in finding a solution to the issue of sectarian parading in Northern Ireland, then what we produced would have to be home-grown, rather than imported in my back pocket from London. So I have acted far more as a convener than as a traditional chairman, leaving both sides to reach their own compromises and agreements. They have done astonishing work, showing real leadership on this very difficult issue, which still retains the capacity to destroy Northern Ireland's miraculous but still fragile progress towards peace. As a result we have made real progress and a workable solution to the issue of parading, based on Northern Ireland's democratic institutions, is within reach. At the time of writing our work, which has been going on for a year, hopefully is drawing towards its conclusion. If we succeed, it will, I hope, make a contribution to long-term peace in the land of my upbringing that I will have been privileged to be associated with. But credit for any success must lie wholly with my colleagues from Northern Ireland, whose courage and willingness to compromise has, I believe, laid the foundations of something really important to the future life of Northern Ireland.

———◆———

So, one way or the other, I found myself as busy as I needed to be and very satisfied with my life. It was therefore a considerable and not wholly welcome surprise to arrive back from a weekend in Somerset on 18 June 2007 to find in my House of Lords mailbox a small pink telephone message slip informing me that the Chancellor of the Exchequer's private office had telephoned and asking me to return the call as soon as I got in.

When I got through to Gordon Brown's Secretary she said that the Chancellor, who was within days of taking over as Prime Minister,* had asked if I would go and see him as soon as was convenient. I said I could make lunchtime on Wednesday, and she confirmed that this would be suitable for him too.

I was, of course, extremely curious about this summons, which set off loud alarm bells in my head. There had been much talk in the Press over the previous few days that Gordon Brown had been impressed with the success of the newly elected French President, Nicholas Sarkozy, in attracting outsiders and even members of opposition parties into his Government, and intended to emulate him in putting together a 'Government of all the talents'.

I immediately put in a call to my own Leader, Ming Campbell, told him about the message and asked if he knew what it was about. He said he did and asked me to come up to his office immediately. When I arrived there were others in the office, but he quickly shooed them out and called in my old friend Archy Kirkwood, now his closest adviser.

It immediately became apparent that Mr Brown had, the day before, approached Ming about Lib Dems, including Anthony Lester, Shirley Williams, Alex Carlile and Julia Neuberger, assisting the Government with discrete tasks, such as heading Government Commissions. I said there could be no objections to this kind of thing; members of opposition

* He became PM a week later, on 27 June.

parties had often carried out such roles for the government of the day – indeed I was fulfilling just such a task in Northern Ireland. But Ming revealed that he had also been discussing something much more ambitious – Lib Dems actually taking up roles in the Government itself, as I had planned with Blair, in 1997. One of the matters which had been discussed was that I should join Gordon Brown's Cabinet as Secretary of State for Northern Ireland. I asked him whether there had been any discussion about an agreed policy programme, including Proportional Representation (PR). For, without this, what Brown was offering us was a deadly suicide pill that would diminish our ability to oppose the Government when we needed to and could seriously damage us in the polls. Ming said there had been no policy discussions. The plan under consideration was, as I understood it, simply to add Lib Dems to the Government, starting with me.

I told him I was very opposed to this. I would be completely isolated, and the Party would be gravely weakened. 'Ming this is madness from your point of view – and mine – but most of all it is madness from the point of view of the Party. How long have you been pursuing this, and are you in detailed negotiations with them?'*

He replied that they had been pursuing it over the last couple of days, with Archy setting up meetings between Ming and the Prime Minister through Alistair Darling, who was therefore also in the loop. I repeated that I thought this was deeply dangerous to him and to the Party.

'This simply will not work. How do I observe collective responsibility in Cabinet when Brown's government mounts – as I am sure they will – a further attack on our civil liberties by extending the period a suspect can be held without being charged? I could not support that! But in Cabinet I would have to, or at least stay silent. If you put this forward to the Party they will reject it, and your leadership will be destroyed.'

I then asked Ming whether or not I should in fact see Gordon Brown under the circumstances. Had he told Ming about asking to see me on a one-to-one basis? Both Ming and Archy confirmed that he hadn't. So, I continued, his approach to me had evidently been made behind Ming's back? Surely I should not go ahead with this? Ming thought, however, that it was worth continuing with the meeting with the Chancellor because we did not know what exactly Mr Brown wanted to offer. It might still be something outside Government of the sort they had also discussed – in which case it would be easier to accept.

* The quotations of conversations in this chapter are taken from my diary.

On Wednesday morning the news of the secret Campbell/Brown talks leaked in the Press with a front-page story in the *Guardian*. In an early-morning radio interview responding to the *Guardian* story Ming made it clear that there could be no question of Lib Dems serving in Brown's cabinet, although he had no objection to individuals assisting the Government in other capacities, as members of the opposition had always done with past governments. The Labour Press operation keeps an eagle eye on all the Press and broadcasts, so I therefore presumed that the future Prime Minister's people would be bound to have heard Ming's interview and informed Brown that any possibility of having Lib Dems actually in the Government was now closed off.

I rang Gordon Brown's office in mid-morning expecting to be told that the meeting was off – but was informed, somewhat to my surprise, that it was still on. I naturally presumed that what this meant was that the proposition the Chancellor was going to discuss with me was not a Cabinet post, but some other task outside government, such as the one I was already doing in Northern Ireland.

When I arrived in his outer office in the Treasury at 2 p.m., the Chancellor came out to meet me, led me into private office, where the two of us, without advisers present, exchanged a few pleasantries and then got pretty swiftly down to business. He said he wanted to reach beyond the confines of the Labour Party in forming his new Government and wanted to know if I would be interested in joining his Cabinet as Secretary of State for Northern Ireland?

I was, to be honest, somewhat taken aback.

Had he discussed this with Ming? He said he had. Did Ming know he was putting this proposition to me today? He confirmed that he didn't.

'Well in these matters, Gordon, I take orders from my boss, and that is Ming. If he asked me to do this I would consider it. But I want you to know that I would say to him that I think it is nonsense. How can I be in your Cabinet and subject to collective responsibility, when you are about to do further terrible damage to our civil liberties to which I and my party are totally opposed? If I were in your Cabinet I would be subject to collective discipline and could not oppose this, could I?'

'Well, could you stay silent?' he asked. I replied that, on issues such as this, I most certainly could not. Moreover, if I was in his Cabinet, this would also greatly diminish my party's capacity to oppose his Government when it became necessary to do so. The Lib Dems would, I continued, thus be reduced as an opposition, and I would be trapped as an isolated individual in a Cabinet in which the majority would always be against me on many of the key issues which I, as a Lib Dem, felt strongly about. 'Are you sure that this is not what you wanted: to emasculate the Lib Dems, rather than forming a partnership with them?'

He strongly denied this, adding that he thought that somehow, as a peer and dealing with the slightly separated issue of Northern Ireland, I could be excused the disciplines of being a member of the Lib Dems so that I could support his Government. This would, he claimed, send a really important signal about the new politics and about the possibility of a relationship between Labour and the Lib Dems in the future. 'Bernard Kouchner* accepted just such a proposition to join the French Government. Why can't you do the same for ours?', he finished.

I replied. 'I am not Kouchner. I am sorry, but I am just not prepared to be locked in a Lib Dem garden shed in the grounds of your Labour mansion. I believe in partnership politics, but it has to based on policy agreements, not disagreements – on things we both believe in, not just bums on cabinet seats. That is what Tony and I were trying to put together in 1997 – a partnership of principle based on a solid programme for a coalition. This is no such thing. Ten years ago, in 1997, was the right time to do this, and we had the right basis for it. If you really believe in this kind of Government why did you oppose it then?'

'Because I couldn't trust the Lib Dems in government then.'

'And you can, now that you are going to be PM?'

He continued, 'Well if you cannot be in my Cabinet, could you, say, be a Minister for Security for Northern Ireland?'

'Gordon, I wish you success. Britain needs a good government, and I hope you can provide it. But my ambitions do not include being a junior member in a Labour Government.'

Our conversation lasted about half an hour, and we parted on good terms. But I noted in my dairy that night

It was clear that he was surprised at my rejection and hadn't expected it. I suspect that never, in his ten years as Chancellor, has he invited someone into his office to offer them an important job which they then turned down. I suspect he will not forgive me for this. He is not like Blair; he can bear a grudge.

* Bernard Kouchner, former UN Special Representative in Kosovo and, at the time of my meeting with Brown, though a member of the French Socialist party, Foreign Minister in Nicholas Sarkozy's government. (See also page 334)

After this flurry of excitement, Jane and I got back to living our lives: I pretending that I was retired, and Jane pretending that she believed me. But fate, in the form of Afghanistan, had other ideas. In October we left on a long-promised visit to see my brother and sister in Australia. I had not seen them since *This is Your Life* in 2001, and my last trip to see them in Australia had been in 1970, on my way back from studying Chinese in Hong Kong. This time Jane and I planned to spend a few weeks with them in order to be able to get to know their families, too, combining this with a trip to New Zealand, which neither of us had ever visited before.

Jane had always said that she would like to go on a cruise once in her life, to see what it was like. So we decided to see New Zealand by taking a two-week trip on a cruise liner. It was not a good idea. This was not New Zealand's fault – it was wonderful and fully up to expectations – but we very quickly decided that cruise ships were not us. I was bored stiff and spent my time taking it out on the gym equipment, and we got hit by two spells of hurricane-force winds. My wife is neither a good sailor, nor a natural lover of the sea (though she is quite happy sitting, watching it from a safe distance). During the height of the two storms we passed through it was all I could do to persuade her that the time had not come to put on her furs and jewels (metaphorically speaking – she has neither in reality) and repair with me to the poop deck to start singing 'Abide with me'.

So it was with considerable relief that at the end of our cruising we arrived in Melbourne to see my brother and sister, together with Jane's cousin Wendy (who had also emigrated to Australia), standing on the quayside waiting for us. We had a wonderful three weeks with them in the Castlemaine area of Victoria, where my parents had made their home when they emigrated in 1959.

On 14 November, during our first week in Australia, we were sitting under a southern sky blazing with stars, having dinner with my sister Alisoun on her patio, when the phone rang. It was the Downing Street exchange,* they had David Miliband, the new Foreign Secretary, on the line. Was it convenient for him to speak to me? A few moments later they put him through.

---

* The Downing Street exchange is one of the least known but most useful bits of Government. It keeps a record of the contact details and regular movements of all key Government and senior political personnel and prides itself on finding find them anywhere in the world at any time of day or night.

Miliband told me that the US and British Governments had been considering their policy on Afghanistan. Each had separately concluded that there had to be a substantial change in the policy if they were to regain the initiative from the Taliban. In due course the Prime Minister would be making a statement about the new approach the Cabinet had agreed on. The Americans had been doing the same thing in Washington. They had arrived at broadly the same conclusions, one of which was that there ought to be an uprated UN Special Representative of the Secretary General (UNSRSG), who would possibly wear three 'hats': those of the UN, NATO, and the EU (in other words the same person would be the head of all three organisations' missions in Afghanistan). After an extensive review of the candidates they had decided to approach me to see if I would do the job. Was I prepared to consider it?

I replied that I *really* did not want to do this. The last thing in the world that I wanted was to disturb my life, with which I was very content. I had done my bit in Bosnia and was now enjoying writing books and articles and doing a little portfolio of jobs, not least for the Government. So I didn't want to do this at all. However, as I had often said to him in the past, I was an old soldier and could, reluctantly, be drafted, provided I was given the instruments to do the job and the mandate was agreed.

Miliband replied that he understood my position, but that they really wanted me to do this. In the next hour, he continued, Nick Burns (whom I had known from Bosnia and who was the most senior official in the State Department) would ring me with a message from Condi Rice, the US Secretary of State, formally asking me to do the job and giving me further details. Finally, he stressed that I was the US candidate for this job, not the British one. But the whole British Government, from the Prime Minister downwards, hoped that I would consider the US proposition. Perhaps after I had thought about it I would, in the next week or so, let the US and UK Governments know my answer?

Half an hour later Burns, rang. He said that we were in a mess in Afghanistan. We had to turn things round; they were relying on me to do it. I repeated that I really did *not* want to do this; I wasn't even certain that it could be done, now. However, as I had said to David Miliband, if they gave me the tools to do the job then – given that young men who had no option were being sent there, and that many of them were dying – I could not refuse.

Burns emphasised that this would not be the same as Bosnia: I would not have the Bonn powers. I replied that I fully understood that. Afghanistan was a sovereign state with a sovereign government. The international community's job would be to help it, not to do things for it. I asked him to thank the Secretary (Condi Rice) for her confidence and promised to give her proposal thought and send him an email in a couple of days giving my response.

Jane and I spent much of the night talking about this bombshell that had dropped so suddenly into our lives. Jane was, of course, very unhappy at the prospect of my being away for another two years (this time she would not be able to come with me) and concerned about the security aspects of the job. But she was, as always, very philosophical. As she put it, if young Marines had no choice but to go there and risk their lives, then however much neither of us wanted this, we couldn't easily say no.

Apart from the prospect of being parted from the family and the personal disruption to my life, my assessment at the time was that the job they were asking me to do was virtually undoable, and I had no particular wish to end my public career on a task for which failure was the most likely outcome. On the other hand, given my experiences in Bosnia and elsewhere, if they would give me the tools necessary for a fighting chance of success, I would not be able to look at myself in the mirror if, for purely personal reasons, I were to say No on such an important issue.

So I drew up a list of conditions I believed were necessary for success, the most critical of which was that I must have the right to give political advice to the American General commanding NATO and US troops in Afghanistan. I then sent these back to Burns by email, saying that if they would accept them, then I would seriously consider their proposals; if not, they should look for someone else. I told Jane that I believed I had pitched my demands so high that the Americans were bound to say no – especially on the right to advise US commanders.

Over the next weeks, however, all the conditions I asked for, including the right to advise US commanders, were agreed by the US and UK Governments. One of my stipulations was that President Hamid Karzai, the head of the Afghan Government should agree to my appointment – I had always criticised the fact that far too often the international community imposed its nominees on host countries without any consultation with, let alone agreement from, the countries concerned.

Jane and I returned to Britain at the end of November and shortly afterwards I met the British Ambassador in Kabul, Sherard Cowper-Coles, for coffee in the Lords. He piled on the emotional pressure, 'We are going to hell in a handcart out there. We are appealing to you to do it.' I replied that it was no sort of incentive to be asked to do this on the basis that I was the drowning man's last straw. The real question was, could we succeed? He thought we still could, but only if the international community started to get its act together, soon.

I had another conversation with Nick Burns shortly afterwards and sought his assurance that Karzai knew of this plan and was prepared to support me, telling him that the job would become completely impossible unless I had the full support and co-operation of the elected Afghan Government. He assured me that Karzai was fully on board and, indeed, enthusiastic.

In early December I started putting together a small team to help me prepare for the job, which, it was decided, should begin at the end of March 2008. Ian Patrick came back to join me again, shaking his head and saying, 'I am afraid I am just not going to let you go out there alone – you will just get yourself into too much trouble.'

I was also joined by one of the brightest of my old OHR Bosnia colleagues, Daniel Korski, and by an extremely able US State Department official, Caitlin Hayden, who was sent over from Washington to help. We set up a small office in the Foreign Office and, with informal help from some of my old Bosnian team (including Ed Llewellyn, who was now working for David Cameron, and who Cameron kindly agreed could provide me with occasional advice) and the assistance of senior Foreign Office officials (including, crucially, some of my old employers), we put together a plan.

Three months before Miliband's phone call to me in Australia, I had written a number of articles saying that I thought we were well on our way to losing in Afghanistan. But by the time we had finished assembling our plan (which included three key priorities – security, the rule of law and improving governance – to which all our efforts and all our aid would be exclusively directed), I concluded that success was still just possible, given enough determination and a good deal of luck. Nevertheless, I wanted to warn Prime Minister Brown and Foreign Secretary Miliband what the bottom line in Afghanistan could still turn out to be. And so I wrote them a very blunt, confidential minute which I sent to them both just before Christmas. This is reprinted in the Appendix.

On 11 December, I flew out to for a secret meeting with Hamid Karzai in Kuwait. He was there for discussions with the Kuwaiti Government and staying in the official palace set aside for important visitors, where it was agreed I should meet him for breakfast on 12 December.

President Karzai is an impressive-looking man, although quite feline and with a curiously soft handshake. He showed me into a room in which there was a table groaning with a huge breakfast and sat me down beside him. Around the table were all the members of his Cabinet: his Foreign Minister, and the Ministers of the Interior, Defence, Finance, and Information. It was very obvious that this was a job interview, and they were the selection panel. I had brought (at Cowper-Coles' suggestion) a jar of honey, which Karzai apparently loves, and a teddy bear for his son, to whom he is devoted (the Foreign Office firmly instructed me on no account to ask after his wife, as this is considered very bad form in Afghan society). Over breakfast we talked about India and Simla, where I spent my early years and where he went to school, about poetry, which he loves (I had tried to find him a copy of John Donne's work, but there were none in Heathrow), and about Britain. He greatly admires Tony Blair, and told me he had profound respect for the Prince of Wales, with whom he had spent some time.

Breakfast over, we then left the table and went into a drawing room next door for the more substantive part of our discussions. His Cabinet arranged themselves around the walls, and he brought them in one after the other to ask me questions. I stressed that this was not the same as my job in Bosnia. Afghanistan was fully sovereign, and my job would be not to govern but to support him and his Government in the policies they had decided on.

At one stage I called him a politician, and he objected, saying that he thought 'politician' was a dirty word. I said that I didn't see it that way; a politician was a patriot who used politics to help his country. In Afghanistan, he said, politics was more about manipulation and serving yourself than serving the country.

We discussed how to co-ordinate better the aid flowing into Afghanistan and the necessity of ensuring more of it went through the Afghan system, rather than directly to bilateral aid projects. I told him I thought one of the most overwhelming failures of our Afghan operation was the international community's complete inability to coordinate its activities, and said I saw my job as ensuring this happened in future, so that we could better support him and his government. At the end Karzai accompanied me outside, shook me by the hand and said, 'I really hope we will work together.'

It is in the nature of these kinds of societies, and especially true of Afghanistan, that they are always polite to guests. So whether or not we really got on well, or whether this was just the usual politeness, I was unable to tell. But when I got back to the UK Nick Burns called to say they (the US) were already receiving reports that the meeting had gone well. Karzai had said he felt that he could work with me.

Burns then asked me directly whether I would take the job. I said I would, on the basis that the US and UK Government agreed with the plan we had assembled, that the UN Secretary General, Ban Ki Moon, was happy, and that Karzai was too. I confirmed this formally in a letter to Condi Rice shortly afterwards.

Our Christmas was spent with our grandchildren skiing in the Savoie. It was overshadowed, but not spoilt, by the fact that I would be leaving for Afghanistan shortly afterwards, and we would not be seeing each other much for the next two years.

On 14 January 2008 I discreetly flew out to see the UN Secretary General in the margins of a conference he was attending in Madrid. We had an hour-long meeting in which we discussed the job and how I proposed to do it, at the end of which he confirmed that President Karzai was keen for me to do the job, and that he, too, hoped that I would accept it. I confirmed that, on this basis, I would. As I left I asked him to inform Karzai and get his final agreement, after which I would telephone him myself and arrange to meet him again as soon as possible, for we had much to discuss together.

On the way back from Madrid I got a call from Ban's Chief of Staff, saying that the Secretary General had spoken to Karzai, and he was very happy and wanted to make progress as soon as possible. Would I now please speak to the Afghan President and arrange to meet him as soon as possible? I eventually managed to reach Karzai late on the evening of 15 January. We had a brief conversation during which he said he was delighted that I had accepted the job, and we orally shook hands on it. He suggested that we should meet again at the World Economic Forum at Davos, which he was attending the following week.

Almost immediately after this phone call, things started to go seriously wrong. First of all I started to get mysterious reports from Afghanistan that Karzai had been turned and was now opposed to my taking the job. Then deeply damaging anti-British reports started appearing in the Afghan

Press, including one in a Government-controlled newspaper comparing me to Sir William Macnaghten, the head of the British Mission in Kabul killed in the slaughter that ended the First Afghan war of 1842, and posed the question, 'Who would be our Akbar Khan?' (the man who killed him). They even dragged up my family history on the Northwest Frontier and the legend about my great grandmother escaping the 1842 'Massacre in the Snows' by the skin of her teeth and suggesting I was coming to Afghanistan to avenge her. The Afghan Press was clearly being stirred up, especially the Government-controlled papers.

It was agreed that Condi Rice should see Karzai in Davos to sort things out. But before she could, Karzai, immediately he arrived at the Davos Conference, launched into an anti-British attack which especially criticised British soldiers fighting in Helmand.

I rang Ambassador Cowper-Coles to ask him his view. Was I being used as a stick to beat Britain? Or was Britain being used to get a message through to me that Karzai had changed his mind and did not want me to take the job? I thought the latter. The Ambassador confirmed that this was his view, too. I was the target, not the United Kingdom.

At the Condi Rice meeting President Karzai, sinuously avoided making a commitment one way or the other to the US proposal, now also backed by the UN Secretary General, that I should take up this post. But his Government at all other levels (including the Afghan Ambassador at the UN) made it publicly clear that they didn't want me to.

By Friday (22 February) I had reached the conclusion that I would have to withdraw. One of the conditions necessary if I was to have any chance of success – that I could work constructively with the Afghan Government – was now plainly not in place. Moreover, I could not, allow my name to be used in a way which was damaging to British interests in Afghanistan.

So the following day I rang the head of the Foreign Office, Sir Peter Ricketts, and told him I would be ringing the US Secretary of State to tell her that, under the circumstances, I felt I should withdraw my name. He said he was very sorry, but, in the circumstances, thought this the right thing to do.

Next I put a call through to Burns, who said he would speak to Condi Rice about my decision. Later that day he got back to me saying that the Secretary had one question for me. If she forced Karzai to take me, could I turn the relationship round? I replied that I didn't think so. Karzai was so mercurial that, though it might be possible to turn things round for a day or two, no one could know what would happen after that. And anyway, even if she persuaded him, it would be a Pyrrhic victory, since I would clearly be going to Kabul against the wishes of the Afghan President and Government, and perhaps even, after what had happened, a large section of Afghanistan's Pashtun population too. This would make what was already going to be a very, very difficult job simply impossible. I concluded that, under the circumstances, I was sure I had no alternative but to withdraw my name, which I would do publicly the following day. Shortly afterwards Condi Rice called, thanked me and expressed her concern about what had happened and the implications for Afghanistan.

●

Why did President Karzai change his mind so suddenly? Here I have to stray into the realms of speculation.

Some have told me that they believed they could detect the hand of Zalmay ('Zal') Khalilzad, the US Ambassador at the UN in New York behind this. Khalilzad, himself an Afghan by origin, is said to have designs on the Afghan Presidency and to be planning to put his name forward for the 2009 Presidential elections. According to this version of events, he strongly advised Karzai to say no to the US proposition that I should do this job, knowing that this would weaken Karzai in American eyes and thus give Khalilzad a clearer run at the Presidency, perhaps even with the support of Washington. Though this is certainly the kind of convoluted conspiracy theory that would be satisfyingly appealing to most in Afghanistan, where conspiracy theorising is the national sport, it has been firmly denied by Khalilzad himself.

In my view, the reasons for Karzai's sudden U-turn are much more likely to be connected with the internal politics of Afghanistan and the forthcoming Presidential elections. Among President Karzai's own people, the Pashtuns, a little bashing of the British, their ancient colonial enemy, always goes down well. More importantly, President Karzai, who has lost a lot of support amongst the other, non-Pashtun, elements in Afghanistan, has consequently become increasingly dependent on Pashtun votes for his re-election as President, and hence on those who can mobilise votes amongst the Pashtun tribes. To these elements of Afghan society the prospect of the international community speaking with a united voice, especially if that meant mounting a determined attack on corruption, as we had done in Bosnia, may not have been welcome.

Whatever the reasons for all this, my family were absolutely delighted.

Jane immediately declared Hamid Karzai her world number one favourite person after Nelson Mandela and gave his picture pride of place on the door of the kitchen fridge – to which she says a ritual thank you every morning. For my part I was glad and relieved too, but with reservations. At the start, I had really not wanted to do this, so now I was, overall, happy I could return to pretending to be retired. But, I confess, as we prepared our plans a bit of me had been drawn into the new enterprise ahead. At least initially, therefore, part of me was disappointed not to be back in the game, working on problems once again and working, once again, with people half my age. But all that is in the past now, and we have got back to the life we were so enjoying before that fateful October-night phone call in Australia.

I remain involved with a couple of commercial enterprises, which I love. I am able, when called upon, to help the Lib Dems and support their gifted new Leader, Nick Clegg. I can also see my family and my grandchildren more regularly than I used to. I am writing again and listening to music I haven't been able to listen to for ages. And, of course, there is our glorious Somerset cottage garden and my friends in the little community of Norton Sub Hamdon, whose name I carry as my title in the House of Lords.

I have always considered that one of the key factors that determine one's quality of life is the quality of your friends, and especially your neighbours. Here Jane and I have been extraordinarily lucky, too. For we have, living either side of us, two neighbours who have become close friends and the constant companions of nearly all the Somerset bit of our lives. Steph and John Bailey and Sally and Steve Radley made the long journey to see us in Bosnia (twice), have come on holiday with us in France, are regular companions in sampling the wares of the local Somerset hostelries and have been outstanding and generous neighbours, whose company I am now at last able to enjoy to the full.

As that NATO interrogator said, all those years ago in my SBS days, being idle is the worst of all punishments for me. So, once again, I am fortunate that, what with one thing and another, I find myself busy enough to keep out of both mischief and boredom. I still find myself working hours almost as long as they used to be and spending almost as much time on aircraft and in trains as I always did. But these days, Jane is mostly able to come with me.

And that, at our time of life, is just the way it should be.

The Galloping Horse

L OOKING BACK, I see that I have led an exceptionally fortunate and varied life – a life of the sort which is probably no longer available to younger generations in Britain. I have taken a lot of risks, some of them very foolish. But in the end they seemed to have worked out as well as, or better than, I had any right to expect.

And now I have all I need or could wish for, and am very content.

Except for one thing. I cannot work out where it all went, this feast that has been laid before me and which I have devoured with such voracious appetite.

I cannot somehow find the way to connect the eighteen-year-old of that sunny May morning in 1959, standing by the side of the Exe estuary on the little station halt at the Commando Training Centre Royal Marines, and the person I seem to have become now. In one sense or another, all lives are journeys. For me that scene of fifty years ago, which is still very fresh in my mind, marks the beginning of an odyssey which has led through many different adventures to the place in which I now find myself. But, looking back, I have almost no idea how I got from there to here. For mine has not been, in any sense, a planned life. It has been a haphazard one: its course may from time to time have been altered by my will, but its overall shape appears to me to owe more to providence than intention. I seem to have lived like one of those seventeenth-century merchant adventurers who sailed out of the great port of Bristol to search the seven seas for opportunity and adventure. And now, thanks to good fortune, favourable winds and excellent friends, I am returning with an ample store of treasure and a huge cargo of memories.

Our greatest treasure, of course, is our family. Perhaps things are changing now for modern politicians, and, if so, that is a very good thing – politics and family life have not easily mixed in the past, as the bleak record of breakdown, drug problems and worse amongst the children of politicians shows. But our children have ended up, not just as fine human beings to be proud of, but also as our greatest friends.

This is almost all down to their strengths and their mother's skills. For I was not, I fear, a very good father in the conventional sense, at least until I realised that I could not control their lives or live them for them. And now my son, a much respected junior-school teacher who lives nearby, has a daughter, Annie Rose, whose regular visits to us are one of the most eagerly anticipated events of our life. We see our daughter, who also teaches (but in France), and her two children, Matthias and Lois, more rarely, which is painful. But this does not diminish the debt I feel I owe to fortune for them, or the joy of being with them when we can.

Ask me what was the pinnacle of it all, and I would not hesitate with the answer: 9 June 1983, the night we won Yeovil at the general election. For there is no privilege greater than representing the community you live in, and love, in Parliament. The only one that perhaps comes close, is to stand before your fellow citizens at election time as one amongst three Party Leaders who have the chance to put before our countrymen our visions for their future. And I have been fortunate enough to do that, too. But I also cannot now imagine my life without the little, beautiful country of Bosnia and Herzegovina and its remarkable people being a part of it

But how did it all happen? Where has it all gone?

Lao Tse said that a man's life passes before him with the speed of a galloping horse. And, content though I am, so it sadly seems.

Appendix
Afghanistan appreciation, 15 December 2007

1. We do not have enough troops, aid or international will to make Afghanistan much different from what it has been for the last 1,000 years – a society built around the gun, drugs and tribalism. And even if we had all of these in sufficient quantities, we would not have them for sufficient time – around 25 years or so – to make the aim of fundamentally altering the nature of Afghanistan achievable.

2. In 5–10 years time it seems very probable that troop numbers and aid in Afghanistan will, at best, be half what they are now. The international community will have other priorities, and Afghanistan will no longer be at the top of its agenda.

3. So our task now is to shape our actions towards the kind of Afghanistan which can be managed on these diminished resources.

4. This will be an Afghanistan in which:

• Guns will, especially in the south, probably still be a greater factor in the exercise of power than the ballot box.

• There will still be tension, especially in the south, between governance through tribal democracy and government through formal Western-style democratic structures, with the former being more influential than the latter, unless we can find a way to synergise the two

• War lords, especially in the south, will still be a feature of Afghan governance and government.

• Drugs, especially in the south, will still be a feature of Afghan life and the Afghan economy.

• Corruption will still be deeply embedded in government.

• The Taliban will still exist as an armed force, especially in the south. Because here the insurgency is actually *not* about Al Qaeda but about deeply conservative Islamic Pashtun nationalism, with most locals preferring the Taliban, even if they do nasty things to them, to foreign troops, even if they do nice things for them.

5. We may, if we are really successful, be able to diminish the effects of the above, but we will not be able to eradicate them.

6. Progress in diminishing the insurgency will require a two-pronged strategy. On the military side we will need to be ruthless about attacking their structures, even at the risk of collateral damage. They need to know that we will do whatever is necessary, and for however long, to defeat them. On the political side we will need to be equally focused on providing a

better alternative that can deliver improvements in Afghan lives. Very bad cop to all insurgents, very good cop to all those who aren't, is our motto.

7. So, politically, governance is the key. But it has to be governance with the grain of Afghan traditions and in tune with what is achievable. Under-promising and over-delivering is a shining virtue; *vice versa*, a mortal sin. So we have to abandon the notion that we can make Afghanistan into a well-governed state, with gender-aware citizens and European-standard human rights. It raises expectations we cannot fulfil and wastes resources better deployed elsewhere. A better-governed state is the limit of the achievable.

8. On the military side we also need to understand that we probably cannot defeat the Taliban – probably only the Afghan people can do this. And at present, especially in the south, they do not seem ready to do so. Nor can we force them. They change their mind on this in their own time, not ours. The best we can do is give them the space, help where we can and hope for the best.

9. To expect to do more than 5, 7 and 8 above, is to set ourselves up for defeat.

10. These truths will be deeply shocking to the politicians and their publics who initiated and still, mostly, support this operation. But that does not make them less true.

11. So one of our tasks is, gently, to lower expectations in the Western world and bring our ambitions back into the range of the achievable. This will certainly be difficult and may well make those who attempt it, unpopular.

12. There is one thing we have achieved, however, and, with skill and a ruthless prioritisation of resources, ought to be able to continue to achieve even with diminished resources. That is denying the Islamic jihadists the use of Afghanistan for the kind of activities they conducted there prior to 9/11. Islamic jihadist fighters may be taking part in the insurgency in Afghanistan, but they are no longer using the country for bases, recruitment and training. These activities are now taking place over the border in Pakistan.

13. So the realistic aim in Afghanistan, with current resources, is not victory, but containment. Our success will be measured not in making things different but making them better; not in final defeat of the jihadists, but in preventing them from using Afghanistan as a space for their activity. These two aims will be difficult enough to achieve; but they are at least achievable.

Index

(Unattributed subheadings refer to Paddy Ashdown.)